The Standard Edition of the Complete Psychological Works of Sigmund Freud

Volume IV
(1900)
The Interpretation of Dreams
(First Part)

TRANSLATED FROM THE GERMAN UNDER
THE GENERAL EDITORSHIP OF
James Strachey

IN COLLABORATION WITH
Anna Freud

ASSISTED BY
Alix Strachey and Alan Tyson

VINTAGE BOOKS
London

THE HOGARTH PRESS
AND THE INSTITUTE OF PSYCHOANALYSIS

Published by Vintage 2001

18

Translation and editorial matter
Copyright © The Institute of Psychoanalysis 1953

First published in Great Britain in 1953 by
The Hogarth Press
Reprinted with corrections 1958

Vintage
Random House, 20 Vauxhall Bridge Road,
London SW1V 2SA

www.vintage-books.co.uk

Addresses for companies within The Random House Group Limited
can be found at: www.randomhouse.co.uk/offices.htm

The Random House Group Limited Reg. No. 954009

A CIP catalogue record for this book
is available from the British Library

ISBN 9780099426554

Penguin Random House is committed to a sustainable future for
our business, our readers and our planet. This book is made from
Forest Stewardship Council® certified paper.

Printed and bound in Great Britain by Clays Ltd, Elcograf S.p.A.

THE STANDARD EDITION OF THE COMPLETE PSYCHOLOGICAL WORKS OF SIGMUND FREUD

VOLUME IV

DIE

TRAUMDEUTUNG

VON

D^R. SIGM. FREUD.

––––––

»FLECTERE SI NEQUEO SUPEROS, ACHERONTA MOVEBO.«

————◄►◄►————

LEIPZIG UND WIEN.

FRANZ DEUTICKE.

1900.

CONTENTS

VOLUME FOUR

THE INTERPRETATION OF DREAMS (1900)

ON DREAMS (1901)

The Frontispiece is a reproduction of the title-page of the
First Edition

THE INTERPRETATION OF DREAMS

(1900)

Flectere si nequeo superos, Acheronta movebo

EDITOR'S INTRODUCTION

BIBLIOGRAPHICAL

(*a*) GERMAN EDITIONS:

1900   *Die Traumdeutung.* Leipzig and Vienna: Franz Deuticke. Pp. iv + 375.

1909   2nd ed. (Enlarged and revised.) Same publishers. Pp. vi + 389.

1911   3rd ed. (Enlarged and revised.) Same publishers. Pp. x + 418.

1914   4th ed. (Enlarged and revised.) Same publishers. Pp. x + 498.

1919   5th ed. (Enlarged and revised.) Same publishers. Pp. ix + 474.

1921   6th ed.⎫ (Reprints of 5th ed. except for new preface
1922   7th ed.⎭ and revised bibliography.) Pp. vii + 478.

1925   Vol. II and part of Vol. III of Freud, *Gesammelte Schriften.* (Enlarged and revised.) Leipzig, Vienna and Zurich: Internationaler Psychoanalytischer Verlag. Pp. 543 and 1–185.

1930   8th ed. (Enlarged and revised.) Leipzig and Vienna: Franz Deuticke. Pp. x + 435.

1942   In Double Volume II & III of Freud, *Gesammelte Werke.* (Reprint of 8th ed.) London: Imago Publishing Co. Pp. xv and 1–642.

(*b*) ENGLISH TRANSLATIONS:

1913   By A. A. Brill. London: George Allen & Co.; New York: The Macmillan Co. Pp. xiii + 510.

1915   2nd ed. London: George Allen & Unwin; New York: The Macmillan Co. Pp. xiii + 510.

1932   3rd ed. (Completely revised and largely rewritten by various unspecified hands.) London: George Allen & Unwin; New York: The Macmillan Co. Pp. 600.

1938 In *The Basic Writings of Sigmund Freud*. Pp. 181–549. (Reprint of 3rd ed. with almost the whole of Chapter I omitted.) New York: Random House.

The present, entirely new, translation is by James Strachey.

ACTUALLY *Die Traumdeutung* made its first appearance in 1899. The fact is mentioned by Freud at the beginning of his second paper on Josef Popper (1932c): 'It was in the winter of 1899 that my book on the interpretation of dreams (though its title-page was post-dated into the new century) at length lay before me.' But we now have more precise information from his correspondence with Wilhelm Fliess (Freud, 1950a). In his letter of November 5, 1899 (Letter 123), Freud announces that 'yesterday at length the book appeared'; and from the preceding letter it seems that Freud himself had received two advance copies about a fortnight earlier, one of which he had sent to Fliess as a birthday present.

The Interpretation of Dreams was one of the two books—the *Three Essays on the Theory of Sexuality* (1905d) was the other —which Freud kept more or less systematically 'up to date' as they passed through their series of editions. After the third edition of the present work, the changes in it were not indicated in any way; and this produced a somewhat confusing effect on the reader of the later editions, since the new material some-times implied a knowledge of modifications in Freud's views dating from times long subsequent to the period at which the book was originally written. In an attempt to get over this difficulty, the editors of the first collected edition of Freud's works (the *Gesammelte Schriften*) reprinted the first edition of *The Interpretation of Dreams* in its original form in one volume, and put into a second volume all the material that had been added subsequently. Unfortunately, however, the work was not carried out very systematically, for the additions themselves were not dated and thereby much of the advantage of the plan was sacrificed. In subsequent editions a return was made to the old, undifferentiated single volume.

By far the greater number of additions dealing with any single subject are those concerned with symbolism in dreams. Freud explains in his 'History of the Psycho-Analytic Move-ment' (1914d), as well as at the beginning of Chapter VI,

Section E (p. 350), of the present work, that he arrived late at a full realization of the importance of this side of the subject. In the first edition, the discussion of symbolism was limited to a few pages and a single specimen dream (giving instances of sexual symbolism) at the end of the Section on 'Considerations of Representability' in Chapter VI. In the second edition (1909), nothing was added to this Section; but, on the other hand, several pages on sexual symbolism were inserted at the end of the Section on 'Typical Dreams' in Chapter V. These were very considerably expanded in the third edition (1911), while the original passage in Chapter VI still remained unaltered. A reorganization was evidently overdue, and in the fourth edition (1914) an entirely new Section on Symbolism was introduced into Chapter VI, and into this the material on the subject that had accumulated in Chapter V was now transplanted, together with a quantity of entirely fresh material. No changes in the *structure* of the book were made in later editions, though much further matter was added. After the two-volume version (1925)—that is, in the eighth edition (1930)—some passages in the Section on 'Typical Dreams' in Chapter V, which had been altogether dropped at an earlier stage, were re-inserted.

In the fourth, fifth, sixth and seventh editions (that is from 1914 to 1922), two essays by Otto Rank (on 'Dreams and Creative Writing' and 'Dreams and Myths') were printed at the end of Chapter VI, but were subsequently omitted.

There remain the bibliographies. The first edition contained a list of some eighty books, to the great majority of which Freud refers in the text. This was left unchanged in the second and third editions, but in the third a second list was added, of some forty books written since 1900. Thereafter both lists began to increase rapidly, till in the eighth edition the first list contained some 260 works and the second over 200. At this stage only a minority of the titles in the first (pre-1900) list were of books actually mentioned in Freud's text; while, on the other hand, the second (post-1900) list (as may be gathered from Freud's own remarks in his various prefaces) could not really keep pace with the production of analytic or quasi-analytic writings on the subject. Furthermore, quite a number of works quoted by Freud in the text were not to be found in *either* list. It seems probable that, from the third edition onwards, Otto Rank became chiefly responsible for these bibliographies. (See also p. 714.)

(2)

HISTORICAL

The publication of Freud's correspondence with Fliess enables us to follow the composition of *The Interpretation of Dreams* in some detail. In his 'History of the Psycho-Analytic Movement' (1914*d*), Freud wrote, looking back upon his leisurely rate of publication in earlier days: '*The Interpretation of Dreams*, for instance, was finished in all essentials at the beginning of 1896 but was not written down until the summer of 1899.' Again, in the introductory remarks to his paper on the psychological consequences of the anatomical distinction between the sexes (1925*j*), he wrote: 'My *Interpretation of Dreams* and my "Fragment of an Analysis of a Case of Hysteria" [1905*e*] . . . were suppressed by me—if not for the nine years enjoined by Horace —at all events for four or five years before I allowed them to be published.' We are now in a position to amplify and in certain respects to correct these later recollections, on the basis of the author's contemporary evidence.

Apart from a number of scattered references to the subject— which, in his correspondence, go back at least as early as 1882— the first important published evidence of Freud's interest in dreams occurs in the course of a long footnote to the first of his case histories (that of Frau Emmy von N., under the date of May 15) in Breuer and Freud's *Studies on Hysteria* (1895). He is discussing the fact that neurotic patients seem to be under a necessity to bring into association with one another any ideas that happen to be simultaneously present in their minds. He goes on: 'Not long ago I was able to convince myself of the strength of this compulsion towards association from some observations made in a different field. For several weeks I found myself obliged to exchange my usual bed for a harder one, in which I had more numerous or more vivid dreams, or in which, it may be, I was unable to reach the normal depth of sleep. In the first quarter of an hour after waking I remembered all the dreams I had had during the night, and I took the trouble to write them down and try to solve them. I succeeded in tracing all these dreams back to two factors: (1) to the necessity for working out any ideas which I had only dwelt upon cursorily during the day—which had only been touched upon and not finally dealt with; and (2) to the compulsion to link together any ideas that might be present in the same state of consciousness. The senseless and contradictory character of the dreams could be traced back to the uncontrolled ascendancy of this latter factor.'

This passage cannot unfortunately be exactly dated. The preface to the volume was written in April 1895. A letter of June 22, 1894 (Letter 19), seems to imply that the case histories were already finished then, and this was quite certainly so by March 4, 1895. Freud's letter of that date (Letter 22) is of particular interest, as giving the first hint of the theory of wish-fulfilment: in the course of it he quotes the story of the medical student's 'dream of convenience' which is included on p. 125 of the present volume. It was not, however, until July 24, 1895, that the analysis of his own dream of Irma's injection—the specimen dream of Chapter II—established that theory definitely in Freud's mind. (See Letter 137 of June 12, 1900.) In September of this same year (1895) Freud wrote the first part of his 'Project for a Scientific Psychology' (published as an Appendix to the Fliess correspondence) and Sections 19, 20 and 21 of this 'Project' constitute a first approach to a coherent theory of dreams. It already includes many important elements which re-appear in the present work, such as (1) the wish-fulfilling character of dreams, (2) their hallucinatory character, (3) the regressive functioning of the mind in hallucinations and dreams (this had already been indicated by Breuer in his theoretical contribution to *Studies on Hysteria*), (4) the fact that the state of sleep involves motor paralysis, (5) the nature of the mechanism of displacement in dreams and (6) the similarity between the mechanisms of dreams and of neurotic symptoms. More than all this, however, the 'Project' gives a clear indication of what is probably the most momentous of the discoveries given to the world in *The Interpretation of Dreams*—the distinction between the two different modes of mental functioning, the Primary and Secondary Processes.

This, however, is far from exhausting the importance of the 'Project' and of the letters to Fliess written in connection with it towards the end of 1895. It is no exaggeration to say that much of the seventh chapter of *The Interpretation of Dreams*, and, indeed, of Freud's later 'metapsychological' studies, has only become fully intelligible since the publication of the 'Project'.

Students of Freud's theoretical writings have been aware that even in his profoundest psychological speculations little or no discussion is to be found upon some of the *most* fundamental of the concepts of which he makes use: such concepts, for instance, as 'mental energy', 'sums of excitation', 'cathexis', 'quantity', 'quality', 'intensity', and so on. Almost the only explicit approach to a discussion of these concepts among Freud's published works is the penultimate sentence of his first paper on the 'Neuro-Psychoses of Defence' (1894*a*), in which he lays down a hypothesis that 'in mental functions something is to be distinguished—a quota of affect or sum of excitation—which possesses all the characteristics of a quantity (though we have no means of measuring it), which is capable of increase, diminution, displacement and discharge, and which is spread over the memory-traces of ideas somewhat as an electric charge is spread over the surface of a body'. The paucity of explanation of such basic notions in Freud's later writings suggests that he was taking it for granted that they were as much a matter of course to his readers as they were to himself; and we owe it as a debt of gratitude to the posthumously published correspondence with Fliess that it throws so much light precisely upon these obscurities.

It is, of course, impossible to enter here into any detailed discussion of the subject, and the reader must be referred to the volume itself (Freud, 1950*a*) and to Dr. Kris's illuminating introduction to it.[1] The crux of the position can, however, be indicated quite simply. The essence of Freud's 'Project' lay in the notion of combining into a single whole two theories of different origin. The first of these was derived ultimately from the physiological school of Helmholtz, of which Freud's teacher, the physiologist Brücke, was a principal member. According to this theory, neurophysiology, and consequently psychology, was governed by purely chemico-physical laws. Such, for instance, was the 'law of constancy', frequently mentioned both by Freud and Breuer and expressed in these terms in 1892 (in a posthumously published draft, Breuer and Freud, 1940): 'The nervous system endeavours to keep constant something in its functional condition that may be described as the "sum of excitation".' The greater part of the theoretical contribution made by Breuer

[1] Bernfeld's paper on 'Freud's Earliest Theories' (1944) is also of great interest in this connection.

(another disciple of the Helmholtz school) to the *Studies on Hysteria* was an elaborate construction along these lines. The second main theory called into play by Freud in his 'Project' was the anatomical doctrine of the neurone, which was becoming accepted by neuro-anatomists at the end of the eighties. (The term 'neurone' was only introduced, by Waldeyer, in 1891.) This doctrine laid it down that the functional unit of the central nervous system was a distinct cell, having no direct anatomical continuity with adjacent cells. The opening sentences of the 'Project' show clearly how its basis lay in a combination of these two theories. Its aim, wrote Freud, was 'to represent psychical processes as quantitatively determined states of specifiable material particles'. He went on to postulate that these 'material particles' were the neurones and that what distinguished their being in a state of activity from their being in a state of rest was a 'quantity' which was 'subject to the general laws of motion'. Thus a neurone might either be 'empty' or 'filled with a certain quantity', that is 'cathected'.[1] 'Nervous excitation' was to be interpreted as a 'quantity' flowing through a system of neurones, and such a current might either be resisted or facilitated according to the state of the 'contact-barriers' between the neurones. (It was only later, in 1897, that the term 'synapse' was introduced by Foster and Sherrington.) The functioning of the whole nervous system was subject to a general principle of 'inertia', according to which neurones always tend to get rid of any 'quantity' with which they may be filled—a principle correlative with the principle of 'constancy'. Using these and similar concepts as his bricks, Freud constructed a highly complicated and extraordinarily ingenious working model of the mind as a piece of neurological machinery.

A principal part was played in Freud's scheme by a hypothetical division of the neurones into three classes or systems, differentiated according to their modes of functioning. Of these the first two were concerned respectively with *external* stimuli and *internal* excitations. Both of these operated on a purely *quantitative* basis; that is to say, their actions were wholly deter-

[1] It must be emphasized that these speculations of Freud's date from a period many years before any systematic investigations had been made into the nature of nervous impulses and the conditions governing their transmission.

mined by the magnitude of the nervous excitations impinging on them. The third system was correlated with the *qualitative* differences which distinguish conscious sensations and feelings. This division of the neurones into three systems was the basis of elaborate physiological explanations of such things as the working of memory, the perception of reality, the process of thought, and also the phenomena of dreaming and of neurotic disorder.

But obscurities and difficulties began to accumulate and, during the months after writing the 'Project', Freud was continually emending his theories. As time passed, his interest was gradually diverted from neurological and theoretical on to psychological and clinical problems, and he eventually abandoned the entire scheme. And when some years later, in the seventh chapter of the present book, he took the theoretical problem up once more—though he certainly never gave up his belief that ultimately a physical groundwork for psychology would be established—the neuro-physiological basis was ostensibly dropped. Nevertheless—and this is why the 'Project' is of importance to readers of *The Interpretation of Dreams*—much of the general pattern of the earlier scheme, and many of its elements, were carried over into the new one. The systems of neurones were replaced by *psychical* systems or agencies; a hypothetical 'cathexis' of psychical energy took the place of the physical 'quantity'; the principle of inertia became the basis of the pleasure (or, as Freud here called it, the unpleasure) principle. Moreover, some of the detailed accounts of psychical processes given in the seventh chapter owe much to their physiological forerunners and can be more easily understood by reference to them. This applies, for instance, to the description of the laying down of memory-traces in the 'mnemic systems', to the discussion of the nature of wishes and of the different ways of satisfying them, and to the stress laid upon the part played by verbal thought-processes in the making of adjustments to the demands of reality.

All of this is enough largely to justify Freud's assertion that *The Interpretation of Dreams* 'was finished in all essentials at the beginning of 1896'. Nevertheless, we are now in a position to add some qualifications. Thus, the existence of the Oedipus complex was only established during the summer and autumn of 1897 (Letters 64 to 71); and though this was not in itself a direct contribution to the theory of dreams, it nevertheless played a large part in emphasizing the *infantile* roots of the unconscious wishes underlying dreams. Of more obvious theoretical importance was the discovery of the omnipresence in dreams of the wish to sleep. This was announced by Freud as late as on June 9, 1899 (Letter 108). Again, the first hint at the process of 'secondary revision' seems to be given in a letter of July 7, 1897 (Letter 66). The similarity in structure between dreams and neurotic symptoms had, as we have seen, already been remarked on in the 'Project' in 1895, and was alluded to at intervals up to the autumn of 1897. Curiously enough, however, it seems thereafter to have been forgotten; for it is announced on January 3, 1899 (Letter 101), as a new discovery and as an explanation of why the book had so long remained unfinished.

The Fliess correspondence enables us to follow the actual process of composition in some detail. The idea of writing the book is first mentioned by Freud in May 1897, but quickly put on one side, probably because his interest began to be centred at that time on his self-analysis, which was to lead during the summer to his discovery of the Oedipus complex. At the end of the year the book was taken up once more, and in the early months of 1898 a first draft of the whole work seems to have been completed, with the exception of the first chapter.[1] Work upon it came to a standstill in June of that year and was not resumed after the summer vacation. On October 23, 1898 (Letter 99), Freud writes that the book 'remains stationary, unchanged; I have no motive for preparing it for publication, and the gap in the psychology [i.e. Chapter VII] as well as the gap left by removing the completely analysed sample dream [cf. p. xx] are obstacles to my finishing it which I have not yet overcome'. There was a pause of many months, till suddenly, and, as Freud himself writes, 'for no particular reason', the book began to stir again towards the end of May 1899. Thereafter it proceeded rapidly. The first chapter, dealing with the literature, which had always been a bug-bear

---

[1] This must be what is alluded to in a passage on p. 477 of the present work, in which Freud remarks that he had 'postponed the printing of the finished manuscript for more than a year'. Actually the first chapter had still to be written.

to Freud, was finished in June and the first pages sent to the printer. The revision of the middle chapters was completed by the end of August, and the last, psychological, chapter was entirely re-written and the final pages despatched early in September.

Both the manuscript and the proofs were regularly submitted by Freud to Fliess for his criticism. He seems to have had considerable influence on the final shape of the book, and to have been responsible for the omission (evidently on grounds of discretion) of an analysis of one important dream of Freud's own (cf. p. xix). But the severest criticisms came from the author himself, and these were directed principally against the style and literary form. 'I think', he wrote on September 21, 1899 (Letter 119), when the book was finished, 'my self-criticism was not entirely unjustified. Somewhere hidden within me I too have some fragmentary sense of form, some appreciation of beauty as a species of perfection; and the involved sentences of my book on dreams, bolstered up on indirect phrases and with sidelong glances at their subject-matter, have gravely affronted some ideal within me. And I am scarcely wrong in regarding this lack of form as a sign of an incomplete mastery of the material.'

But in spite of these self-criticisms, and in spite of the depression which followed the almost total neglect of the book by the outside world—only 351 copies were sold in the first six years after publication—*The Interpretation of Dreams* was always regarded by Freud as his most important work: 'Insight such as this', as he wrote in his preface to the third English edition, 'falls to one's lot but once in a lifetime.'

(3)

THE PRESENT ENGLISH EDITION

The present translation is based on the eighth (1930) German edition, the last published during its author's life. At the same time, it differs from all previous editions (both German and English) in an important respect, for it is in the nature of a 'Variorum' edition. An effort has been made to indicate, with dates, every alteration of substance introduced into the book since its first issue. Wherever material has been dropped or greatly modified in later editions, the cancelled passage or earlier version is given in a footnote. The only exception is that Rank's two appendices to Chapter VI have been omitted. The question of their inclusion was seriously considered; but it was decided against doing so. The essays are entirely self-contained and have no direct connections with Freud's book; they would have filled another fifty pages or so; and they would be particularly unenlightening to English readers, since they deal in the main with German literature and German mythology.

The bibliographies have been entirely recast. The first of these contains a list of every work actually referred to in the text or footnotes. This bibliography is also arranged to serve as an Author Index. The second bibliography contains all the works in the German pre-1900 list *not* actually quoted by Freud. It has seemed worth while to print this, since no other comparably full bibliography of the older literature on dreams is easily accessible. Writings *after* 1900, apart from those actually quoted and consequently included in the first bibliography, have been disregarded. A warning must, however, be issued in regard to both my lists. Investigation has shown a very high proportion of errors in the German bibliographies. These have been corrected wherever possible; but quite a number of the entries have proved to be untraceable in London, and these (which are distinguished by an asterisk) must be regarded as suspect.

Editorial additions are printed in square brackets. Many readers will no doubt be irritated by the number of references and other explanatory notes. The references, however, are essentially to Freud's own writings, and very few will be found to other authors (apart, of course, from references made by Freud himself). In any case, the fact must be faced that *The Interpretation of Dreams* is one of the major classics of scientific literature and that the time has come to treat it as such. It is the editor's hope and belief that actually the references, and more particularly the cross-references to other parts of the work itself, will make it easier for serious students to follow the intricacies of the material. Readers in search of mere entertainment—if there are any such—must steel themselves to disregard these parentheses.

A word must be added upon the translation itself. Great attention has had, of course, to be paid to the details of the wording of the text of dreams. Where the English rendering strikes the reader as unusually stiff, he may assume that the stiffness has been imposed by some verbal necessity determined by the interpretation that is to follow. Where there are inconsistencies between different versions of the text of the same dream, he may assume that there are parallel inconsistencies in the original. These verbal difficulties culminate in the fairly frequent instances in which an interpretation depends entirely upon a pun. There are three methods of dealing with such situations. The translator can omit the dream entirely, or he can replace it by another parallel dream, whether derived from his own experience or fabricated *ad hoc*. These two methods have been the ones adopted in the main in the earlier translations of the book. But there are serious objections to them. We must once more remember that we are dealing with a scientific classic. What we want to hear about are the examples chosen by Freud—not by someone else. Accordingly the present translator has adopted the pedantic and tiresome third alternative of keeping the original German pun and laboriously explaining it in a square bracket or footnote. Any amusement that might be got out of it completely evaporates in the process. But that, unfortunately, is a sacrifice that has to be made.

Help in the laborious task of proof-reading has been generously given (among others) by Mrs. R. S. Partridge and Dr. C. F. Rycroft. Mrs. Partridge is also largely responsible for the index. The revision of the bibliographies has in the main been carried out by Mr. G. Talland.

Finally, the editor's thanks are due to Dr. Ernest Jones for his constant advice and encouragement. The first volume of his Freud biography will be found to throw invaluable light on the background of this work as a whole, as well as on many of its details.

Preface to the First Edition

I HAVE attempted in this volume to give an account of the interpretation of dreams; and in doing so I have not, I believe, trespassed beyond the sphere of interest covered by neuropathology. For psychological investigation shows that the dream is the first member of a class of abnormal psychical phenomena of which further members, such as hysterical phobias, obsessions and delusions, are bound for practical reasons to be a matter of concern to physicians. As will be seen in the sequel, dreams can make no such claim to practical importance; but their theoretical value as a paradigm is on the other hand proportionately greater. Anyone who has failed to explain the origin of dream-images can scarcely hope to understand phobias, obsessions or delusions or to bring a therapeutic influence to bear on them.

But the same correlation that is responsible for the importance of the subject must also bear the blame for the deficiencies of the present work. The broken threads which so frequently interrupt my presentation are nothing less than the many points of contact between the problem of the formation of dreams and the more comprehensive problems of psychopathology. These cannot be treated here, but, if time and strength allow and further material comes to hand, will form the subject of later communications.

The difficulties of presentation have been further increased by the peculiarities of the material which I have had to use to illustrate the interpreting of dreams. It will become plain in the course of the work itself why it is that none of the dreams already reported in the literature of the subject or collected from unknown sources could be of any use for my purposes. The only dreams open to my choice were my own and those of my patients undergoing psycho-analytic treatment. But I was precluded from using the latter material by the fact that in its case the dream-processes were subject to an undesirable complication owing to the added presence of neurotic features. But if I was to report my own dreams, it inevitably followed that I should have to reveal to the public gaze more of the intimacies of my mental life than I liked, or than is normally necessary for any writer who is a man of science and not a poet. Such was the painful but unavoidable necessity; and I have submitted to it rather than totally abandon the possibility of giving the evidence for my psychological findings. Naturally, however, I have been unable to resist the temptation of taking the edge off some of my indiscretions by omissions and substitutions. But whenever this has happened, the value of my instances has been very definitely diminished. I can only express a hope that readers of this book will put themselves in my difficult situation and treat me with indulgence, and further, that anyone who finds any sort of reference to himself in my dreams may be willing to grant me the right of freedom of thought—in my dream-life, if nowhere else

Preface to the Second Edition

IF within ten years of the publication of this book (which is very far from being an easy one to read) a second edition is called for, this is not due to the interest taken in it by the professional circles to whom my original preface was addressed. My psychiatric colleagues seem to have taken no trouble to overcome the initial bewilderment created by my new approach to dreams. The professional philosophers have become accustomed to polishing off the problems of dream-life (which they treat as a mere appendix to conscious states) in a few sentences—and usually in the same ones; and they have evidently failed to notice that we have something here from which a number of inferences can be drawn that are bound to transform our psychological theories. The attitude adopted by reviewers in the scientific periodicals could only lead one to suppose that my work was doomed to be sunk into complete silence; while the small group of gallant supporters, who practise medical psycho-analysis under my guidance and who follow my example in interpreting dreams and make use of their interpretations in treating neurotics, would never have exhausted the first edition of the book. Thus it is that I feel indebted to a wider circle of educated and curious-minded readers, whose interest has led me to take up once more after nine years this difficult, but in many respects fundamental, work.

I am glad to say that I have found little to change in it. Here and there I have inserted some new material, added some fresh points of detail derived from my increased experience, and at some few points recast my statements. But the essence of what I have written about dreams and their interpretation, as well as about the psychological theorems to be deduced from them —all this remains unaltered: subjectively at all events, it has stood the test of time. Anyone who is acquainted with my other writings (on the aetiology and mechanism of the psycho-neuroses) will know that I have never put forward inconclusive opinions as though they were established facts, and that I have always sought to modify my statements so that they may keep in step with my advancing knowledge. In the sphere of dream-life I have been able to leave my original assertions unchanged. During the long years in which I have been working at the problems of the neuroses I have often been in doubt and sometimes been shaken in my convictions. At such times it has always been the *Interpretation of Dreams* that has given me back my certainty. It is thus a sure instinct which has led my many scientific opponents to refuse to follow me more especially in my researches upon dreams.

An equal durability and power to withstand any far-reaching alterations during the process of revision has been shown by the *material* of the book, consisting as it does of dreams of my own which have for the most part been overtaken or made valueless by the march of events and by which I illustrated the rules of dream-interpretation. For this book has a further subjective significance for me personally—a significance which I only grasped after I had completed it. It was, I found, a portion of my own self-analysis, my reaction to my father's death—that is to say, to the most important event, the most poignant loss, of a man's life. Having discovered that this was so, I felt unable to obliterate the traces of the experience.[1] To my readers, however, it will be a matter of indifference upon what particular material they learn to appreciate the importance of dreams and how to interpret them.

Wherever I have found it impossible to incorporate some essential addition into the original context, I have indicated its more recent date by enclosing it in square brackets.[2]

BERCHTESGADEN, *Summer* 1908

[1] [Freud's father had died in 1896. Some account of his feelings at the time will be found in his letter to Fliess of November 2, 1896. (Freud 1950a, Letter 50.)]

[2] [*Footnote added* 1914.] In later editions [from the fourth onwards] these were omitted.

Preface to the Third Edition

NINE years elapsed between the first and second editions of this book, but after scarcely more than a single year a third edition has become necessary. This new turn of events may please me; but just as formerly I was unwilling to regard the neglect of my book by readers as evidence of its worthlessness, so I cannot claim that the interest which is now being taken in it is a proof of its excellence.

Even the *Interpretation of Dreams* has not been left untouched by the advance of scientific knowledge. When I wrote it in 1899, my theory of sexuality was not yet in existence and the analysis of the more complicated forms of psycho-neurosis was only just beginning. It was my hope that dream-interpretation would help to make possible the psychological analysis of neuroses; since then a deeper understanding of neuroses has reacted in turn upon our view of dreams. The theory of dream-interpretation has itself developed further in a direction on which insufficient stress had been laid in the first edition of this book. My own experience, as well as the works of Wilhelm Stekel and others, have since taught me to form a truer estimate of the extent and importance of symbolism in dreams (or rather in unconscious thinking). Thus in the course of these years much has accumulated which demands attention. I have endeavoured to take these innovations into account by making numerous interpolations in the text and by additional footnotes. If these additions threaten at times to burst the whole framework of the book or if I have not everywhere succeeded in bringing the original text up to the level of our present knowledge, I must ask the reader's indulgence for these deficiencies: they are the results and signs of the present increasingly rapid development of our science. I may even venture to prophesy in what other directions later editions of this book—if any should be needed—will differ from the present one. They will have on the one hand to afford a closer contact with the copious material presented in imaginative writing, in myths, in linguistic usage and in folklore; while on the other hand they will have to deal in greater detail than has here been possible with the relations of dreams to neuroses and mental diseases.

Herr Otto Rank has given me valuable assistance in selecting the additional matter and has been entirely responsible for correcting the proofs. I owe my thanks to him and to many others for their contributions and corrections.

VIENNA, *Spring* 1911

Preface to the Fourth Edition

LAST year (1913) Dr. A. A. Brill of New York produced an English translation of this book (*The Interpretation of Dreams*, G. Allen & Co., London).

On this occasion Dr. Otto Rank has not only corrected the proofs but has also contributed two self-contained chapters to the text—the appendices to Chapter VI.

VIENNA, *June* 1914

Preface to the Fifth Edition

INTEREST in the *Interpretation of Dreams* has not flagged even during the World War, and while it is still in progress a new edition has become necessary. It has not been possible, however, to notice fully publications since 1914; neither Dr. Rank nor I have any knowledge of foreign works since that date.

A Hungarian translation, prepared by Dr. Hollós and Dr. Ferenczi, is on the point of appearing. In 1916–17 my *Introductory Lectures on Psycho-Analysis* were published in Vienna by Hugo Heller. The central section of these, comprising eleven lectures, is devoted to an account of dreams which aims at being more elementary and at being in closer contact with the theory of the neuroses than the present work. On the whole it is in the nature of an epitome of the *Interpretation of Dreams*, though at certain points it enters into greater detail.

I have not been able to bring myself to embark upon any fundamental revision of this book, which might bring it up to the level of our present psycho-analytic views but would on the other hand destroy its historic character. I think, however, that after an existence of nearly twenty years it has accomplished its task.

BUDAPEST-STEINBRUCH, *July* 1918

Preface to the Sixth Edition

OWING to the difficulties in which the book trade is placed at present, this new edition has long been in demand, and the preceding edition has, for the first time, been reprinted without any alterations. Only the bibliography at the end of the volume has been completed and brought up to date by Dr. Otto Rank.

Thus my assumption that after an existence of nearly twenty years this book had accomplished its task has not been confirmed. On the contrary, I might say that it has a new task to perform. If its earlier function was to offer some information on the nature of dreams, now it has the no less important duty of dealing with the obstinate misunderstandings to which that information is subject.

Vienna, *April* 1921

Preface to the Eighth Edition

DURING the interval between the publication of the last (seventh) edition of this book in 1922 and the present one, my *Gesammelte Schriften* [Collected Writings] have been issued in Vienna by the Internationaler Psychoanalytischer Verlag. The second volume of that collection consists of an exact reprint of the first edition of the *Interpretation of Dreams*, while the third volume contains all the additions that have since been made to it. The translations of the book which have appeared during the same interval are based upon the usual, single-volume, form of the work: a French one by I. Meyerson published under the title of *La science des rêves* in the 'Bibliothèque de Philosophie Contemporaine' in 1926; a Swedish one by John Landquist, *Drömtydning* (1927); and a Spanish one by Luis López-Ballesteros y de Torres [1922], which occupies Volumes VI and VII of the *Obras Completas*. The Hungarian translation, which I thought was on the point of completion as long ago as in 1918, has even now not appeared.[1]

In the present revised edition of the work I have again treated it essentially as an historic document and I have only made such alterations in it as were suggested by the clarification and deepening of my own opinions. In accordance with this, I have finally given up the idea of including a list of works on the problems of dreams published since the book's first appearance, and that section has now been dropped. The two essays which Otto Rank contributed to earlier editions, on 'Dreams and Creative Writing' and 'Dreams and Myths', have also been omitted. [See p. xxi.]

VIENNA, *December* 1929

[1] [It was published in 1934.—During Freud's lifetime, in addition to the translations mentioned in these prefaces, a Russian version appeared in 1913, a Japanese one in 1930 and a Czech one in 1938.]

Preface to the Third (Revised) English Edition[1]

In 1909 G. Stanley Hall invited me to Clark University, in Worcester, to give the first lectures on psycho-analysis. In the same year Dr. Brill published the first of his translations of my writings, which were soon followed by further ones. If psycho-analysis now plays a role in American intellectual life, or if it does so in the future, a large part of this result will have to be attributed to this and other activities of Dr. Brill's.

His first translation of *The Interpretation of Dreams* appeared in 1913. Since then much has taken place in the world, and much has been changed in our views about the neuroses. This book, with the new contribution to psychology which surprised the world when it was published (1900), remains essentially unaltered. It contains, even according to my present-day judgement, the most valuable of all the discoveries it has been my good fortune to make. Insight such as this falls to one's lot but once in a lifetime.

VIENNA, *March* 15, 1931

[1] [This is not included in the German editions and no German text is extant. It is here reprinted exactly from the 1932 English edition.]

CHAPTER I

THE SCIENTIFIC LITERATURE DEALING WITH THE PROBLEMS OF DREAMS[1]

In the pages that follow I shall bring forward proof that there is a psychological technique which makes it possible to interpret dreams, and that, if that procedure is employed, every dream reveals itself as a psychical structure which has a meaning and which can be inserted at an assignable point in the mental activities of waking life. I shall further endeavour to elucidate the processes to which the strangeness and obscurity of dreams are due and to deduce from those processes the nature of the psychical forces by whose concurrent or mutually opposing action dreams are generated. Having gone thus far, my description will break off, for it will have reached a point at which the problem of dreams merges into more comprehensive problems, the solution of which must be approached upon the basis of material of another kind.

I shall give by way of preface a review of the work done by earlier writers on the subject as well as of the present position of the problems of dreams in the world of science, since in the course of my discussion I shall not often have occasion to revert to those topics. For, in spite of many thousands of years of effort, the scientific understanding of dreams has made very little advance—a fact so generally admitted in the literature that it seems unnecessary to quote instances in support of it. In these writings, of which a list appears at the end of my work, many stimulating observations are to be found and a quantity of interesting material bearing upon our theme, but little or nothing that touches upon the essential nature of dreams or that offers a final solution of any of their enigmas. And still less, of course, has passed into the knowledge of educated laymen.

It may be asked[2] what view was taken of dreams in prehistoric times by primitive races of men and what effect dreams

---

[1] [*Footnote added* in second to seventh editions:] Up to the date of the first publication of this book (1900).

[2] [This paragraph and the next were added in 1914.]

may have had upon the formation of their conceptions of the world and of the soul; and this is a subject of such great interest that it is only with much reluctance that I refrain from dealing with it in this connection. I must refer my readers to the standard works of Sir John Lubbock, Herbert Spencer, E. B. Tylor and others, and I will only add that we shall not be able to appreciate the wide range of these problems and speculations until we have dealt with the task that lies before us here—the interpretation of dreams.

The prehistoric view of dreams is no doubt echoed in the attitude adopted towards dreams by the peoples of classical antiquity.[1] They took it as axiomatic that dreams were connected with the world of superhuman beings in whom they believed and that they were revelations from gods and daemons. There could be no question, moreover, that for the dreamer dreams had an important purpose, which was as a rule to foretell the future. The extraordinary variety in the content of dreams and in the impression they produced made it difficult, however, to have any uniform view of them and made it necessary to classify dreams into numerous groups and subdivisions according to their importance and trustworthiness. The position adopted towards dreams by individual philosophers in antiquity was naturally dependent to some extent upon their attitude towards divination in general.

In the two works of Aristotle which deal with dreams, they have already become a subject for psychological study. We are told that dreams are not sent by the gods and are not of a divine character, but that they are 'daemonic', since nature is 'daemonic' and not divine. Dreams, that is, do not arise from supernatural manifestations but follow the laws of the human spirit, though the latter, it is true, is akin to the divine. Dreams are defined as the mental activity of the sleeper in so far as he is asleep.[2]

[1] [Footnote added 1914:] What follows is based on Büchsenschütz's scholarly study (1868).

[2] [De divinatione per somnum, II (Trans., 1935, 377), and De somniis, III (Trans., 1935, 365).—In the first edition (1900) this paragraph ran: 'The first work in which dreams were treated as a subject for psychological study seems to be that of Aristotle (On Dreams and their Interpretation). Aristotle declares that dreams are of a "daemonic" but not of a "divine" nature; no doubt this distinction has some great significance if we knew how to translate it correctly.' The next paragraph ended with the sen-

Aristotle was aware of some of the characteristics of dream-life. He knew, for instance, that dreams give a magnified construction to small stimuli arising during sleep. 'Men think that they are walking through fire and are tremendously hot, when there is only a slight heating about certain parts.'[1] And from this circumstance he draws the conclusion that dreams may very well betray to a physician the first signs of some bodily change which has not been observed in waking.[2]

Before the time of Aristotle, as we know, the ancients regarded dreams not as a product of the dreaming mind but as something introduced by a divine agency; and already the two opposing currents, which we shall find influencing opinions of dream-life at every period of history, were making themselves felt. The distinction was drawn between truthful and valuable dreams, sent to the sleeper to warn him or foretell the future, and vain, deceitful and worthless dreams, whose purpose it was to mislead or destroy him.

Gruppe (1906, **2**, 930)[3] quotes a classification of dreams on these lines made by Macrobius and Artemidorus [of Daldis (see p. 98 *n.*)]: 'Dreams were divided into two classes. One class was supposed to be influenced by the present or past, but to have no future significance. It included the ἐνύπνια or *insomnia*, which gave a direct representation of a given idea or of its opposite—e.g. of hunger or of its satiation—, and the φαντάσματα, which lent a fantastic extension to the given idea—e.g. the nightmare or *ephialtes*. The other class, on the contrary, was supposed to determine the future. It included (1) direct prophecies received in a dream (the χρηματισμός or *oraculum*), (2) previsions of some future event (the ὅραμα or *visio*) and (3) symbolic dreams, which needed interpretation (the ὄνειρος or *somnium*). This theory persisted for many centuries.'

tence: 'My own insufficient knowledge and my lack of specialist assistance prevent my entering more deeply into Aristotle's treatise.' These passages were altered into their present form in 1914; and a note in *Gesammelte Schriften*, **3** (1925), 4, points out that in fact Aristotle wrote not one but two works on the subject.]

[1] [*De divinatione*, I (*Trans.*, 1935, 375).]

[2] [*Footnote added* 1914:] The Greek physician Hippocrates deals with the relation of dreams to illnesses in one of the chapters of his famous work [*Ancient Medicine*, X (*Trans.*, 1923, 31). See also *Regimen*, IV, 88, passim. (*Trans.*, 1931, 425, etc.)]

[3] [This paragraph was added as a footnote in 1911 and included in the text in 1914.]

This variation in the value that was to be assigned to dreams [1] was closely related to the problem of 'interpreting' them. Important consequences were in general to be expected from dreams. But dreams were not all immediately comprehensible and it was impossible to tell whether a particular unintelligible dream might not be making some important announcement. This provided an incentive for elaborating a method by which the unintelligible content of a dream might be replaced by one that was comprehensible and significant. In the later years of antiquity Artemidorus of Daldis was regarded as the greatest authority on the interpretation of dreams, and the survival of his exhaustive work [*Oneirocritica*] must compensate us for the loss of the other writings on the same subject. [2]

The pre-scientific view of dreams adopted by the peoples of antiquity was certainly in complete harmony with their view of the universe in general, which led them to project into the external world as though they were realities things which in fact enjoyed reality only within their own minds. Moreover, their view of dreams took into account the principal impression produced upon the waking mind in the morning by what is left of a dream in the memory: an impression of something alien, arising from another world and contrasting with the remaining contents of the mind. Incidentally, it would be a mistake to suppose that the theory of the supernatural origin of dreams is without its supporters in our own days. We may leave on one side pietistic and mystical writers, who, indeed, are perfectly justified in remaining in occupation of what is left of the once wide domain of the supernatural so long as that field is not conquered by scientific explanation. But apart from them, one comes across clear-headed men, without any extravagant ideas, who seek to support their religious faith in the existence and

---

[1] [This paragraph was added in 1914.]

[2] [*Footnote added* 1914:] For the further history of dream-interpretation in the Middle Ages see Diepgen (1912) and the monographs of Förster (1910 and 1911), Gotthard (1912), etc. Dream-interpretation among the Jews has been discussed by Almoli (1848), Amram (1901), and Löwinger (1908); also, quite recently and taking account of psychoanalytic findings, by Lauer (1913). Information upon dream-interpretation among the Arabs has been given by Drexl (1909), Schwarz (1913) and the missionary Tfinkdji (1913); among the Japanese by Miura (1906) and Iwaya (1902); among the Chinese by Secker (1909–10); and among the people of India by Negelein (1912).

activity of superhuman spiritual forces precisely by the inexplicable nature of the phenomena of dreaming. (Cf. Haffner, 1887.) The high esteem in which dream-life is held by some schools of philosophy (by the followers of Schelling,[1] for instance) is clearly an echo of the divine nature of dreams which was undisputed in antiquity. Nor are discussions of the premonitory character of dreams and their power to foretell the future at an end. For attempts at giving a psychological explanation have been inadequate to cover the material collected, however decidedly the sympathies of those of a scientific cast of mind may incline against accepting any such beliefs.

It is difficult to write a history of the scientific study of the problems of dreams because, however valuable that study may have been at a few points, no line of advance in any particular direction can be traced. No foundation has been laid of secure findings upon which a later investigator might build; but each new writer examines the same problems afresh and begins again, as it were, from the beginning. If I attempted to take those who have written on the question in chronological order and to give a summary of their views upon the problems of dreams, I should have to abandon any hope of giving a comprehensive general picture of the present state of knowledge of the subject. I have therefore chosen to frame my account according to topics rather than authors and, as I raise each dream-problem in turn, I shall bring forward whatever material the literature contains for its solution.

Since, however, it has been impossible for me to cover the whole of the literature of the subject, widely scattered as it is and trenching upon many other fields, I must ask my readers to be satisfied so long as no fundamental fact and no important point of view is overlooked in my description.

Until recently most writers on the subject have felt obliged to treat sleep and dreams as a single topic, and as a rule they have dealt in addition with analogous conditions on the fringe

[1] [The chief exponent of the pantheistic 'Philosophy of Nature', popular in Germany during the early part of the nineteenth century.—Freud often recurred to the question of the occult significance of dreams. Cf. Freud 1922a, 1925i (Part 3) and 1933a (Lecture 30). An allegedly premonitory dream is discussed in Freud 1941c [1899], printed as an Appendix to this work, p. 623. See also pp. 65 and 621 below.]

of pathology, and dream-like states, such as hallucinations, visions and so on. The latest works, on the contrary, show a preference for a restricted theme and take as their subject, perhaps, some isolated question in the field of dream-life. I should be glad to see in this change of attitude the expression of a conviction that in such obscure matters it will only be possible to arrive at explanations and agreed results by a series of detailed investigations. A piece of detailed research of that kind, predominantly psychological in character, is all I have to offer in these pages. I have had little occasion to deal with the problem of sleep, for that is essentially a problem of physiology, even though one of the characteristics of the state of sleep must be that it brings about modifications in the conditions of functioning of the mental apparatus. The literature on the subject of sleep is accordingly disregarded in what follows.

The questions raised by a scientific enquiry into the phenomena of dreams as such may be grouped under the headings which follow, though a certain amount of overlapping cannot be avoided.

THE RELATION OF DREAMS TO WAKING LIFE

The unsophisticated waking judgement of someone who has just woken from sleep assumes that his dreams, even if they did not themselves come from another world, had at all events carried him off into another world. The old physiologist Burdach (1838, 499), to whom we owe a careful and shrewd account of the phenomena of dreams, has given expression to this conviction in a much-quoted passage: 'In dreams, daily life, with its labours and pleasures, its joys and pains, is never repeated. On the contrary, dreams have as their very aim to free us from it. Even when our whole mind has been filled with something, when we are torn by some deep sorrow or when all our intellectual power is absorbed in some problem, a dream will do no more than enter into the tone of our mood and represent reality in symbols.' I. H. Fichte (1864, 1, 541), in the same sense, actually speaks of 'complementary dreams' and describes them as one of the secret benefactions of the self-healing nature of the spirit.[1] Strümpell (1877, 16) writes to similar effect in his study on the nature and origin of dreams— a work which is widely and deservedly held in high esteem: 'A man who dreams is removed from the world of waking consciousness.' So too (ibid., 17): 'In dreams our memory of the ordered contents of waking consciousness and of its normal behaviour is as good as completely lost.' And again (ibid., 19) he writes that 'the mind is cut off in dreams, almost without memory, from the ordinary content and affairs of waking life'.

The preponderant majority of writers, however, take a contrary view of the relation of dreams to waking life. Thus Haffner (1887, 245): 'In the first place, dreams carry on waking life. Our dreams regularly attach themselves to the ideas that have been in our consciousness shortly before. Accurate observation will almost always find a thread which connects a dream with the experiences of the previous day.' Weygandt (1893, 6) specifically contradicts Burdach's statement which I have just quoted: 'For it may often, and apparently in the majority of

---

[1] [This sentence was added in 1914.]

dreams, be observed that they actually lead us back to ordinary life instead of freeing us from it.' Maury (1878, 51) advances a concise formula: 'Nous rêvons de ce que nous avons vu, dit, désiré ou fait';[1] while Jessen, in his book on psychology (1855, 530), remarks at somewhat greater length: 'The content of a dream is invariably more or less determined by the individual personality of the dreamer, by his age, sex, class, standard of education and habitual way of living, and by the events and experiences of his whole previous life.'

The most uncompromising attitude on this question[2] is adopted by J. G. E. Maass, the philosopher (1805, [1, 168 and 173]), quoted by Winterstein (1912): 'Experience confirms our view that we dream most frequently of the things on which our warmest passions are centred. And this shows that our passions must have an influence on the production of our dreams. The ambitious man dreams of the laurels he has won (or imagines he has won) or of those he has still to win; while the lover is busied in his dreams with the object of his sweet hopes. . . . All the sensual desires and repulsions that slumber in the heart can, if anything sets them in motion, cause a dream to arise from the ideas that are associated with them or cause those ideas to intervene in a dream that is already present.'

The same view was taken in antiquity on the dependence of the content of dreams upon waking life. Radestock (1879, 134) tells us how before Xerxes started on his expedition against Greece, he was given sound advice of a discouraging kind but was always urged on again by his dreams; whereupon Artabanus, the sensible old Persian interpreter of dreams, observed to him pertinently that as a rule dream-pictures contain what the waking man already thinks.

Lucretius' didactic poem *De rerum natura* contains the following passage (IV, 962):

> Et quo quisque fere studio devinctus adhaeret
> aut quibus in rebus multum sumus ante morati
> atque in ea ratione fuit contenta magis mens,
> in somnis eadem plerumque videmur obire;
> causidici causas agere et componere leges,
> induperatores pugnare ac proelia obire . . .[3]

---

[1] ['We dream of what we have seen, said, desired or done.']

[2] [This paragraph was added in 1914.]

[3] ['And whatever be the pursuit to which one clings with devotion, whatever the things on which we have been occupied much in the past,

Cicero (*De divinatione*, II, lxvii, 140) writes to exactly the same effect as Maury so many years later: 'Maximeque reliquiae rerum earum moventur in animis et agitantur de quibus vigilantes aut cogitavimus aut egimus.'[1]

The contradiction between these two views upon the relation between dream-life and waking life seems in fact insoluble. It is therefore relevant at this point to recall the discussion of the subject by Hildebrandt (1875, 8 ff.), who believes that it is impossible to describe the characteristics of dreams at all except by means of 'a series of [three] contrasts which seem to sharpen into contradictions'. 'The first of these contrasts', he writes, 'is afforded on the one hand by the completeness with which dreams are secluded and separated from real and actual life and on the other hand by their constant encroachment upon each other and their constant mutual dependence. A dream is something completely severed from the reality experienced in waking life, something, as one might say, with an hermetically sealed existence of its own, and separated from real life by an impassable gulf. It sets us free from reality, extinguishes our normal memory of it and places us in another world and in a quite other life-story which in essentials has nothing to do with our real one. . . .' Hildebrandt goes on to show how when we fall asleep our whole being with all its forms of existence 'disappears, as it were, through an invisible trap-door'. Then, perhaps, the dreamer may make a sea-voyage to St. Helena in order to offer Napoleon, who is a prisoner there, a choice bargain in Moselle wines. He is received most affably by the ex-Emperor and feels almost sorry when he wakes and the interesting illusion is destroyed. But let us compare the situation in the dream, proceeds Hildebrandt, with reality. The dreamer has never been a wine-merchant and has never wished to be. He has never gone on a sea-voyage, and if he did, St. Helena would be the last place he would choose to go to. He nourishes no sympathetic feelings whatever towards Napoleon, but on the contrary a fierce patriotic hatred. And, on top of all the mind being thus more intent upon that pursuit, it is generally the same things that we seem to encounter in dreams: pleaders to plead their cause and collate laws, generals to contend and engage battle . . .' (Rouse's translation in the Loeb Classical Library, 1924, 317.)]

[1] ['Then especially do the remnants of our waking thoughts and deeds move and stir within the soul.' (Falconer's translation in the Loeb Classical Library, 1922, 527.)]

the rest, the dreamer was not even born when Napoleon died on the island; so that to have any personal relations with him was beyond the bounds of possibility. Thus the dream-experience appears as something alien inserted between two sections of life which are perfectly continuous and consistent with each other.

'And yet', continues Hildebrandt [ibid., 10], 'what appears to be the contrary of this is equally true and correct. In spite of everything, the most intimate relationship goes hand in hand, I believe, with the seclusion and separation. We may even go so far as to say that whatever dreams may offer, they derive their material from reality and from the intellectual life that revolves around that reality. . . . Whatever strange results they may achieve, they can never in fact get free from the real world; and their most sublime as well as their most ridiculous structures must always borrow their basic material either from what has passed before our eyes in the world of the senses or from what has already found a place somewhere in the course of our waking thoughts—in other words from what we have already experienced either externally or internally.'

THE MATERIAL OF DREAMS—MEMORY IN DREAMS

All the material making up the content of a dream is in some way derived from experience, that is to say, has been reproduced or remembered in the dream—so much at least we may regard as an undisputed fact. But it would be a mistake to suppose that a connection of this kind between the content of a dream and reality is bound to come to light easily, as an immediate result of comparing them. The connection requires, on the contrary, to be looked for diligently, and in a whole quantity of cases it may long remain hidden. The reason for this lies in a number of peculiarities which are exhibited by the faculty of memory in dreams and which, though generally remarked upon, have hitherto resisted explanation. It will be worth while to examine these characteristics more closely.

It may happen that a piece of material occurs in the content of a dream which in the waking state we do not recognize as forming a part of our knowledge or experience. We remember, of course, having dreamt the thing in question, but we cannot remember whether or when we experienced it in real life. We are thus left in doubt as to the source which has been drawn upon by the dream and are tempted to believe that dreams have a power of independent production. Then at last, often after a long interval, some fresh experience recalls the lost memory of the other event and at the same time reveals the source of the dream. We are thus driven to admit that in the dream we knew and remembered something which was beyond the reach of our waking memory.[1]

A particularly striking example of this is given by Delbœuf [1885, 107 ff.] from his own experience. He saw in a dream the courtyard of his house covered with snow and found two small lizards half-frozen and buried under it. Being an animal-lover, he picked them up, warmed them and carried them back to the

---

[1] [*Footnote added* 1914:] Vaschide (1911) remarks that it has often been observed that in dreams people speak foreign languages more fluently and correctly than in waking life.

little hole in the masonry where they belonged. He further gave them a few leaves of a small fern which grew on the wall and of which, as he knew, they were very fond. In the dream he knew the name of the plant: *Asplenium ruta muralis*. The dream proceeded and, after a digression, came back to the lizards. Delbœuf then saw to his astonishment two new ones which were busy on the remains of the fern. He then looked round him and saw a fifth and then a sixth lizard making their way to the hole in the wall, until the whole roadway was filled with a procession of lizards, all moving in the same direction . . . and so on.

When he was awake, Delbœuf knew the Latin names of very few plants and an *Asplenium* was not among them. To his great surprise he was able to confirm the fact that a fern of this name actually exists. Its correct name is *Asplenium ruta muraria*, which had been slightly distorted in the dream. It was hardly possible that this could be a coincidence; and it remained a mystery to Delbœuf how he had acquired his knowledge of the name '*Asplenium*' in his dream.

The dream occurred in 1862. Sixteen years later, while the philosopher was on a visit to one of his friends, he saw a little album of pressed flowers of the sort that are sold to foreigners as mementos in some parts of Switzerland. A recollection began to dawn on him—he opened the herbarium, found the *Asplenium* of his dream and saw its Latin name written underneath it in his own handwriting. The facts could now be established. In 1860 (two years before the lizard dream) a sister of this same friend had visited Delbœuf on her honeymoon. She had with her the album, which was to be a gift to her brother, and Delbœuf took the trouble to write its Latin name under each dried plant, at the dictation of a botanist.

Good luck, which made this example so well worth recording, enabled Delbœuf to trace yet another part of the content of the dream to its forgotten source. One day in 1877 he happened to take up an old volume of an illustrated periodical and in it he found a picture of the whole procession of lizards which he had dreamed of in 1862. The volume was dated 1861 and Delbœuf remembered having been a subscriber to the paper from its first number.

The fact that dreams have at their command memories which are inaccessible in waking life is so remarkable and of such theoretical importance that I should like to draw still more attention to it by relating some further 'hypermnesic' dreams. Maury [1878, 142] tells us how for some time the word 'Mussidan' kept coming into his head during the day. He knew nothing about it except that it was the name of a town in France. One night he dreamt that he was talking to someone who told him he came from Mussidan, and who, on being asked where that was, replied that it was a small town in the Department of Dordogne. When he woke up, Maury had no belief in the information given him in the dream; he learnt from a gazetteer, however, that it was perfectly correct. In this case the fact of the dream's superior knowledge was confirmed, but the forgotten source of that knowledge was not discovered.

Jessen (1855, 551) reports a very similar event in a dream dating from remoter times: 'To this class belongs among others a dream of the elder Scaliger (quoted by Hennings, 1784, 300) who wrote a poem in praise of the famous men of Verona. A man who called himself Brugnolus appeared to him in a dream and complained that he had been overlooked. Although Scaliger could not remember having ever heard of him, he wrote some verses on him. His son learnt later in Verona that someone named Brugnolus had in fact been celebrated there as a critic.'

The Marquis d'Hervey de St. Denys [1867, 305],[1] quoted by Vaschide (1911, 232 f.), describes a hypermnesic dream which has a special peculiarity, for it was followed by another dream which completed the recognition of what was at first an unidentified memory: 'I once dreamt of a young woman with golden hair, whom I saw talking to my sister while showing her some embroidery. She seemed very familiar to me in the dream and I thought I had seen her very often before. After I woke up, I still had her face very clearly before me but I was totally unable to recognize it. I then went to sleep once more and the dream-picture was repeated. . . . But in this second dream I spoke to the fair-haired lady and asked her if I had not had the pleasure of meeting her before somewhere. "Of course," she replied, "don't you remember the *plage* at Pornic?" I immediately woke up again and I was then able to recollect clearly all the details associated with the attractive vision in the dream.'

[1] [This paragraph and the next were added in 1914.]

The same author [ibid., 306] (quoted again by Vaschide, ibid., 233–4) tells how a musician of his acquaintance once heard in a dream a tune which seemed to him entirely new. It was not until several years later that he found the same tune in an old collected volume of musical pieces, though he still could not remember ever having looked through it before.

I understand that Myers [1892] has published a whole collection of hypermnesic dreams of this kind in the *Proceedings* of the Society for Psychical Research; but these are unluckily inaccessible to me.

No one who occupies himself with dreams can, I believe, fail to discover that it is a very common event for a dream to give evidence of knowledge and memories which the waking subject is unaware of possessing. In my psycho-analytic work with nervous patients, of which I shall speak later, I am in a position several times a week to prove to patients from their dreams that they are really quite familiar with quotations, obscene words and so on, and make use of them in their dreams, though they have forgotten them in their waking life. I will add one more innocent case of hypermnesia in a dream, because of the great ease with which it was possible to trace the source of the knowledge that was accessible only in the dream.

One of my patients dreamt in the course of a fairly lengthy dream that he had ordered a '*Kontuszówka*' while he was in a café. After telling me this, he asked me what a '*Kontuszówka*' was, as he had never heard the name. I was able to tell him in reply that it was a Polish liqueur, and that he could not have invented the name as it had long been familiar to me from advertisements on the hoardings. At first he would not believe me; but some days later, after making his dream come true in a café, he noticed the name on a hoarding at a street corner which he must have gone past at least twice a day for several months.

I have noticed myself [1] from my own dreams how much it is a matter of chance whether one discovers the source of particular elements of a dream. Thus, for several years before completing this book, I was pursued by the picture of a church tower of very simple design, which I could not remember ever having seen. Then I suddenly recognized it, with absolute certainty, at a small station on the line between Salzburg and

[1] [This paragraph was added in 1909.]

Reichenhall. That was during the second half of the eighteen-nineties and I had travelled over the line for the first time in 1886. During later years, when I was already deeply absorbed in the study of dreams, the frequent recurrence in my dreams of the picture of a particular unusual-looking place became a positive nuisance to me. In a specific spatial relation to myself, on my left-hand side, I saw a dark space out of which there glimmered a number of grotesque sandstone figures. A faint recollection, which I was unwilling to credit, told me it was the entrance to a beer-cellar. But I failed to discover either the meaning of the dream-picture or its origin. In 1907 I happened to be in Padua, which, to my regret, I had not been able to visit since 1895. My first visit to that lovely University town had been a disappointment, as I had not been able to see Giotto's frescoes in the Madonna dell' Arena. I had turned back half-way along the street leading there, on being told that the chapel was closed on that particular day. On my second visit, twelve years later, I decided to make up for this and the first thing I did was to set off towards the Arena chapel. In the street leading to it, on my left-hand side as I walked along and in all probability at the point at which I had turned back in 1895, I came upon the place I had seen so often in my dreams, with the sandstone figures that formed part of it. It was in fact the entrance to the garden of a restaurant.

One of the sources from which dreams derive material for reproduction—material which is in part neither remembered nor used in the activities of waking thought—is childhood experience. I will quote only a few of the authors who have noticed and stressed this fact.

Hildebrandt (1875, 23): 'I have already expressly admitted that dreams sometimes bring back to our minds, with a wonderful power of reproduction, very remote and even forgotten events from our earliest years.'

Strümpell (1877, 40): 'The position is even more remarkable when we observe how dreams sometimes bring to light, as it were, from beneath the deepest piles of débris under which the earliest experiences of youth are buried in later times, pictures of particular localities, things or people, completely intact and with all their original freshness. This is not limited to experiences which created a lively impression when they occurred or enjoy a high degree of psychical importance and return later in a dream as genuine recollections at which waking consciousness will rejoice. On the contrary, the depths of memory in dreams also include pictures of people, things, localities and events dating from the earliest times, which either never possessed any psychical importance or more than a slight degree of vividness, or which have long since lost what they may have possessed of either, and which consequently seem completely alien and unknown alike to the dreaming and waking mind till their earlier origin has been discovered.'

Volkelt (1875, 119): 'It is especially remarkable how readily memories of childhood and youth make their way into dreams. Dreams are continually reminding us of things which we have ceased to think of and which have long ceased to be important to us.'

Since dreams have material from childhood at their command, and since, as we all know, that material is for the most part blotted out by gaps in our conscious faculty of memory, these circumstances give rise to interesting hypermnesic dreams, of which I will once more give a few examples.

Maury (1878, 92) relates how when he was a child he used often to go from Meaux, which was his birthplace, to the neighbouring village of Trilport, where his father was superintending the building of a bridge. One night in a dream he found himself in Trilport and was once more playing in the village street. A man came up to him who was wearing a sort of uniform. Maury asked him his name and he replied that he was called C. and was a watchman at the bridge. Maury awoke feeling sceptical as to the correctness of the memory, and asked an old maid-servant, who had been with him since his childhood, whether she could remember a man of that name. 'Why, yes,' was the reply, 'he was the watchman at the bridge when your father was building it.'

Maury (ibid., 143–4) gives another equally well corroborated example of the accuracy of a memory of childhood emerging in a dream. It was dreamt by a Monsieur F., who as a child had lived at Montbrison. Twenty-five years after leaving it, he decided to revisit his home and some friends of the family whom he had not since met. During the night before his departure he dreamt that he was already at Montbrison and, near the town, met a gentleman whom he did not know by sight but who told him he was Monsieur T., a friend of his father's. The dreamer was aware that when he was a child he had known someone of that name, but in his waking state no longer remembered what he looked like. A few days later he actually reached Montbrison, found the locality which in his dream had seemed unknown to him, and there met a gentleman whom he at once recognized as the Monsieur T. in the dream. The real person, however, looked much older than he had appeared in the dream.

At this point I may mention a dream of my own, in which what had to be traced was not an impression but a connection. I had a dream of someone who I knew in my dream was the doctor in my native town. His face was indistinct, but was confused with a picture of one of the masters at my secondary school, whom I still meet occasionally. When I woke up I could not discover what connection there was between these two men. I made some enquiries from my mother, however, about this doctor who dated back to the earliest years of my childhood, and learnt that he had only one eye. The schoolmaster whose figure had covered that of the doctor in the dream, was also one-eyed. It was thirty-eight years since I had seen the doctor, and so far as I know I had never thought of him in my waking life, though a scar on my chin might have reminded me of his attentions.[1]

A number of writers, on the other hand, assert that elements are to be found in most dreams, which are derived from the very last few days before they were dreamt; and this sounds like an attempt to counterbalance the laying of too much weight upon the part played in dream-life by experiences in childhood. Thus Robert (1886, 46) actually declares that normal dreams are as a rule concerned only with the impressions of the past few days. We shall find, however, that the theory of dreams constructed by Robert makes it essential for him to bring forward

[1] [The last clause of this sentence was added in 1909, appears in all later editions up to 1922, but was afterwards omitted. The reference to this same man on p. 275 below only makes sense if it alludes to this omitted clause. The accident that caused the scar is mentioned in the disguised autobiographical case history in Freud (1899a), and the event itself is probably described below on p. 560. This dream plays an important part in a letter to Fliess of October 15, 1897 (Freud, 1950a, Letter 71); it is also described in Freud, 1916-17, Lecture 13.]

the most recent impressions and leave the oldest out of sight. None the less the fact stated by him remains correct, as I am able to confirm from my own investigations. An American writer, Nelson [1888, 380 f.], is of the opinion that the impressions most frequently employed in a dream arise from the day next but one before the dream occurs, or from the day preceding that one—as though the impressions of the day *immediately* before the dream were not sufficiently attenuated or remote.

Several writers who are anxious not to cast doubts on the intimate connection between the content of dreams and waking life have been struck by the fact that impressions with which waking thoughts are intensely occupied only appear in dreams after they have been pushed somewhat aside by the workings of daytime thought. Thus, after the death of someone dear to them, people do not as a rule dream of him to begin with, while they are overwhelmed by grief (Delage, 1891, [40]). On the other hand one of the most recent observers, Miss Hallam (Hallam and Weed, 1896, 410–11), has collected instances to the contrary, thus asserting the right of each of us to psychological individualism in this respect.

The third, most striking and least comprehensible characteristic of memory in dreams is shown in the *choice* of material reproduced. For what is found worth remembering is not, as in waking life, only what is most important, but on the contrary what is most indifferent and insignificant as well. On this point I will quote those writers who have given the strongest expression to their astonishment.

Hildebrandt (1875, 11): 'For the remarkable thing is that dreams derive their elements not from major and stirring events nor the powerful and compelling interests of the preceding day, but from incidental details, from the worthless fragments, one might say, of what has been recently experienced or of the remoter past. A family bereavement, which has moved us deeply and under whose immediate shadow we have fallen asleep late at night, is blotted out of our memory till with our first waking moment it returns to it again with disturbing violence. On the other hand, a wart on the forehead of a stranger whom we met in the street and to whom we gave no second thought after passing him *has* a part to play in our dream. . . .'

Strümpell (1877, 39): 'There are cases in which the analysis of a dream shows that some of its components are indeed derived from experiences of the previous day or its predecessor, but experiences so unimportant and trivial from the point of view of waking consciousness that they were forgotten soon after they occurred. Experiences of this kind include, for instance, remarks accidentally overheard, or another person's actions inattentively observed, or passing glimpses of people or things, or odd fragments of what one has read, and so on.'

Havelock Ellis (1899, 727): 'The profound emotions of waking life, the questions and problems on which we spread our chief voluntary mental energy, are not those which usually present themselves at once to dream consciousness. It is, so far as the immediate past is concerned, mostly the trifling, the incidental, the "forgotten" impressions of daily life which reappear in our dreams. The psychic activities that are awake most intensely are those that sleep most profoundly.'

Binz (1878, 44–5) actually makes this particular peculiarity of memory in dreams the occasion for expressing his dissatisfaction with the explanations of dreams which he himself has supported: 'And the natural dream raises similar problems. Why do we not always dream of the mnemic impressions of the day we have just lived through? Why do we often, without any apparent motive, plunge instead into the remote and almost extinct past? Why does consciousness so often in dreams receive the impression of *indifferent* mnemic images, while the brain-cells, just where they carry the most sensitive marks of what has been experienced, lie for the most part silent and still, unless they have been stirred into fresh activity shortly before, during waking life?'

It is easy to see how the remarkable preference shown by the memory in dreams for indifferent, and consequently unnoticed, elements in waking experience is bound to lead people to overlook in general the dependence of dreams upon waking life and at all events to make it difficult in any particular instance to prove that dependence. Thus Miss Whiton Calkins (1893, 315), in her statistical study of her own and her collaborator's dreams, found that in eleven per cent of the total there was no visible connection with waking life. Hildebrandt (1875, [12 f.]) is unquestionably right in asserting that we should be able to explain the genesis of every dream-image if we devoted enough

time and trouble to tracing its origin. He speaks of this as 'an
exceedingly laborious and thankless task. For as a rule it ends
in hunting out every kind of utterly worthless psychical event
from the remotest corners of the chambers of one's memory,
and in dragging to light once again every kind of completely
indifferent moment of the past from the oblivion in which it
was buried in the very hour, perhaps, after it occurred.' I can
only regret that this keen-sighted author allowed himself to be
deterred from following the path which had this inauspicious
beginning; if he had followed it, it would have led him to the
very heart of the explanation of dreams.

The way in which the memory behaves in dreams is undoubtedly of the greatest importance for any theory of memory
in general. It teaches us that 'nothing which we have once
mentally possessed can be entirely lost' (Scholz, 1893, 59); or,
as Delbœuf [1885, 115] puts it, 'que toute impression même
la plus insignifiante, laisse une trace inaltérable, indéfiniment
susceptible de reparaître au jour'.[1] This is a conclusion to which
we are also driven by many pathological phenomena of mental
life. Certain theories about dreams which we shall mention
later seek to account for their absurdity and incoherence by a
partial forgetting of what we know during the day. When we
bear in mind the extraordinary efficiency that we have just
seen exhibited by memory in dreams we shall have a lively
sense of the contradiction which these theories involve.

It might perhaps occur to us that the phenomenon of
dreaming could be reduced entirely to that of memory: dreams,
it might be supposed, are a manifestation of a reproductive
activity which is at work even in the night and which is an end
in itself. This would tally with statements such as those made
by Pilcz (1899), according to which there is a fixed relation
observable between the time at which a dream occurs and its
content—impressions from the remotest past being reproduced
in dreams during deep sleep, while more recent impressions
appear towards morning. But views of this sort are inherently
improbable owing to the manner in which dreams deal with the
material that is to be remembered. Strümpell [1877, 18] rightly
points out that dreams do not reproduce experiences. They

[1] ['That even the most insignificant impression leaves an unalterable
trace, which is indefinitely capable of revival.']

take one step forward, but the next step in the chain is omitted, or appears in an altered form, or is replaced by something entirely extraneous. Dreams yield no more than *fragments* of reproductions; and this is so general a rule that theoretical conclusions may be based on it. It is true that there are exceptional cases in which a dream repeats an experience with as much completeness as is attainable by our waking memory. Delbœuf [1885, 239 f.] tells how one of his university colleagues [1] had a dream which reproduced in all its details a dangerous carriage-accident he had had, with an almost miraculous escape. Miss Calkins (1893) mentions two dreams whose content was an exact reproduction of an event of the previous day, and I shall myself have occasion later to report an example I came across of a childhood experience re-appearing in a dream without modification. [See pp. 189 and 198.][2]

[1] [In the first edition the words 'who is now teaching in Vienna' appeared here but they were cut out in 1909. In *Ges. Schr.* 3 (1925), 8, Freud remarks that 'the words were no doubt rightly omitted, especially as the man in question had died'.]

[2] [*Footnote added* 1909:] Subsequent experience leads me to add that it by no means rarely happens that innocent and unimportant actions of the previous day are repeated in a dream: such, for instance, as packing a trunk, preparing food in the kitchen, and so on. What the dreamer is himself stressing in dreams of this kind is not, however, the content of the memory but the fact of its being 'real': 'I really *did* do all that yesterday.' [Cf. below pp. 187 and 372. The topics discussed in this and the preceding section are taken up again in the first two sections of Chapter V (p. 163 ff.).]

THE STIMULI AND SOURCES OF DREAMS

There is a popular saying that 'dreams come from indigestion' and this helps us to see what is meant by the stimuli and sources of dreams. Behind these concepts lies a theory according to which dreams are a result of a disturbance of sleep: we should not have had a dream unless something disturbing had happened during our sleep, and the dream was a reaction to that disturbance.

Discussions upon the exciting causes of dreams occupy a very large space in the literature of the subject. The problem could obviously only arise after dreams had become a subject of biological investigation. The ancients, who believed that dreams were inspired by the gods, had no need to look around for their stimulus: dreams emanated from the will of divine or daemonic powers and their content arose from the knowledge or purpose of those powers. Science was immediately faced by the question of whether the stimulus to dreaming was always the same or whether there could be many kinds of such stimuli; and this involved the consideration of whether the explanation of the causation of dreams fell within the province of psychology or rather of physiology. Most authorities seem to agree in assuming that the causes that disturb sleep—that is, the sources of dreaming—may be of many kinds and that somatic stimuli and mental excitations alike may come to act as instigators of dreams. Opinions differ widely, however, in the preference they show for one or the other source of dreams and in the order of importance which they assign to them as factors in the production of dreams.

Any complete enumeration of the sources of dreams leads to a recognition of four kinds of source; and these have also been used for the classification of dreams themselves. They are: (1) external (objective) sensory excitations; (2) internal (subjective) sensory excitations; (3) internal (organic) somatic stimuli; and (4) purely psychical sources of stimulation.

1. EXTERNAL SENSORY STIMULI

The younger Strümpell [1883–4; Engl. trans. (1912, **2**, 160)], the son of the philosopher whose book on dreams has already given us several hints upon their problems, published a well-known account of his observations upon one of his patients who was afflicted with general anaesthesia of the surface of his body and paralysis of several of his higher sense organs. If the few of this man's sensory channels which remained open to the external world were closed, he would fall asleep. Now when we ourselves wish to go to sleep we are in the habit of trying to produce a situation similar to that of Strümpell's experiment. We close our most important sensory channels, our eyes, and try to protect the other senses from all stimuli or from any modification of the stimuli acting on them. We then fall asleep, even though our plan is never completely realized. We cannot keep stimuli completely away from our sense organs nor can we completely suspend the excitability of our sense organs. The fact that a fairly powerful stimulus will awaken us at any time is evidence that 'even in sleep the soul is in constant contact with the extra-corporeal world'.[1] The sensory stimuli that reach us during sleep may very well become sources of dreams.

Now there are a great number of such stimuli, ranging from the unavoidable ones which the state of sleep itself necessarily involves or must tolerate from time to time, to the accidental, rousing stimuli which may or do put an end to sleep. A bright light may force its way into our eyes, or a noise may make itself heard, or some strong-smelling substance may stimulate the mucous membrane of our nose. By unintentional movements during our sleep we may uncover some part of our body and expose it to sensations of chill, or by a change in posture we may ourselves bring about sensations of pressure or contact. We may be stung by a gnat, or some small mishap during the night may impinge upon several of our senses at once. Attentive observers have collected a whole series of dreams in which there has been such a far-reaching correspondence between a stimulus noticed on waking and a portion of the content of the dream that it has been possible to identify the stimulus as the source of the dream.

I will quote from Jessen (1855, 527 f.) a collection of dreams

[1] [Cf. Burdach's remarks on p. 52 f.]

of this kind which may be traced back to objective, and more or less accidental, sensory stimulation.

'Every noise that is indistinctly perceived arouses corresponding dream-images. A peal of thunder will set us in the midst of a battle; the crowing of a cock may turn into a man's cry of terror; the creaking of a door may produce a dream of burglars. If our bed-clothes fall off in the night, we may dream, perhaps, of walking about naked or of falling into water. If we are lying cross-wise in bed and push our feet over the edge, we may dream that we are standing on the brink of a frightful precipice or that we are falling over a cliff. If our head happens to get under the pillow, we dream of being beneath a huge overhanging rock which is on the point of burying us under its weight. Accumulations of semen lead to lascivious dreams, local pains produce ideas of being ill-treated, attacked or injured. . . .

'Meier (1758, 33) once dreamt that he was overpowered by some men who stretched him out on his back on the ground and drove a stake into the earth between his big toe and the next one. While he was imagining this in the dream he woke up and found that a straw was sticking between his toes. On another occasion, according to Hennings (1784, 258), when Meier had fastened his shirt rather tight round his neck, he dreamt that he was being hanged. Hoffbauer [(1796, 146)] dreamt when he was a young man of falling down from a high wall, and when he woke up found that his bedstead had collapsed and that he had really fallen on to the floor. . . . Gregory reports that once, when he was lying with his feet on a hot-water-bottle, he dreamt he had climbed to the top of Mount Etna and that the ground there was intolerably hot. Another man, who was sleeping with a hot poultice on his head, dreamt that he was being scalped by a band of Red Indians; while a third, who was wearing a damp night-shirt, imagined that he was being dragged through a stream. An attack of gout that came on suddenly during sleep caused the patient to believe he was in the hands of the Inquisition and being tortured on the rack. (Macnish [1835, 40].)'

The argument based on the similarity between the stimulus and the content of the dream gains in strength if it is possible deliberately to convey a sensory stimulus to the sleeper and produce in him a dream corresponding to that stimulus. According to Macnish (loc. cit.), quoted by Jessen (1855, 529), experiments of this sort had already been made by Girou de Buzareingues [1848, 55]. 'He left his knee uncovered and dreamt that he was travelling at night in a mail coach. He remarks upon this that travellers will no doubt be aware how cold one's knees become at night in a coach. Another time he left his head uncovered at the back and dreamt that he was taking part in a religious ceremony in the open air. It must be explained that in the country in which he lived it was the custom always to keep the head covered except in circumstances such as these.'

Maury (1878, [154–6]) brings forward some new observations of dreams produced in himself. (A number of other experiments were unsuccessful.)

(1) His lips and the tip of his nose were tickled with a feather.—He dreamt of a frightful form of torture: a mask made of pitch was placed on his face and then pulled off, so that it took his skin off with it.

(2) A pair of scissors was sharpened on a pair of pliers.—He heard bells pealing, followed by alarm-bells, and he was back in the June days of 1848.

(3) He was given some eau-de-cologne to smell.—He was in Cairo, in Johann Maria Farina's shop. Some absurd adventures followed, which he could not reproduce.

(4) He was pinched lightly on the neck.—He dreamt he was being given a mustard plaster and thought of the doctor who had treated him as a child.

(5) A hot iron was brought close to his face.—He dreamt that the 'chauffeurs'[1] had made their way into the house and were forcing its inhabitants to give up their money by sticking their feet into braziers of hot coal. The Duchess of Abrantès, whose secretary he was in the dream, then appeared.

(8) A drop of water was dropped on his forehead.—He was in Italy, was sweating violently and was drinking white Orvieto wine.

(9) Light from a candle was repeatedly shone upon him through a sheet of red paper.—He dreamt of the weather and of the heat, and was once again in a storm he had experienced in the English Channel.

[1] The 'chauffeurs' [heaters] were bands of robbers in La Vendée [at the time of the French Revolution], who made use of the method of torture described above.

Other attempts at producing dreams experimentally have been reported by Hervey de Saint-Denys [1867, 268 f. and 376 f.], Weygandt (1893) and others.

Many writers have commented upon 'the striking facility with which dreams are able to weave a sudden impression from the world of the senses into their own structure so that it comes as what appears to be a pre-arranged catastrophe that has been gradually led up to.' (Hildebrandt, 1875, [36].) 'In my youth', this author goes on, 'I used to make use of an alarm-clock in order to be up regularly at a fixed hour. It must have happened hundreds of times that the noise produced by this instrument fitted into an ostensibly lengthy and connected dream as though the whole dream had been leading up to that one event and had reached its appointed end in what was a logically indispensable climax.' [Ibid., 37.]

I shall quote three of these alarm-clock dreams presently in another connection. [P. 27 f.]

Volkelt (1875, 108 f.) writes: 'A composer once dreamt that he was giving a class and was trying to make a point clear to his pupils. When he had done, he turned to one of the boys and asked him if he had followed. The boy shouted back like a lunatic: "Oh ja! [Oh yes!]" He began to reprove the boy angrily for shouting, but the whole class broke out into cries first of "Orja!", then of "Eurjo!" and finally of "Feuerjo!"[1] At this point he was woken up by actual cries of "Feuerjo!" in the street.'

Garnier (1865, [1, 476]) tells how Napoleon I was woken by a bomb-explosion while he was asleep in his carriage. He had a dream that he was once more crossing the Tagliamento under the Austrian bombardment, and at last started up with a cry: 'We are undermined!'[2]

A dream dreamt by Maury (1878, 161) has become famous. He was ill and lying in his room in bed, with his mother sitting beside him, and dreamt that it was during the Reign of Terror. After witnessing a number of frightful scenes of murder, he was finally himself brought before the revolutionary tribunal. There he saw Robespierre, Marat, Fouquier-Tinville and the rest of the grim heroes of those terrible days. He was questioned by

---

[1] [The first two of these last three exclamations are meaningless; the third is the conventional cry for an alarm of fire.]

[2] [Further considered below on pp. 233 f. and 497 f.]

them, and, after a number of incidents which were not retained
in his memory, was condemned, and led to the place of execu-
tion surrounded by an immense mob. He climbed on to the
scaffold and was bound to the plank by the executioner. It was
tipped up. The blade of the guillotine fell. He felt his head
being separated from his body, woke up in extreme anxiety—
and found that the top of the bed had fallen down and had
struck his cervical vertebrae just in the way in which the blade
of the guillotine would actually have struck them.

This dream was the basis of an interesting discussion between
Le Lorrain (1894) and Egger (1895) in the *Revue philosophique*.
The question raised was whether and how it was possible
for a dreamer to compress such an apparently superabundant
quantity of material into the short period elapsing between his
perceiving the rousing stimulus and his waking.[1]

Examples of this kind leave an impression that of all the
sources of dreams the best confirmed are objective sensory
stimuli during sleep. Moreover they are the only sources whatever taken into account by laymen. If an educated man, who is
unacquainted with the literature of dreams, is asked how dreams
arise, he will infallibly answer with a reference to some instance
he has come across in which a dream was explained by an objective sensory stimulus discovered after waking. Scientific enquiry,
however, cannot stop there. It finds an occasion for further
questions in the observed fact that the stimulus which impinges
on the senses during sleep does not appear in the dream in its
real shape but is replaced by another image in some way related
to it. But the relation connecting the stimulus of the dream to
the dream which is its result is, to quote Maury's words (1854,
72), 'une affinité quelconque, mais qui n'est pas unique et
exclusive.'[2] Let us consider in this connection three of Hildebrandt's alarm-clock dreams (1875, 37 f.). The question they
raise is why the same stimulus should have provoked three such
different dreams and why it should have provoked these rather
than any other.

'I dreamt, then, that one spring morning I was going for a
walk and was strolling through the green fields till I came to a
neighbouring village, where I saw the villagers in their best

[1] [Further discussed below, pp. 64 and 496 f.]
[2] ['An affinity of some kind, but one which is not unique and
exclusive.']

clothes, with hymn-books under their arms, flocking to the church. Of course! It was Sunday, and early morning service would soon be beginning. I decided I would attend it; but first, as I was rather hot from walking, I went into the churchyard which surrounded the church, to cool down. While I was reading some of the tombstones, I heard the bell-ringer climbing up the church tower and at the top of it I now saw the little village bell which would presently give the signal for the beginning of devotions. For quite a while it hung there motionless, then it began to swing, and suddenly its peal began to ring out clear and piercing—so clear and piercing that it put an end to my sleep. But what was ringing was the alarm-clock.

'Here is another instance. It was a bright winter's day and the streets were covered with deep snow. I had agreed to join a party for a sleigh-ride; but I had to wait a long time before news came that the sleigh was at the door. Now followed the preparations for getting in—the fur rug spread out, the foot-muff put ready—and at last I was sitting in my seat. But even then the moment of departure was delayed till a pull at the reins gave the waiting horses the signal. Then off they started, and, with a violent shake, the sleigh bells broke into their familiar jingle—with such violence, in fact, that in a moment the cobweb of my dream was torn through. And once again it was only the shrill sound of the alarm-clock.

'And now yet a third example. I saw a kitchen-maid, carrying several dozen plates piled on one another, walking along the passage to the dining-room. The column of china in her arms seemed to me in danger of losing its balance. "Take care," I exclaimed, "or you'll drop the whole load." The inevitable rejoinder duly followed: she was quite accustomed to that kind of job, and so on. And meanwhile my anxious looks followed the advancing figure. Then—just as I expected—she stumbled at the threshold and the fragile crockery slipped and rattled and clattered in a hundred pieces on the floor. But the noise continued without ceasing, and soon it seemed no longer to be a clattering; it was turning into a ringing—and the ringing, as my waking self now became aware, was only the alarm-clock doing its duty.'

The question of why the mind mistakes the nature of objective sensory stimuli in dreams receives almost the same answer from Strümpell (1877, [103]) as from Wundt (1874, [659 f.]):

the mind receives stimuli that reach it during sleep under conditions favourable to the formation of illusions. A sense-impression is recognized by us and correctly interpreted—that is, it is placed in the group of memories to which, in accordance with all our previous experiences, it belongs—provided the impression is sufficiently strong, clear and lasting and provided we have sufficient time at our disposal for considering the matter. If these conditions are not fulfilled, we mistake the object which is the source of the impression: we form an illusion about it. 'If someone goes for a walk in the open country and has an indeterminate perception of a distant object, he may at first believe it to be a horse.' On a closer view he may be led to interpret it as a cow lying down, and the image may finally resolve itself definitely into a group of people sitting on the ground. The impressions received by the mind from external stimuli during sleep are of a similarly indeterminate nature; and on their basis the mind forms illusions, since a greater or smaller number of mnemic images are aroused by the impression and it is through them that it acquires its psychical value. From *which* of the many groups of memories concerned the related images shall be aroused and *which* of the possible associative connections shall accordingly be put into action—these questions too, on Strümpell's theory, are indeterminable and are, as it were, left open to the arbitrary decision of the mind.

At this point we are faced with a choice between two alternatives. We may admit it as a fact that it is impossible to follow the laws governing the formation of dreams any further; and we may accordingly refrain from enquiring whether there may not be other determinants governing the interpretation put by the dreamer upon the illusion called up by the sense-impression. Or, on the other hand, we may have a suspicion that the sensory stimulus which impinges on the sleeper plays only a modest part in generating his dream and that other factors determine the choice of the mnemic images which are to be aroused in him. In fact, if we examine Maury's experimentally produced dreams (which I have related in such detail for this very reason), we shall be tempted to say that the experiment in fact accounts for the origin of only one element of the dreams; the rest of their content seems too self-contained, too definite in its details, to be explicable solely by the necessity for fitting in with the element experimentally introduced from outside. Indeed, one begins to have doubts about the illusion theory and about the power of objective impressions to give a shape to dreams when one finds that those impressions are sometimes subjected in dreams to the most peculiar and far-fetched interpretations. Thus Simon (1888) tells us of a dream in which he saw some gigantic figures seated at table and clearly heard the frightful snapping noise made by their jaws coming together as they chewed. When he awoke he heard the beat of a horse's hooves galloping past his window. The noise made by the horse's hooves may have suggested ideas from a group of memories connected with *Gulliver's Travels*—the giants of Brobdingnag and the virtuous Houyhnhnms—if I may venture on an interpretation without the dreamer's assistance. Is it not probable, then, that the choice of such an unusual group of memories as these was facilitated by motives other than the objective stimulus alone?[1]

2. INTERNAL (SUBJECTIVE) SENSORY EXCITATIONS

In spite of any objections to the contrary, it has to be admitted that the part played by objective sensory excitations during sleep in provoking dreams remains indisputable. And if such stimuli may appear, from their nature and frequency, insufficient to explain *every* dream-image, we shall be encouraged to seek for other sources of dreams analogous to them in their operation. I cannot say when the idea first cropped up of taking *internal* (subjective) excitations of the sense organs into account alongside of the *external* sensory stimuli. It is, however, the case that this is done, more or less explicitly, in all the more recent discussions of the aetiology of dreams. 'An essential part is also played, I believe,' writes Wundt (1874, 657), 'in the production of the illusions that occur in dreams by the subjective visual and auditory sensations which are familiar to us in the waking state as the formless areas of luminosity which become visible to us when our field of vision is darkened, as ringing or buzzing

[1] [*Footnote added* 1911:] The appearance of gigantic figures in a dream gives grounds for supposing that some scene from the dreamer's childhood is involved. [Cf. p. 408.]—[*Added* 1925 :] Incidentally, the interpretation given in the text, pointing to a reminiscence of *Gulliver's Travels*, is a good example of what an interpretation ought *not* to be. The interpreter of a dream should not give free play to his own ingenuity and neglect the dreamer's associations.

in the ears, and so on. Especially important among these are the subjective excitations of the retina. It is in this way that is to be explained the remarkable tendency of dreams to conjure up before the eyes similar or identical objects in large numbers. We see before us innumerable birds or butterflies or fishes or coloured beads or flowers, etc. Here the luminous dust in the darkened field of vision has taken on a fantastic shape, and the numerous specks of which it consists are incorporated into the dream as an equal number of separate images; and these, on account of their mobility, are regarded as *moving* objects.—This is no doubt also the basis of the great fondness shown by dreams for animal figures of every sort; for the immense variety of such forms can adjust itself easily to the particular form assumed by the subjective luminous images.'

As sources of dream-images, subjective sensory excitations have the obvious advantage of not being dependent, like objective ones, upon external chance. They are ready to hand, as one might say, whenever they are needed as an explanation. But they are at a disadvantage compared with objective sensory stimuli in that the part they play in instigating a dream is scarcely or not at all open to confirmation, as is the case with objective stimuli, by observation and experiment. The chief evidence in favour of the power of subjective sensory excitations to instigate dreams is provided by what are known as 'hypnagogic hallucinations', or, to use Johannes Müller's term (1826), 'imaginative visual phenomena'. These are images, often very vivid and rapidly changing, which are apt to appear—quite habitually in some people—during the period of falling asleep; and they may also persist for a time after the eyes have been opened. Maury, who was subject to them in a high degree, has made an exhaustive examination of them and maintains (as did Müller [ibid., 49 f.] before him) their connection and indeed their identity with dream-images. In order to produce them, he says (Maury, 1878, 59 f.), a certain amount of mental passivity, a relaxation of the strain of attention, is necessary. It is enough, however, to fall into a lethargic state of this kind for no more than a second (provided that one has the necessary predisposition) in order to have a hypnagogic hallucination. After this one may perhaps wake up again and the process may be repeated several times until one finally falls asleep. Maury found that if he then woke up once more after not too long an

interval, he was able to detect in his dream the same images
that had floated before his eyes as hypnagogic hallucinations
before he fell asleep. (Ibid., 134 f.) This was the case on one
occasion with a number of grotesque figures with distorted
faces and strange *coiffures* which pestered him with extreme per-
tinacity while he was going to sleep and which he remembered
having dreamt about after he woke. Another time, when he was
suffering from hunger owing to having put himself on a light
diet, he had a hypnagogic vision of a plate and a hand armed
with a fork which was helping itself to some of the food from the
plate. In the dream which followed he was sitting at a well-
spread table and heard the noise made by the diners with their
forks. Yet another time, when he went to sleep with his eyes in
an irritated and painful state, he had a hypnagogic hallucination of some microscopically small signs which he could only
decipher one by one with the greatest difficulty; he was woken
from his sleep an hour later and remembered a dream in which
there was an open book printed in very small type which he
was reading painfully.

Auditory hallucinations of words, names, and so on can
also occur hypnagogically in the same way as visual images,
and may then be repeated in a dream—just as an overture
announces the principal themes which are to be heard in the
opera that is to follow.

A more recent observer of hypnagogic hallucinations,
G. Trumbull Ladd (1892), has followed the same lines as
Müller and Maury. After some practice he succeeded in being
able to wake himself suddenly without opening his eyes, from
two to five minutes after gradually falling asleep. He thus had
an opportunity of comparing the retinal sensations which were
just disappearing with the dream-images persisting in his
memory. He declares that it was possible in every case to
recognize an internal relation between the two, for the luminous
points and lines of the idioretinal light provided, as it were, an
outline drawing or diagram of the figures mentally perceived in
the dream. For instance, an arrangement of the luminous points
in the retina in parallel lines corresponded to a dream in which
he had been seeing, clearly spread out in front of him, some
lines of print which he was engaged in reading. Or, to use his
own words, 'the clearly printed page which I was reading in
my dream faded away into an object that appeared to my

waking consciousness like a section of an actual page of print
when seen through an oval hole in a piece of paper at too great
a distance to distinguish more than an occasional fragment of a
word, and even that dimly'. Ladd is of opinion (though he does
not underestimate the part played in the phenomenon by
central [cerebral] factors) that scarcely a single visual dream
occurs without the participation of material provided by intra-
ocular retinal excitation. This applies especially to dreams
occurring soon after falling asleep in a dark room, while the
source of stimulus for dreams occurring in the morning shortly
before waking is the objective light which penetrates the eyes in
a room that is growing light. The changing, perpetually shifting
character of the excitation of the idioretinal light corresponds
precisely to the constantly moving succession of images shown
us by our dreams. No one who attaches importance to these
observations of Ladd's will underestimate the part played in
dreams by these subjective sources of stimulation, for, as we
know, visual images constitute the principal component of our
dreams. The contributions from the other senses, except for that
of hearing, are intermittent and of less importance.

3. INTERNAL ORGANIC SOMATIC STIMULI

Since we are now engaged in looking for sources of dreams
inside the organism instead of outside it, we must bear in mind
that almost all our internal organs, though they give us scarcely
any news of their working so long as they are in a healthy state,
become a source of what are mainly distressing sensations when
they are in what we describe as states of excitation, or during
illnesses. These sensations must be equated with the sensory or
painful stimuli reaching us from the outside. The experience of
ages is reflected in—to take an example—Strümpell's remarks
on the subject (1877, 107): 'During sleep the mind attains a far
deeper and wider sensory consciousness of somatic events than
during the waking state. It is obliged to receive and be affected
by impressions of stimuli from parts of the body and from
changes in the body of which it knows nothing when awake.'
So early a writer as Aristotle regarded it as quite possible that
the beginnings of an illness might make themselves felt in
dreams before anything could be noticed of it in waking life,
owing to the magnifying effect produced upon impressions by
dreams. (See above, p. 3.) Medical writers, too, who were

certainly far from believing in the prophetic power of dreams, have not disputed their significance as premonitors of illness. (Cf. Simon, 1888, 31, and many earlier writers.[1])

Instances of the diagnostic power of dreams seem to be vouched for in more recent times. Thus Tissié (1898, 62 f.) quotes from Artigues (1884, 43) the story of a forty-three-year-old woman, who, while apparently in perfect health, was for some years tormented by anxiety-dreams. She was then medically examined and found to be in the early stages of an affection of the heart, to which she eventually succumbed.

Pronounced disorders of the internal organs obviously act as instigators of dreams in a whole number of cases. The frequency of anxiety-dreams in diseases of the heart and lungs is generally recognized. Indeed, this side of dream-life is placed in the foreground by so many authorities that I am content with a mere reference to the literature: Radestock [1879, 70], Spitta [1882, 241 f.], Maury [1878, 33 f.], Simon (1888), Tissié [1898, 60 ff.]. Tissié is even of the opinion that the particular organ affected gives a characteristic impress to the content of the dream. Thus the dreams of those suffering from diseases of the heart are usually short and come to a terrifying end at the moment of waking; their content almost always includes a situation involving a horrible death. Sufferers from diseases of the lungs dream of suffocation, crowding and fleeing, and are remarkably subject to the familiar nightmare. (It may be remarked, incidentally, that Börner (1855) has succeeded in provoking the latter experimentally by lying on his face or covering the respiratory

---

[1] [*Footnote added* 1914:] Apart from the diagnostic value ascribed to dreams (e.g. in the works of Hippocrates [see above p. 3 *n.*]), their *therapeutic* importance in antiquity must also be borne in mind. In Greece there were dream oracles, which were regularly visited by patients in search of recovery. A sick man would enter the temple of Apollo or Aesculapius, would perform various ceremonies there, would be purified by lustration, massage and incense, and then, in a state of exaltation, would be stretched on the skin of a ram that had been sacrificed. He would then fall asleep and would dream of the remedies for his illness. These would be revealed to him either in their natural form or in symbols and pictures which would afterwards be interpreted by the priests. For further information upon therapeutic dreams among the Greeks see Lehmann (1908, 1, 74), Bouché-Leclercq (1879–1882), Hermann (1858, §41, 262 ff., and 1882, §38, 356), Böttinger (1795, 163 ff.), Lloyd (1877), Döllinger (1857, 130).—[A comment on the 'diagnostic' value of dreams will be found near the beginning of Freud, 1917*d*.]

apertures.) In the case of digestive disorders dreams contain ideas connected with enjoyment of food or disgust. Finally, the influence of sexual excitement on the content of dreams can be adequately appreciated by everyone from his own experience and provides the theory that dreams are instigated by organic stimuli with its most powerful support.

No one, moreover, who goes through the literature of the subject can fail to notice that some writers, such as Maury [1878, 451 f.] and Weygandt (1893), were led to the study of dream problems by the effect of their own illnesses upon the content of their dreams.

Nevertheless, though these facts are established beyond a doubt, their importance for the study of the sources of dreams is not so great as might have been hoped. Dreams are phenomena which occur in healthy people—perhaps in everyone, perhaps every night—and it is obvious that organic illness cannot be counted among its indispensable conditions. And what we are concerned with is not the origin of certain special dreams but the source that instigates the ordinary dreams of normal people.

We need only go a step further, however, in order to come upon a source of dreams more copious than any we have so far considered, one indeed which seems as though it could never run dry. If it is established that the interior of the body when it is in a diseased state becomes a source of stimuli for dreams, and if we admit that during sleep the mind, being diverted from the external world, is able to pay more attention to the interior of the body, then it seems plausible to suppose that the internal organs do not need to be diseased before they can cause excitations to reach the sleeping mind—excitations which are somehow turned into dream-images. While we are awake we are aware of a diffuse general sensibility or coenaesthesia, but only as a vague quality of our mood; to this feeling, according to medical opinion, all the organic systems contribute a share. At night, however, it would seem that this same feeling, grown into a powerful influence and acting through its various components, becomes the strongest and at the same time the commonest source for instigating dream-images. If this is so, it would only remain to investigate the laws according to which the organic stimuli turn into dream-images.

We have here reached the theory of the origin of dreams which is preferred by all the medical authorities. The obscurity in which the centre of our being (the '*moi splanchnique*', as Tissié [1898, 23] calls it) is veiled from our knowledge and the obscurity surrounding the origin of dreams tally too well not to be brought into relation to each other. The line of thought which regards vegetative organic sensation as the constructor of dreams has, moreover, a particular attraction for medical men since it allows of a single aetiology for dreams and mental diseases, whose manifestations have so much in common; for coenaesthetic changes and stimuli arising from the internal organs are also held largely responsible for the origin of the psychoses. It is not surprising, therefore, that the origin of the theory of somatic stimulation may be traced back to more than one independent source.

The line of argument developed by the philosopher Schopenhauer in 1851 has had a decisive influence on a number of writers. Our picture of the universe, in his view, is arrived at by our intellect taking the impressions that impinge on it from outside and remoulding them into the forms of time, space and causality. During the daytime the stimuli from the interior of the organism, from the sympathetic nervous system, exercise at the most an unconscious effect upon our mood. But at night, when we are no longer deafened by the impressions of the day, those which arise from within are able to attract attention— just as at night we can hear the murmuring of a brook which is drowned by daytime noises. But how is the intellect to react to these stimuli otherwise than by carrying out its own peculiar function on them? The stimuli are accordingly remodelled into forms occupying space and time and obeying the rules of causality, and thus dreams arise [cf. Schopenhauer, 1862, 1, 249 ff.]. Scherner (1861) and after him Volkelt (1875) endeavoured subsequently to investigate in more detail the relation between somatic stimuli and dream-images, but I shall postpone my consideration of these attempts till we reach the section dealing with the various theories about dreams. [See below, p. 83 ff.]

Krauss [1859, 255], the psychiatrist, in an investigation carried through with remarkable consistency, traces the origin alike of dreams and of deliria[1] and delusions to the same factor, namely to organically determined sensations. It is scarcely possible to think of any part of the organism which might not be

[1] [Perhaps 'hallucinations'; see p. 59 *n*.]

the starting-point of a dream or of a delusion. Organically determined sensations 'may be divided into two classes: (1) those constituting the general mood (coenaesthesia) and (2) the specific sensations immanent in the principal systems of the vegetative organism. Of these latter five groups are to be distinguished: (a) muscular, (b) respiratory, (c) gastric, (d) sexual and (e) peripheral sensations.' Krauss supposes that the process by which dream-images arise on the basis of somatic stimuli is as follows. The sensation that has been aroused evokes a cognate image, in accordance with some law of association. It combines with the image into an organic structure, to which, however, consciousness reacts abnormally. For it pays no attention to the *sensation*, but directs the whole of it to the accompanying *images* —which explains why the true facts were for so long misunderstood. Krauss has a special term for describing this process: the 'trans-substantiation' of sensations into dream-images.

The influence of organic somatic stimuli upon the formation of dreams is almost universally accepted to-day; but the question of the laws that govern the relation between them is answered in very various ways, and often by obscure pronouncements. On the basis of the theory of somatic stimulation, dream-interpretation is thus faced with the special problem of tracing back the content of a dream to the organic stimuli which caused it; and, if the rules for interpretation laid down by Scherner (1861) are not accepted, one is often faced with the awkward fact that the only thing that reveals the existence of the organic stimulus is precisely the content of the dream itself.

There is a fair amount of agreement, however, over the interpretation of various forms of dreams that are described as 'typical', because they occur in large numbers of people and with very similar content. Such are the familiar dreams of falling from a height, of teeth falling out, of flying and of embarrassment at being naked or insufficiently clad. This last dream is attributed simply to the sleeper's perceiving that he has thrown off his bedclothes in his sleep and is lying exposed to the air. The dream of teeth falling out is traced back to a 'dental stimulus', though this does not necessarily imply that the excitation of the teeth is a pathological one. According to Strümpell [1877, 119] the flying dream is the image which is found appropriate by the mind as an interpretation of the stimulus produced by the rising and sinking of the lobes of the lungs at times when cutaneous sensations in the thorax have ceased to be conscious: it is this latter circumstance that leads to the feeling which is attached to the idea of floating. The dream of falling from a height is said to be due to an arm falling away from the body or a flexed knee being suddenly extended at a time when the sense of cutaneous pressure is beginning to be no longer conscious; the movements in question cause the tactile sensations to become conscious once more, and the transition to consciousness is represented psychically by the dream of falling (ibid., 118). The obvious weakness of these attempted explanations, plausible though they are, lies in the fact that, without any other evidence, they can make successive hypotheses that this or that group of organic sensations enters or disappears from mental perception, till a constellation has been reached which affords an explanation of the dream. I shall later have occasion to return to the question of typical dreams and their origin. [Cf. pp. 241 ff. and 384 ff.]

Simon (1888, 34 f.) has attempted to deduce some of the rules governing the way in which organic stimuli determine the resultant dreams by comparing a series of similar dreams. He asserts that if an organic apparatus which normally plays a part in the expression of an emotion is brought by some extraneous cause during sleep into the state of excitation which is usually produced by the emotion, then a dream will arise which will contain images appropriate to the emotion in question. Another rule lays it down that if during sleep an organ is in a state of activity, excitation or disturbance, the dream will produce images related to the performance of the function which is discharged by the organ concerned.

Mourly Vold (1896) has set out to prove experimentally in one particular field the effect on the production of dreams which is asserted by the theory of somatic stimulation. His experiments consisted in altering the position of a sleeper's limbs and comparing the resultant dreams with the alterations made. He states his findings as follows:

(1) The position of a limb in the dream corresponds approximately to its position in reality. Thus, we dream of the limb being in a static condition when it is so actually.

(2) If we dream of a limb moving, then one of the positions passed through in the course of completing the movement invariably corresponds to the limb's actual position.

(3) The position of the dreamer's own limb may be ascribed in the dream to some other person.

(4) The dream may be of the movement in question being *hindered*.

(5) The limb which is in the position in question may appear in the dream as an animal or monster, in which case a certain analogy is established between them.

(6) The position of a limb may give rise in the dream to thoughts which have some connection with the limb. Thus, if the fingers are concerned, we dream of numbers.

I should be inclined to conclude from findings such as these that even the theory of somatic stimulation has not succeeded in completely doing away with the apparent absence of determination in the choice of what dream-images are to be produced.[1]

4. Psychical Sources of Stimulation

When we were dealing with the relations of dreams to waking life and with the material of dreams, we found that the most ancient and the most recent students of dreams were united in believing that men dream of what they do during the daytime and of what interests them while they are awake [p. 7 f.]. Such an interest, carried over from waking life into sleep, would not only be a mental bond, a link between dreams and life, but would also provide us with a further source of dreams and one not to be despised. Indeed, taken in conjunction with the interests that develop during sleep—the stimuli that impinge on the sleeper—it might be enough to explain the origin of all dream-images. But we have also heard the opposite asserted, namely that dreams withdraw the sleeper from the interests of daytime and that, as a rule, we only start dreaming of the things that have most struck us during the day, after they have lost the spice of actuality in waking life. [Pp. 7 and 18.] Thus at every step we take in our analysis of dream-life we come to feel that it is impossible to make generalizations without covering ourselves by such qualifying phrases as 'frequently', 'as a rule' or 'in most cases', and without being prepared to admit the validity of exceptions.

[1] [*Footnote added* 1914:] This author has since produced a two-volume report on his experiments (1910 and 1912), which is referred to below. [See p. 223 *n*.]

If it were a fact that waking interests, along with internal and external stimuli during sleep, sufficed to exhaust the aetiology of dreams, we ought to be in a position to give a satisfactory account of the origin of every element of a dream: the riddle of the sources of dreams would be solved, and it would only remain to define the share taken respectively by psychical and somatic stimuli in any particular dream. Actually no such complete explanation of a dream has ever yet been achieved, and anyone who has attempted it has found portions (and usually very numerous portions) of the dream regarding whose origin he could find nothing to say. Daytime interests are clearly not such far-reaching psychical sources of dreams as might have been expected from the categorical assertions that everyone continues to carry on his daily business in his dreams.

No other psychical sources of dreams are known. So it comes about that all the explanations of dreams given in the literature of the subject—with the possible exception of Scherner's, which will be dealt with later [see p. 83]—leave a great gap when it comes to assigning an origin for the ideational images which constitute the most characteristic material of dreams. In this embarrassing situation, a majority of the writers on the subject have tended to reduce to a minimum the part played by psychical factors in instigating dreams, since those factors are so hard to come at. It is true that they divide dreams into two main classes—those 'due to nervous stimulation' and those 'due to association', of which the latter have their source exclusively in reproduction [of material already experienced] (cf. Wundt, 1874, 657 f.). Nevertheless they cannot escape a doubt 'whether any dream can take place without being given an impetus by some somatic stimulus' (Volkelt, 1875, 127). It is difficult even to give a description of purely associative dreams. 'In associative dreams proper, there can be no question of any such solid core [derived from somatic stimulation]. Even the very centre of the dream is only loosely put together. The ideational processes, which in any dream are ungoverned by reason or common sense, are here no longer even held together by any relatively important somatic or mental excitations, and are thus abandoned to their own kaleidoscopic changes and to their own jumbled confusion.' (Ibid., 118.) Wundt (1874, 656–7), too, seeks to minimize the psychical factor in the instigation of dreams. He declares that there seems to be no justification for regarding the phantasms of dreams as pure hallucinations; most dream-images are probably in fact illusions, since they arise from faint sense-impressions, which never cease during sleep. Weygandt (1893, 17) has adopted this same view and made its application general. He asserts of *all* dream-images 'that their primary causes are sensory stimuli and that only later do reproductive associations become attached to them'. Tissié (1898, 183) goes even further in putting a limit to the psychical sources of stimulation: 'Les rêves d'origine absolument psychique n'existent pas'; and (ibid., 6) 'les pensées de nos rêves nous viennent du dehors. . . .'[1]

Those writers who, like that eminent philosopher Wundt, take up a middle position do not fail to remark that in most dreams somatic stimuli and the psychical instigators (whether unknown or recognized as daytime interests) work in co-operation.

We shall find later that the enigma of the formation of dreams can be solved by the revelation of an unsuspected psychical source of stimulation. Meanwhile we shall feel no surprise at the over-estimation of the part played in forming dreams by stimuli which do not arise from mental life. Not only are they easy to discover and even open to experimental confirmation; but the somatic view of the origin of dreams is completely in line with the prevailing trend of thought in psychiatry to-day. It is true that the dominance of the brain over the organism is asserted with apparent confidence. Nevertheless, anything that might indicate that mental life is in any way independent of demonstrable organic changes or that its manifestations are in any way spontaneous alarms the modern psychiatrist, as though a recognition of such things would inevitably bring back the days of the Philosophy of Nature, [see p. 5 *n.*] and of the metaphysical view of the nature of mind. The suspicions of the psychiatrists have put the mind, as it were, under tutelage, and they now insist that none of its impulses shall be allowed to suggest that it has any means of its own. This behaviour of theirs only shows how little trust they really have in the validity of a causal connection between the somatic and the mental. Even when investigation shows that the primary exciting cause of a phenomenon is psychical, deeper research

[1] ['Dreams of purely psychical origin do not exist.' 'The thoughts in our dreams reach us from outside.']

will one day trace the path further and discover an organic basis for the mental event. But if at the moment we cannot see beyond the mental, that is no reason for denying its existence.[1]

[1] [The topics in this section are taken up again in Section C of Chapter V (p. 220 ff.).]

WHY DREAMS ARE FORGOTTEN AFTER WAKING

It is a proverbial fact that dreams melt away in the morning. They can, of course, be remembered; for we only know dreams from our memory of them after we are awake. But we very often have a feeling that we have only remembered a dream in part and that there was more of it during the night; we can observe, too, how the recollection of a dream, which was still lively in the morning, will melt away, except for a few small fragments, in the course of the day; we often know we have dreamt, without knowing *what* we have dreamt; and we are so familiar with the fact of dreams being liable to be forgotten, that we see no absurdity in the possibility of someone having had a dream in the night and of his not being aware in the morning either of what he has dreamt or even of the fact that he has dreamt at all. On the other hand, it sometimes happens that dreams show an extraordinary persistence in the memory. I have analysed dreams in my patients which occurred twenty-five and more years earlier; and I can remember a dream of my own separated by at least thirty-seven years from to-day and yet as fresh as ever in my memory. All of this is very remarkable and not immediately intelligible.

The most detailed account of the forgetting of dreams is the one given by Strümpell [1877, 79 f.]. It is evidently a complex phenomenon, for Strümpell traces it back not to a single cause but to a whole number of them.

In the first place, all the causes that lead to forgetting in waking life are operative for dreams as well. When we are awake we regularly forget countless sensations and perceptions at once, because they were too weak or because the mental excitation attaching to them was too slight. The same holds good of many dream-images: they are forgotten because they are too weak, while stronger images adjacent to them are remembered. The factor of intensity, however, is certainly not in itself enough to determine whether a dream-image shall be recollected. Strümpell [1877, 82] admits, as well as other writers (e.g. Calkins, 1893, 312), that we often forget dream-images

which we know were very vivid, while a very large number
which are shadowy and lacking in sensory force are among
those retained in the memory. Moreover when we are awake
we tend easily to forget an event which occurs only once and
more readily to notice what can be perceived repeatedly. Now
most dream-images are unique experiences;[1] and that fact will
contribute impartially towards making us forget all dreams.
Far more importance attaches to a third cause of forgetting. If
sensations, ideas, thoughts, and so on, are to attain a certain
degree of susceptibility to being remembered, it is essential that
they should not remain isolated but should be arranged in
appropriate concatenations and groupings. If a short line of
verse is divided up into its component words and these are
mixed up, it becomes very hard to remember. 'If words are
properly arranged and put into the relevant order, one word
will help another, and the whole, being charged with meaning,
will be easily taken up by the memory and retained for a long
time. It is in general as difficult and unusual to retain what is
nonsensical as it is to retain what is confused and disordered.'
[Strümpell, 1877, 83.] Now dreams are in most cases lacking
in intelligibility and orderliness. The compositions which constitute dreams are barren of the qualities which would make it
possible to remember them, and they are forgotten because as a
rule they fall to pieces a moment later. Radestock (1879, 168),
however, claims to have observed that it is the most peculiar
dreams that are best remembered, and this, it must be admitted,
would scarcely tally with what has just been said.

Strümpell [1877, 82 f.] believes that certain other factors
derived from the relation between dreaming and waking life
are of still greater importance in causing dreams to be forgotten. The liability of dreams to be forgotten by waking consciousness is evidently only the counterpart of the fact which
has been mentioned earlier [p. 21] that dreams scarcely ever
take over ordered recollections from waking life, but only
details selected from them, which they tear from the psychical
context in which they are usually remembered in the waking
state. Thus dream-compositions find no place in the company
of the psychical sequences with which the mind is filled. There
is nothing that can help us to remember them. 'In this way

[1] Dreams that recur periodically have often been observed. Cf. the
collection given by Chabaneix (1897). [Cf. p. 190.]

'ream-structures are, as it were, lifted above the floor of our
ıental life and float in psychical space like clouds in the sky,
:attered by the first breath of wind.' (Strümpell, 1877, 87.)
.\fter waking, moreover, the world of the senses presses forward
and at once takes possession of the attention with a force which
very few dream-images can resist; so that here too we have another factor tending in the same direction. Dreams give way
before the impressions of a new day just as the brilliance of the
stars yields to the light of the sun.

Finally, there is another fact to be borne in mind as likely to
lead to dreams being forgotten, namely that most people take
very little interest in their dreams. Anyone, such as a scientific
investigator, who pays attention to his dreams over a period of
time will have more dreams than usual—which no doubt
means that he remembers his dreams with greater ease and
frequency.

Two further reasons why dreams should be forgotten, which
Benini [1898, 155–6] quotes as having been brought forward by
Bonatelli [1880] as additions to those mentioned by Strümpell,
seem in fact to be already covered by the latter. They are (1)
that the alteration in coenaesthesia between the sleeping and
waking states is unfavourable to reciprocal reproduction between
them; and (2) that the different arrangement of the ideational
material in dreams makes them untranslatable, as it were, for
waking consciousness.

In view of all these reasons in favour of dreams being forgotten, it is in fact (as Strümpell himself insists [1877, 6]) very
remarkable that so many of them are retained in the memory.
The repeated attempts by writers on the subject to lay down
the rules governing the recollection of dreams amount to an
admission that here too we are faced by something puzzling and
unexplained. Certain particular characteristics of the recollection of dreams have been rightly emphasized recently (cf.
Radestock, 1879, [169], and Tissié, 1898, [148 f.]), such as the
fact that when a dream seems in the morning to have been forgotten, it may nevertheless be recollected during the course of
the day, if its content, forgotten though it is, is touched upon
by some chance perception.

But the recollection of dreams in general is open to an objection which is bound to reduce their value very completely in
critical opinion. Since so great a proportion of dreams is lost

altogether, we may well doubt whether our memory of what is left of them may not be falsified.

These doubts as to the accuracy of the reproduction of dreams are also expressed by Strümpell (1877, [119]): 'Thus it may easily happen that waking consciousness unwittingly makes interpolations in the memory of a dream: we persuade ourselves that we have dreamt all kinds of things that were not contained in the actual dreams.'

Jessen (1855, 547) writes with special emphasis on this point: 'Moreover, in investigating and interpreting coherent and consistent dreams a particular circumstance must be borne in mind which, as it seems to me, has hitherto received too little attention. In such cases the truth is almost always obscured by the fact that when we recall dreams of this kind to our memory we almost always—unintentionally and without noticing the fact —fill in the gaps in the dream-images. It is seldom or never that a coherent dream was in fact as coherent as it seems to us in memory. Even the most truth-loving of men is scarcely able to relate a noteworthy dream without some additions or embellishments. The tendency of the human mind to see everything connectedly is so strong that in memory it unwittingly fills in any lack of coherence there may be in an incoherent dream.'

Some remarks made by Egger [1895, 41], though they were no doubt arrived at independently, read almost like a translation of this passage from Jessen: '. . . L'observation des rêves a ses difficultés spéciales et le seul moyen d'éviter tout erreur en pareille matière est de confier au papier sans le moindre retard ce que l'on vient d'éprouver et de remarquer; sinon, l'oubli vient vite ou total ou partiel; l'oubli total est sans gravité; mais l'oubli partiel est perfide; car si l'on se met ensuite à raconter ce que l'on n'a pas oublié, on est exposé à compléter par imagination les fragments incohérents et disjoints fournis par la mémoire . . .; on devient artiste à son insu, et le récit périodiquement répété s'impose à la créance de son auteur, qui, de bonne foi, le présente comme un fait authentique, dûment établi selon les bonnes méthodes. . . .'[1]

[1] ['There are peculiar difficulties in observing dreams, and the only way of escaping all errors in such matters is to put down upon paper with the least possible delay what we have just experienced or observed. Otherwise forgetfulness, whether total or partial, quickly supervenes.

Very similar ideas are expressed by Spitta (1882, 338), who seems to believe that it is not until we try to reproduce a dream that we introduce order of any kind into its loosely associated elements: we 'change things that are merely juxtaposed into sequences or causal chains, that is to say, we introduce a process of logical connection which is lacking in the dream.'

Since the only check that we have upon the validity of our memory is objective confirmation, and since that is unobtainable for dreams, which are our own personal experience and of which the only source we have is our recollection, what value can we still attach to our memory of dreams?[1]

Total forgetfulness is not serious; but partial forgetfulness is treacherous. For if we then proceed to give an account of what we have not forgotten, we are liable to fill in from our imagination the incoherent and disjointed fragments furnished by memory. . . . We unwittingly become creative artists; and the tale, if it is repeated from time to time, imposes itself on its author's own belief, and he ends by offering it in good faith as an authentic fact duly and legitimately established.']

[1] [The questions raised in this section are taken up in Chapter VII, Section A (p. 512 ff.).]

THE DISTINGUISHING PSYCHOLOGICAL
CHARACTERISTICS OF DREAMS

Our scientific consideration of dreams starts off from the assumption that they are products of our own mental activity. Nevertheless the finished dream strikes us as something alien to us. We are so little obliged to acknowledge our responsibility for it that [in German] we are just as ready to say '*mir hat geträumt*' ['I had a dream', literally 'a dream came to me'] as '*ich habe geträumt*' ['I dreamt']. What is the origin of this feeling that dreams are extraneous to our minds? In view of our discussion upon the sources of dreams, we must conclude that the strangeness cannot be due to the material that finds its way into their content, since that material is for the most part common to dreaming and waking life. The question arises whether in dreams there may not be modifications in the processes of the mind which produce the impression we are discussing; and we shall therefore make an attempt at drawing a picture of the psychological attributes of dreams.

No one has emphasized more sharply the essential difference between dreaming and waking life or drawn more far-reaching conclusions from it than G. T. Fechner in a passage in his *Elemente der Psychophysik* (1889, **2**, 520–1). In his opinion, 'neither the mere lowering of conscious mental life below the main threshold', nor the withdrawal of attention from the influences of the external world, are enough to explain the characteristics of dream-life as contrasted with waking life. He suspects, rather, that *the scene of action of dreams is different from that of waking ideational life*. 'If the scene of action of psycho-physical activity were the same in sleeping and waking, dreams could, in my view, only be a prolongation at a lower degree of intensity of waking ideational life and, moreover, would necessarily be of the same material and form. But the facts are quite otherwise.'

It is not clear what Fechner had in mind in speaking of this change of location of mental activity; nor, so far as I know, has anyone else pursued the path indicated by his words. We may,

I think, dismiss the possibility of giving the phrase an anatomical interpretation and supposing it to refer to physiological cerebral localization or even to the histological layers of the cerebral cortex. It may be, however, that the suggestion will eventually prove to be sagacious and fertile, if it can be applied to a *mental* apparatus built up of a number of agencies arranged in a series one behind the other.[1]

Other writers have contented themselves with drawing attention to the more tangible of the distinguishing characteristics of dream-life and with taking them as a starting-point for attempts at more far-reaching explanations.

It has justly been remarked that one of the principal peculiarities of dream-life makes its appearance during the very process of falling asleep and may be described as a phenomenon heralding sleep. According to Schleiermacher (1862, 351), what characterizes the waking state is the fact that thought-activity takes place in *concepts* and not in *images*. Now dreams think essentially in images; and with the approach of sleep it is possible to observe how, in proportion as voluntary activities become more difficult, involuntary ideas arise, all of which fall into the class of images. Incapacity for ideational work of the kind which we feel as intentionally willed and the emergence (habitually associated with such states of abstraction) of images —these are two characteristics which persevere in dreams and which the psychological analysis of dreams forces us to recognize as essential features of dream-life. We have already seen [p. 31 ff.] that these images—hypnagogic hallucinations—are themselves identical in their content with dream-images.[2]

Dreams, then, think predominantly in visual images—but not exclusively. They make use of auditory images as well, and, to a lesser extent, of impressions belonging to the other senses. Many things, too, occur in dreams (just as they normally do in waking life) simply as thoughts or ideas—probably, that is to say, in the form of residues of verbal presentations. Nevertheless,

[1] [This idea is taken up and developed in Chapter VII, Section B, of the present work (p. 535 ff.).]

[2] [*Footnote added* 1911:] Silberer (1909) has given some nice examples of the way in which, in a drowsy state, even abstract thoughts become converted into pictorial plastic images which seek to express the same meaning. [*Added* 1925:] I shall have occasion to return to this discovery in another connection. [See pp. 344 f. and 503 ff.]

what are truly characteristic of dreams are only those elements of their content which behave like images, which are more like perceptions, that is, than they are like mnemic presentations. Leaving on one side all the arguments, so familiar to psychiatrists, on the nature of hallucinations, we shall be in agreement with every authority on the subject in asserting that dreams *hallucinate*—that they replace thoughts by hallucinations. In this respect there is no distinction between visual and acoustic presentations: it has been observed that if one falls asleep with the memory of a series of musical notes in one's mind, the memory becomes transformed into an hallucination of the same melody; while, if one then wakes up again—and the two states may alternate more than once during the process of dropping asleep—the hallucination gives way in turn to the mnemic presentation, which is at once fainter and qualitatively different from it.

The transformation of ideas into hallucinations is not the only respect in which dreams differ from corresponding thoughts in waking life. Dreams construct a *situation* out of these images; they represent an event which is actually happening; as Spitta (1882, 145) puts it, they 'dramatize' an idea. But this feature of dream-life can only be fully understood if we further recognize that in dreams—as a rule, for there are exceptions which require special examination—we appear not to *think* but to *experience*; that is to say, we attach complete belief to the hallucinations. Not until we wake up does the critical comment arise that we have not experienced anything but have merely been thinking in a peculiar way, or in other words dreaming. It is this characteristic that distinguishes true dreams from day-dreaming, which is never confused with reality.

Burdach (1838, 502 f.) summarizes the features of dream-life which we have so far discussed in the following words: 'These are among the essential features of dreams: (*a*) In dreams the subjective activity of our minds appears in an objective form, for our perceptive faculties regard the products of our imagination as though they were sense impressions. . . . (*b*) Sleep signifies an end of the authority of the self. Hence falling asleep brings a certain degree of passivity along with it. . . . The images that accompany sleep can occur only on condition that the authority of the self is reduced.'

The next thing is to try to explain the belief which the mind accords to dream-hallucinations, a belief which can only arise after some kind of 'authoritative' activity of the self has ceased. Strümpell (1877) argues that in this respect the mind is carrying out its function correctly and in conformity with its own mechanism. Far from being mere presentations, the elements of dreams are true and real mental experiences of the same kind as arise in a waking state through the agency of the senses. (Ibid., 34.) The waking mind produces ideas and thoughts in verbal images and in speech; but in dreams it does so in true sensory images. (Ibid., 35.) Moreover, there is a spatial consciousness in dreams, since sensations and images are assigned to an external space, just as they are in waking. (Ibid., 36.) It must therefore be allowed that in dreams the mind is in the same relation to its images and perceptions as it is in waking. (Ibid., 43.) If it is nevertheless in error in so doing, that is because in the state of sleep it lacks the criterion which alone makes it possible to distinguish between sense-perceptions arising from without and from within. It is unable to submit its dream-images to the only tests which could prove their objective reality. In addition to this, it disregards the distinction between images which are only interchangeable *arbitrarily* and cases where the element of arbitrariness is absent. It is in error because it is unable to apply the law of causality to the content of its dreams. (Ibid., 50–1.) In short, the fact of its having turned away from the external world is also the reason for its belief in the subjective world of dreams.

Delbœuf (1885, 84) arrives at the same conclusion after somewhat different psychological arguments. We believe in the reality of dream-images, he says, because in our sleep we have no other impressions with which to compare them, because we are detached from the external world. But the reason why we believe in the truth of these hallucinations is not because it is impossible to put them to the test *within* the dream. A dream can seem to offer us such tests: it can let us touch the rose that we see—and yet we are dreaming. In Delbœuf's opinion there is only one valid criterion of whether we are dreaming or awake, and that is the purely empirical one of the fact of waking up. I conclude that everything I experienced between falling asleep and waking up was illusory, when, on awaking, I find that I am lying undressed in bed. During sleep I took the dream-images as real owing to my mental habit (which cannot be put to sleep) of assuming the existence of an external world with which I contrast my own ego.[1]

Detachment from the external world seems thus to be regarded as the factor determining the most marked features of dream-life. It is therefore worth while quoting some penetrating remarks made long ago by Burdach which throw light on the relations between the sleeping mind and the external world and which are calculated to prevent our setting too great store by the conclusions drawn in the last few pages. 'Sleep', he writes, 'can occur only on condition that the mind is not irritated by sensory stimuli. . . . But the actual precondition of sleep is not so much absence of sensory stimuli as absence of

[1] Haffner (1887, 243) attempts, like Delbœuf, to explain the activity of dreaming by the modification which the introduction of an abnormal condition must inevitably produce in the otherwise correct functioning of an intact mental apparatus; but he gives a somewhat different account of that condition. According to him the first mark of a dream is its independence of space and time, i.e. the fact of a presentation being emancipated from the position occupied by the subject in the spatial and temporal order of events. The second basic feature of dreams is connected with this—namely, the fact that hallucinations, phantasies and imaginary combinations are confused with external perceptions. 'All the higher powers of the mind—in particular the formation of concepts and the powers of judgement and inference on the one hand and free self-determination on the other hand—are attached to sensory images and have at all times a background of such images. It follows, therefore, that these higher activities too take their part in the disorderliness of the dream-images. I say "take their part", since in themselves our powers of judgement and of will are in no way altered in sleep. Our activities are just as clear-sighted and just as free as in waking life. Even in his dreams a man cannot violate the laws of thought as such —he cannot, for instance, regard as identical things that appear to him as contraries, and so on. So too in dreams he can only desire what he looks upon as a good (*sub ratione boni*). But the human spirit is led astray in dreams in its *application* of the laws of thought and of will through confusing one idea with another. Thus it comes about that we are guilty of the grossest contradictions in dreams, while at the same time we can make the clearest judgements, draw the most logical inferences and come to the most virtuous and saintly decisions. . . . Lack of orientation is the whole secret of the flights taken by our imagination in dreams, and lack of critical reflection and of communication with other people is the main source of the unbridled extravagance exhibited in dreams by our judgements as well as by our hopes and wishes.' (Ibid., 18.) [The problem of 'reality-testing' is considered later, on p. 566.]

interest in them.[1] Some sense impressions may actually be necessary in order to calm the mind. Thus the miller can only sleep so long as he hears the clacking of his mill; and anyone who feels that burning a night-light is a necessary precaution, finds it impossible to get to sleep in the dark.' (Burdach, 1838, 482.)

'In sleep the mind isolates itself from the external world and withdraws from its own periphery. . . . Nevertheless connection is not broken off entirely. If we could not hear or feel while we were actually asleep, but only after we had woken up, it would be impossible to wake us at all. . . . The persistence of sensation is proved even more clearly by the fact that what rouses us is not always the mere sensory strength of an impression but its psychical context: a sleeping man is not aroused by an indifferent word, but if he is called by name he wakes. . . . Thus the mind in sleep distinguishes between sensations. . . . It is for that reason that the absence of a sensory stimulus can wake a man if it is related to something of ideational importance to him; so it is that the man with the night-light wakes if it is extinguished and the miller is roused if his mill comes to a stop. He is awakened, that is, by the cessation of a sensory activity; and this implies that that activity was perceived by him, but, since it was indifferent, or rather satisfying, did not disturb his mind.' (Ibid., 485-6.)

Even if we disregard these objections—and they are by no means trifling ones—, we shall have to confess that the features of dream-life which we have considered hitherto, and which have been ascribed to its detachment from the external world, do not account completely for its strange character. For it should be possible otherwise to turn the hallucinations in a dream back into ideas, and its situations into thoughts, and in that way to solve the problem of dream-interpretation. And that in fact is what we are doing when, after waking, we reproduce a dream from memory; but, whether we succeed in making this re-translation wholly or only in part, the dream remains no less enigmatic than before.

And indeed all the authorities unhesitatingly assume that yet other and more deep-going modifications of the ideational material of waking life take place in dreams. Strümpell (1877,

[1] [*Footnote added* 1914:] Cf. the '*désintérêt*' which Claparède (1905, 306 f.) regards as the mechanism of falling asleep.

27–8) has endeavoured to put his finger on one such modification in the following passage: 'With the cessation of sensory
functioning and of normal vital consciousness, the mind loses
the soil in which its feelings, desires, interests and activities are
rooted. The psychical states, too,—feelings, interests, judgements of value—, which are linked to mnemic images in waking
life, are subjected to . . . an obscuring pressure, as a result of
which their connection with those images is broken; perceptual
images of things, persons, places, events and actions in waking
life are reproduced separately in great numbers, but none of
them carries its *psychical value* along with it. That value is detached from them and they thus float about in the mind at their
own sweet will. . . .' According to Strümpell, the fact of images
being denuded of their psychical value (which in turn goes
back to detachment from the external world) plays a principal
part in creating the impression of strangeness which distinguishes dreams from actual life in our memory.

We have seen [cf. p. 49] that falling asleep at once involves
the loss of one of our mental activities, namely our power of
giving intentional guidance to the sequence of our ideas. We
are now faced by the suggestion, which is in any case a plausible
one, that the effects of the state of sleep may extend over *all* the
faculties of the mind. Some of these seem to be entirely suspended; but the question now arises whether the rest continue
to operate normally and whether under such conditions they
are *capable* of normal work. And here it may be asked whether
the distinguishing features of dreams cannot be explained by
the lowering of psychical efficiency in the sleeping state—a
notion which finds support in the impression made by dreams
on our waking judgement. Dreams are disconnected, they
accept the most violent contradictions without the least objection, they admit impossibilities, they disregard knowledge which
carries great weight with us in the daytime, they reveal us as
ethical and moral imbeciles. Anyone who when he was awake
behaved in the sort of way that is shown in situations in dreams
would be considered insane. Anyone who when he was awake
talked in the sort of way that people talk in dreams or described the sort of thing that happens in dreams would
give us the impression of being muddle-headed or feeble-
minded. It seems to be no more than putting the truth into
words when we express our very low opinion of mental activity

in dreams and assert that in dreams the higher intellectual
faculties in particular are suspended or at all events gravely
impaired.

The authorities display unusual unanimity—exceptions will
be treated later [p. 59 ff.]—in expressing opinions of this kind
on dreams; and these judgements lead directly to a particular
theory or explanation of dream-life. But it is time for me to
leave generalities and to give instead a series of quotations from
various writers—philosophers and physicians—upon the psychological characteristics of dreams.

According to Lemoine (1855), the 'incoherence' of dream-
images is the one essential characteristic of dreams.

Maury (1878, 163) agrees with him: 'Il n'y a pas de rêves
absolument raisonnables et qui ne contiennent quelque incohérence, quelque anachronisme, quelque absurdité.'[1]

Spitta [1882, 193] quotes Hegel as saying that dreams are
devoid of all objective and reasonable coherence.

Dugas [1897a, 417] writes: 'Le rêve c'est l'anarchie psychique
affective et mentale, c'est le jeu des fonctions livrées à elles-
mêmes et s'exerçant sans contrôle et sans but; dans le rêve
l'esprit est un automate spirituel.'[2]

Even Volkelt (1875, 14), whose theory is far from regarding
psychical activity during sleep as purposeless, speaks of 'the
relaxing, disconnecting and confusing of ideational life, which
in the waking state is held together by the logical force of the
central ego.'

The *absurdity* of the associations of ideas that occur in dreams
could scarcely be criticized more sharply than it was by Cicero
(*De divinatione*, II, [lxxi, 146]): 'Nihil tam praepostere, tam in-
condite, tam monstruose cogitari potest, quod non possimus
somniare.'[3]

Fechner (1889, **2**, 522) writes: 'It is as though psychological
activity had been transported from the brain of a reasonable
man into that of a fool.'

[1] ['There are no dreams that are *absolutely* reasonable and that do not
contain *some* incoherence, anachronism or absurdity.']

[2] ['A dream is psychical, emotional and mental anarchy; it is the play
of functions left to their own devices and acting without control or
purpose; in dreams the spirit becomes a spiritual automaton.']

[3] ['There is no imaginable thing too absurd, too involved, or too
abnormal for us to dream about it.' (Falconer's translation in the Loeb
Classical Library, 1922, 533.)]

Radestock (1879, 145): 'In fact it seems impossible to detect any fixed laws in this crazy activity. After withdrawing from the strict policing exercised over the course of waking ideas by the rational will and the attention, dreams melt into a mad whirl of kaleidoscopic confusion.'

Hildebrandt (1875, 45): 'What astonishing leaps a dreamer may make, for instance, in drawing inferences! How calmly he is prepared to see the most familiar lessons of experience turned upside down. What laughable contradictions he is ready to accept in the laws of nature and society before, as we say, things get beyond a joke and the excessive strain of nonsense wakes him up. We calculate without a qualm that three times three make twenty; we are not in the least surprised when a dog quotes a line of poetry, or when a dead man walks to his grave on his own legs, or when we see a rock floating on the water; we proceed gravely on an important mission to the Duchy of Bernburg or to the Principality of Liechtenstein to inspect their naval forces; or we are persuaded to enlist under Charles XII shortly before the battle of Poltava.'

Binz (1878, 33), having in mind the theory of dreams which is based upon such impressions as these, writes: 'The content of at least nine out of ten dreams is nonsensical. We bring together in them people and things that have no connection whatever with one another. Next moment there is a shift in the kaleidoscope and we are faced by a new grouping, more senseless and crazy, if possible, than the last. And so the changing play of the incompletely sleeping brain goes on, till we awake and clasp our forehead and wonder whether we still possess the capacity for rational ideas and thoughts.'

Maury (1878, 50) finds a parallel to the relation between dream-images and waking thoughts which will be highly significant to physicians: 'La production de ces images que chez l'homme éveillé fait le plus souvent naître la volonté, correspond, pour l'intelligence, à ce que sont pour la motilité certains mouvements que nous offre la chorée et les affections paralytiques . . .'[1] He further regards dreams as 'toute une

---

[1] ['The production of these images (which in a waking person are usually provoked by the will) corresponds in the sphere of intelligence to the place taken in the sphere of motion by some of the movements observable in chorea and paralytic disorders.']

série de dégradations de la faculté pensante et raisonnante'.
(Ibid., 27.)[1]

It is scarcely necessary to quote the writers who repeat
Maury's opinion in relation to the various higher mental functions. Strümpell (1877, 26), for instance, remarks that in dreams
—even, of course, where there is no manifest nonsense—there
is an eclipse of all the logical operations of the mind which are
based on relations and connections. Spitta (1882, 148) declares
that ideas that occur in dreams seem to be completely withdrawn from the law of causality. Radestock (1879, [153–4])
and other writers insist upon the weakness of judgement and
inference characteristic of dreams. According to Jodl (1896,
123), there is no critical faculty in dreams, no power of correcting one set of perceptions by reference to the general content of consciousness. The same author remarks that 'every
kind of conscious activity occurs in dreams, but only in an incomplete, inhibited and isolated fashion.' The contradictions
with our waking knowledge in which dreams are involved are
explained by Stricker (1879, 98) and many others as being due
to facts being forgotten in dreams or to logical relations between ideas having disappeared. And so on, and so on.

Nevertheless, the writers who in general take so unfavourable
a view of psychical functioning in dreams allow that a certain
remnant of mental activity still remains in them. This is explicitly admitted by Wundt, whose theories have had a determining influence on so many other workers in this field. What,
it may be asked, is the nature of the remnant of normal mental
activity which persists in dreams? There is fairly general agreement that the reproductive faculty, the memory, seems to have
suffered least, and indeed that it shows a certain superiority to
the same function in waking life (see Section B above), though
some part of the absurdities of dreaming seems to be explicable
by its forgetfulness. In the opinion of Spitta (1882, 84 f.) the
part of the mind which is not affected by sleep is the life of the
sentiments and it is this which directs dreams. By 'sentiment'
['*Gemüt*'] he means 'the stable assemblage of feelings which
constitutes the innermost subjective essence of a human being'.

Scholz (1893, 64) believes that one of the mental activities
operating in dreams is a tendency to subject the dream-

[1] ['A whole series of degradations of the thinking and reasoning
faculty.']

material to 're-interpretation in allegorical terms'. Siebeck too
(1877, 11) sees in dreams a faculty of the mind for 'wider
interpretation', which is exercised upon all sensations and perceptions. There is particular difficulty in assessing the position
in dreams of what is ostensibly the highest of the psychical
functions, that of consciousness. Since all that we know of
dreams is derived from consciousness, there can be no doubt
of its persisting in them; yet Spitta (1882, 84–5) believes that
what persists in dreams is only consciousness and not *self*-
consciousness. Delbœuf (1885, 19), however, confesses that he
is unable to follow the distinction.

The laws of association governing the sequence of ideas hold
good of dream-images, and indeed their dominance is even
more clearly and strongly expressed in dreams. 'Dreams', says
Strümpell (1877, 70), 'run their course, as it seems, according
to the laws either of bare ideas or of organic stimuli accompanying such ideas—that is, without being in any way affected by
reflection or commonsense or aesthetic taste or moral judgement.' [See pp. 54 f. and 222.]

The authors whose views I am now giving picture the process
of forming dreams in some such way as this. The totality of the
sensory stimuli generated during sleep from the various sources
which I have already enumerated [see Section C above] arouse
in the mind in the first place a number of ideas, which are
represented in the form of hallucinations or more properly,
according to Wundt [see p. 41], of illusions, in view of their
derivation from external and internal stimuli. These ideas
become linked together according to the familiar laws of
association and, according to the same laws, call up a further
series of ideas (or images). The whole of this material is then
worked over, so far as it will allow, by what still remain in
operation of the organizing and thinking faculties of the mind.
(See, for instance, Wundt [1874, 658] and Weygandt [1893].)
All that remain undiscovered are the motives which decide
whether the calling-up of images arising from non-external
sources shall proceed along one chain of associations or another.

It has often been remarked, however, that the associations
connecting dream-images with one another are of a quite
special kind and differ from those which operate in waking
thought. Thus Volkelt (1875, 15) writes: 'In dreams the associations seem to play at catch-as-catch-can in accordance with

chance similarities and connections that are barely perceptible. Every dream is stuffed full of slovenly and perfunctory associations of this kind.' Maury (1878, 126) attaches very great importance to this feature of the way in which ideas are linked in dreams, since it enables him to draw a close analogy between dream-life and certain mental disorders. He specifies two main features of a '*délire*': '(1) une action spontanée et comme automatique de l'esprit; (2) une association vicieuse et irrégulière des idées.'[1] Maury himself gives two excellent instances of dreams of his own in which dream-images were linked together merely through a similarity in the sound of words. He once dreamt that he was on a pilgrimage (*pélerinage*) to Jerusalem or Mecca; after many adventures he found himself visiting *Pell*etier, the chemist, who, after some conversation, gave him a zinc shovel (*pelle*); in the next part of the dream this turned into a great broad-sword. (Ibid., 137.) In another dream he was walking along a highway and reading the number of *kilo*metres on the milestones; then he was in a grocer's shop where there was a big pair of scales, and a man was putting *kilo*gramme weights into the scale in order to weigh Maury; the grocer then said to him: 'You're not in Paris but on the island of *Gilolo*.' Several other scenes followed, in which he saw a *Lo*belia flower, and then General *Lo*pez, of whose death he had read shortly before. Finally, while he was playing a game of *lo*tto, he woke up. (Ibid., 126.)[2]

We shall no doubt be prepared to find, however, that this low estimate of psychical functioning in dreams has not been allowed to pass without contradiction—though contradiction on this point would seem to be no easy matter. For instance, Spitta (1882, 118), one of the disparagers of dream-life, insists that the same psychological laws which regulate waking life also hold good in dreams; and another, Dugas (1897*a*), declares that 'le rêve n'est pas déraison ni même irraison pure'.[3] But

---

[1] ['(1) A mental act which is spontaneous and as it were automatic; (2) an invalid and irregular association of ideas.'—*N.B.* In French (and similarly in German) psychiatry '*délire*' has the meaning of a delusional state.]

[2] [*Footnote added* 1909:] At a later stage [p. 531 *n*.] we shall come to understand the meaning of dreams such as this which are filled with alliterations and similar-sounding first syllables.

[3] ['Dreams are not contrary to reason or even entirely lacking in reason.']

such assertions carry little weight so long as their authors make
no attempt to reconcile them with their own descriptions of the
psychical anarchy and disruption of every function that prevail
in dreams. It seems, however, to have dawned upon some other
writers that the madness of dreams may not be without method
and may even be simulated, like that of the Danish prince on
whom this shrewd judgement was passed. These latter writers
cannot have judged by appearances; or the appearance presented to them by dreams must have been a different one.

Thus Havelock Ellis (1899, 721), without dwelling on the
apparent absurdity of dreams, speaks of them as 'an archaic
world of vast emotions and imperfect thoughts', the study of
which might reveal to us primitive stages in the evolution of
mental life.

The same view[1] is expressed by James Sully (1893, 362) in
a manner that is both more sweeping and more penetrating.
His words deserve all the more attention when we bear in mind
that he was more firmly convinced, perhaps, than any other
psychologist that dreams have a disguised meaning. 'Now
our dreams are a means of conserving these successive [earlier]
personalities. *When asleep we go back to the old ways of looking at
things and of feeling about them, to impulses and activities which long
ago dominated us.*'

The sagacious Delbœuf (1885, 222) declares (though he puts
himself in the wrong by not giving any refutation of the material
which contradicts his thesis): 'Dans le sommeil, hormis la perception, toutes les facultés de l'esprit, intelligence, imagination,
mémoire, volonté, moralité, restent intactes dans leur essence;
seulement elles s'appliquent à des objets imaginaires et mobiles.
Le songeur est un acteur qui joue à volonté les fous et les sages,
les bourreaux et les victimes, les nains et les géants, les démons
et les anges.'[2]

The most energetic opponent of those who seek to depreciate
psychical functioning in dreams seems to be the Marquis
d'Hervey de Saint-Denys [1867], with whom Maury carried

---

[1] [This paragraph was added in 1914.]

[2] ['In sleep, all the mental faculties (except for perception)—intelligence, imagination, memory, will and morality—remain essentially
intact; they are merely applied to imaginary and unstable objects. A
dreamer is an actor who at his own will plays the parts of madmen and
philosophers, of executioners and their victims, of dwarfs and giants, of
demons and angels.']

on a lively controversy, and whose book, in spite of all my efforts, I have not succeeded in procuring.[1] Maury (1878, 19) writes of him: 'M. le Marquis d'Hervey prête à l'intelligence durant le sommeil, toute sa liberté d'action et d'attention et il ne semble faire consister le sommeil que dans l'occlusion des sens, dans leur fermeture au monde extérieur; en sorte que l'homme qui dort ne se distingue guère, selon sa manière de voir, de l'homme qui laisse vaguer sa pensée en se bouchant les sens; toute la différence qui sépare alors la pensée ordinaire de celle du dormeur c'est que, chez celui-ci, l'idée prend une forme visible, objective et ressemble, à s'y méprendre, à la sensation déterminée par les objets extérieurs; le souvenir revêt l'apparence du fait présent.'[2] To this Maury adds 'qu'il y a une différence de plus et capitale à savoir que les facultés intellectuelles de l'homme endormi n'offrent pas l'équilibre qu'elles gardent chez l'homme éveillé.'[3]

Vaschide (1911, 146 f.)[4] gives us a clearer account of Hervey de Saint-Denys' book and quotes a passage from it [1867, 35] upon the apparent incoherence of dreams: 'L'image du rêve est la copie de l'idée. Le principal est l'idée; la vision n'est qu'accessoire. Ceci établi, il faut savoir suivre la marche des idées, il faut savoir analyser le tissu des rêves; l'incohérence devient alors compréhensible, les conceptions les plus fantasques deviennent des faits simples et parfaitement logiques. . . . Les rêves les plus bizarres trouvent même une explication des plus logiques quand on sait les analyser.'[5]

[1] [This work, by a famous sinologist, was published anonymously.]
[2] ['The Marquis d'Hervey attributes complete liberty of action and attention to the intelligence during sleep, and he seems to think that sleep consists merely in the blocking of the senses, in their being closed to the external world. So that on his view a sleeping man would hardly be different from a man who shut off his senses and allowed his thoughts to wander; the only distinction between ordinary thoughts and those of a sleeper would be that, in the latter, ideas assume a visible and objective shape and are indistinguishable from sensations determined by external objects, while memories take on the appearance of present events.']
[3] ['There is a further distinction and one of capital importance: namely, that the intellectual faculties of a sleeping man do not exhibit the balance maintained in a man who is awake.']
[4] [This paragraph and the next were added in 1914.]
[5] ['Dream-images are copies of ideas. The essential thing is the idea, the vision is a mere accessory. When this is once established, we must know how to follow the sequence of the ideas, we must know how to

Johan Stärcke (1913, 243) has pointed out that a similar explanation of the incoherence of dreams was put forward by an earlier writer, Wolf Davidson (1799, 136), whose work was unknown to me: 'The remarkable leaps taken by our ideas in dreams all have their basis in the law of association; sometimes, however, these connections occur in the mind very obscurely, so that our ideas often seem to have taken a leap when in fact there has been none.'

The literature of the subject thus shows a very wide range of variation in the value which it assigns to dreams as psychical products. This range extends from the deepest disparagement, of the kind with which we have become familiar, through hints at a yet undisclosed worth, to an overvaluation which ranks dreams far higher than any of the functions of waking life. Hildebrandt (1875, 19 f.), who, as we have heard [see above, p. 9], has summed up the whole of the psychological features of dream-life in three antinomies, makes use of the two extreme ends of this range of values for his third paradox: 'it is a contrast between an intensification of mental life, an enhancement of it that not infrequently amounts to virtuosity, and, on the other hand, a deterioration and enfeeblement which often sinks below the level of humanity. As regards the former, there are few of us who could not affirm, from our own experience, that there emerges from time to time in the creations and fabrics of the genius of dreams a depth and intimacy of emotion, a tenderness of feeling, a clarity of vision, a subtlety of observation, and a brilliance of wit such as we should never claim to have at our permanent command in our waking lives. There lies in dreams a marvellous poetry, an apt allegory, an incomparable humour, a rare irony. A dream looks upon the world in a light of strange idealism and often enhances the effects of what it sees by its deep understanding of their essential nature. It pictures earthly beauty to our eyes in a truly heavenly splendour and clothes dignity with the highest majesty, it shows us our everyday fears in the ghastliest shape and turns our amusement into jokes of

analyse the texture of dreams; their incoherence then becomes intelligible, and the most fantastic notions become simple and perfectly logical facts . . . . We can even find a most logical explanation for the strangest dreams if we know how to analyse them.'—This is not in fact a verbatim quotation from Hervey de Saint-Denys, but a paraphrase by Vaschide.]

indescribable pungency. And sometimes, when we are awake
and still under the full impact of an experience like one of these,
we cannot but feel that never in our life has the real world
offered us its equal.'

We may well ask whether the disparaging remarks quoted
on earlier pages and this enthusiastic eulogy can possibly relate
to the same thing. Is it that some of our authorities have overlooked the nonsensical dreams and others the profound and
subtle ones? And if dreams of both kinds occur, dreams that
justify both estimates, may it not be a waste of time to look for
any distinguishing psychological feature of dreams? Will it not
be enough to say that in dreams *anything* is possible—from the
deepest degradation of mental life to an exaltation of it which
is rare in waking hours? However convenient a solution of this
kind might be, what lies against it is the fact that all of the
efforts at research into the problem of dreams seem to be based
on a conviction that some distinguishing feature *does* exist,
which is universally valid in its essential outline and which
would clear these apparent contradictions out of the way.

There can be no doubt that the psychical achievements of
dreams received readier and warmer recognition during the
intellectual period which has now been left behind, when
the human mind was dominated by philosophy and not by the
exact natural sciences. Pronouncements such as that by Schu-
bert (1814, 20 f.) that dreams are a liberation of the spirit from
the power of external nature, a freeing of the soul from the
bonds of the senses, and similar remarks by the younger Fichte
(1864, 1, 143 f.) [1] and others, all of which represent dreams as
an elevation of mental life to a higher level, seem to us now to
be scarcely intelligible; to-day they are repeated only by
mystics and pietists. [2] The introduction of the scientific mode of
thought has brought along with it a reaction in the estimation of
dreams. Medical writers in especial tend to regard psychical
activity in dreams as trivial and valueless; while philosophers
and non-professional observers—amateur psychologists—whose

[1] Cf. Haffner (1887) and Spitta (1882, 11 f.).
[2] [*Footnote added* 1914:] That brilliant mystic Du Prel, one of the few
authors for whose neglect in earlier editions of this book I should wish
to express my regret, declares that the gateway to metaphysics, so far as
men are concerned, lies not in waking life but in the dream. (Du Prel,
1885, 59.)

contributions to this particular subject are not to be despised, have (in closer alignment with popular feeling) retained a belief in the psychical value of dreams. Anyone who is inclined to take a low view of psychical functioning in dreams will naturally prefer to assign their source to somatic stimulation; whereas those who believe that the dreaming mind retains the greater part of its waking capacities have of course no reason for denying that the stimulus to dreaming can arise within the dreaming mind itself.

Of the superior faculties which even a sober comparison may be inclined to attribute to dream-life, the most marked is that of memory; we have already [in Section B above] discussed at length the not uncommon evidence in favour of this view. Another point of superiority in dream-life, often praised by earlier writers,—that it rises superior to distance in time and space—may easily be shown to have no basis in fact. As Hildebrandt (1875, [25]) points out, this advantage is an illusory one; for dreaming rises superior to time and space in precisely the same way as does waking thought, and for the very reason that it is merely a form of thought. It has been claimed for dreams that they enjoy yet another advantage over waking life in relation to time—that they are independent of the passage of time in yet another respect. Dreams such as the one dreamt by Maury of his own guillotining (see above, p. 26 f.) seem to show that a dream is able to compress into a very short space of time an amount of perceptual matter far greater than the amount of ideational matter that can be dealt with by our waking mind. This conclusion has however been countered by various arguments; since the papers by Le Lorrain (1894) and Egger (1895) on the apparent duration of dreams, a long and interesting discussion on the subject has developed, but it seems unlikely that the last word has yet been said on this subtle question and the deep implications which it involves.[1]

Reports of numerous cases as well as the collection of instances made by Chabaneix (1897) seem to put it beyond dispute that dreams can carry on the intellectual work of daytime and bring it to conclusions which had not been reached during the day, and that they can resolve doubts and problems and be

[1] [Footnote added 1914:] A further bibliography and a critical discussion of these problems will be found in Tobowolska (1900). [Cf. also p. 496 f.]

the source of new inspiration for poets and musical composers. But though the *fact* may be beyond dispute, its implications are open to many doubts, which raise matters of principle.[1]

Lastly, dreams are reputed to have the power of divining the future. Here we have a conflict in which almost insuperable scepticism is met by obstinately repeated assertions. No doubt we shall be acting rightly in not insisting that this view has no basis at all in fact, since it is possible that before long a number of the instances cited may find an explanation within the bounds of natural psychology.[2]

[1] [*Footnote added* 1914:] Cf. the criticism in Havelock Ellis (1911, 265). [See also below, p. 564.]

[2] [Cf. the posthumously published paper by Freud (1941*c*) printed as an Appendix at the end of this work (p. 623).]

THE MORAL SENSE IN DREAMS

For reasons which will only become apparent after my own investigations into dreams have been taken into account, I have isolated from the subject of the psychology of dreams the special problem of whether and to what extent moral dispositions and feelings extend into dream-life. Here too we are met by the same contradictory views which, curiously enough, we have found adopted by different authors in regard to all the other functions of the mind during dreams. Some assert that the dictates of morality have no place in dreams, while others maintain no less positively that the moral character of man persists in his dream-life.

Appeal to the common experience of dreams seems to establish beyond any doubt the correctness of the former of these views. Jessen (1855, 553) writes: 'Nor do we become better or more virtuous in sleep. On the contrary, conscience seems to be silent in dreams, for we feel no pity in them and may commit the worst crimes—theft, violence and murder—with complete indifference and with no subsequent feelings of remorse.'

Radestock (1879, 164): 'It should be borne in mind that associations occur and ideas are linked together in dreams without any regard for reflection, common sense, aesthetic taste or moral judgement. Judgement is extremely weak and ethical indifference reigns supreme.'

Volkelt (1875, 23): 'In dreams, as we are all aware, proceedings are especially unbridled in sexual matters. The dreamer himself is utterly shameless and devoid of any moral feeling or judgement; moreover, he sees everyone else, including those for whom he has the deepest respect, engaged in acts with which he would be horrified to associate them while he was awake, even in his thoughts.'

In diametrical opposition to these, we find statements such as Schopenhauer's [1862, 1, 245] that everyone who figures in a dream acts and speaks in complete accordance with his character. K. P. Fischer (1850, 72 f.), quoted by Spitta (1882, 188), declares that subjective feelings and longings, or affects and passions, reveal themselves in the freedom of dream-life, and that people's moral characteristics are reflected in their dreams.

Haffner (1884, 251): 'With rare exceptions . . . a virtuous man will be virtuous in his dreams as well; he will resist temptations and will keep himself aloof from hatred, envy, anger and all other vices. But a sinful man will as a rule find in his dreams the same images that he had before his eyes while he was awake.'

Scholz [Jewett's translation, 1893, 62]: 'In dreams is truth: in dreams we learn to know ourselves as we are in spite of all the disguises we wear to the world, [whether they be ennobling or humiliating]. . . . The honourable man cannot commit a crime in dreams, or if he does he is horrified over it as over something contrary to his nature. The Roman Emperor who put a man to death who had dreamt that he had assassinated the ruler, was justified in so doing if he reasoned that the thoughts one has in dreams, one has, too, when awake. The common expression "I wouldn't dream of such a thing" has a doubly correct significance when it refers to something which can have no lodgement in our hearts or mind.' (Plato, on the contrary, thought that the best men are those who only *dream* what other men *do* in their waking life.)[1]

Pfaff (1868, [9]), quoted by Spitta (1882, 192), alters the wording of a familiar saying: 'Tell me some of your dreams, and I will tell you about your inner self.'

The problem of morality in dreams is taken as the centre of interest by Hildebrandt, from whose small volume I have already quoted so much—for, of all the contributions to the study of dreams which I have come across, it is the most perfect in form and the richest in ideas. Hildebrandt [1875, 54] too lays it down as a rule that the purer the life the purer the dream, and the more impure the one the more impure the other. He believes that man's moral nature persists in dreams. 'Whereas', he writes, 'even the grossest mistake in arithmetic, even the most romantic reversal of scientific laws, even the most ridiculous anachronism fails to upset us or even to arouse our suspicions, yet we never lose sight of the distinction between good and evil, between right and wrong or between virtue and vice.

[1] [This sentence was added in 1914. Cf. also p. 620. The reference is no doubt to the opening sections of Book IX of the *Republic*. (*Trans.*, 1871, 409 f.)]

However much of what accompanies us in the daytime may drop away in our sleeping hours, Kant's categorical imperative is a companion who follows so close at our heels that we cannot be free of it even in sleep. . . . But this can only be explained by the fact that what is fundamental in man's nature, his moral being, is too firmly fixed to be affected by the kaleidoscopic shuffling to which the imagination, the reason, the memory and other such faculties must submit in dreams.' (Ibid., 45 f.)

As the discussion of this subject proceeds, however, both groups of writers begin to exhibit remarkable shifts and inconsistencies in their opinions. Those who maintain that the moral personality of man ceases to operate in dreams should, in strict logic, lose all interest in immoral dreams. They could rule out any attempt at holding a dreamer responsible for his dreams, or at deducing from the wickedness of his dreams that he had an evil streak in his character, just as confidently as they would reject a similar attempt at deducing from the absurdity of his dreams that his intellectual activities in waking life were worthless. The other group, who believe that the 'categorical imperative' extends to dreams, should logically accept unqualified responsibility for immoral dreams. We could only hope for their sake that they would have no such reprehensible dreams of their own to upset their firm belief in their own moral character.

It appears, however, that no one is as confident as all that of how far he is good or bad, and that no one can deny the recollection of immoral dreams of his own. For writers in both groups, irrespective of the opposition between their opinions on dream-morality, make efforts at explaining the origin of immoral dreams; and a fresh difference of opinion develops, according as their origin is sought in the functions of the mind or in deleterious effects produced on the mind by somatic causes. Thus the compelling logic of facts forces the supporters of both the responsibility and the irresponsibility of dream-life to unite in recognizing that the immorality of dreams has a specific psychical source.

Those who believe that morality extends to dreams are, however, all careful to avoid assuming *complete* responsibility for their dreams. Thus Haffner (1887, 250) writes: 'We are not responsible for our dreams, since our thought and will have been deprived in them of the basis upon which alone our life possesses truth and reality . . . For that reason no dream-wishes or dream-actions can be virtuous or sinful.' Nevertheless, he goes on, men are responsible for their sinful dreams in so far as they cause them indirectly. They have the duty of morally cleansing their minds not only in their waking life but more especially before going to sleep.

Hildebrandt [1875, 48 f.] presents us with a far deeper analysis of this mingled rejection and acceptance of responsibility for the moral content of dreams. He argues that in considering the immoral appearance of dreams allowance must be made for the dramatic form in which they are couched, for their compression of the most complicated processes of reflection into the briefest periods of time, as well as for the way in which, as even he admits, the ideational elements of dreams become confused and deprived of their significance. He confesses that he has the greatest hesitation, nevertheless, in thinking that all responsibility for sins and faults in dreams can be repudiated.

'When we are anxious to disown some unjust accusation, especially one that relates to our aims and intentions, we often use the phrase "I should never dream of such a thing". We are in that way expressing, on the one hand, our feeling that the region of dreams is the most remote and furthest in which we are answerable for our thoughts, since thoughts in that region are so loosely connected with our essential self that they are scarcely to be regarded as ours; but nevertheless, since we feel obliged expressly to deny the existence of these thoughts in this region, we are at the same time admitting indirectly that our self-justification would not be complete unless it extended so far. And I think that in this we are speaking, although unconsciously, the language of truth.' (Ibid., 49.)

'It is impossible to think of any action in a dream for which the original motive has not in some way or other—whether as a wish, or desire or impulse—passed through the waking mind.' We must admit, Hildebrandt proceeds, that this original impulse was not invented by the dream; the dream merely copied it and spun it out, it merely elaborated in dramatic form a scrap of historical material which it had found in us; it merely dramatized the Apostle's words: 'Whosoever hateth his brother is a murderer.' [1 John iii, 15.] And although after we have awoken, conscious of our moral strength, we may smile at the whole elaborate structure of the sinful dream, yet the original material from which the structure was derived will fail to raise a smile.

We feel responsible for the dreamer's errors—not for the whole amount of them, but for a certain percentage. 'In short, if we understand in this scarcely disputable sense Christ's saying that "out of the heart proceed evil thoughts" [Matt. xv, 19], we can hardly escape the conviction that a sin committed in a dream bears with it at least an obscure minimum of guilt.' (Hildebrandt, 1875, 51 ff.)

Thus Hildebrandt finds the source of immorality in dreams in the germs and hints of evil impulses which, in the form of temptations, pass through our minds during the day; and he does not hesitate to include these immoral elements in his estimate of a person's moral value. These same thoughts, as we know, and this same estimate of them, are what have led the pious and saintly in every age to confess themselves miserable sinners.[1]

There can of course be no doubt as to the general existence of such incompatible ideas; they occur in most people and in spheres other than that of ethics. Sometimes, however, they have been judged less seriously. Spitta (1882, 194) quotes some remarks by Zeller [1818, 120–1], which are relevant in this connection: 'A mind is seldom so happily organized as to possess complete power at every moment and not to have the regular and clear course of its thoughts constantly interrupted not only by inessential but by positively grotesque and non-sensical ideas. Indeed, the greatest thinkers have had to complain of this dreamlike, teasing and tormenting rabble of ideas, which have disturbed their deepest reflections and their most solemn and earnest thoughts.'

A more revealing light is thrown upon the psychological position of these incompatible thoughts by another remark of Hildebrandt's (1875, 55), to the effect that dreams give us an occasional glimpse into depths and recesses of our nature to which we usually have no access in our waking state. Kant expresses the same idea in a passage in his *Anthropologie* [1798][2]

[1] [*Footnote added* 1914:] It is of some interest to learn the attitude of the Inquisition to our problem. In Caesar Carena's *Tractatus de Officio sanctissimae Inquisitionis* 1659, the following passage occurs: 'If anyone speaks heresies in a dream, the inquisitors should take occasion to enquire into his way of life, for what occupies a man during the day is wont to come again in his sleep.' (Communicated by Dr. Ehniger, St. Urban, Switzerland.)

[2] [Not traceable.]

in which he declares that dreams seem to exist in order to show us our hidden natures and to reveal to us, not what we are, but what we might have been if we had been brought up differently. Radestock (1879, 84), too, says that dreams often do no more than reveal to us what we would not admit to ourselves and that it is therefore unfair of us to stigmatize them as liars and deceivers. Erdmann [1852, 115] writes: 'Dreams have never shown me what I ought to think of a man; but I have occasionally learnt from a dream, greatly to my own astonishment, what I *do* think of a man and how I feel towards him.' Similarly I. H. Fichte (1864, **1**, 539) remarks: 'The nature of our dreams gives a far more truthful reflection of our whole disposition than we are able to learn of it from self-observation in waking life.'[1]

It will be seen that the emergence of impulses which are foreign to our moral consciousness is merely analogous to what we have already learnt—the fact that dreams have access to ideational material which is absent in our waking state or plays but a small part in it. Thus Benini (1898) writes: 'Certe nostre inclinazioni che si credevano soffocate e spente da un pezzo, si ridestano; passioni vecchie e sepolte rivivono; cose e persone a cui non pensiamo mai, ci vengono dinanzi.'[2] And Volkelt (1875, 105): 'Ideas, too, which have entered waking consciousness almost unnoticed and have perhaps never again been called to memory, very frequently announce their presence in the mind through dreams.' At this point, finally, we may recall Schleiermacher's assertion [see above, p. 49] that the act of falling asleep is accompanied by the appearance of 'involuntary ideas' or images.

We may, then, class together under the heading of 'involuntary ideas' the whole of the ideational material the emergence of which, alike in immoral and in absurd dreams, causes us so much bewilderment. There is, however, one important point of difference: involuntary ideas in the moral sphere contradict our usual attitude of mind, whereas the others merely strike us as strange. No step has yet been taken towards a deeper knowledge which would resolve this distinction.

The question next arises as to the *significance* of the appearance

---

[1] [The two last sentences were added in 1914.]

[2] ['Certain of our desires which have seemed for a time to be stifled and extinguished are re-awakened; old and buried passions come to life again; things and persons of whom we never think appear before us.']

of involuntary ideas in dreams, as to the light which the emergence during the night of these morally incompatible impulses
throws upon the psychology of the waking and dreaming mind.
And here we find a fresh division of opinion and yet another
different grouping of the authorities. The line of thought
adopted by Hildebrandt and others who share his fundamental
position inevitably leads to the view that immoral impulses
possess a certain degree of power even in waking life, though
it is an inhibited power, unable to force its way into action, and
that in sleep something is put out of action which acts like an
inhibition in the daytime and has prevented us from being
aware of the existence of such impulses. Thus dreams would
reveal the true nature of man, though not his *whole* nature, and
they would constitute one means of rendering the hidden
interior of the mind accessible to our knowledge. Only upon
some such premises as these can Hildebrandt [1875, 56] base
his attribution to dreams of warning powers, which draw our
attention to moral infirmities in our mind, just as physicians
admit that dreams can bring unobserved physical illnesses to
our conscious notice. So, too, Spitta must be adopting this view
when, in speaking [1882, 193 f.] of the sources of excitation
which impinge upon the mind (at puberty, for instance), he
consoles the dreamer with the assurance that he will have done
all that lies within his power if he leads a strictly virtuous life
in his waking hours, and if he takes care to suppress sinful
thoughts whenever they arise and to prevent their maturing and
turning into acts. According to this view we might define the
'involuntary ideas' as ideas which had been 'suppressed' during
the day, and we should have to regard their emergence as a
genuine mental phenomenon.

Other writers, however, regard this last conclusion as unjustifiable. Thus Jessen (1855) believes that involuntary ideas, both
in dreams and in waking, and in feverish and other delirious
conditions, 'have the character of a volitional activity that has
been put to rest and of a more or less mechanical succession of
images and ideas provoked by internal impulses'. All that an
immoral dream proves as to the dreamer's mental life is, in
Jessen's view, that on some occasion he had cognizance of the
ideational content in question; it is certainly no evidence of a
mental impulse of the dreamer's own.

As regards another writer, Maury, it would almost seem as

though he too attributes to the dreaming condition a capacity, not for the arbitrary destruction of mental activity, but for analysing it into its components. He writes as follows of dreams which transgress the bounds of morality: 'Ce sont nos penchants qui parlent et qui nous font agir, sans que la conscience nous retienne, bien que parfois elle nous avertisse. J'ai mes défauts et mes penchants vicieux; à l'état de veille je tâche de lutter contre eux, et il m'arrive assez souvent de n'y pas succomber. Mais dans mes songes j'y succombe toujours ou pour mieux dire j'agis par leur impulsion, sans crainte et sans remords. . . . Evidemment les visions qui se déroulent devant ma pensée et qui constituent le rêve, me sont suggérées par les incitations que je ressens et que ma volonté absente ne cherche pas à refouler.' (Maury, 1878, 113.) [1]

No one who believes in the capacity of dreams to reveal an immoral tendency of the dreamer's which is really present though suppressed or concealed, could express his view more precisely than in Maury's words: 'En rêve l'homme se révèle donc tout entier à soi-même dans sa nudité et sa misère natives. Dès qu'il suspend l'exercice de sa volonté, il devient le jouet de toutes les passions contres lesquelles, à l'état de veille, la conscience, le sentiment de l'honneur, la crainte nous défendent.' (Ibid., 165.) [2] In another passage we find these pertinent sentences: 'Dans le songe, c'est surtout l'homme instinctif qui se révèle. . . . L'homme revient pour ainsi dire à l'état de nature quand il rêve; mais moins les idées acquises ont pénétré dans son esprit, plus les penchants en désaccord avec elles conservent encore sur lui l'influence dans le rêve.' (Ibid., 462.) [3] He goes on

[1] ['It is our impulses that are speaking and making us act, while our conscience does not hold us back, though it sometimes warns us. I have my faults and my vicious impulses; while I am awake I try to resist them, and quite often I succeed in not yielding to them. But in my dreams I *always* yield to them, or rather I act under their pressure without fear or remorse. . . . The visions which unroll before my mind and which constitute a dream are clearly suggested by the urges which I feel and which my absent will does not attempt to repress.']

[2] ['Thus in dreams a man stands self-revealed in all his native nakedness and poverty. As soon as he suspends the exercise of his will, he becomes the plaything of all the passions against which he is defended while he is awake by his conscience, his sense of honour and his fears.']

[3] ['What is revealed in dreams is primarily the man of instinct. . . . Man may be said to return in his dreams to a state of nature. But the less his mind has been penetrated by acquired ideas, the more it remains influenced in dreams by impulses of a contrary nature.']

to relate by way of example how in his dreams he is not infrequently the victim of the very superstition which he has been attacking in his writings with particular vehemence.

These penetrating reflections of Maury's, however, lose their value in the investigation of dream-life owing to the fact that he regards the phenomena which he has observed with such accuracy as no more than proofs of an *'automatisme psychologique'* which, in his view, dominates dreams and which he looks upon as the exact opposite of mental activity.

Stricker (1879, [51]) writes: 'Dreams do not consist solely of illusions. If, for instance, one is afraid of robbers in a dream, the robbers, it is true, are imaginary—but the fear is real.' This calls our attention to the fact that *affects* in dreams cannot be judged in the same way as the remainder of their content; and we are faced by the problem of what part of the psychical processes occurring in dreams is to be regarded as real, that is to say, has a claim to be classed among the psychical processes of waking life.[1]

[1] [The question of affects in dreams is discussed in Section H of Chapter VI (p. 460 ff.). The whole topic of moral responsibility for dreams is touched upon below on p. 620 f. and considered at greater length in Section B of Freud 1925*i*.]

THEORIES OF DREAMING AND ITS FUNCTION

Any disquisition upon dreams which seeks to explain as many as possible of their observed characteristics from a particular point of view, and which at the same time defines the position occupied by dreams in a wider sphere of phenomena, deserves to be called a theory of dreams. The various theories will be found to differ in that they select one or the other characteristic of dreams as the essential one and take it as the point of departure for their explanations and correlations. It need not necessarily be possible to infer a *function* of dreaming (whether utilitarian or otherwise) from the theory. Nevertheless, since we have a habit of looking for teleological explanations, we shall be more ready to accept theories which are bound up with the attribution of a function to dreaming.

We have already made the acquaintance of several sets of views which deserve more or less to be called theories of dreams in this sense of the term. The belief held in antiquity that dreams were sent by the gods in order to guide the actions of men was a complete theory of dreams, giving information on everything worth knowing about them. Since dreams have become an object of scientific research a considerable number of theories have been developed, including some that are extremely incomplete.

Without attempting any exhaustive enumeration, we may try to divide theories of dreams into the following three rough groups, according to their underlying assumptions as to the amount and nature of psychical activity in dreams.

(1) There are the theories, such as that of Delbœuf [1885, 221 f.], according to which the whole of psychical activity continues in dreams. The mind, they assume, does not sleep and its apparatus remains intact; but, since it falls under the conditions of the state of sleep, which differ from those of waking life, its normal functioning necessarily produces different results during sleep. The question arises in regard to these theories whether they are capable of deriving all the distinctions between

dreams and waking thought from the conditions of the state of sleep. Moreover, there is no possibility of their being able to suggest any *function* for dreaming; they offer no reason why we should dream, why the complicated mechanism of the mental apparatus should continue to operate even when set in circumstances for which it appears undesigned. Either dreamless sleep or, if disturbing stimuli intervene, awakening, would seem to be the only expedient reactions—rather than the third alternative of dreaming.

(2) There are the theories which, on the contrary, presuppose that dreams imply a lowering of psychical activity, a loosening of connections, and an impoverishment of the material accessible. These theories must imply the attribution to sleep of characteristics quite different from those suggested, for instance, by Delbœuf. Sleep, according to such theories, has a far-reaching influence upon the mind; it does not consist merely in the mind being shut off from the external world; it forces its way, rather, into the mental mechanism and throws it temporarily out of use. If I may venture on a simile from the sphere of psychiatry, the first group of theories construct dreams on the model of paranoia, while the second group make them resemble mental deficiency or confusional states.

The theory according to which only a fragment of mental activity finds expression in dreams, since it has been paralysed by sleep, is by far the most popular with medical writers and in the scientific world generally. In so far as any general interest may be supposed to exist in the explanation of dreams, this may be described as the ruling theory. It is to be remarked how easily this theory avoids the worst stumbling-block in the way of any explanation of dreams—the difficulty of dealing with the contradictions involved in them. It regards dreams as a result of a partial awakening—'a gradual, partial and at the same time highly abnormal awakening', to quote a remark of Herbart's upon dreams (1892, 307). Thus, this theory can make use of a series of conditions of ever-increasing wakefulness, culminating in the completely waking state, in order to account for the series of variations in efficiency of mental functioning in dreams, ranging from the inefficiency revealed by their occasional absurdity up to fully concentrated intellectual functioning. [See p. 180.]

Those who find that they cannot dispense with a statement in terms of physiology, or to whom a statement in such terms seems more scientific, will find what they want in the account given by Binz (1878, 43): 'This condition' (of torpor) 'comes to an end in the early hours of the morning, but only by degrees. The products of fatigue which have accumulated in the albumen of the brain gradually diminish; more and more of them are decomposed or eliminated by the unceasing flow of the blood-stream. Here and there separate groups of cells begin to emerge into wakefulness, while the torpid state still persists all around them. The isolated work of these separate groups now appears before our clouded consciousness, unchecked by other portions of the brain which govern the process of association. For that reason the images produced, which correspond for the most part to material impressions of the more recent past, are strung together in a wild and irregular manner. The number of the liberated brain-cells constantly grows and the senselessness of the dreams correspondingly diminishes.'

This view of dreaming as an incomplete, partial waking state is no doubt to be found in the writings of every modern physiologist and philosopher. The most elaborate exposition of it is given by Maury (1878, 6 f.). It often appears as though that author imagined that the waking or sleeping state could be shifted from one anatomical region to another, each particular anatomical region being linked to one particular psychical function. I will merely remark at this point that, even if the theory of partial waking were confirmed, its details would still remain very much open to discussion.

This view naturally leaves no room for assigning any function to dreaming. The logical conclusion that follows from it as to the position and significance of dreams is correctly stated by Binz (1878, 35): 'Every observed fact forces us to conclude that dreams must be characterized as *somatic* processes, which are in every case useless and in many cases positively pathological. . . .'

The application to dreams of the term 'somatic', which is italicized by Binz himself, has more than one bearing. It alludes, in the first place, to the *aetiology* of dreams which seemed particularly plausible to Binz when he studied the experimental production of dreams by the use of toxic substances. For theories of this kind involve a tendency to limit the instigation of dreams so far as possible to somatic causes. Put in its most

extreme form the view is as follows. Once we have put ourselves to sleep by excluding all stimuli, there is no need and
no occasion for dreaming until the morning, when the process
of being gradually awakened by the impact of fresh stimuli
might be reflected in the phenomenon of dreaming. It is im-
practicable, however, to keep our sleep free from stimuli; they
impinge upon the sleeper from all sides—like the germs of life
of which Mephistopheles complained[1]—from without and from
within and even from parts of his body which are quite unnoticed in waking life. Thus sleep is disturbed; first one corner
of the mind is shaken into wakefulness and then another; the
mind functions for a brief moment with its awakened portion
and is then glad to fall asleep once more. Dreams are a reaction
to the disturbance of sleep brought about by a stimulus—a
reaction, incidentally, which is quite superfluous.

But the description of dreaming—which, after all is said and
done, remains a function of the mind—as a somatic process
implies another meaning as well. It is intended to show that
dreams are unworthy to rank as psychical processes. Dreaming
has often been compared with 'the ten fingers of a man who
knows nothing of music wandering over the keys of a piano'
[Strümpell, 1877, 84; cf. p. 222 below]; and this simile shows as
well as anything the sort of opinion that is usually held of
dreaming by representatives of the exact sciences. On this view
a dream is something wholly and completely incapable of interpretation; for how could the ten fingers of an unmusical player
produce a piece of music?

Even in the distant past there was no lack of critics of the
theory of partial waking. Thus Burdach (1838, 508 f.) wrote:
'When it is said that dreams are a partial waking, in the first
place this throws no light either on waking or on sleeping, and
in the second place it says no more than that some mental
forces are active in dreams while others are at rest. But vari-
ability of this kind occurs throughout life.'

This ruling theory, which regards dreams as a somatic process, underlies a most interesting hypothesis put forward for the

[1] [In his first conversation with Faust (Part I, Scene 3), Mephistopheles complained bitterly that his destructive efforts were perpetually
frustrated by the emergence of thousands of fresh germs of life. The
whole passage is quoted by Freud in a footnote to Section VI of *Civilization and its Discontents* (1930a).]

first time by Robert in 1886. It is particularly attractive since it is able to suggest a function, a utilitarian purpose, for dreaming. Robert takes as the groundwork of his theory two facts of observation which we have already considered in the course of our examination of the material of dreams (see above, p. 18 ff.), namely that we dream so frequently of the most trivial daily impressions and that we so rarely carry over into our dreams our important daily interests. Robert (1886, 10) asserts that it is universally true that things which we have thoroughly thought out never become instigators of dreams but only things which are in our minds in an uncompleted shape or which have merely been touched upon by our thoughts in passing: 'The reason why it is usually impossible to explain dreams is precisely because they are caused by sensory impressions of the preceding day which failed to attract enough of the dreamer's attention.' [Ibid., 19–20.] Thus the condition which determines whether an impression shall find its way into a dream is whether the process of working over the impression was interrupted or whether the impression was too unimportant to have a right to be worked over at all.

Robert describes dreams as 'a somatic process of excretion of which we become aware in our mental reaction to it'. [Ibid., 9.] Dreams are excretions of thoughts that have been stifled at birth. 'A man deprived of the capacity for dreaming would in course of time become mentally deranged, because a great mass of uncompleted, unworked-out thoughts and superficial impressions would accumulate in his brain and would be bound by their bulk to smother the thoughts which should be assimilated into his memory as completed wholes.' [Ibid., 10.] Dreams serve as a safety-valve for the over-burdened brain. They possess the power to heal and relieve. (Ibid., 32.)

We should be misunderstanding Robert if we were to ask him how it can come about that the mind is relieved through the presentation of ideas in dreams. What Robert is clearly doing is to infer from these two features of the material of dreams that by some means or other an expulsion of worthless impressions is accomplished during sleep as a *somatic* process, and that dreaming is not a special sort of psychical process but merely the information we receive of that expulsion. Moreover, excretion is not the only event which occurs in the mind at night. Robert himself adds that, besides this, the suggestions arising during the previous day are worked out and that 'whatever parts of the undigested thoughts are not excreted are bound together into a rounded whole by threads of thought borrowed from the imagination and thus inserted in the memory as a harmless imaginative picture.' (Ibid., 23.)

But Robert's theory is diametrically opposed to the ruling one in its estimate of the nature of the *sources* of dreams. According to the latter, there would be no dreaming at all if the mind were not being constantly wakened by external and internal sensory stimuli. But in Robert's view the impulsion to dreaming arises in the mind itself—in the fact of its becoming overloaded and requiring relief; and he concludes with perfect logic that causes derived from somatic conditions play a subordinate part as determinants of dreams, and that such causes would be quite incapable of provoking dreams in a mind in which there was no material for the construction of dreams derived from waking consciousness. The only qualification he makes is to admit that the phantasy-images arising in dreams out of the depths of the mind may be affected by nervous stimuli. (Ibid., 48.) After all, therefore, Robert does not regard dreams as so completely dependent upon somatic events. Nevertheless, in his view dreams are not psychical processes, they have no place among the psychical processes of waking life; they are somatic processes occurring every night in the apparatus that is concerned with mental activity, and they have as their function the task of protecting that apparatus from excessive tension—or, to change the metaphor—of acting as scavengers of the mind.[1]

Another writer, Yves Delage, bases his theory on the same features of dreams, as revealed in the choice of their material; and it is instructive to notice the way in which a slight variation in his view of the same things leads him to conclusions of a very different bearing.

Delage (1891, 41) tells us that he experienced in his own person, on the occasion of the death of someone of whom he was fond, the fact that we do *not* dream of what has occupied all our thoughts during the day, or not until it has begun to give place

---

[1] [Robert's theory is further discussed on pp. 164 *n.*, 177 f. and 579. —In the course of a footnote to *Studies on Hysteria* (Breuer and Freud, 1895), quoted in the Editor's Introduction to this volume, p. xiv f., Freud accepted this theory of Robert's as describing one of the two main factors in the production of dreams.]

to other daytime concerns. His investigations among other people confirmed him in the general truth of this fact. He makes what would be an interesting observation of this kind, if it should prove to have general validity, on the dreams of young married couples: 'S'ils ont été fortement épris, presque jamais ils n'ont rêvé l'un de l'autre avant le mariage ou pendant la lune de miel; et s'ils ont rêvé d'amour c'est pour être infidèles avec quelque personne indifférente ou odieuse.'[1] [Ibid., 41.] What, then, do we dream of? Delage identifies the material that occurs in our dreams as consisting of fragments and residues of the preceding days and of earlier times. Everything that appears in our dreams, even though we are inclined at first to regard it as a creation of our dream-life, turns out, when we have examined it more closely, to be unrecognized reproduction [of material already experienced]—'souvenir inconscient'.[2] But this ideational material possesses a common characteristic: it originates from impressions which probably affected our senses more strongly than our intelligence or from which our attention was diverted very soon after they emerged. The less conscious and at the same time the more powerful an impression has been, the more chance it has of playing a part in the next dream.

Here we have what are essentially the same two categories of impressions as are stressed by Robert: the trivial ones and those that have not been dealt with. Delage, however, gives the situation a different turn, for he holds that it is because these impressions have not been dealt with that they are capable of producing dreams, not because they are trivial. It is true in a certain sense that trivial impressions, too, have not been dealt with completely; being in the nature of fresh impressions, they are 'autant de ressorts tendus'[3] which are released during sleep. A powerful impression which happens to have met with some check in the process of being worked over or which has been purposely held under restraint has more claim to play a part in dreams than an impression which is weak and almost unnoticed. The psychical energy which has been stored up during

---

[1] ['If they were deeply in love, they almost never dreamt of each other before marriage or during their honeymoon; and if they had erotic dreams they were unfaithful in them with some indifferent or repellent person.']

[2] ['Unconscious memory.']

[3] ['They are so many springs under tension.']

the daytime by being inhibited and suppressed becomes the
motive force for dreams at night. Psychical material that has
been suppressed comes to light in dreams. [Ibid., 1891, 43.][1]

At this point, unluckily, Delage interrupts his train of thought.
He can attribute only the smallest share in dreams to any
independent psychical activity; and thus he brings his theory
into line with the ruling theory of the partial awakening of the
brain: 'En somme le rêve est le produit de la pensée errante,
sans but et sans direction, se fixant successivement sur les
souvenirs, qui ont gardé assez d'intensité pour se placer sur sa
route et l'arrêter au passage, établissant entre eux un lien tantôt
faible et indécis, tantôt plus fort et plus serré, selon que
l'activité actuelle du cerveau est plus ou moins abolie par le
sommeil.' [Ibid., 46.][2]

(3) We may place in a third group those theories which
ascribe to the dreaming mind a capacity and inclination for
carrying out special psychical activities of which it is largely or
totally incapable in waking life. The putting of these faculties
into force usually provides dreaming with a utilitarian function.
Most of the estimates formed of dreaming by earlier writers on
psychology fall into this class. It will be enough, however, for
me to quote a sentence from Burdach (1838, 512). Dreaming,
he writes, 'is a natural activity of the mind which is not limited
by the power of individuality, which is not interrupted by self-
consciousness and which is not directed by self-determination,
but which is the freely operating vitality of the sensory centres.'

This revelling of the mind in the free use of its own forces is
evidently regarded by Burdach and the rest as a condition in

[1] [*Footnote added* 1909:] Anatole France expresses exactly the same
idea in *Le lys rouge*: 'Ce que nous voyons la nuit, ce sont les restes mal-
heureux de ce que nous avons négligé dans la veille. Le rêve est souvent la
revanche des choses qu'on méprise ou le reproche des êtres abandonnés.'
['What we see during the night are the miserable remnants of what we
have neglected during the previous day. A dream is often a retaliation
on the part of what we despise or a reproach on the part of those we
have deserted.']

[2] ['In short, dreams are the product of thought wandering without
purpose or direction, attaching itself in turn to memories which have
retained enough intensity to stand in its way and interrupt its course,
and linking them together by a bond which is sometimes weak and
vague and sometimes stronger and closer, according as the brain's
activity at the moment is abolished by sleep to a greater or less extent.']

which the mind is refreshed and collects new strength for the day's work—in which, in fact, it enjoys a sort of holiday. Thus Burdach [ibid., 514] quotes with approval the charming words in which the poet Novalis praises the reign of dreams: 'Dreams are a shield against the humdrum monotony of life; they set imagination free from its chains so that it may throw into confusion all the pictures of everyday existence and break into the unceasing gravity of grown men with the joyful play of a child. Without dreams we should surely grow sooner old; so we may look on them—not, perhaps as a gift from on high—but as a precious recreation, as friendly companions on our pilgrimage to the grave.' [*Heinrich von Ofterdingen* (1802), Part I, Chap. 1.]

The reviving and healing function of dreams is described with still more insistence by Purkinje (1846, 456): 'These functions are performed especially by productive dreams. They are the easy play of the imagination and have no connection with the affairs of daytime. The mind has no wish to prolong the tensions of waking life; it seeks to relax them and to recover from them. It produces above all conditions contrary to the waking ones. It cures sorrow by joy, cares by hopes and pictures of happy distraction, hatred by love and friendliness, fear by courage and foresight; it allays doubt by conviction and firm faith, and vain expectation by fulfilment. Many of the spirit's wounds which are being constantly re-opened during the day are healed by sleep, which covers them and shields them from fresh injury. The healing action of time is based partly on this.' We all have a feeling that sleep has a beneficial effect upon mental activities, and the obscure working of the popular mind refuses to let itself be robbed of its belief that dreaming is one of the ways in which sleep dispenses its benefits.

The most original and far-reaching attempt to explain dreaming as a special activity of the mind, capable of free expansion only during the state of sleep, was that undertaken by Scherner in 1861. His book is written in a turgid and high-flown style and is inspired by an almost intoxicated enthusiasm for his subject which is bound to repel anyone who cannot share in his fervour. It puts such difficulties in the way of an analysis of its contents that we turn with relief to the clearer and briefer exposition of Scherner's doctrines given by the philosopher Volkelt. 'Suggestive gleams of meaning proceed like lightning-flashes out of these mystical agglomerations, these clouds of glory and splendour—but they do not illuminate a philosopher's path.' It is in these terms that Scherner's writings are judged even by his disciple. [Volkelt, 1875, 29.]

Scherner is not one of those who believe that the capacities of the mind continue undiminished in dream-life. He himself [in Volkelt's words (ibid., 30)] shows how the centralized core of the ego—its spontaneous energy—is deprived of its nervous force in dreams, how as a result of this decentralization the processes of cognition, feeling, willing and ideation are modified, and how the remnants of these psychical functions no longer possess a truly mental character but become nothing more than mechanisms. But by way of contrast, the mental activity which may be described as 'imagination', liberated from the domination of reason and from any moderating control, leaps into a position of unlimited sovereignty. Though dream-imagination makes use of recent waking memories for its building material, it erects them into structures bearing not the remotest resemblance to those of waking life; it reveals itself in dreams as possessing not merely reproductive but *productive* powers. [Ibid., 31.] Its characteristics are what lend their peculiar features to dreams. It shows a preference for what is immoderate, exaggerated and monstrous. But at the same time, being freed from the hindrances of the categories of thought, it gains in pliancy, agility and versatility. It is susceptible in the subtlest manner to the shades of the tender feelings and to passionate emotions, and promptly incorporates our inner life into external plastic pictures. Imagination in dreams is without the power of conceptual speech. It is obliged to paint what it has to say pictorially, and, since there are no concepts to exercise an attenuating influence, it makes full and powerful use of the pictorial form. Thus, however clear its speech may be, it is diffuse, clumsy and awkward. The clarity of its speech suffers particularly from the fact that it has a dislike of representing an object by its proper image, and prefers some extraneous image which will express only that particular one of the object's attributes which it is seeking to represent. Here we have the 'symbolizing activity' of the imagination. . . . [Ibid., 32.] Another very important point is that dream-imagination never depicts things completely, but only in outline and even so only in the roughest fashion. For this reason its paintings seem like inspired sketches. It does not halt, however, at the mere representation of an object; it is under an internal necessity to involve the dream-ego to a greater or less extent with the object and thus produce an *event*. For instance, a dream caused by a visual stimulus may represent gold coins in the street; the dreamer will pick them up delightedly and carry them off. [Ibid., 33.]

The material with which dream-imagination accomplishes its artistic work is principally, according to Scherner, provided by the organic somatic stimuli which are so obscure during the daytime. (See above, p. 33 ff.) Thus the excessively fantastic hypothesis put forward by Scherner and the perhaps unduly sober doctrines of Wundt and other physiologists, which are poles asunder in other respects, are entirely at one in regard to their theory of the sources and instigators of dreams. According to the physiological view, however, the mental reaction to the internal somatic stimuli is exhausted with the provoking of certain ideas appropriate to the stimuli; these ideas give rise to others along associative lines and at this point the course of psychical events in dreams seems to be at an end. According to Scherner, on the other hand, the somatic stimuli do no more than provide the mind with material of which it can make use for its imaginative purposes. The formation of dreams only begins, in Scherner's eyes, at the point which the other writers regard as its end.

What dream-imagination does to the somatic stimuli cannot, of course, be regarded as serving any useful purpose. It plays about with them, and pictures the organic sources, from which the stimuli of the dream in question have arisen, in some kind of plastic symbolism. Scherner is of the opinion—though here Volkelt [1875, 37] and others refuse to follow him—that dream-imagination has one particular favourite way of representing the organism as a whole: namely as a house. Fortunately, however, it does not seem to be restricted to this one method of representation. On the other hand, it may make use of a whole row of houses to indicate a single organ; for instance, a very long street of houses may represent a stimulus from the intestines. Again, separate portions of a house may stand for separate portions of the body; thus, in a dream caused by a headache, the head may be represented by the ceiling of a room covered with disgusting, toad-like spiders. [Ibid., 33 f.]

Leaving this house-symbolism on one side, any number of

other kinds of things may be used to represent the parts of the body from which the stimulus to the dream has arisen. 'Thus the breathing lung will be symbolically represented by a blazing furnace, with flames roaring with a sound like the passage of air; the heart will be represented by hollow boxes or baskets, the bladder by round, bag-shaped objects or, more generally, by hollow ones. A dream caused by stimuli arising from the male sexual organs may cause the dreamer to find the top part of a clarinet in the street or the mouth-piece of a tobacco-pipe, or again, a piece of fur. Here the clarinet and the tobacco-pipe represent the approximate shape of the male organ, while the fur stands for the pubic hair. In the case of a sexual dream in a woman, the narrow space where the thighs come together may be represented by a narrow courtyard surrounded by houses, while the vagina may be symbolized by a soft, slippery and very narrow foot-path leading across the yard, along which the dreamer has to pass, in order, perhaps, to take a gentleman a letter.' (Ibid., 34.) It is of special importance that, at the end of dreams with a somatic stimulus, such as these, the dream-imagination often throws aside its veil, as it were, by openly revealing the organ concerned or its function. Thus a dream 'with a dental stimulus' usually ends by the dreamer picturing himself pulling a tooth out of his mouth. [Ibid., 35.]

Dream-imagination may, however, not merely direct its attention to the *form* of the stimulating organ; it may equally well symbolize the substance contained in that organ. In this way, a dream with an intestinal stimulus may lead the dreamer along muddy streets, or one with a urinary stimulus may lead him to a foaming stream. Or the stimulus as such, the nature of the excitement it produces, or the object it desires, may be symbolically represented. Or the dream-ego may enter into concrete relations with the symbols of its own state; for instance, in the case of painful stimuli the dreamer may engage in a desperate struggle with fierce dogs or savage bulls, or a woman in a sexual dream may find herself pursued by a naked man. [Ibid., 35 f.] Quite apart from the wealth of the means that it employs, the symbolizing activity of the imagination remains the central force in every dream. [Ibid., 36.] The task of penetrating more deeply into the nature of this imagination and of finding a place for it in a system of philosophical thought is attempted by Volkelt in the pages of his book. But, though it is well and feelingly written, it remains excessively hard to understand for anyone whose early education has not prepared him for a sympathetic grasp of the conceptual constructions of philosophy.

There is no utilitarian function attached to Scherner's symbolizing imagination. The mind plays in its sleep with the stimuli that impinge upon it. One might almost suspect that it plays with them mischievously. But I might also be asked whether my detailed examination of Scherner's theory of dreams can serve any utilitarian purpose, since its arbitrary character and its disobedience to all the rules of research seem only too obvious. By way of rejoinder, I might register a protest against the arrogance which would dismiss Scherner's theory unexamined. His theory is built upon the impression made by his dreams upon a man who considered them with the greatest attention and seems to have had a great personal gift for investigating the obscure things of the mind. Moreover it deals with a subject that for thousands of years has been regarded by mankind as enigmatic, no doubt, but also as important in itself and its implications—a subject to the elucidation of which exact science, on its own admission, has contributed little apart from an attempt (in direct opposition to popular feeling) to deny it any meaning or significance. And finally it may honestly be said that in attempting to explain dreams it is not easy to avoid being fantastic. Ganglion cells can be fantastic too. The passage which I quoted on p. 77 from a sober and exact investigator like Binz, and which describes the way in which the dawn of awakening steals over the mass of sleeping cells in the cerebral cortex, is no less fantastic—and no less improbable—than Scherner's attempts at interpretation. I hope to be able to show that behind the latter there is an element of reality, though it has only been vaguely perceived and lacks the attribute of universality which should characterize a theory of dreams. Meanwhile the contrast between Scherner's theory and the medical one will show us the extremes between which explanations of dream-life doubtfully oscillate to this very day.[1]

[1] [Scherner's theories are further discussed on pp. 224 ff. and 346.]

THE RELATIONS BETWEEN DREAMS AND MENTAL DISEASES

When we speak of the relation of dreams to mental disorders we may have three things in mind: (1) aetiological and clinical connections, as when a dream represents a psychotic state, or introduces it, or is left over from it; (2) modifications to which dream-life is subject in cases of mental disease; and (3) intrinsic connections between dreams and psychoses, analogies pointing to their being essentially akin. These numerous relations between the two groups of phenomena were a favourite topic among medical writers in earlier times and have become so once again to-day, as is shown by the bibliographies of the subject collected by Spitta [1882, 196 f. and 319 f.], Radestock [1879, 217], Maury [1878, 124 f.] and Tissié [1898, 77 f.]. Quite recently Sante de Sanctis has turned his attention to this subject.[1] It will be enough for the purpose of my thesis if I do no more than touch upon this important question.

As regards the clinical and aetiological connections between dreams and psychoses, the following observations may be given as samples. Hohnbaum [1830, 124], quoted by Krauss [1858, 619], reports that a first outbreak of delusional insanity often originates in an anxious or terrifying dream, and that the dominant idea is connected with the dream. Sante de Sanctis brings forward similar observations in cases of paranoia and declares that in some of these the dream was the 'vraie cause déterminante de la folie'.[2] The psychosis, says de Sanctis, may come to life at a single blow with the appearance of the opera-tive dream which brings the delusional material to light; or it may develop slowly in a series of further dreams, which have still to overcome a certain amount of doubt. In one of his cases

---

[1] [*Footnote added* 1914:] Among later writers who deal with these rela-tions are Féré [1887], Ideler [1862], Lasègue [1881], Pichon [1896], Régis [1894], Vespa [1897], Giessler [1888, etc.], Kazowsky [1901], Pachantoni [1909], etc.

[2] ['The true determining cause of insanity.']

the significant dream was followed by mild hysterical attacks and later by a condition of anxious melancholia. Féré [1886] (quoted by Tissié, 1898 [78]) reports a dream which resulted in a hysterical paralysis. In these instances the dreams are represented as the aetiology of the mental disorder; but we should be doing equal justice to the facts if we said that the mental disorder made its first appearance in dream-life, that it first broke through in a dream. In some further examples the pathological symptoms are contained in dream-life, or the psychosis is limited to dream-life. Thus Thomayer (1897) draws attention to certain anxiety-dreams which he thinks should be regarded as equivalents of epileptic fits. Allison [1868] (quoted by Radestock, 1879 [225]) has described a 'nocturnal insanity', in which the patient appears completely healthy during the day but is regularly subject at night to hallucinations, fits of frenzy, etc. Similar observations are reported by de Sanctis [1899, 226] (a dream of an alcoholic patient which was equivalent to a paranoia, and which represented voices accusing his wife of unfaithfulness) and Tissié. The latter (1898, [147 ff.]) gives copious recent examples in which acts of a pathological nature, such as conduct based on delusional premises and obsessive impulses, were derived from dreams. Guislain [1833] describes a case in which sleep was replaced by an intermittent insanity.

There can be no doubt that alongside of the psychology of dreams physicians will some day have to turn their attention to a *psychopathology* of dreams.

In cases of recovery from mental diseases it can often be quite clearly observed that, while functioning is normal during the day, dream-life is still under the influence of the psychosis. According to Krauss (1859, 270), Gregory first drew attention to this fact. Macario [1847], quoted by Tissié [1898, 89], describes how a manic patient, a week after his complete recovery was still subject in his dreams to the flight of ideas and the violent passions which were characteristic of his illness.

Very little research has hitherto been carried out into the modifications occurring in dream-life during chronic psychoses.[1] On the other hand, attention was long ago directed to the

[1] [This question was later examined by Freud himself (1922b, end of Section B).]

underlying kinship between dreams and mental disorders, exhibited in the wide measure of agreement between their manifestations. Maury (1854, 124) tells us that Cabanis (1802) was the first to remark on them, and after him Lélut [1852], J. Moreau (1855) and, in particular, Maine de Biran [1834, 111 ff.] the philosopher. No doubt the comparison goes back still earlier. Radestock (1879, 217) introduces the chapter in which he deals with it by a number of quotations drawing an analogy between dreams and madness. Kant writes somewhere [1764]: 'The madman is a waking dreamer.' Krauss (1859, 270) declares that 'insanity is a dream dreamt while the senses are awake'. Schopenhauer [1862, 1, 246] calls dreams a brief madness and madness a long dream. Hagen [1846, 812] describes delirium as dream-life induced not by sleep but by illness. Wundt [1878, 662] writes: 'We ourselves, in fact, can experience in dreams almost all the phenomena to be met with in insane asylums.'

Spitta (1882, 199), in much the same way as Maury (1854), enumerates as follows the different points of agreement which constitute the basis for this comparison: '(1) Self-consciousness is suspended or at least retarded, which results in a lack of insight into the nature of the condition, with consequent inability to feel surprise and loss of moral consciousness. (2) Perception by the sense organs is modified: being diminished in dreams but as a rule greatly increased in insanity. (3) Interconnection of ideas occurs exclusively according to the laws of association and reproduction; ideas thus fall into sequences automatically and there is a consequent lack of proportion in the relation between ideas (exaggerations and illusions). All this leads to (4) an alteration or in some cases a reversal of personality and occasionally of character traits (perverse conduct).'

Radestock (1879, 219) adds a few more features—analogies between the *material* in the two cases: 'The majority of hallucinations and illusions occur in the region of the senses of sight and hearing and of coenaesthesia. As in the case of dreams, the senses of smell and taste provide the fewest elements.—Both in patients suffering from fever and in dreamers memories arise from the remote past; both sleeping and sick men recollect things which waking and healthy men seem to have forgotten.' The analogy between dreams and psychoses is only fully appreciated when it is seen to extend to the details of expressive movement and to particular characteristics of facial expression.

'A man tormented by physical and mental suffering obtains from dreams what reality denies him: health and happiness. So too in mental disease there are bright pictures of happiness, grandeur, eminence and wealth. The supposed possession of property and the imaginary fulfilment of wishes—the with-holding or destruction of which actually affords a psychological basis for insanity—often constitute the chief content of a delirium. A woman who has lost a loved child experiences the joys of motherhood in her delirium; a man who has lost his money believes himself immensely rich; a girl who has been deceived feels that she is tenderly loved.'

(This passage from Radestock is actually a summary of an acute observation made by Griesinger (1861, 106), who shows quite clearly that ideas in dreams and in psychoses have in common the characteristic of being *fulfilments of wishes*. My own researches have taught me that in this fact lies the key to a psychological theory of both dreams and psychoses.)

'The chief feature of dreams and of insanity lies in their eccentric trains of thought and their weakness of judgement.' In both states [Radestock continues] we find an over-valuation of the subject's own mental achievements which seems senseless to a sober view; the rapid sequence of ideas in dreams is paralleled by the flight of ideas in psychoses. In both there is a complete lack of sense of time. In dreams the personality may be split—when, for instance, the dreamer's own knowledge is divided between two persons and when, in the dream, the extraneous ego corrects the actual one. This is precisely on a par with the splitting of the personality that is familiar to us in hallucinatory paranoia; the dreamer too hears his own thoughts pronounced by extraneous voices. Even chronic delusional ideas have their analogy in stereotyped recurrent pathological dreams (*le rêve obsédant*).—It not infrequently happens that after re-covering from a delirium patients will say that the whole period of their illness seems to them like a not unpleasant dream: indeed they will sometimes tell us that even during the illness they have occasionally had a feeling that they are only caught up in a dream—as is often the case in dreams occurring in sleep.

After all this, it is not surprising that Radestock sums up his views, and those of many others, by declaring that 'insanity, an abnormal pathological phenomenon, is to be regarded as an intensification of the periodically recurrent normal condition of dreaming'. (Ibid., 228.)

Krauss (1859, 270 f.) has sought to establish what is perhaps a still more intimate connection between dreams and insanity than can be demonstrated by an analogy between these external manifestations. This connection he sees in their aetiology or rather in the sources of their excitation. The fundamental element common to the two states lies according to him, as we have seen [p. 36 f.], in organically determined sensations, in sensations derived from somatic stimuli, in the coenaesthesia which is based upon contributions arising from all the organs. (Cf. Peisse, 1857, 2, 21, quoted by Maury, 1878, 52.)

The indisputable analogy between dreams and insanity, extending as it does down to their characteristic details, is one of the most powerful props of the medical theory of dream-life, which regards dreaming as a useless and disturbing process and as the expression of a reduced activity of the mind. Nevertheless it is not to be expected that we shall find the ultimate explanation of dreams in the direction of mental disorders; for the unsatisfactory state of our knowledge of the origin of these latter conditions is generally recognized. It is quite likely, on the contrary, that a modification of our attitude towards dreams will at the same time affect our views upon the internal mechanism of mental disorders and that we shall be working towards an explanation of the psychoses while we are endeavouring to throw some light on the mystery of dreams.[1]

---

[1] [A discussion of the relation between dreams and psychoses will be found in Lecture 29 of the *New Introductory Lectures* (Freud, 1933a).]

The fact that I have not extended my account of the literature dealing with the problems of dreams to cover the period between the first and second editions of this book stands in need of a justification. It may strike the reader as an unsatisfactory one, but for me it was none the less decisive. The motives which led me to give any account at all of the way in which earlier writers have dealt with dreams were exhausted with the completion of this introductory chapter; to continue the task would have cost me an extraordinary effort—and the result would have been of very little use or instruction. For the intervening nine years have produced nothing new or valuable either in factual material or in opinions that might throw light on the subject. In the majority of publications that have appeared during the interval my work has remained unmentioned and unconsidered. It has, of course, received least attention from those who are engaged in what is described as 'research' into dreams, and who have thus provided a shining example of the repugnance to learning anything new which is characteristic of men of science. In the ironical words of Anatole France, '*les savants ne sont pas curieux*'. If there were such a thing in science as a right to retaliate, I should certainly be justified in my turn in disregarding the literature that has been issued since the publication of this book. The few notices of it that have appeared in scientific periodicals show so much *lack* of understanding and so much *mis*understanding that my only reply to the critics would be to suggest their reading the book again—or perhaps, indeed, merely to suggest their reading it.

A large number of dreams have been published and analysed in accordance with my directions in papers by physicians who have decided to adopt the psycho-analytic therapeutic procedure, as well as by other authors.[1] In so far as these writings have gone beyond a mere confirmation of my views I have included their findings in the course of my exposition. I have

[1] [In the 1909 and 1911 editions only, there was a parenthesis at this point containing the names of Jung, Abraham, Riklin, Muthmann and Stekel. In 1909 only, the next sentence read : 'But these publications have merely confirmed my views and not added anything to them.']

added a second bibliography at the end of the volume containing a list of the most important works that have appeared since this book was first published.[1] The extensive monograph on dreams by Sante de Sanctis (1899), of which a German translation appeared soon after its issue, was published almost simultaneously with my *Interpretation of Dreams*, so that neither I nor the Italian author was able to comment upon each other's work. I have unfortunately been unable to escape the conclusion that his painstaking volume is totally deficient in ideas—so much so, in fact, that it would not even lead one to suspect the existence of the problems with which I have dealt.

Only two publications require to be mentioned which come near to my own treatment of the problems of dreams. Hermann Swoboda (1904), a youthful philosopher, has undertaken the task of extending to psychical events the discovery of a biological periodicity (in 23-day and 28-day periods) made by Wilhelm Fliess [1906].[2] In the course of his highly imaginative work he has endeavoured to use this key for the solution, among other problems, of the riddle of dreams. His findings would seem to under-estimate the significance of dreams; the subject-matter of a dream, on his view, is to be explained as an assemblage of all the memories which, on the night on which it is dreamt, complete one of the biological periods, whether for the first or for the *n*th time. A personal communication from the author led me at first to suppose that he himself no longer took this theory seriously, but it seems that this was a mistaken conclusion on my part.[3] At a later stage [see below, p. 166 ff.] I shall report upon some observations which I made in connection with Swoboda's suggestion but which led me to no convincing conclusion. I was the more pleased when, in an unexpected quarter, I made the chance discovery of a view of dreams which coincides entirely with the core of my own theory. It is impossible, for chronological reasons, that the statement in question can have been influenced by my book. I must there-

---

[1] [See the Editor's Introduction, pp. xiii and xxi.]

[2] [An account of Fliess's theories and of his relations with Swoboda is given in Section IV of Kris's introduction to Freud's correspondence with Fliess (Freud, 1950a).]

[3] [In its present form this sentence dates from 1911. In 1909 it read: 'A personal communication from the author to the effect that he himself no longer supports these views exempts me from giving them serious consideration.' The following sentence was added in 1911.]

fore hail it as the single discoverable instance in the literature
of the subject of an independent thinker who is in agreement
with the essence of my theory of dreams. The book which contains the passage upon dreaming which I have in mind appeared
in its second edition in 1900 under the title of *Phantasien eines
Realisten* by 'Lynkeus'. [First edition, 1899.][1]

POSTSCRIPT, 1914

The preceding plea of justification was written in 1909. I am
bound to admit that since then the situation has changed;
my contribution to the interpretation of dreams is no longer
neglected by writers on the subject. The new state of affairs,
however, has now made it quite out of the question for me to
extend my previous account of the literature. *The Interpretation
of Dreams* has raised a whole series of fresh considerations and
problems which have been discussed in a great variety of ways.
I cannot give an account of these works, however, before I have
expounded those views of my own on which they are based. I
have therefore dealt with whatever seems to me of value in the
latest literature at its appropriate place in the course of the
discussion which now follows.

[1] [*Footnote added* 1930:] Cf. my paper on Josef Popper-Lynkeus and
the theory of dreams (1923*f*). [Freud wrote a further paper on the subject (1932*c*). The passage referred to in the text above will be found
quoted in full below in a footnote on p. 308 f.]

CHAPTER II

THE METHOD OF INTERPRETING DREAMS: AN ANALYSIS OF A SPECIMEN DREAM

THE title that I have chosen for my work makes plain which of the traditional approaches to the problem of dreams I am inclined to follow. The aim which I have set before myself is to show that dreams are capable of being interpreted; and any contributions I may be able to make towards the solution of the problems dealt with in the last chapter will only arise as by-products in the course of carrying out my proper task. My presumption that dreams can be interpreted at once puts me in opposition to the ruling theory of dreams and in fact to every theory of dreams with the single exception of Scherner's [p. 83 ff.]; for 'interpreting' a dream implies assigning a 'meaning' to it—that is, replacing it by something which fits into the chain of our mental acts as a link having a validity and importance equal to the rest. As we have seen, the scientific theories of dreams leave no room for any problem of interpreting them, since in their view a dream is not a mental act at all, but a somatic process signalizing its occurrence by indications registered in the mental apparatus. Lay opinion has taken a different attitude throughout the ages. It has exercised its indefeasible right to behave inconsistently; and, though admitting that dreams are unintelligible and absurd, it cannot bring itself to declare that they have no significance at all. Led by some obscure feeling, it seems to assume that, in spite of everything, every dream has a meaning, though a hidden one, that dreams are designed to take the place of some other process of thought, and that we have only to undo the substitution correctly in order to arrive at this hidden meaning.

Thus the lay world has from the earliest times concerned itself with 'interpreting' dreams and in its attempts to do so it has made use of two essentially different methods.

The first of these procedures considers the content of the dream as a whole and seeks to replace it by another content which is intelligible and in certain respects analogous to the original one. This is '*symbolic*' dream-interpreting; and it inevitably breaks down when faced by dreams which are not merely unintelligible but also confused. An example of this procedure is to be seen in the explanation of Pharaoh's dream propounded by Joseph in the Bible. The seven fat kine followed by seven lean kine that ate up the fat kine—all this was a symbolic substitute for a prophecy of seven years of famine in the land of Egypt which should consume all that was brought forth in the seven years of plenty. Most of the artificial dreams constructed by imaginative writers are designed for a symbolic interpretation of this sort: they reproduce the writer's thoughts under a disguise which is regarded as harmonizing with the recognized characteristics of dreams.[1] The idea of dreams being chiefly concerned with the future and being able to foretell it— a remnant of the old prophetic significance of dreams—provides a reason for transposing the meaning of the dream, when it has been arrived at by symbolic interpretation, into the future tense. It is of course impossible to give instructions upon the *method* of arriving at a symbolic interpretation. Success must be a question of hitting on a clever idea, of direct intuition, and for that reason it was possible for dream-interpretation by means of symbolism to be exalted into an artistic activity dependent on the possession of peculiar gifts.[2]

The second of the two popular methods of interpreting dreams is far from making any such claims. It might be described as the '*decoding*' method, since it treats dreams as a kind of cryptography in which each sign can be translated into another sign having a known meaning, in accordance with a fixed key. Suppose, for instance, that I have dreamt of a letter

[1] [*Footnote added* 1909:] I found by chance in *Gradiva*, a story written by Wilhelm Jensen, a number of artificial dreams which were perfectly correctly constructed and could be interpreted just as though they had not been invented but had been dreamt by real people. In reply to an enquiry, the author confirmed the fact that he had no knowledge of my theory of dreams. I have argued that the agreement between my researches and this writer's creations is evidence in favour of the correctness of my analysis of dreams. (See Freud, 1907*a*.)

[2] [*Footnote added* 1914:] Aristotle [*De divinatione per somnum*, II (*Trans.*, 1935, 383)] remarked in this connection that the best interpreter of dreams was the man who could best grasp similarities; for dreampictures, like pictures on water, are pulled out of shape by movement, and the most successful interpreter is the man who can detect the truth from the misshapen picture. (Büchsenschütz, 1868, 65.)

and also of a funeral. If I consult a 'dream-book', I find that
'letter' must be translated by 'trouble' and 'funeral' by
'betrothal'. It then remains for me to link together the key-
words which I have deciphered in this way and, once more, to
transpose the result into the future tense. An interesting modification of the process of decoding, which to some extent corrects
the purely mechanical character of its method of transposing, is
to be found in the book written upon the interpretation of
dreams [*Oneirocritica*] by Artemidorus of Daldis.[1] This method
takes into account not only the content of the dream but also the
character and circumstances of the dreamer; so that the same
dream-element will have a different meaning for a rich man,
a married man or, let us say, an orator, from what it has for a

---

[1] [*Footnote added* 1914:] Artemidorus of Daldis, who was probably
born at the beginning of the second century A.D., has left us the most
complete and painstaking study of dream-interpretation as practised in
the Graeco-Roman world. As Theodor Gomperz (1866, 7 f.) points out,
he insisted on the importance of basing the interpretation of dreams on
observation and experience, and made a rigid distinction between his
own art and others that were illusory. The principle of his interpretative
art, according to Gomperz, is identical with magic, the principle of
association. A thing in a dream means what it recalls to the mind—to
the dream-interpreter's mind, it need hardly be said. An insuperable
source of arbitrariness and uncertainty arises from the fact that the
dream-element may recall *various* things to the interpreter's mind and
may recall something different to different interpreters. The technique
which I describe in the pages that follow differs in one essential respect
from the ancient method: it imposes the task of interpretation upon the
dreamer himself. It is not concerned with what occurs to the *interpreter*
in connection with a particular element of the dream, but with what
occurs to the *dreamer.*—Recent reports, however, from a missionary,
Father Tfinkdji (1913, [516–17 and 523]), show that modern dream-
interpreters in the East also make free use of the dreamer's collaboration. He writes as follows of dream-interpreters among the Arabs of
Mesopotamia: 'Pour interprêter exactement un songe, les oniromanciens les plus habiles s'informent de ceux qui les consultent de toutes les
circonstances qu'ils regardent nécessaires pour la bonne explication. . . .
En un mot, nos oniromanciens ne laissent aucune circonstance leur
échapper et ne donnent l'interprétation désirée avant d'avoir parfaitement saisi et reçu toutes les interrogations désirables.' ['In órder to give
a precise interpretation of a dream, the most skilful dream-diviners find
out from those who consult them all the circumstances which they consider essential in order to arrive at a right explanation. . . . In short,
these dream-diviners do not allow a single point to escape them and only
give their interpretation after they have completely mastered the replies
to all the necessary enquiries.'] Among these enquiries are habitually

poor man, a bachelor or a merchant. The essence of the decoding procedure, however, lies in the fact that the work of interpretation is not brought to bear on the dream as a whole but on each portion of the dream's content independently, as though the dream were a geological conglomerate in which each fragment of rock required a separate assessment. There can be no question that the invention of the decoding method of interpretation was suggested by disconnected and confused dreams.[1]

It cannot be doubted for a moment that neither of the two popular procedures for interpreting dreams can be employed for a scientific treatment of the subject. The symbolic method is restricted in its application and incapable of being laid down

included questions as to the dreamer's closest family relations—his parents, wife and children—as well as such a typical formula as: 'Habuistine in hac nocte copulam conjugalem ante vel post somnium?' ['Did you copulate with your wife that night before or after you had the dream?'] —'L'idée dominante dans l'interprétation des songes consiste à expliquer le rêve par son opposée.' ['The principal idea in interpreting dreams lies in explaining a dream by its opposite.']

[1] [Footnote added 1909:] Dr. Alfred Robitsek has pointed out to me that the oriental 'dream-books' (of which ours are wretched imitations) base the greater number of their interpretations of dream-elements upon similarity of sounds and resemblance between words. The fact that these connections inevitably disappear in translation accounts for the unintelligibility of the renderings in our own popular dream-books. The extraordinarily important part played by punning and verbal quibbles in the ancient civilizations of the East may be studied in the writings of Hugo Winckler [the famous archaeologist].—[Added 1911:] The nicest instance of a dream-interpretation which has reached us from ancient times is based on a play upon words. It is told by Artemidorus [Book IV, Chap. 24; Krauss's translation, 1881, 255]: 'I think too that Aristander gave a most happy interpretation to Alexander of Macedon when he had surrounded Tyre [Τύρος] and was besieging it but was feeling uneasy and disturbed because of the length of time the siege was taking. Alexander dreamt he saw a satyr [σάτυρος] dancing on his shield. Aristander happened to be in the neighbourhood of Tyre, in attendance on the king during his Syrian campaign. By dividing the word for satyr into σά and τύρος he encouraged the king to press home the siege so that he became master of the city.' (σά Τύρος = Tyre is thine.)—Indeed, dreams are so closely related to linguistic expression that Ferenczi [1910] has truly remarked that every tongue has its own dream-language. It is impossible as a rule to translate a dream into a foreign language and this is equally true, I fancy, of a book such as the present one. [Added 1930:] Nevertheless, Dr. A. A. Brill of New York, and others after him, have succeeded in translating The Interpretation of Dreams.

on general lines. In the case of the decoding method everything depends on the trustworthiness of the 'key'—the dream-book, and of this we have no guarantee. Thus one might feel tempted to agree with the philosophers and the psychiatrists and, like them, rule out the problem of dream-interpretation as a purely fanciful task.[1]

But I have been taught better. I have been driven to realize that here once more we have one of those not infrequent cases in which an ancient and jealously held popular belief seems to be nearer the truth than the judgement of the prevalent science of to-day. I must affirm that dreams really have a meaning and that a scientific procedure for interpreting them is possible.

My knowledge of that procedure was reached in the following manner. I have been engaged for many years (with a therapeutic aim in view) in unravelling certain psychopathological structures—hysterical phobias, obsessional ideas, and so on. I have been doing so, in fact, ever since I learnt from an important communication by Josef Breuer that as regards these structures (which are looked on as pathological symptoms) unravelling them coincides with removing them.[2] (Cf. Breuer and Freud, 1895.) If a pathological idea of this sort can be traced back to the elements in the patient's mental life from which it originated, it simultaneously crumbles away and the patient is freed from it. Considering the impotence of our other therapeutic efforts and the puzzling nature of these disorders, I felt tempted to follow the path marked out by Breuer, in spite of every difficulty, till a complete explanation was reached. I shall have on another occasion to report at length upon the form finally taken by this procedure and the results of my labours. It was in the course of these psycho-analytic studies that I came upon dream-interpretation. My patients were pledged to communicate to me every idea or thought that occurred to them in connection with some particular subject; amongst other things they told me their dreams and so taught

---

[1] After I had completed my manuscript I came across a work by Stumpf (1899) which agrees with my views in seeking to prove that dreams have a meaning and can be interpreted. He effects his interpretations, however, by means of a symbolism of an allegorical character without any guarantee of the general validity of his procedure.

[2] ['*Auflösung*' and '*Lösung*' in the original.]

me that a dream can be inserted into the psychical chain that has to be traced backwards in the memory from a pathological idea. It was then only a short step to treating the dream itself as a symptom and to applying to dreams the method of interpretation that had been worked out for symptoms.

This involves some psychological preparation of the patient. We must aim at bringing about two changes in him: an increase in the attention he pays to his own psychical perceptions and the elimination of the criticism by which he normally sifts the thoughts that occur to him. In order that he may be able to concentrate his attention on his self-observation it is an advantage for him to lie in a restful attitude and shut his eyes.[1] It is necessary to insist explicitly on his renouncing all criticism of the thoughts that he perceives. We therefore tell him that the success of the psycho-analysis depends on his noticing and reporting whatever comes into his head and not being misled, for instance, into suppressing an idea because it strikes him as unimportant or irrelevant or because it seems to him meaningless. He must adopt a completely impartial attitude to what occurs to him, since it is precisely his critical attitude which is responsible for his being unable, in the ordinary course of things, to achieve the desired unravelling of his dream or obsessional idea or whatever it may be.

I have noticed in my psycho-analytical work that the whole frame of mind of a man who is reflecting is totally different from that of a man who is observing his own psychical processes. In reflection there is one more psychical activity at work than in the most attentive self-observation, and this is shown amongst other things by the tense looks and wrinkled forehead of a person pursuing his reflections as compared with the restful expression of a self-observer. In both cases attention [2] must be concentrated, but the man who is reflecting is also exercising his *critical* faculty; this leads him to reject some of the ideas that occur to him after perceiving them, to cut short others without following the trains of thought which they would open up to

---

[1] [The stress upon the advisability of shutting the eyes (a remnant of the old hypnotic procedure) was very soon dropped. See, for instance, the account of psycho-analytic technique in Freud (1904a), where it is specifically mentioned that the analyst does *not* ask the patient to shut his eyes.]

[2] [The function of attention is discussed below (p. 593).]

him, and to behave in such a way towards still others that they never become conscious at all and are accordingly suppressed before being perceived. The self-observer on the other hand need only take the trouble to suppress his critical faculty. If he succeeds in doing that, innumerable ideas come into his consciousness of which he could otherwise never have got hold. The material which is in this way freshly obtained for his self-perception makes it possible to interpret both his pathological ideas and his dream-structures. What is in question, evidently, is the establishment of a psychical state which, in its distribution of psychical energy (that is, of mobile attention), bears some analogy to the state before falling asleep—and no doubt also to hypnosis. As we fall asleep, 'involuntary ideas' emerge, owing to the relaxation of a certain deliberate (and no doubt also critical) activity which we allow to influence the course of our ideas while we are awake. (We usually attribute this relaxation to 'fatigue'.) As the involuntary ideas emerge they change into visual and acoustic images. (Cf. the remarks by Schleiermacher and others quoted above on pp. 49 f. [and 71 f.].)[1] In the state used for the analysis of dreams and pathological ideas, the patient purposely and deliberately abandons this activity and employs the psychical energy thus saved (or a portion of it) in attentively following the involuntary thoughts which now emerge, and which—and here the situation differs from that of falling asleep—retain the character of ideas. *In this way the 'involuntary' ideas are transformed into 'voluntary' ones.*

The adoption[2] of the required attitude of mind towards ideas that seem to emerge 'of their own free will' and the abandonment of the critical function that is normally in operation against them seem to be hard of achievement for some people. The 'involuntary thoughts' are liable to release a most violent resistance, which seeks to prevent their emergence. If we may trust that great poet and philosopher Friedrich Schiller, however, poetic creation must demand an exactly similar attitude. In a passage in his correspondence with Körner—we

---

[1] [*Footnote added* 1919:] Silberer (1909, 1910 and 1912) has made important contributions to dream-interpretation by directly observing this transformation of ideas into visual images. [See below, pp. 344 f. and 503 f.]

[2] [This paragraph was added in 1909, and the first sentence of the next paragraph modified accordingly.]

have to thank Otto Rank for unearthing it—Schiller (writing on December 1, 1788) replies to his friend's complaint of insufficient productivity: 'The ground for your complaint seems to me to lie in the constraint imposed by your reason upon your imagination. I will make my idea more concrete by a simile. It seems a bad thing and detrimental to the creative work of the mind if Reason makes too close an examination of the ideas as they come pouring in—at the very gateway, as it were. Looked at in isolation, a thought may seem very trivial or very fantastic; but it may be made important by another thought that comes after it, and, in conjunction with other thoughts that may seem equally absurd, it may turn out to form a most effective link. Reason cannot form any opinion upon all this unless it retains the thought long enough to look at it in connection with the others. On the other hand, where there is a creative mind, Reason—so it seems to me—relaxes its watch upon the gates, and the ideas rush in pell-mell, and only then does it look them through and examine them in a mass.— You critics, or whatever else you may call yourselves, are ashamed or frightened of the momentary and transient extravagances which are to be found in all truly creative minds and whose longer or shorter duration distinguishes the thinking artist from the dreamer. You complain of your unfruitfulness because you reject too soon and discriminate too severely.'

Nevertheless, what Schiller describes as a relaxation of the watch upon the gates of Reason, the adoption of an attitude of uncritical self-observation, is by no means difficult. Most of my patients achieve it after their first instructions. I myself can do so very completely, by the help of writing down my ideas as they occur to me. The amount of psychical energy by which it is possible to reduce critical activity and increase the intensity of self-observation varies considerably according to the subject on which one is trying to fix one's attention.

Our first step in the employment of this procedure teaches us that what we must take as the object of our attention is not the dream as a whole but the separate portions of its content. If I say to a patient who is still a novice: 'What occurs to you in connection with this dream?', as a rule his mental horizon becomes a blank. If, however, I put the dream before him cut up into pieces, he will give me a series of associations to each piece, which might be described as the 'background thoughts' of that particular part of the dream. Thus the method of dream-interpretation which I practise already differs in this first important respect from the popular, historic and legendary method of interpretation by means of symbolism and approximates to the second or 'decoding' method. Like the latter, it employs interpretation *en détail* and not *en masse*; like the latter, it regards dreams from the very first as being of a composite character, as being conglomerates of psychical formations. [Cf. pp. 418 f. and 449.][1]

In the course of my psycho-analyses of neurotics I must already have analysed over a thousand dreams; but I do not propose to make use of this material in my present introduction to the technique and theory of dream-interpretation. Apart from the fact that such a course would be open to the objection that these are the dreams of neuropaths, from which no valid inferences could be made as to the dreams of normal people, there is quite another reason which forces this decision upon me. The subject to which these dreams of my patients lead up is always, of course, the case history which underlies their neurosis. Each dream would therefore necessitate a lengthy introduction and an investigation of the nature and aetiological determinants of the psychoneuroses. But these questions are in themselves novelties and highly bewildering and would distract attention from the problem of dreams. On the contrary, it is my intention to make use of my present elucidation of dreams as a preliminary step towards solving the more difficult problems of the psychology of the neuroses.[2] If, however, I forego my principal material, the dreams of my neurotic patients, I must not be too particular about what is left to me. All that remains are such dreams as have been reported to me

[1] [The technique of dream-interpretation is further discussed below (p. 522 ff.). See also the first two sections of Freud (1923c). The quite other question of the part played by dream-interpretation in the technique of therapeutic psycho-analysis is considered in Freud (1911e).]

[2] [At the beginning of Section E of Chapter VII, Freud reflects upon the difficulties imposed upon his exposition of the subject by this programme, which is already laid down in his preface to the first edition (p. xxiii). As he points out on p. 146 and again on p. 151 n., he is often led into disregarding it. In spite of his declared intention, he makes use of many of his patients' dreams, and more than once (e.g. on p. 149 f.) enters into a discussion of the mechanism of neurotic symptoms.]

from time to time by normal persons of my acquaintance, and such others as have been quoted as instances in the literature dealing with dream-life. Unluckily, however, none of these dreams are accompanied by the analysis without which I cannot discover a dream's meaning. My procedure is not so convenient as the popular decoding method which translates any given piece of a dream's content by a fixed key. I, on the contrary, am prepared to find that the same piece of content may conceal a different meaning when it occurs in various people or in various contexts. Thus it comes about that I am led to my own dreams, which offer a copious and convenient material, derived from an approximately normal person and relating to multifarious occasions of daily life. No doubt I shall be met by doubts of the trustworthiness of 'self-analyses' of this kind; and I shall be told that they leave the door open to arbitrary conclusions. In my judgement the situation is in fact more favourable in the case of *self*-observation than in that of other people; at all events we may make the experiment and see how far self-analysis takes us with the interpretation of dreams. But I have other difficulties to overcome, which lie within myself. There is some natural hesitation about revealing so many intimate facts about one's mental life; nor can there be any guarantee against misinterpretation by strangers. But it must be possible to overcome such hesitations. 'Tout psychologiste', writes Delbœuf [1885], 'est obligé de faire l'aveu même de ses faiblesses s'il croit par là jeter du jour sur quelque problème obscur.'[1] And it is safe to assume that my readers too will very soon find their initial interest in the indiscretions which I am bound to make replaced by an absorbing immersion in the psychological problems upon which they throw light.[2]

Accordingly I shall proceed to choose out one of my own dreams and demonstrate upon it my method of interpretation. In the case of every such dream some remarks by way of preamble will be necessary.—And now I must ask the reader

[1] ['Every psychologist is under an obligation to confess even his own weaknesses, if he thinks that it may throw light upon some obscure problem.']

[2] I am obliged to add, however, by way of qualification of what I have said above, that in scarcely any instance have I brought forward the *complete* interpretation of one of my own dreams, as it is known to me. I have probably been wise in not putting too much faith in my readers' discretion.

to make my interests his own for quite a while, and to plunge, along with me, into the minutest details of my life; for a transference of this kind is peremptorily demanded by our interest in the hidden meaning of dreams.

PREAMBLE

During the summer of 1895 I had been giving psycho-analytic treatment to a young lady who was on very friendly terms with me and my family. It will be readily understood that a mixed relationship such as this may be a source of many disturbed feelings in a physician and particularly in a psychotherapist. While the physician's personal interest is greater, his authority is less; any failure would bring a threat to the old-established friendship with the patient's family. This treatment had ended in a partial success; the patient was relieved of her hysterical anxiety but did not lose all her somatic symptoms. At that time I was not yet quite clear in my mind as to the criteria indicating that a hysterical case history was finally closed, and I proposed a solution to the patient which she seemed unwilling to accept. While we were thus at variance, we had broken off the treatment for the summer vacation.—One day I had a visit from a junior colleague, one of my oldest friends, who had been staying with my patient, Irma, and her family at their country resort. I asked him how he had found her and he answered: 'She's better, but not quite well.' I was conscious that my friend Otto's words, or the tone in which he spoke them, annoyed me. I fancied I detected a reproof in them, such as to the effect that I had promised the patient too much; and, whether rightly or wrongly, I attributed the supposed fact of Otto's siding against me to the influence of my patient's relatives, who, as it seemed to me, had never looked with favour on the treatment. However, my disagreeable impression was not clear to me and I gave no outward sign of it. The same evening I wrote out Irma's case history, with the idea of giving it to Dr. M. (a common friend who was at that time the leading figure in our circle) in order to justify myself. That night (or more probably the next morning) I had the following dream, which I noted down immediately after waking.[1]

[1] [*Footnote added* 1914:] This is the first dream which I submitted to a detailed interpretation. [Freud describes some first groping attempts at the analysis of his own dreams in *Studies on Hysteria* (Breuer and Freud,

DREAM OF JULY 23RD–24TH, 1895

A large hall—numerous guests, whom we were receiving.—Among them was Irma. I at once took her on one side, as though to answer her letter and to reproach her for not having accepted my 'solution' yet. I said to her: 'If you still get pains, it's really only your fault.' She replied: 'If you only knew what pains I've got now in my throat and stomach and abdomen—it's choking me'—I was alarmed and looked at her. She looked pale and puffy. I thought to myself that after all I must be missing some organic trouble. I took her to the window and looked down her throat, and she showed signs of recalcitrance, like women with artificial dentures. I thought to myself that there was really no need for her to do that.—She then opened her mouth properly and on the right I found a big white[1] patch; at another place I saw extensive whitish grey scabs upon some remarkable curly structures which were evidently modelled on the turbinal bones of the nose.—I at once called in Dr. M., and he repeated the examination and confirmed it. . . . Dr. M. looked quite different from usual; he was very pale, he walked with a limp and his chin was clean-shaven. . . . My friend Otto was now standing beside her as well, and my friend Leopold was percussing her through her bodice and saying: 'She has a dull area low down on the left.' He also indicated that a portion of the skin on the left shoulder was infiltrated. (I noticed this, just as he did, in spite of her dress.) . . . M. said: 'There's no doubt it's an infection, but no matter; dysentery will supervene and the toxin will be eliminated.' . . . We were directly aware, too, of the origin of the infection. Not long before, when she was feeling unwell, my friend Otto had given her an injection of a preparation of propyl, propyls . . . propionic acid . . . trimethylamin (and I saw before me the formula for this printed in heavy type). . . . Injections of that sort ought not to be made so thoughtlessly. . . . And probably the syringe had not been clean.

This dream has one advantage over many others. It was immediately clear what events of the previous day provided its starting-point. My preamble makes that plain. The news which Otto had given me of Irma's condition and the case history

1895). They will be found mentioned in the course of the long footnote attached to the entry of May 15 in the Case History of Frau Emmy von N. This passage is quoted in full in the Editor's Introduction (p. xiv f.).]

[1] [The word 'white' is omitted, no doubt accidentally, in the 1942 edition only.]

which I had been engaged in writing till far into the night continued to occupy my mental activity even after I was asleep. Nevertheless, no one who had only read the preamble and the content of the dream itself could have the slightest notion of what the dream meant. I myself had no notion. I was astonished at the symptoms of which Irma complained to me in the dream, since they were not the same as those for which I had treated her. I smiled at the senseless idea of an injection of propionic acid and at Dr. M.'s consoling reflections. Towards its end the dream seemed to me to be more obscure and compressed than it was at the beginning. In order to discover the meaning of all this it was necessary to undertake a detailed analysis.

ANALYSIS

The hall—numerous guests, whom we were receiving. We were spending that summer at Bellevue, a house standing by itself on one of the hills adjoining the Kahlenberg.[1] The house had formerly been designed as a place of entertainment and its reception-rooms were in consequence unusually lofty and hall-like. It was at Bellevue that I had the dream, a few days before my wife's birthday. On the previous day my wife had told me that she expected that a number of friends, including Irma, would be coming out to visit us on her birthday. My dream was thus anticipating this occasion: it was my wife's birthday and a number of guests, including Irma, were being received by us in the large hall at Bellevue.

I reproached Irma for not having accepted my solution; I said: 'If you still get pains, it's your own fault.' I might have said this to her in waking life, and I may actually have done so. It was my view at that time (though I have since recognized it as a wrong one) that my task was fulfilled when I had informed a patient of the hidden meaning of his symptoms: I considered that I was not responsible for whether he accepted the solution or not—though this was what success depended on. I owe it to this mistake, which I have now fortunately corrected, that my life was made easier at a time when, in spite of all my inevitable ignorance, I was expected to produce therapeutic successes.—I noticed, however, that the words which I spoke to Irma in the dream showed that I was specially anxious not to be responsible for the pains

[1] [A hill which is a favourite resort in the immediate neighbourhood of Vienna.]

which she still had. If they were her fault they could not be mine. Could it be that the purpose of the dream lay in this direction?

Irma's complaint: pains in her throat and abdomen and stomach; it was choking her. Pains in the stomach were among my patient's symptoms but were not very prominent; she complained more of feelings of nausea and disgust. Pains in the throat and abdomen and constriction of the throat played scarcely any part in her illness. I wondered why I decided upon this choice of symptoms in the dream but could not think of an explanation at the moment.

She looked pale and puffy. My patient always had a rosy complexion. I began to suspect that someone else was being substituted for her.

I was alarmed at the idea that I had missed an organic illness. This, as may well be believed, is a perpetual source of anxiety to a specialist whose practice is almost limited to neurotic patients and who is in the habit of attributing to hysteria a great number of symptoms which other physicians treat as organic. On the other hand, a faint doubt crept into my mind—from where, I could not tell—that my alarm was not entirely genuine. If Irma's pains had an organic basis, once again I could not be held responsible for curing them; my treatment only set out to get rid of *hysterical* pains. It occurred to me, in fact, that I was actually *wishing* that there had been a wrong diagnosis; for, if so, the blame for my lack of success would also have been got rid of.

I took her to the window to look down her throat. She showed some recalcitrance, like women with false teeth. I thought to myself that really there was no need for her to do that. I had never had any occasion to examine Irma's oral cavity. What happened in the dream reminded me of an examination I had carried out some time before of a governess: at a first glance she had seemed a picture of youthful beauty, but when it came to opening her mouth she had taken measures to conceal her plates. This led to recollections of other medical examinations and of little secrets revealed in the course of them—to the satisfaction of neither party. '*There was really no need for her to do that*' was no doubt intended in the first place as a compliment to Irma; but I suspected that it had another meaning besides. (If one carries out an analysis attentively, one gets a feeling of whether or not one has exhausted all the background thoughts that are to be expected.)

The way in which Irma stood by the window suddenly reminded me of another experience. Irma had an intimate woman friend of whom I had a very high opinion. When I visited this lady one evening I had found her by a window in the situation reproduced in the dream, and her physician, the same Dr. M., had pronounced that she had a diphtheritic membrane. The figure of Dr. M. and the membrane reappear later in the dream. It now occurred to me that for the last few months I had had every reason to suppose that this other lady was also a hysteric. Indeed, Irma herself had betrayed the fact to me. What did I know of her condition? One thing precisely: that, like my Irma of the dream, she suffered from hysterical choking. So in the dream I had replaced my patient by her friend. I now recollected that I had often played with the idea that she too might ask me to relieve her of her symptoms. I myself, however, had thought this unlikely, since she was of a very reserved nature. She was *recalcitrant*, as was shown in the dream. Another reason was that *there was no need for her to do it*: she had so far shown herself strong enough to master her condition without outside help. There still remained a few features that I could not attach either to Irma or to her friend: *pale; puffy; false teeth*. The false teeth took me to the governess whom I have already mentioned; I now felt inclined to be satisfied with *bad* teeth. I then thought of someone else to whom these features might be alluding. She again was not one of my patients, nor should I have liked to have her as a patient, since I had noticed that she was bashful in my presence and I could not think she would make an amenable patient. She was usually pale, and once, while she had been in specially good health, she had looked puffy.[1] Thus I had been comparing my patient Irma with two other people who would also have been recalcitrant to treatment. What could the reason have been for my having exchanged her in the dream for her friend? Perhaps it was that I should have *liked* to exchange her: either I felt more sympathetic towards her friend

[1] The still unexplained complaint about *pains in the abdomen* could also be traced back to this third figure. The person in question was, of course, my own wife; the pains in the abdomen reminded me of one of the occasions on which I had noticed her bashfulness. I was forced to admit to myself that I was not treating either Irma or my wife very kindly in this dream; but it should be observed by way of excuse that I was measuring them both by the standard of the good and amenable patient.

or had a higher opinion of her intelligence. For Irma seemed to
me foolish because she had not accepted my solution. Her friend
would have been wiser, that is to say she would have yielded
sooner. She would then have *opened her mouth properly*, and have
told me more than Irma.[1]

*What I saw in her throat: a white patch and turbinal bones with
scabs on them.* The white patch reminded me of diphtheritis and
so of Irma's friend, but also of a serious illness of my eldest
daughter's almost two years earlier and of the fright I had had
in those anxious days. The scabs on the turbinal bones recalled
a worry about my own state of health. I was making frequent
use of cocaine at that time to reduce some troublesome nasal
swellings, and I had heard a few days earlier that one of my
women patients who had followed my example had developed
an extensive necrosis of the nasal mucous membrane. I had been
the first to recommend the use of cocaine, in 1885,[2] and this
recommendation had brought serious reproaches down on me.
The misuse of that drug had hastened the death of a dear friend
of mine. This had been before 1895 [the date of the dream].

I at once called in Dr. M., and he repeated the examination. This
simply corresponded to the position occupied by M. in our
circle. But the '*at once*' was sufficiently striking to require a
special explanation.[3] It reminded me of a tragic event in my
practice. I had on one occasion produced a severe toxic state in
a woman patient by repeatedly prescribing what was at that
time regarded as a harmless remedy (sulphonal), and had hur-
riedly turned for assistance and support to my experienced senior
colleague. There was a subsidiary detail which confirmed the
idea that I had this incident in mind. My patient—who succumbed to the poison—had the same name as my eldest daughter.

---

[1] I had a feeling that the interpretation of this part of the dream
was not carried far enough to make it possible to follow the whole of its
concealed meaning. If I had pursued my comparison between the three
women, it would have taken me far afield.—There is at least one spot
in every dream at which it is unplumbable—a navel, as it were, that
is its point of contact with the unknown. [Cf. p. 525.]

[2] [This is a misprint (which occurs in every German edition) for
'1884', the date of Freud's first paper on cocaine. A full account of
Freud's work in connection with cocaine will be found in Chapter VI of
the first volume of Ernest Jones's life of Freud. From this it appears that
the 'dear friend' was Fleischl von Marxow (see p. 482 *n.*). Further indirect allusions to this episode will be found on pp. 170 f., 206, 216 f. and
484.]

484.]   [3] [See below, p. 513.]

It had never occurred to me before, but it struck me now almost like an act of retribution on the part of destiny. It was as though the replacement of one person by another was to be continued in another sense: this Mathilde for that Mathilde, an eye for an eye and a tooth for a tooth. It seemed as if I had been collecting all the occasions which I could bring up against myself as evidence of lack of medical conscientiousness.

Dr. M. was pale, had a clean-shaven chin and walked with a limp. This was true to the extent that his unhealthy appearance often caused his friends anxiety. The two other features could only apply to someone else. I thought of my elder brother, who lives abroad, who is clean-shaven and whom, if I remembered right, the M. of the dream closely resembled. We had had news a few days earlier that he was walking with a limp owing to an arthritic affection of his hip. There must, I reflected, have been some reason for my fusing into one the two figures in the dream. I then remembered that I had a similar reason for being in an ill-humour with each of them: they had both rejected a certain suggestion I had recently laid before them.

My friend Otto was now standing beside the patient and my friend Leopold was examining her and indicated that there was a dull area low down on the left. My friend Leopold was also a physician and a relative of Otto's. Since they both specialized in the same branch of medicine, it was their fate to be in competition with each other, and comparisons were constantly being drawn between them. Both of them acted as my assistants for years while I was still in charge of the neurological out-patients' department of a children's hospital.[1] Scenes such as the one represented in the dream used often to occur there. While I was discussing the diagnosis of a case with Otto, Leopold would be examining the child once more and would make an unexpected contribution to our decision. The difference between their characters was like that between the bailiff Bräsig and his friend Karl[2]: one was distinguished for his quickness, while the other was slow but sure. If in the dream I was contrasting Otto with the prudent Leopold, I was evidently doing so to the advantage of the

---

[1] [For details of this hospital see Section II of Kris's introduction to the Fliess correspondence (Freud, 1950a).]

[2] [The two chief figures in the once popular novel, *Ut mine Stromtid*, written in Mecklenburg dialect, by Fritz Reuter (1862–4). There is an English translation, *An Old Story of my Farming Days* (London, 1878).]

latter. The comparison was similar to the one between my disobedient patient Irma and the friend whom I regarded as wiser
than she was. I now perceived another of the lines along which
the chain of thought in the dream branched off: from the sick
child to the children's hospital.—*The dull area low down on the
left* seemed to me to agree in every detail with one particular
case in which Leopold had struck me by his thoroughness. I
also had a vague notion of something in the nature of a metastatic affection; but this may also have been a reference to the
patient whom I should have liked to have in the place of Irma.
So far as I had been able to judge, she had produced an
imitation of a tuberculosis.

A portion of the skin on the left shoulder was infiltrated. I saw at
once that this was the rheumatism in my own shoulder, which
I invariably notice if I sit up late into the night. Moreover the
wording in the dream was most ambiguous: '*I noticed this, just
as he did.* . . .' I noticed it in my own body, that is. I was struck,
too, by the unusual phrasing: 'a portion of the skin was infiltrated'. We are in the habit of speaking of 'a left upper posterior
infiltration', and this would refer to the lung and so once more
to tuberculosis.

In spite of her dress. This was in any case only an interpolation.
We naturally used to examine the children in the hospital undressed: and this would be a contrast to the manner in which
adult female patients have to be examined. I remembered that
it was said of a celebrated clinician that he never made a physical
examination of his patients except through their clothes. Further than this I could not see. Frankly, I had no desire to penetrate more deeply at this point.

*Dr. M. said: 'It's an infection, but no matter. Dysentery will super-
vene and the toxin will be eliminated.'* At first this struck me as
ridiculous. But nevertheless, like all the rest, it had to be carefully analysed. When I came to look at it more closely it seemed
to have some sort of meaning all the same. What I discovered
in the patient was a local diphtheritis. I remembered from the
time of my daughter's illness a discussion on diphtheritis and
diphtheria, the latter being the general infection that arises
from the local diphtheritis. Leopold indicated the presence
of a general infection of this kind from the existence of a
dull area, which might thus be regarded as a metastatic
focus. I seemed to think, it is true, that metastases like this do

not in fact occur with diphtheria: it made me think rather of pyaemia.

No matter. This was intended as a consolation. It seemed to fit into the context as follows. The content of the preceding part of the dream had been that my patient's pains were due to a severe organic affection. I had a feeling that I was only trying in that way to shift the blame from myself. Psychological treatment could not be held responsible for the persistence of diphtheritic pains. Nevertheless I had a sense of awkwardness at having invented such a severe illness for Irma simply in order to clear myself. It looked so cruel. Thus I was in need of an assurance that all would be well in the end, and it seemed to me that to have put the consolation into the mouth precisely of Dr. M. had not been a bad choice. But here I was taking up a superior attitude towards the dream, and this itself required explanation.

And why was the consolation so nonsensical?

Dysentery. There seemed to be some remote theoretical notion that morbid matter can be eliminated through the bowels. Could it be that I was trying to make fun of Dr. M.'s fertility in producing far-fetched explanations and making unexpected pathological connections? Something else now occurred to me in relation to dysentery. A few months earlier I had taken on the case of a young man with remarkable difficulties associated with defaecating, who had been treated by other physicians as a case of 'anaemia accompanied by malnutrition'. I had recognized it as a hysteria, but had been unwilling to try him with my psychotherapeutic treatment and had sent him on a sea voyage. Some days before, I had had a despairing letter from him from Egypt, saying that he had had a fresh attack there which a doctor had declared was dysentery. I suspected that the diagnosis was an error on the part of an ignorant practitioner who had allowed himself to be taken in by the hysteria. But I could not help reproaching myself for having put my patient in a situation in which he might have contracted some organic trouble on top of his hysterical intestinal disorder. Moreover, 'dysentery' sounds not unlike 'diphtheria'—a word of ill omen which did not occur in the dream.[1]

Yes, I thought to myself, I must have been making fun of

[1] [The German words '*Dysenterie*' and '*Diphtherie*' are more alike than the English ones.]

Dr. M. with the consoling prognosis 'Dysentery will supervene, etc.': for it came back to me that, years before, he himself had told an amusing story of a similar kind about another doctor. Dr. M. had been called in by him for consultation over a patient who was seriously ill, and had felt obliged to point out, in view of the very optimistic view taken by his colleague, that he had found albumen in the patient's urine. The other, however, was not in the least put out: '*No matter*', he had said, 'the albumen will soon be eliminated!'—I could no longer feel any doubt, therefore, that this part of the dream was expressing derision at physicians who are ignorant of hysteria. And, as though to confirm this, a further idea crossed my mind: 'Does Dr. M. realize that the symptoms in his patient (Irma's friend) which give grounds for fearing tuberculosis also have a hysterical basis? Has he spotted this hysteria? or has he been taken in by it?'

But what could be my motive for treating this friend of mine so badly? That was a very simple matter. Dr. M. was just as little in agreement with my 'solution' as Irma herself. So I had already revenged myself in this dream on two people: on Irma with the words 'If you still get pains, it's your own fault', and on Dr. M. by the wording of the nonsensical consolation that I put into his mouth.

We were directly aware of the origin of the infection. This direct knowledge in the dream was remarkable. Only just before we had had no knowledge of it, for the infection was only revealed by Leopold.

When she was feeling unwell, my friend Otto had given her an injection. Otto had in fact told me that during his short stay with Irma's family he had been called in to a neighbouring hotel to give an injection to someone who had suddenly felt unwell. These injections reminded me once more of my unfortunate friend who had poisoned himself with cocaine [see p. 111 *n.*]. I had advised him to use the drug internally [i.e. orally] only, while morphia was being withdrawn; but he had at once given himself cocaine *injections*.

A preparation of propyl . . . propyls . . . propionic acid. How could I have come to think of this? During the previous evening, before I wrote out the case history and had the dream, my wife had opened a bottle of liqueur, on which the word 'Ananas'[1]

---

[1] I must add that the sound of the word 'Ananas' bears a remarkable resemblance to that of my patient Irma's family name.

appeared and which was a gift from our friend Otto: for he has a habit of making presents on every possible occasion. It was to be hoped, I thought to myself, that some day he would find a wife to cure him of the habit.[1] This liqueur gave off such a strong smell of fusel oil that I refused to touch it. My wife suggested our giving the bottle to the servants, but I—with even greater prudence—vetoed the suggestion, adding in a philanthropic spirit that there was no need for *them* to be poisoned either. The smell of fusel oil (amyl . . .) evidently stirred up in my mind a recollection of the whole series—propyl, methyl, and so on—and this accounted for the propyl preparation in the dream. It is true that I carried out a substitution in the process: I dreamt of propyl after having smelt amyl. But substitutions of this kind are perhaps legitimate in organic chemistry.

Trimethylamin. I saw the chemical formula of this substance in my dream, which bears witness to a great effort on the part of my memory. Moreover, the formula was printed in heavy type, as though there had been a desire to lay emphasis on some part of the context as being of quite special importance. What was it, then, to which my attention was to be directed in this way by trimethylamin? It was to a conversation with another friend who had for many years been familiar with all my writings during the period of their gestation, just as I had been with his.[2] He had at that time confided some ideas to me on the subject of the chemistry of the sexual processes, and had mentioned among other things that he believed that one of the products of sexual metabolism was trimethylamin. Thus this substance led me to sexuality, the factor to which I attributed the greatest importance in the origin of the nervous disorders which it was my aim to cure. My patient Irma was a young widow; if I wanted to find an excuse for the failure of my treatment in her case, what I could best appeal to would no doubt be this fact

---

[1] [*Footnote added* 1909, but omitted again from 1925 onwards:] In this respect the dream did not turn out to be prophetic. But in another respect it *was*. For my patient's 'unsolved' gastric pains, for which I was so anxious not to be blamed, turned out to be the forerunners of a serious disorder caused by gall-stones.

[2] [This was Wilhelm Fliess, the Berlin biologist and nose and throat specialist, who exercised a great influence on Freud during the years immediately preceding the publication of this book, and who figures frequently, though as a rule anonymously, in its pages. See Freud (1950a).]

of her widowhood, which her friends would be so glad to see changed. And how strangely, I thought to myself, a dream like this is put together! The other woman, whom I had as a patient in the dream instead of Irma, was also a young widow.

I began to guess why the formula for trimethylamin had been so prominent in the dream. So many important subjects converged upon that one word. Trimethylamin was an allusion not only to the immensely powerful factor of sexuality, but also to a person whose agreement I recalled with satisfaction whenever I felt isolated in my opinions. Surely this friend who played so large a part in my life must appear again elsewhere in these trains of thought. Yes. For he had a special knowledge of the consequences of affections of the nose and its accessory cavities; and he had drawn scientific attention to some very remarkable connections between the turbinal bones and the female organs of sex. (Cf. the three curly structures in Irma's throat.) I had had Irma examined by him to see whether her gastric pains might be of nasal origin. But he suffered himself from suppurative rhinitis, which caused me anxiety; and no doubt there was an allusion to this in the pyaemia which vaguely came into my mind in connection with the metastases in the dream.[1]

Injections of that sort ought not to be made so thoughtlessly. Here an accusation of thoughtlessness was being made directly against my friend Otto. I seemed to remember thinking something of the same kind that afternoon when his words and looks had appeared to show that he was siding against me. It had been some such notion as: 'How easily his thoughts are influenced! How thoughtlessly he jumps to conclusions!'—Apart from this, this sentence in the dream reminded me once more of my dead friend who had so hastily resorted to cocaine injections. As I have said, I had never contemplated the drug being given by injection. I noticed too that in accusing Otto of thoughtlessness in handling chemical substances I was once more touching upon the story of the unfortunate Mathilde, which gave grounds for the same accusation against myself. Here I was evidently collecting instances of my conscientiousness, but also of the reverse.

---

[1] [The analysis of this part of the dream is further elaborated below (p. 294 f.). It had already been used by Freud as an example of the mechanism of displacement in Section 21 of Part I of his very early 'Project for a Scientific Psychology', written in the autumn of 1895 and printed as an Appendix to Freud (1950a).]

And probably the syringe had not been clean. This was yet another accusation against Otto, but derived from a different source. I had happened the day before to meet the son of an old lady of eighty-two, to whom I had to give an injection of morphia twice a day.[1] At the moment she was in the country and he told me that she was suffering from phlebitis. I had at once thought it must be an infiltration caused by a dirty syringe. I was proud of the fact that in two years I had not caused a single infiltration; I took constant pains to be sure that the syringe was clean. In short, I was conscientious. The phlebitis brought me back once more to my wife, who had suffered from thrombosis during one of her pregnancies; and now three similar situations came to my recollection involving my wife, Irma and the dead Mathilde. The identity of these situations had evidently enabled me to substitute the three figures for one another in the dream.

I have now completed the interpretation of the dream.[2] While I was carrying it out I had some difficulty in keeping at bay all the ideas which were bound to be provoked by a comparison between the content of the dream and the concealed thoughts lying behind it. And in the meantime the 'meaning' of the dream was borne in upon me. I became aware of an intention which was carried into effect by the dream and which must have been my motive for dreaming it. The dream fulfilled certain wishes which were started in me by the events of the previous evening (the news given me by Otto and my writing out of the case history). The conclusion of the dream, that is to say, was that I was not responsible for the persistence of Irma's pains, but that Otto was. Otto had in fact annoyed me by his remarks about Irma's incomplete cure, and the dream gave me my revenge by throwing the reproach back on to him. The dream acquitted me of the responsibility for Irma's condition by showing that it was due to other factors—it produced a whole series of reasons. The dream represented a particular

[1] [This old lady makes frequent appearances in Freud's writings at this period. See below, p. 239, and *The Psychopathology of Everyday Life* (1901*b*), Chapter VIII(*b* and *g*) and Chapter XII(C*b*). Her death is reported in a letter to Fliess of July 8, 1901 (Freud, 1950*a*, Letter 145).]

[2] [*Footnote added* 1909:] Though it will be understood that I have not reported everything that occurred to me during the process of interpretation.

state of affairs as I should have wished it to be. *Thus its content was the fulfilment of a wish and its motive was a wish.*

Thus much leapt to the eyes. But many of the details of the dream also became intelligible to me from the point of view of wish-fulfilment. Not only did I revenge myself on Otto for being too hasty in taking sides against me by representing him as being too hasty in his medical treatment (in giving the injection); but I also revenged myself on him for giving me the bad liqueur which had an aroma of fusel oil. And in the dream I found an expression which united the two reproaches: the injection was of a preparation of propyl. This did not satisfy me and I pursued my revenge further by contrasting him with his more trustworthy competitor. I seemed to be saying: 'I like *him* better than *you*.' But Otto was not the only person to suffer from the vials of my wrath. I took revenge as well on my disobedient patient by exchanging her for one who was wiser and less recalcitrant. Nor did I allow Dr. M. to escape the consequences of his contradiction but showed him by means of a clear allusion that he was an ignoramus on the subject. ('*Dysentery will supervene,* etc.') Indeed I seemed to be appealing from him to someone else with greater knowledge (to my friend who had told me of trimethylamin) just as I had turned from Irma to her friend and from Otto to Leopold. 'Take these people away! Give me three others of my choice instead! Then I shall be free of these undeserved reproaches!' The groundlessness of the reproaches was proved for me in the dream in the most elaborate fashion. *I* was not to blame for Irma's pains, since she herself was to blame for them by refusing to accept my solution. *I* was not concerned with Irma's pains, since they were of an organic nature and quite incurable by psychological treatment. Irma's pains could be satisfactorily explained by her widowhood (cf. the trimethylamin) which *I* had no means of altering. Irma's pains had been caused by Otto giving her an incautious injection of an unsuitable drug—a thing *I* should never have done. Irma's pains were the result of an injection with a dirty needle, like my old lady's phlebitis—whereas *I* never did any harm with my injections. I noticed, it is true, that these explanations of Irma's pains (which agreed in exculpating me) were not entirely consistent with one another, and indeed that they were mutually exclusive. The whole plea—for the dream was nothing else—reminded one vividly of the defence put forward by the man who was charged by one of his neighbours with having given him back a borrowed kettle in a damaged condition. The defendant asserted first, that he had given it back undamaged; secondly, that the kettle had a hole in it when he borrowed it; and thirdly, that he had never borrowed a kettle from his neighbour at all. So much the better: if only a single one of these three lines of defence were to be accepted as valid, the man would have to be acquitted.[1]

Certain other themes played a part in the dream, which were not so obviously connected with my exculpation from Irma's illness: my daughter's illness and that of my patient who bore the same name, the injurious effect of cocaine, the disorder of my patient who was travelling in Egypt, my concern about my wife's health and about that of my brother and of Dr. M., my own physical ailments, my anxiety about my absent friend who suffered from suppurative rhinitis. But when I came to consider all of these, they could all be collected into a single group of ideas and labelled, as it were, 'concern about my own and other people's health—professional conscientiousness'. I called to mind the obscure disagreeable impression I had had when Otto brought me the news of Irma's condition. This group of thoughts that played a part in the dream enabled me retrospectively to put this transient impression into words. It was as though he had said to me: 'You don't take your medical duties seriously enough. You're not conscientious; you don't carry out what you've undertaken.' Thereupon, this group of thoughts seemed to have put itself at my disposal, so that I could produce evidence of how highly conscientious I was, of how deeply I was concerned about the health of my relations, my friends and my patients. It was a noteworthy fact that this material also included some disagreeable memories, which supported my friend Otto's accusation rather than my own vindication. The material was, as one might say, impartial; but nevertheless there was an unmistakable connection between this more extensive group of thoughts which underlay the dream and the narrower subject of the dream which gave rise to the wish to be innocent of Irma's illness.

I will not pretend that I have completely uncovered the

[1] [This anecdote is discussed by Freud in relation to this passage in Chapter II, Section 8, and Chapter VII, Section 2, of his book on jokes. (Freud, 1905c.)]

meaning of this dream or that its interpretation is without a gap. I could spend much more time over it, derive further information from it and discuss fresh problems raised by it. I myself know the points from which further trains of thought could be followed. But considerations which arise in the case of every dream of my own restrain me from pursuing my interpretative work. If anyone should feel tempted to express a hasty condemnation of my reticence, I would advise him to make the experiment of being franker than I am. For the moment I am satisfied with the achievement of this one piece of fresh knowledge. If we adopt the method of interpreting dreams which I have indicated here, we shall find that dreams really have a meaning and are far from being the expression of a fragmentary activity of the brain, as the authorities have claimed. *When the work of interpretation has been completed, we perceive that a dream is the fulfilment of a wish.*[1]

---

[1] [In a letter to Fliess on June 12, 1900 (Freud, 1950*a*, Letter 137), Freud describes a later visit to Bellevue, the house where he had this dream. 'Do you suppose', he writes, 'that some day a marble tablet will be placed on the house, inscribed with these words?—

> In This House, on July 24th, 1895
> the Secret of Dreams was Revealed
> to Dr. Sigm. Freud

At the moment there seems little prospect of it.']

CHAPTER III

A DREAM IS THE FULFILMENT OF
A WISH

WHEN, after passing through a narrow defile, we suddenly emerge upon a piece of high ground, where the path divides and the finest prospects open up on every side, we may pause for a moment and consider in which direction we shall first turn our steps.[1] Such is the case with us, now that we have surmounted the first interpretation of a dream. We find ourselves in the full daylight of a sudden discovery. Dreams are not to be likened to the unregulated sounds that rise from a musical instrument struck by the blow of some external force instead of by a player's hand [cf. p. 78]; they are not meaningless, they are not absurd; they do not imply that one portion of our store of ideas is asleep while another portion is beginning to wake. On the contrary, they are psychical phenomena of complete validity—fulfilments of wishes; they can be inserted into the chain of intelligible waking mental acts; they are constructed by a highly complicated activity of the mind.

But no sooner have we begun to rejoice at this discovery than we are assailed by a flood of questions. If, as we are told by dream-interpretation, a dream represents a fulfilled wish, what is the origin of the remarkable and puzzling form in which the wish-fulfilment is expressed? What alteration have the dream-thoughts undergone before being changed into the manifest dream which we remember when we wake up? How does that alteration take place? What is the source of the material that has been modified into the dream? What is the source of the

[1] [In a letter to Fliess of August 6, 1899 (Freud, 1950a, Letter 114), Freud describes the opening chapters of this book as follows: 'The whole thing is planned on the model of an imaginary walk. First comes the dark wood of the authorities (who cannot see the trees), where there is no clear view and it is easy to go astray. Then there is a cavernous defile through which I lead my readers—my specimen dream with its peculiarities, its details, its indiscretions and its bad jokes—and then, all at once, the high ground and the open prospect and the question: "Which way do you want to go?" ']

many peculiarities that are to be observed in the dream-thoughts—such, for instance, as the fact that they may be mutually contradictory? (Cf. the analogy of the borrowed kettle on p. 120.) Can a dream tell us anything new about our internal psychical processes? Can its content correct opinions we have held during the day?

I propose that for the moment we should leave all these questions on one side and pursue our way further along one particular path. We have learnt that a dream can represent a wish as fulfilled. Our first concern must be to enquire whether this is a universal characteristic of dreams or whether it merely happened to be the content of the particular dream (the dream of Irma's injection) which was the first that we analysed. For even if we are prepared to find that every dream has a meaning and a psychical value, the possibility must remain open of this meaning not being the same in every dream. Our first dream was the fulfilment of a wish; a second one might turn out to be a fulfilled fear; the content of a third might be a reflection; while a fourth might merely reproduce a memory. Shall we find other wishful dreams besides this one? or are there perhaps no dreams but wishful ones?

It is easy to prove that dreams often reveal themselves without any disguise as fulfilments of wishes; so that it may seem surprising that the language of dreams was not understood long ago. For instance, there is a dream that I can produce in myself as often as I like—experimentally, as it were. If I eat anchovies or olives or any other highly salted food in the evening, I develop thirst during the night which wakes me up. But my waking is preceded by a dream; and this always has the same content, namely, that I am drinking. I dream I am swallowing down water in great gulps, and it has the delicious taste that nothing can equal but a cool drink when one is parched with thirst. Then I wake up and have to have a real drink. This simple dream is occasioned by the thirst which I become aware of when I wake. The thirst gives rise to a wish to drink, and the dream shows me that wish fulfilled. In doing so it is performing a function—which it was easy to divine. I am a good sleeper and not accustomed to be woken by any physical need. If I can succeed in appeasing my thirst by *dreaming* that I am drinking, then I need not wake up in order to quench it. This, then, is a dream of convenience. Dreaming has taken the place of action, as it often does elsewhere in life. Unluckily my need for water to quench my thirst cannot be satisfied by a dream in the same way as my thirst for revenge against my friend Otto and Dr. M.; but the good intention is there in both cases. Not long ago this same dream of mine showed some modification. I had felt thirsty even before I fell asleep, and I had emptied a glass of water that stood on the table beside my bed. A few hours later during the night I had a fresh attack of thirst, and this had inconvenient results. In order to provide myself with some water I should have had to get up and fetch the glass standing on the table by my wife's bed. I therefore had an appropriate dream that my wife was giving me a drink out of a vase; this vase was an Etruscan cinerary urn which I had brought back from a journey to Italy and had since given away. But the water in it tasted so salty (evidently because of the ashes in the urn) that I woke up. It will be noticed how conveniently everything was arranged in this dream. Since its only purpose was to fulfil a wish, it could be completely egoistical. A love of comfort and convenience is not really compatible with consideration for other people. The introduction of the cinerary urn was probably yet another wish-fulfilment. I was sorry that the vase was no longer in my possession—just as the glass of water on my wife's table was out of my reach. The urn with its ashes fitted in, too, with the salty taste in my mouth which had now grown stronger and which I knew was bound to wake me.[1]

[1] Weygandt (1893, 41) was aware of the occurrence of thirst dreams, for he writes: 'The sensation of thirst is perceived with greater precision than any other; it always gives rise to an idea of its being quenched. The manner in which the thirst is represented as being quenched in the dream varies, and derives its special form from some near-by memory. Another general feature in these cases is that immediately after the idea of the thirst being quenched there follows a disappointment over the small effect produced by the imaginary refreshment.' Weygandt, however, overlooks the fact that this reaction of a dream to a stimulus is one which holds good universally. Other people who are attacked by thirst in the night may wake up without having had a dream; but that is no objection to my experiment. It merely shows that they are worse sleepers than I am.—[*Added* 1914:] Compare in this connection Isaiah xxix, 8: 'It shall even be as when an hungry man dreameth, and, behold, he eateth; but he awaketh, and his soul is empty: or as when a thirsty man dreameth, and, behold, he drinketh; but he awaketh, and, behold, he is faint, and his soul hath appetite.'

Dreams of convenience like these were very frequent in my youth. Having made it a practice as far back as I can remember to work late into the night, I always found it difficult to wake early. I used then to have a dream of being out of bed and standing by the washing-stand; after a while I was no longer able to disguise from myself the fact that I was really still in bed, but in the meantime I had had a little more sleep. A slothful dream of this kind, which was expressed in a particularly amusing and elegant form, has been reported to me by a young medical colleague who seems to share my liking for sleep. The landlady of his lodgings in the neighbourhood of the hospital had strict instructions to wake him in time every morning but found it no easy job to carry them out. One morning sleep seemed peculiarly sweet. The landlady called through the door: 'Wake up, Herr Pepi! it's time to go to the hospital!' In response to this he had a dream that he was lying in bed in a room in the hospital, and that there was a card over the bed on which was written: 'Pepi H., medical student, age 22.' While he was dreaming, he said to himself 'As I'm already *in* the hospital, there's no need for me to go there'—and turned over and went on sleeping. In this way he openly confessed the motive for his dream.[1]

Here is another dream in which once again the stimulus produced its effect during actual sleep. One of my women patients, who had been obliged to undergo an operation on her jaw which had taken an unfavourable course, was ordered by her doctors to wear a cooling apparatus on the side of her face day and night. But as soon as she fell asleep she used to throw it off. One day, after she had once more thrown the apparatus on the floor, I was asked to speak to her seriously about it. 'This time I really couldn't help it,' she answered. 'It was because of a dream I had in the night. I dreamt I was in a box at the opera and very much enjoying the performance. But Herr Karl Meyer was in the nursing-home and complaining bitterly of pains in his jaw. So I told myself that as I hadn't any pain I didn't need the apparatus; and I threw it away.' The dream of this poor sufferer seems almost like a concrete representation of a phrase that sometimes forces its way on to people's lips in unpleasant

[1] [This dream was reported by Freud in a letter to Fliess, dated March 4, 1895 (Freud, 1950a, Letter 22)—the earliest recorded hint at the wish-fulfilment theory.]

situations: 'I must say I could think of something more agreeable than this.' The dream gives a picture of this more agreeable
thing. The Herr Karl Meyer on to whom the dreamer transplanted her pains was the most indifferent young man of her
acquaintance that she could call to mind.

The wish-fulfilment can be detected equally easily in some
other dreams which I have collected from normal people. A
friend of mine, who knows my theory of dreams and has told
his wife of it, said to me one day: 'My wife has asked me to
tell you that she had a dream yesterday that she was having her
period. You can guess what that means.' I could indeed guess
it. The fact that this young married woman dreamt that she
was having her period meant that she had missed her period.
I could well believe that she would have been glad to go on
enjoying her freedom a little longer before shouldering the
burden of motherhood. It was a neat way of announcing her
first pregnancy. Another friend of mine wrote and told me that,
not long before, his wife had dreamt that she had noticed some
milk stains on the front of her vest. This too was an announcement of pregnancy, but not of a first one. The young mother
was wishing that she might have more nourishment to give her
second child than she had had for her first.

A young woman had been cut off from society for weeks on
end while she nursed her child through an infectious illness.
After the child's recovery, she had a dream of being at a party
at which, among others, she met Alphonse Daudet, Paul
Bourget, and Marcel Prévost; they were all most affable to her
and highly amusing. All of the authors resembled their portraits, except Marcel Prévost, of whom she had never seen a
picture; and he looked like . . . the disinfection officer who had
fumigated the sick-room the day before and who had been her
first visitor for so long. Thus it seems possible to give a complete
translation of the dream: 'It's about time for something more
amusing than this perpetual sick-nursing.'

These examples will perhaps be enough to show that dreams
which can only be understood as fulfilments of wishes and which
bear their meaning upon their faces without disguise are to be
found under the most frequent and various conditions. They are
mostly short and simple dreams, which afford a pleasant contrast to the confused and exuberant compositions that have in
the main attracted the attention of the authorities. Neverthe-

less, it will repay us to pause for a moment over these simple dreams. We may expect to find the very simplest forms of dreams in *children*, since there can be no doubt that their psychical productions are less complicated than those of adults. Child psychology, in my opinion, is destined to perform the same useful services for adult psychology that the investigation of the structure or development of the lower animals has performed for research into the structure of the higher classes of animals. Few deliberate efforts have hitherto been made to make use of child psychology for this purpose.

The dreams of young children are frequently[1] pure wish-fulfilments and are in that case[2] quite uninteresting compared with the dreams of adults. They raise no problems for solution; but on the other hand they are of inestimable importance in proving that, in their essential nature, dreams represent fulfilments of wishes. I have been able to collect a few instances of such dreams from material provided by my own children.

I have to thank an excursion which we made to the lovely village of Hallstatt[3] in the summer of 1896 for two dreams: one of these was dreamt by my daughter, who was then eight and a half, and the other by her brother of five and a quarter. I must explain by way of preamble that we had been spending the summer on a hillside near Aussee, from which, in fine weather, we enjoyed a splendid view of the Dachstein. The Simony Hütte could be clearly distinguished through a telescope. The children made repeated attempts at seeing it through the telescope—I cannot say with what success. Before our excursion I had told the children that Hallstatt lay at the foot of the Dachstein. They very much looked forward to the day. From Hallstatt we walked up the Echerntal, which delighted the children with its succession of changing landscapes. One of them, however, the five-year-old boy, gradually became fretful. Each time a new

---

[1] [This word was added in 1911. The following comment upon this qualifying adverb appears in *Gesammelte Schriften*, 3 (1925), 21: 'Experience has shown that distorted dreams, which stand in need of interpretation, are already found in children of four or five; and this is in full agreement with our theoretical views on the determining conditions of distortion in dreams.']

[2] [Before 1911: 'for that reason'.]

[3] [In the Salzkammergut district of Upper Austria.—'Echerntal' (below) is misprinted 'Escherntal' in all the German editions.]

mountain came into view he asked if that was the Dachstein and I had to say 'No, only one of the foothills.' After he had asked the question several times, he fell completely silent; and he refused point-blank to come with us up the steep path to the waterfall. I thought he was tired. But next morning he came to me with a radiant face and said: 'Last night I dreamt we were at the Simony Hütte.' I understood him then. When I had spoken about the Dachstein, he had expected to climb the mountain in the course of our excursion to Hallstatt and to find himself at close quarters with the hut which there had been so much talk about in connection with the telescope. But when he found that he was being fobbed off with foothills and a water-fall, he felt disappointed and out of spirits. The dream was a compensation. I tried to discover its details, but they were scanty: 'You have to climb up steps for six hours'—which was what he had been told.

The same excursion stirred up wishes in the eight-and-a-half-year-old girl as well—wishes which had to be satisfied in a dream. We had taken our neighbour's twelve-year-old son with us to Hallstatt. He was already a full-blown gallant, and there were signs that he had engaged the young lady's affections. Next morning she told me the following dream: 'Just fancy! I had a dream that Emil was one of the family and called you "Father" and "Mother" and slept with us in the big room like the boys. Then Mother came in and threw a handful of big bars of chocolate, wrapped up in blue and green paper, under our beds.' Her brothers, who have evidently not inherited a faculty for understanding dreams, followed the lead of the authorities and declared that the dream was nonsense. The girl herself defended one part of the dream at least; and it throws light on the theory of the neuroses to learn *which* part. 'Of course it's nonsense Emil being one of the family; but the part about the bars of chocolate isn't.' It had been precisely on that point that I had been in the dark, but the girl's mother now gave me the explanation. On their way home from the station the children had stopped in front of a slot-machine from which they were accustomed to obtain bars of chocolate of that very kind, wrapped in shiny metallic paper. They had wanted to get some; but their mother rightly decided that the day had already fulfilled enough wishes and left this one over to be fulfilled by the dream. I myself had not observed the incident. But the part of the dream which had been proscribed by my daughter was immediately clear to me. I myself had heard our well-behaved guest telling the children on the walk to wait till Father and Mother caught up with them. The little girl's dream turned this temporary kinship into permanent adoption. Her affection was not yet able to picture any other forms of companionship than those which were represented in the dream and which were based on her relation to her brothers. It was of course impossible to discover without questioning her why the bars of chocolate were thrown under the beds.

A friend of mine has reported a dream to me which was very much like my son's. The dreamer was an eight-year-old girl. Her father had started off with several children on a walk to Dornbach,[1] with the idea of visiting the Rohrer Hütte. As it was getting late, however, he had turned back, promising the children to make up for the disappointment another time. On their way home they had passed the sign-post that marks the path up to the Hameau. The children had then asked to be taken up to the Hameau; but once again for the same reason they had to be consoled with the promise of another day. Next morning the eight-year-old girl came to her father and said in satisfied tones: 'Daddy, I dreamt last night that you went with us to the Rohrer Hütte and the Hameau.' In her impatience she had anticipated the fulfilment of her father's promises.

Here is an equally straightforward dream, provoked by the beauty of the scenery at Aussee in another of my daughters, who was at that time three and a quarter. She had crossed the lake for the first time, and the crossing had been too short for her: when we reached the landing-stage she had not wanted to leave the boat and had wept bitterly. Next morning she said: 'Last night I went on the lake.' Let us hope that her dream-crossing had been of a more satisfying length.

My eldest boy, then eight years old, already had dreams of his phantasies coming true: he dreamt that he was driving in a chariot with Achilles and that Diomede was the charioteer. As may be guessed, he had been excited the day before by a book on the legends of Greece which had been given to his elder sister.

If I may include words spoken by children in their sleep under the heading of dreams, I can at this point quote one of the most

[1] [In the hills just outside Vienna.]

youthful dreams in my whole collection. My youngest daughter, then nineteen months old, had had an attack of vomiting one morning and had consequently been kept without food all day. During the night after this day of starvation she was heard calling out excitedly in her sleep: 'Anna Fweud, stwawbewwies, wild stwawbewwies, omblet, pudden!' At that time she was in the habit of using her own name to express the idea of taking possession of something. The menu included pretty well everything that must have seemed to her to make up a desirable meal. The fact that strawberries appeared in it in two varieties was a demonstration against the domestic health regulations. It was based upon the circumstance, which she had no doubt observed, that her nurse had attributed her indisposition to a surfeit of strawberries. She was thus retaliating in her dream against this unwelcome verdict.[1]

Though we think highly of the happiness of childhood because it is still innocent of sexual desires, we should not forget what a fruitful source of disappointment and renunciation, and consequently what a stimulus to dreaming, may be provided by the other of the two great vital instincts.[2] Here is another instance of this. My nephew, aged 22 months, had been entrusted with the duty of congratulating me on my birthday and of presenting me with a basket of cherries, which are still scarcely in season at that time of year. He seems to have found the task a hard

---

[1] The same feat was accomplished shortly afterwards by a dream produced by this little girl's grandmother—their combined ages came to some seventy years. She had been obliged to go without food for a whole day on account of a disturbance due to a floating kidney. During the following night, no doubt imagining herself back in the heyday of her girlhood, she dreamt that she had been 'asked out' to both of the principal meals and been served at both with the most appetizing delicacies.— [The little girl's dream had been reported to Fliess not long after its occurrence (Freud, 1950a, Letter 73 of October 31, 1897).]

[2] [Footnote added 1911:] A closer study of the mental life of children has taught us, to be sure, that sexual instinctual forces, in infantile form, play a large enough part, and one that has been too long overlooked, in the psychical activity of children. Closer study, too, has given us grounds for feeling some doubt in regard to the happiness of childhood as it has been constructed by adults in retrospect. Cf. my *Three Essays on the Theory of Sexuality* (1905d).—[The remarkable inconsistency between this sentence in the text and several other passages (e.g. on p. 256 ff. below) is commented on in the editor's preface to the last-mentioned work in the seventh volume of the Standard Edition.]

one, for he kept on repeating 'Chewwies in it' but could not be
induced to hand the present over. However, he found a means
of compensation. He had been in the habit every morning of
telling his mother that he had a dream of the 'white soldier'—
a Guards officer in his white cloak whom he had once gazed
at admiringly in the street. On the day after his birthday
sacrifice he awoke with a cheerful piece of news, which could
only have originated from a dream: 'Hermann eaten all the
chewwies!'[1]

I do not myself know what animals dream of. But a proverb,
to which my attention was drawn by one of my students, does

---

[1] [*Footnote added* 1911:] The fact should be mentioned that children
soon begin to have more complicated and less transparent dreams, and
that, on the other hand, adults in certain circumstances often have
dreams of a similarly simple, infantile character. The wealth of unexpected material that may occur in the dreams of children of four or five
is shown by examples in my 'Analysis of a Phobia in a Five-Year-Old
Boy' (1909*b*) and in Jung (1910*a*).—[*Added* 1914:] For analytical interpretations of children's dreams see also von Hug-Hellmuth (1911 and
1913), Putnam (1912), van Raalte (1912), Spielrein (1913) and Tausk
(1913). Children's dreams are also reported by Bianchieri (1912), Buse-
mann (1909 and 1910), Doglia and Bianchieri (1910–11) and, in particular, Wiggam (1909), who lays stress on their trend towards wish-
fulfilment.—[*Added* 1911:] On the other hand, dreams of an infantile type
seem to occur in adults with special frequency when they find themselves
in unusual external circumstances. Thus Otto Nordenskjöld (1904, **1**,
336 f.) writes as follows of the members of his expedition while they were
wintering in the Antarctic: 'The direction taken by our innermost
thoughts was very clearly shown by our dreams, which were never more
vivid or numerous than at this time. Even those of us who otherwise
dreamt but rarely had long stories to tell in the morning when we
exchanged our latest experiences in this world of the imagination. They
were all concerned with the outside world which was now so remote from
us, though they were often adapted to our actual circumstances. One of
my companions had a particularly characteristic dream of being back in
his school class-room, where it was his task to skin miniature seals which
had been specially prepared for instructional purposes. Eating and
drinking, however, were the pivot round which our dreams most often
revolved. One of us, who had a special gift for attending large luncheon
parties during the night, was proud if he was able to report in the morning that he had "got through a three-course dinner". Another of us
dreamt of tobacco, of whole mountains of tobacco; while a third dreamt
of a ship in full sail coming in across open water. Yet another dream is
worth repeating. The postman brought round the mail and gave a long
explanation of why we had had to wait so long for it: he had delivered

claim to know. 'What', asks the proverb, 'do geese dream of?'
And it replies: 'Of maize.'[1] The whole theory that dreams are
wish-fulfilments is contained in these two phrases.[2]

It will be seen that we might have arrived at our theory of
the hidden meaning of dreams most rapidly merely by following

it at the wrong address and had only succeeded in recovering it with
great difficulty. We dreamt, of course, of still more impossible things.
But there was a most striking lack of imaginativeness shown by almost
all the dreams that I dreamt myself or heard described. It would certainly be of great psychological interest if all these dreams could be
recorded. And it will easily be understood how much we longed for
sleep, since it could offer each one of us everything that he most eagerly
desired.' [This passage is much abbreviated in the English translation
of Nordenskjöld's book (1905, 290).—*Added* 1914:] According to Du
Prel (1885, 231), 'Mungo Park, when he was almost dying of thirst on
one of his African journeys, dreamt unceasingly of the well-watered
valleys and meadows of his home. Similarly, Baron Trenck suffering
torments of hunger while he was a prisoner in the fortress at Magdeburg,
dreamt of being surrounded by sumptuous meals; and George Back,
who took part in Franklin's first expedition, when he was almost dying
of starvation as a result of his fearful privations, dreamt constantly and
regularly of copious meals.'

[1] [*Footnote added* 1911:] A Hungarian proverb quoted by Ferenczi
[1910] goes further and declares that 'pigs dream of acorns and geese
dream of maize'.—[*Added* 1914:] A Jewish proverb runs: 'What do hens
dream of?—Of millet.' (Bernstein and Segel, 1908, 116.)

[2] [*Footnote added* 1914:] I am far from seeking to maintain that I am
the first writer to have had the idea of deriving dreams from wishes.
(Cf. the opening sentences of my next chapter.) Those who attach any
importance to anticipations of this kind may go back to classical antiquity and quote Herophilus, a physician who lived under the first
Ptolemy. According to Büchsenschütz (1868, 33), he distinguished three
sorts of dreams: those which are sent by the gods, those which are
natural and arise when the mind forms a picture of something that is
agreeable to it and will come about, and those which are of a mixed
nature and which arise of their own accord from the emergence of pictures in which we see what we wish for. J. Stärcke (1913, [248]) has
drawn attention to a dream in Scherner's collection which that writer
himself describes as the fulfilment of a wish. Scherner (1861, 239) writes:
'The dreamer's imagination fulfilled her waking wish so promptly,
simply because that wish was emotionally active in her.' Scherner
classes this dream among 'dreams of mood'; alongside it he places
'dreams of erotic yearning' in men and women, and 'dreams of ill-
temper'. There is clearly no question of Scherner attributing any more
importance to wishes in the instigation of dreams than to any other waking mental state: still less is there any question of his having related
wishes to the essential nature of dreaming.

linguistic usage. It is true that common language sometimes speaks of dreams with contempt. (The phrase '*Träume sind Schäume* [Dreams are froth]' seems intended to support the scientific estimate of dreams.) But, on the whole, ordinary usage treats dreams above all as the blessed fulfillers of wishes. If ever we find our expectation surpassed by the event, we exclaim in our delight: 'I should never have imagined such a thing even in my wildest dreams.'[1]

[1] [Children's dreams (including many of those recorded in this chapter) and dreams of an infantile type are discussed in Lecture VIII of Freud's *Introductory Lectures* (1916–17) and more briefly in Section III of his short study *On Dreams* (1901a) (*Standard Ed.*, 5, 643 f.).]

CHAPTER IV

DISTORTION IN DREAMS

IF I proceed to put forward the assertion that the meaning of *every* dream is the fulfilment of a wish, that is to say that there cannot be any dreams but wishful dreams, I feel certain in advance that I shall meet with the most categorical contradiction.

'There is nothing new,' I shall be told, 'in the idea that *some* dreams are to be regarded as wish-fulfilments; the authorities noticed that fact long ago. Cf. Radestock (1879, 137 f.), Volkelt (1875, 110 f.), Purkinje (1846, 456), Tissié (1898, 70), Simon (1888, 42, on the hunger dreams of Baron Trenck while he was a prisoner), and a passage in Griesinger (1845, 89).[1] But to assert that there are no dreams other than wish-fulfilment dreams is only one more unjustifiable generalization, though fortunately one which it is easy to disprove. After all, plenty of dreams occur which contain the most distressing subject-matter but never a sign of any wish-fulfilment. Eduard von Hartmann, the philosopher of pessimism, is probably furthest removed from the wish-fulfilment theory. In his *Philosophie des Unbewussten* (1890, **2**, 344) he writes: "When it comes to dreams, we find all the annoyances of waking life carried over into the state of sleep; the only thing we do *not* find is what can to some extent reconcile an educated man to life—scientific and artistic enjoyment. . . ." But even less disgruntled observers have insisted that pain and unpleasure are more common in dreams than pleasure: for instance, Scholz (1893, 57), Volkelt (1875, 80), and others. Indeed two ladies, Florence Hallam and Sarah Weed (1896, 499), have actually given statistical expression, based on a study of their own dreams, to the preponderance of unpleasure in dreaming. They find that 57·2 per cent of dreams are "disagreeable" and only 28·6 per cent positively "pleasant".

---

[1] [*Footnote added* 1914:] A writer as early as Plotinus, the Neoplatonist, is quoted by Du Prel (1885, 276) as saying: 'When our desires are aroused, imagination comes along and, as it were, presents us with the objects of those desires.' [*Ennead*, iv, 4, 17.]

And apart from these dreams, which carry over into sleep the various distressing emotions of life, there are anxiety-dreams, in which that most dreadful of all unpleasurable feelings holds us in its grasp till we awaken. And the commonest victims of these anxiety-dreams are precisely children,[1] whose dreams you have described as undisguised wish-fulfilments.'

It does in fact look as though anxiety-dreams make it impossible to assert as a general proposition (based on the examples quoted in my last chapter) that dreams are wish-fulfilments; indeed they seem to stamp any such proposition as an absurdity.

Nevertheless, there is no great difficulty in meeting these apparently conclusive objections. It is only necessary to take notice of the fact that my theory is not based on a consideration of the manifest content of dreams but refers to the thoughts which are shown by the work of interpretation to lie behind dreams. We must make a contrast between the *manifest* and the *latent* content of dreams. There is no question that there are dreams whose manifest content is of the most distressing kind. But has anyone tried to interpret such dreams? to reveal the latent thoughts behind them? If not, then the two objections raised against my theory will not hold water: it still remains possible that distressing dreams and anxiety-dreams, when they have been interpreted, may turn out to be fulfilments of wishes.[2]

When in the course of a piece of scientific work we come upon a problem which is difficult to solve, it is often a good plan to

[1] Cf. Debacker (1881) on pavor nocturnus.

[2] [*Footnote added* 1909:] It is hard to credit the obstinacy with which readers and critics of this book shut their eyes to this consideration and overlook the fundamental distinction between the manifest and latent content of dreams.—[*Added* 1914:] On the other hand, nothing in the literature of the subject comes so near to my hypothesis as a passage in James Sully's essay 'The Dream as a Revelation' (1893, 364). The fact that I am only now quoting it for the first time is no sign of disparagement: 'It would seem then, after all, that dreams are not the utter nonsense they have been said to be by such authorities as Chaucer, Shakespeare and Milton. The chaotic aggregations of our night-fancy have a significance and communicate new knowledge. Like some letter in cypher, the dream-inscription when scrutinized closely loses its first look of balderdash and takes on the aspect of a serious, intelligible message. Or, to vary the figure slightly, we may say that, like some palimpsest, the dream discloses beneath its worthless surface-characters traces of an old and precious communication.' [Freud prints the two last sentences in spaced type.]

take up a second problem along with the original one—just as it is easier to crack two nuts together than each separately. Thus we are not only faced by the question 'How can distressing dreams and anxiety-dreams be wish-fulfilments?'; our reflections enable us to add a second question: 'Why is it that dreams with an indifferent content, which turn out to be wish-fulfilments, do not express their meaning undisguised?' Take, for instance, the dream which I treated at such length of Irma's injection. It was not by any means of a distressing nature and interpretation showed it as a striking example of the fulfilment of a wish. But why should it have needed any interpretation at all? Why did it not say what it meant straight out? At first sight the dream of Irma's injection gave no impression that it represented a wish of the dreamer's as fulfilled. My readers will have had no such impression; but neither did I myself before I carried out the analysis. Let us describe this behaviour of dreams, which stands in so much need of explanation, as 'the phenomenon of distortion in dreams'. Thus our second problem is: what is the origin of dream-distortion?

A number of possible solutions of the problem may at once occur to us: as, for instance, that some incapacity exists during sleep for giving direct expression to our dream-thoughts. But the analysis of certain dreams forces us to adopt another explanation of distortion in dreams. I will exemplify this by another dream of my own. Once again this will involve me in a variety of indiscretions; but a thorough elucidation of the problem will compensate for my personal sacrifice.

PREAMBLE.—In the spring of 1897 I learnt that two professors at our university had recommended me for appointment as *professor extraordinarius*.[1] The news surprised and greatly delighted me, since it implied recognition by two eminent men, which could not be put down to any considerations of a personal kind. But I at once warned myself not to attach any

---

[1] [Roughly equivalent to an Assistant Professor. All such appointments in Austria were made by the Minister of Education. The fact of this recommendation is reported by Freud in a letter to Fliess of February 8, 1897 (Freud, 1950a, Letter 58) and the dream itself is mentioned on March 15, 1897 (ibid., Letter 85).—The 'denominational considerations' mentioned below relate, of course, to anti-semitic feeling, which was already rife in Vienna during the last years of the nineteenth century.]

expectations to the event. During the last few years the Ministry had disregarded recommendations of that sort; and several of my colleagues who were my seniors in age and at least my equals in merit had been waiting vainly for appointment. I had no reason to believe that I should be more fortunate. I therefore determined to meet the future with resignation. So far as I knew, I was not an ambitious man; I was following my profession with gratifying success even without the advantages afforded by a title. Moreover there was no question of my pronouncing the grapes sweet or sour: they hung far too high over my head.

One evening I had a visit from a friend—one of the men whose example I had taken as a warning to me. For a considerable time he had been a candidate for promotion to a professorship, a rank which in our society turns its holder into a demi-god to his patients. Less resigned than I was, however, he was in the habit of paying his respects from time to time in the offices of the Ministry with a view to advancing his prospects. He had been paying one of these visits just before calling on me. He told me that on this occasion he had driven the exalted official into a corner and had asked straight out whether the delay over his appointment was not in fact due to denominational considerations. The reply had been that, in view of the present state of feeling, it was no doubt true that, for the moment, His Excellency was not in a position, etc. etc. 'At least I know where I am now,' my friend had concluded. It was not news to me, though it was bound to strengthen my feeling of resignation; for the same denominational considerations applied to my own case.

On the morning after this visit I had the following dream, which was remarkable among other things for its form. It consisted of two thoughts and two pictures—each thought being succeeded by a picture. I shall, however, report only the first half of the dream here, since the other half has no connection with the purpose for which I am describing the dream.

I. . . . *My friend R. was my uncle.—I had a great feeling of affection for him.*

II. *I saw before me his face, somewhat changed. It was as though it had been drawn out lengthways. A yellow beard that surrounded it stood out especially clearly.*

Then followed the two other pieces which I shall pass over
—once more a thought followed by a picture.

The interpretation of the dream took place as follows.

When, during the course of the morning, the dream came
into my head, I laughed aloud and said: 'The dream's nonsense!' But it refused to go away and followed me about all
day, till at last in the evening I began to reproach myself: 'If
one of your patients who was interpreting a dream could find
nothing better to say than that it was nonsense, you would take
him up about it and suspect that the dream had some disagreeable story at the back of it which he wanted to avoid becoming
aware of. Treat yourself in the same way. Your opinion that the
dream is nonsense only means that you have an internal resistance against interpreting it. Don't let yourself be put off like
this.' So I set about the interpretation.

'*R. was my uncle.*' What could that mean? I never had more
than one uncle—Uncle Josef.[1] There was an unhappy story
attached to him. Once—more than thirty years ago,—in his
eagerness to make money, he allowed himself to be involved in
a transaction of a kind that is severely punished by the law, and
he was in fact punished for it. My father, whose hair turned
grey from grief in a few days, used always to say that Uncle
Josef was not a bad man but only a simpleton; those were his
words. So that if my friend R. was my Uncle Josef, what I was
meaning to say was that R. was a simpleton. Hardly credible
and most disagreeable!—But there was the face which I saw in
the dream with its elongated features and yellow beard. My
uncle did in fact have a face like that, elongated and framed in
a handsome fair beard. My friend R. had originally been
extremely dark; but when black-haired people begin to turn
grey they pay for the splendour of their youth. Hair by hair,
their black beards go through an unpleasing change of colour:
first they turn to a reddish brown, then to a yellowish brown,
and only then to a definite grey. My friend R.'s beard was at

---

[1] It is astonishing to observe the way in which my memory—my
waking memory—was narrowed at this point, for the purposes of the
analysis. Actually I have known five of my uncles, and loved and honoured one of them. But at the moment at which I overcame my resistance
to interpreting the dream I said to myself that I never had more
than one uncle—the one that was intended in the dream.

that time passing through this stage—and so, incidentally, was my own, as I had noticed with dissatisfaction. The face that I saw in the dream was at once my friend R.'s and my uncle's. It was like one of Galton's composite photographs. (In order to bring out family likenesses, Galton used to photograph several faces on the same plate [1907, 6 ff. and 221 ff.].) So there could be no doubt that I really did mean that my friend R. was a simpleton—like my Uncle Josef.

I still had no idea at all what could be the purpose of this comparison, against which I continued to struggle. It did not go very deep, after all, since my uncle was a criminal, whereas my friend R. bore an unblemished character . . . except for having been fined for knocking a boy down with his bicycle. Could I have had that crime in mind? That would have been making fun of the comparison. At this point I remembered another conversation which I had had a few days earlier with another colleague, N., and, now I came to think of it, upon the same subject. I had met N. in the street. He too had been recommended for a professorship. He had heard of the honour that had been paid me and had offered me his congratulations on it; but I had unhesitatingly refused to accept them. 'You are the last person,' I had said, 'to make that kind of joke; you know what such a recommendation is worth from your own experience.' 'Who can say?' he had answered—jokingly, it seemed; 'there was something definite against *me*. Don't you know that a woman once started legal proceedings against me? I needn't assure you that the case was dismissed. It was a disgraceful attempt at blackmail; and I had the greatest difficulty in saving the prosecutrix from being punished. But perhaps they may be using this at the Ministry as an excuse for not appointing me. But *you* have an unblemished character.' This told me who the criminal was, and at the same time showed me how the dream was to be interpreted and what its purpose was. My Uncle Josef represented my two colleagues who had not been appointed to professorships—the one as a simpleton and the other as a criminal. I now saw too why they were represented in this light. If the appointment of my friends R. and N. had been postponed for 'denominational' reasons, my own appointment was also open to doubt; if, however, I could attribute the rejection of my two friends to other reasons, which did not apply to me, my hopes would remain untouched. This was the

procedure adopted by my dream: it made one of them, R., into
a simpleton and the other, N., into a criminal, whereas *I* was
neither the one nor the other; thus we no longer had anything
in common; I could rejoice at my appointment to a professorship, and I could avoid drawing the distressing conclusion that
R.'s report of what the high official had said to him must apply
equally to me.

But I felt obliged to proceed still further with my interpretation of the dream; I felt I had not yet finished dealing with it
satisfactorily. I was still uneasy over the light-heartedness with
which I had degraded two of my respected colleagues in order
to keep open my own path to a professorship. My dissatisfaction
with my conduct, however, had diminished since I had come
to realize the worth that was to be attached to expressions in
dreams. I was prepared to deny through thick and thin that I
really considered that R. was a simpleton and that I really dis-
believed N.'s account of the blackmailing affair. Nor did I
believe that Irma was really made dangerously ill through being
injected with Otto's preparation of propyl. In both these cases
what my dreams had expressed was only *my wish that it might
be so*. The assertion in which my wish was realized sounded less
absurd in the later dream than in the earlier one; it made
cleverer use of the actual facts in its construction, like a well-
designed slander of the kind that makes people feel that 'there's
something in it'. For one of the professors in his own faculty
had voted against my friend R., and my friend N. had himself
innocently provided me with the material for my aspersions.
Nevertheless, I must repeat, the dream seemed to me to stand
in need of further elucidation.

I then recalled that there was still a piece of the dream which
the interpretation had not touched. After the idea had occurred
to me that R. was my uncle, I had had a warm feeling of
affection for him in the dream. Where did that feeling belong?
I had naturally never had any feeling of affection for my Uncle
Josef. I had been fond of my friend R. and had esteemed him
for many years; but if I had gone up to him and expressed my
sentiments in terms approaching the degree of affection I had
felt in the dream, there could be no doubt that he would have
been astonished. My affection for him struck me as ungenuine
and exaggerated—like the judgement of his intellectual qualities
which I had expressed by fusing his personality with my uncle's,

though *there* the exaggeration had been in the opposite direction. But a new light began to dawn on me. The affection in the dream did not belong to the latent content, to the thoughts that lay behind the dream; it stood in contradiction to them and was calculated to conceal the true interpretation of the dream. And probably that was precisely its *raison d'être*. I recalled my resistance against embarking on the interpretation, how long I had put it off and how I had declared that the dream was sheer nonsense. My psycho-analytic treatments taught me how a repudiation of that kind was to be interpreted: it had no value as a judgement but was simply an expression of emotion. If my little daughter did not want an apple that was offered to her, she asserted that the apple tasted sour without having tasted it. And if my patients behaved like the child, I knew that they were concerned with an idea which they wanted to repress. The same was true of my dream. I did not want to interpret it, because the interpretation contained something that I was struggling against. When I had completed the interpretation I learnt what it was that I had been struggling against—namely, the assertion that R. was a simpleton. The affection that I felt for R. could not be derived from the latent dream-thoughts; but no doubt it originated from this struggle of mine. If my dream was distorted in this respect from its latent content—and distorted into its opposite,—then the affection that was manifest in the dream served the purpose of this distortion. In other words, distortion was shown in this case to be deliberate and to be a means of *dissimulation*. My dream thoughts had contained a slander against R.; and, in order that I might not notice this, what appeared in the dream was the opposite, a feeling of affection for him.

It seemed as though this might be a discovery of general validity. It is true that, as was shown by the instances quoted in Chapter III, there are some dreams which are undisguised fulfilments of wishes. But in cases where the wish-fulfilment is unrecognizable, where it has been disguised, there must have existed some inclination to put up a defence against the wish; and owing to this defence the wish was unable to express itself except in a distorted shape. I will try to seek a social parallel to this internal event in the mind. Where can we find a similar distortion of a psychical act in social life? Only where two persons are concerned, one of whom possesses a certain degree of power which the second is obliged to take into account. In such a case the second person will distort his psychical acts or, as we might put it, will dissimulate. The politeness which I practise every day is to a large extent dissimulation of this kind; and when I interpret my dreams for my readers I am obliged to adopt similar distortions. The poet complains of the need for these distortions in the words:

> Das Beste, was du wissen kannst,
> Darfst du den Buben doch nicht sagen.[1]

A similar difficulty confronts the political writer who has disagreeable truths to tell to those in authority. If he presents them undisguised, the authorities will suppress his words—after they have been spoken, if his pronouncement was an oral one, but beforehand, if he had intended to make it in print. A writer must beware of the censorship,[2] and on its account he must soften and distort the expression of his opinion. According to the strength and sensitiveness of the censorship he finds himself compelled either merely to refrain from certain forms of attack, or to speak in allusions in place of direct references, or he must conceal his objectionable pronouncement beneath some apparently innocent disguise: for instance, he may describe a dispute between two Mandarins in the Middle Kingdom, when the people he really has in mind are officials in his own country. The stricter the censorship, the more far-reaching will be the disguise and the more ingenious too may be the means employed for putting the reader on the scent of the true meaning.[3]

---

[1] [Mephistopheles, in Goethe's *Faust*, Part I [Scene 4]: 'After all, the best of what you know may not be told to boys.'—These were favourite lines of Freud's. He uses them again on p. 453 below. He had already quoted them in letters to Fliess of December 3, 1897, and February 9, 1898 (Freud, 1950a, Letters 77 and 83); and, towards the end of his life, on the occasion of his reception of the Goethe prize in 1930, he applied them to Goethe himself. (Freud, 1930e).]

[2] [This analogy, which makes its first appearance in this passage in connection with dreams, had already been used in connection with paranoia at the end of Freud's second paper on the neuropsychoses of defence (1896b) and more generally in Section 2 of his chapter on psychotherapy in *Studies on Hysteria* (Breuer and Freud, 1895).]

[3] [*Footnote added* 1919:] Frau Dr. H. von Hug-Hellmuth (1915) has recorded a dream which is perhaps better fitted than any to justify my choice of nomenclature. In this example the dream-distortion adopted the same methods as the postal censorship for expunging passages which

The fact that the phenomena of censorship and of dream-distortion correspond down to their smallest details justifies us in presuming that they are similarly determined. We may there-

were objectionable to it. The postal censorship makes such passages unreadable by blacking them out; the dream censorship replaced them by an incomprehensible mumble.

In order to make the dream intelligible, I must explain that the dreamer, a cultivated and highly esteemed lady, was fifty years of age. She was the widow of an officer of high rank who had died some twelve years previously and was the mother of grown sons, one of whom was in the field at the time of the dream.

Here then is the dream—which deals with 'love services' in war-time. ['*Liebesdienste*' means in the first instance 'services performed for love', i.e. 'unremunerated services'; but the term obviously courts another interpretation.] 'The patient went to Garrison Hospital No. 1 and informed the sentry at the gate that she must speak to the Chief Medical Officer (mentioning a name that was unknown to her) as she wanted to volunteer for service at the hospital. She pronounced the word "service" in such a way that the N.C.O. at once understood that she meant "love service". Since she was an elderly lady, after some hesitation he allowed her to pass. Instead of finding the Chief Medical Officer, however, she reached a large and gloomy apartment in which a number of officers and army doctors were standing and sitting round a long table. She approached a staff surgeon with her request, and he understood her meaning after she had said only a few words. The actual wording of her speech in the dream was: "I and many other women and girls in Vienna are ready to . . ." at this point in the dream her words turned into a mumble ". . . for the troops—officers and other ranks without distinction." She could tell from the expressions on the officers' faces, partly embarrassed and partly sly, that everyone had understood her meaning correctly. The lady went on: "I'm aware that our decision must sound surprising, but we mean it in bitter earnest. No one asks a soldier in the field whether he wishes to die or not." There followed an awkward silence of some minutes. The staff surgeon then put his arm round her waist and said: "Suppose, madam, it actually came to . . . (mumble)." She drew away from him, thinking to herself: "He's like all the rest of them", and replied: "Good gracious, I'm an old woman and I might never come to that. Besides, there's one condition that must be observed: age must be respected. It must never happen that an elderly woman . . . (mumble) . . . a mere boy. That would be terrible." "I understand perfectly," replied the staff surgeon. Some of the officers, and among them one who had been a suitor of hers in her youth, laughed out loud. The lady then asked to be taken to the Chief Medical Officer, with whom she was acquainted, so that the whole matter could be thrashed out; but she found, to her consternation, that she could not recall his name. Nevertheless, the staff surgeon, most politely and respectfully, showed her the way up to the second floor by a very narrow, iron, spiral staircase, which led directly from the room to the upper fore suppose that dreams are given their shape in individual human beings by the operation of two psychical forces (or we may describe them as currents or systems); and that one of these forces constructs the wish which is expressed by the dream, while the other exercises a censorship upon this dream-wish and, by the use of that censorship, forcibly brings about a distortion in the expression of the wish. It remains to enquire as to the nature of the power enjoyed by this second agency which enables it to exercise its censorship. When we bear in mind that the latent dream-thoughts are not conscious before an analysis has been carried out, whereas the manifest content of the dream is consciously remembered, it seems plausible to suppose that the privilege enjoyed by the second agency is that of permitting thoughts to enter consciousness. Nothing, it would seem, can reach consciousness from the first system without passing the second agency; and the second agency allows nothing to pass without exercising its rights and making such modifications as it thinks fit in the thought which is seeking admission to consciousness. Incidentally, this enables us to form a quite definite view of the 'essential nature' of consciousness: we see the process of a thing becoming conscious as a specific psychical act, distinct from and independent of the process of the formation of a presentation or idea; and we regard consciousness as a sense organ which perceives data that arise elsewhere. It can be demonstrated that these basic assumptions are absolutely indispensable to psychopathology. We must, however, postpone our further consideration of them to a later stage. [See Chapter VII, particularly Section F, p. 610 ff.]

If this picture of the two psychical agencies and their relation to consciousness is accepted, there is a complete analogy in political life to the extraordinary affection which I felt in my dream for my friend R., who was treated with such contumely during the dream's interpretation. Let us imagine a society in

storeys of the building. As she went up she heard an officer say: "That's a tremendous decision to make—no matter whether a woman's young or old! Splendid of her!" Feeling simply that she was doing her duty, she walked up an interminable staircase.—The dream was repeated twice in the course of a few weeks, with, as the lady remarked, some quite unimportant and meaningless modifications.'

[Some further comments on this dream will be found in Freud's *Introductory Lectures* (1916–17), Lecture IX.]

which a struggle is in process between a ruler who is jealous of his power and an alert public opinion. The people are in revolt against an unpopular official and demand his dismissal. But the autocrat, to show that he need take no heed of the popular wish, chooses that moment for bestowing a high distinction upon the official, though there is no other reason for doing so. In just the same way my second agency, which commands the approaches to consciousness, distinguished my friend R. by a display of excessive affection simply because the wishful impulses belonging to the first system, for particular reasons of their own on which they were intent at the moment, chose to condemn him as a simpleton.[1]

These considerations may lead us to feel that the interpretation of dreams may enable us to draw conclusions as to the structure of our mental apparatus which we have hoped for in vain from philosophy. I do not propose, however, to follow this line of thought [which is taken up in Chapter VII]; but, having cleared up the matter of distortion in dreams, I shall go back to the problem from which we started. The question raised was how dreams with a distressing content can be resolved into wish-fulfilments. We now see that this is possible if dream-distortion has occurred and if the distressing content serves only to disguise something that is wished for. Bearing in mind our assumption of the existence of two psychical agencies, we can

---

[1] [The analysis of this dream is continued on p. 191 ff.—*Footnote added* 1911:] Hypocritical dreams of this description are not uncommon events in my own case or in that of other people. [They are further discussed below, p. 471 ff.] While I was engaged in working out a certain scientific problem, I was troubled for several nights in close succession by a somewhat confusing dream which had as its subject a reconciliation with a friend whom I had dropped many years before. On the fourth or fifth occasion I at last succeeded in understanding the meaning of the dream. It was an incitement to abandon my last remnants of consideration for the person in question and to free myself from him completely, and it had been hypocritically disguised as its opposite. [Cf. p. 477.] I have reported elsewhere [1910*l*, reprinted below, p. 398 f. *n.*] a 'hypocritical Oedipus dream', dreamt by a man, in which the hostile impulses and death-wishes contained in the dream-thoughts were replaced by manifest affection. Another kind of hypocritical dream will be mentioned below in Chapter VI [p. 473 ff.]. [The friend referred to in this footnote was evidently Fliess. Cf. Section IV of Kris's introduction to Freud's correspondence with Fliess (Freud, 1950*a*).]

further say that distressing dreams do in fact contain something which is distressing to the *second* agency, but something which at the same time fulfils a wish on the part of the *first* agency. They are wishful dreams in so far as every dream arises from the first agency; the relation of the second agency towards dreams is of a *defensive* and not of a *creative* kind.[1] If we were to restrict ourselves to considering what the second agency contributes to dreams, we could never arrive at an understanding of them: all the conundrums which the authorities have observed in dreams would remain unsolved.

The fact that dreams really have a secret meaning which represents the fulfilment of a wish must be proved afresh in each particular case by analysis. I shall therefore select a few dreams with a distressing content and attempt to analyse them. Some of them are the dreams of hysterical patients which require lengthy preambles and an occasional excursus into the psychical processes characteristic of hysteria. But I cannot escape this aggravation of the difficulties of presenting my argument. [See p. 104.]

As I have already explained [p. 100 f.], when I undertake the analytic treatment of a psycho-neurotic patient his dreams are invariably discussed between us. In the course of these discussions I am obliged to give him all the psychological explanations which have enabled me myself to reach an understanding of his symptoms. I am thereupon subjected to a remorseless criticism, certainly no less severe than I have to expect from the members of my own profession. And my patients invariably contradict my assertion that all dreams are fulfilments of wishes. Here, then, are some instances from the material of dreams that have been brought up against me as evidence to the contrary.

'You're always saying to me,' began a clever woman patient of mine, 'that a dream is a fulfilled wish. Well, I'll tell you a dream whose subject was the exact opposite—a dream in which one of my wishes was *not* fulfilled. How do you fit that in with your theory? This was the dream:

[1] [*Footnote added* 1930:] Later [pp. 476 *n.* and 557 ff.] we shall also come across instances in which, on the contrary, a dream expresses a wish on the part of the *second* agency.

'I wanted to give a supper-party, but I had nothing in the house but a little smoked salmon. I thought I would go out and buy something, but remembered then that it was Sunday afternoon and all the shops would be shut. Next I tried to ring up some caterers, but the telephone was out of order. So I had to abandon my wish to give a supper-party.'

I answered, of course, that analysis was the only way of deciding on the meaning of the dream; though I admitted that at first sight it seemed sensible and coherent and looked like the reverse of a wish-fulfilment. 'But what material did the dream arise from? As you know, the instigation to a dream is always to be found in the events of the previous day.'

ANALYSIS.—My patient's husband, an honest and capable wholesale butcher, had remarked to her the day before that he was getting too stout and therefore intended to start on a course of weight-reduction. He proposed to rise early, do physical exercises, keep to a strict diet, and above all accept no more invitations to supper.—She laughingly added that her husband, at the place where he regularly lunched, had made the acquaintance of a painter, who had pressed him to be allowed to paint his portrait, as he had never seen such expressive features. Her husband however had replied in his blunt manner that he was much obliged, but he was sure the painter would prefer a piece of a pretty young girl's behind to the whole of his face.[1] She was very much in love with her husband now and teased him a lot. She had begged him, too, not to give her any caviare.

I asked her what that meant; and she explained that she had wished for a long time that she could have a caviare sandwich every morning but had grudged the expense. Of course her husband would have let her have it at once if she had asked him. But, on the contrary, she had asked him *not* to give her any caviare, so that she could go on teasing him about it.

This explanation struck me as unconvincing. Inadequate reasons like this usually conceal unconfessed motives. They

---

[1] Cf. the phrase 'sitting for one's portrait' and Goethe's lines:

> Und wenn er keinen Hintern hat,
> Wie mag der Edle sitzen?

> [And if he hasn't a behind,
> How can his Lordship sit?
>
> (From 'Totalität', 1814–15.)]

remind one of Bernheim's hypnotized patients. When one of these carries out a post-hypnotic suggestion and is asked why he is acting in this way, instead of saying that he has no idea, he feels compelled to invent some obviously unsatisfactory reason. The same was no doubt true of my patient and the caviare. I saw that she was obliged to create an unfulfilled wish for herself in her actual life; and the dream represented this renunciation as having been put into effect. But why was it that she stood in need of an unfulfilled wish?

The associations which she had so far produced had not been sufficient to interpret the dream. I pressed her for some more. After a short pause, such as would correspond to the over-coming of a resistance, she went on to tell me that the day before she had visited a woman friend of whom she confessed she felt jealous because her (my patient's) husband was constantly singing her praises. Fortunately this friend of hers is very skinny and thin and her husband admires a plumper figure. I asked her what she had talked about to her thin friend. Naturally, she replied, of that lady's wish to grow a little stouter. Her friend had enquired, too: 'When are you going to ask us to another meal? You always feed one so well.'

The meaning of the dream was now clear, and I was able to say to my patient: 'It is just as though when she made this suggestion you said to yourself: "A likely thing! I'm to ask you to come and eat in my house so that you may get stout and attract my husband still more! I'd rather never give another supper-party." What the dream was saying to you was that you were unable to give any supper-parties, and it was thus ful-filling your wish not to help your friend to grow plumper. The fact that what people eat at parties makes them stout had been brought home to you by your husband's decision not to accept any more invitations to supper in the interests of his plan to reduce his weight.' All that was now lacking was some coin-cidence to confirm the solution. The smoked salmon in the dream had not yet been accounted for. 'How,' I asked, 'did you arrive at the salmon that came into your dream?' 'Oh,' she replied, 'smoked salmon is my friend's favourite dish.' I happen to be acquainted with the lady in question myself, and I can confirm the fact that she grudges herself salmon no less than my patient grudges herself caviare.

The same dream admits of another and subtler interpretation, which in fact becomes unavoidable if we take a subsidiary detail into account. (The two interpretations are not mutually contradictory, but both cover the same ground; they are a good instance of the fact that dreams, like all other psychopathological structures, regularly have more than one meaning.) My patient, it will be remembered, at the same time as she was occupied with her dream of the renunciation of a wish, was also trying to bring about a renounced wish (for the caviare sandwich) in real life. Her friend had also given expression to a wish—to become stouter—and it would not have been surprising if my patient had dreamt that her friend's wish was unfulfilled; for my patient's own wish was that her friend's wish (to put on weight) should not be fulfilled. But instead of this she dreamt that one of her *own* wishes was not fulfilled. Thus the dream will acquire a new interpretation if we suppose that the person indicated in the dream was not herself but her friend, that she had put herself in her friend's place, or, as we might say, that she had 'identified' herself with her friend. I believe she had in fact done this; and the circumstance of her having brought about a renounced wish in real life was evidence of this identification.

What is the meaning of hysterical identification? It requires a somewhat lengthy explanation. Identification is a highly important factor in the mechanism of hysterical symptoms. It enables patients to express in their symptoms not only their own experiences but those of a large number of other people; it enables them, as it were, to suffer on behalf of a whole crowd of people and to act all the parts in a play single-handed. I shall be told that this is not more than the familiar hysterical imitation, the capacity of hysterics to imitate any symptoms in other people that may have struck their attention—sympathy, as it were, intensified to the point of reproduction. This, however, does no more than show us the path along which the psychical process in hysterical imitation proceeds. The path is something different from the mental act which proceeds along it. The latter is a little more complicated than the common picture of hysterical imitation; it consists in the unconscious drawing of an inference, as an example will make clear. Supposing a physician is treating a woman patient, who is subject to a particular kind of spasm, in a hospital ward among a number of other patients. He will show no surprise if he finds one morning that this particular kind of hysterical attack has found imitators. He will merely say: 'The other patients have seen it and copied it; it's a case of psychical infection.' That is true; but the psychical infection has occurred along some such lines as these. As a rule, patients know more about one another than the doctor does about any of them; and after the doctor's visit is over they turn their attention to one another. Let us imagine that this patient had her attack on a particular day; then the others will quickly discover that it was caused by a letter from home, the revival of some unhappy love-affair, or some such thing. Their sympathy is aroused and they draw the following inference, though it fails to penetrate into consciousness: 'If a cause like this can produce an attack like this, I may have the same kind of attack since I have the same grounds for having it.' If this inference were capable of entering consciousness, it might possibly give rise to a *fear* of having the same kind of attack. But in fact the inference is made in a different psychical region, and consequently results in the actual realization of the dreaded symptom. Thus identification is not simple imitation but *assimilation* on the basis of a similar aetiological pretension; it expresses a resemblance and is derived from a common element which remains in the unconscious.

Identification is most frequently used in hysteria to express a common *sexual* element. A hysterical woman identifies herself in her symptoms most readily—though not exclusively—with people with whom she has had sexual relations or with people who have had sexual relations with the same people as herself. Linguistic usage takes this into account, for two lovers are spoken of as being 'one'. In hysterical phantasies, just as in dreams, it is enough for purposes of identification that the subject should have *thoughts* of sexual relations without their having necessarily taken place in reality. Thus the patient whose dream I have been discussing was merely following the rules of hysterical processes of thought in expressing her jealousy of her friend (which incidentally she herself knew was unjustified) by taking her place in the dream and identifying herself with her by creating a symptom—the renounced wish. The process might be expressed verbally thus: my patient put herself in her friend's place in the dream because her friend was taking my patient's place with her husband and because she (my patient) wanted to take her friend's place in her husband's high opinion.[1]

A contradiction to my theory of dreams produced by another of my women patients (the cleverest of all my dreamers) was resolved more simply, but upon the same pattern: namely that the non-fulfilment of one wish meant the fulfilment of another. One day I had been explaining to her that dreams are fulfilments of wishes. Next day she brought me a dream in which she was travelling down with her mother-in-law to the place in the country where they were to spend their holidays together. Now I knew that she had violently rebelled against the idea of spending the summer near her mother-in-law and that a few days earlier she had successfully avoided the propinquity she dreaded by engaging rooms in a far distant resort. And now her dream had undone the solution she had wished for: was not this the sharpest possible contradiction of my theory that in dreams wishes are fulfilled? No doubt; and it was only necessary to follow the dream's logical consequence in order to arrive at its interpretation. The dream showed that I was wrong. *Thus it was her wish that I might be wrong, and her dream showed that wish fulfilled.* But her wish that I might be wrong, which was fulfilled in connection with her summer holidays, related in fact to another and more serious matter. For at about the same time I had inferred from the material produced in her analysis that at a particular period of her life something must have occurred that was of importance in determining her illness. She had disputed this, since she had no recollection of it; but soon afterwards it had turned out that I was right. Thus her

[1] I myself regret the insertion into my argument of excerpts from the psychopathology of hysteria. [See p. 104.] Their fragmentary presentation and detachment from their context cannot fail to detract from their enlightening effect. If, however, they serve to indicate the intimate connection between the topic of dreams and that of the psychoneuroses, they will have fulfilled the purpose for which they are inserted.—[This is Freud's first published discussion of identification, though he had referred to it earlier, in his correspondence with Fliess (e.g. in Letter 58 of February 8, 1897, and Manuscript L of May 2, 1897). Though he touched upon the subject here and there in later publications, his first lengthy consideration of it after the present one was more then twenty years later—in Chapter VII of *Group Psychology* (Freud, 1921*c*). The different topic of identification as part of the dream-work is discussed below on p. 320 f.]

wish that I might be wrong, which was transformed into her dream of spending her holidays with her mother-in-law, corresponded to a well-justified wish that the events of which she was then becoming aware for the first time might never have occurred.

I have ventured to interpret—without any analysis, but only by a guess—a small episode which occurred to a friend of mine who was in the same class as I was all through our career at a secondary school. One day he listened to a lecture which I gave before a small audience on the novel idea that dreams were wish-fulfilments. He went home and dreamt that *he had lost all his cases* (he was a barrister) and afterwards arraigned me on the subject. I evaded the issue by telling him that after all one can't win *all* one's cases. But to myself I thought: 'Considering that for eight whole years I sat on the front bench as top of the class while he drifted about somewhere in the middle, he can hardly fail to nourish a wish, left over from his school-days, that some day or other *I* may come a complete cropper.'

A dream of a gloomier kind was also brought up against me by a patient as an objection to the theory of wishful dreams.
The patient, who was a young girl, began thus: 'As you will remember, my sister has only one boy left now—Karl; she lost his elder brother, Otto, while I was still living with her. Otto was my favourite; I more or less brought him up. I'm fond of the little one too, but of course not nearly so fond as I was of the one who died. Last night, then, I dreamt that *I saw Karl lying before me dead. He was lying in his little coffin with his hands folded and with candles all round—in fact just like little Otto, whose death was such a blow to me.* Now tell me, what can that mean? You know me. Am I such a wicked person that I can wish my sister to lose the one child she still has? Or does the dream mean that I would rather Karl were dead than Otto whom I was so much fonder of?'
I assured her that this last interpretation was out of the question. And after reflecting a little I was able to give her the correct interpretation of the dream, which she afterwards confirmed. I was able to do so because I was familiar with the whole of the dreamer's previous history.

The girl had early been left an orphan and had been brought
up in the house of a much older sister. Among the friends who
visited at the house was a man who made a lasting impression
on her heart. For a time it had seemed as though her scarcely
acknowledged relations with him would lead to marriage; but
this happy outcome was brought to nothing by her sister, whose
motives were never fully explained. After the breach the man
ceased to visit the house; and shortly after the death of little
Otto, on to whom she had meanwhile turned her affection, my
patient herself set up on her own. She did not succeed, however,
in freeing herself from her attachment to her sister's friend. Her
pride bade her avoid him; but she was unable to transfer her
love to any of the other admirers who presented themselves
later. Whenever it was announced that the object of her affections, who was by profession a literary man, was to give a
lecture anywhere, she was invariably in the audience; and she
took every possible opportunity of seeing him from a distance
on neutral ground. I remembered that she had told me the
day before that the Professor was going to a particular concert
and that she intended to go to it as well so as to enjoy a glimpse
of him once more. That had been on the day before the dream,
and the concert was to take place on the day on which she told
me the dream. It was therefore easy for me to construct the
correct interpretation, and I asked her whether she could think
of anything that happened after little Otto's death. She
answered at once: 'Of course; the Professor came to see us
again after a long absence, and I saw him once more beside
little Otto's coffin.' This was exactly what I had expected, and
I interpreted the dream in this way: 'If now the other boy were
to die, the same thing would happen. You would spend the
day with your sister and the Professor would be certain to come
to offer his condolences, so that you would see him again under
the same conditions as the other time. The dream means no
more than your wish to see him once more, a wish which you
are inwardly struggling against. I know you have a ticket for
to-day's concert in your pocket. Your dream was a dream of
impatience: it anticipated the glimpse you are to have of him
to-day by a few hours.'

In order to conceal her wish, she had evidently chosen a
situation in which such wishes are usually suppressed, a situation in which one is so much filled with grief that one has no

thought of love. Yet it is quite possible that even in the real
situation of which the dream was an exact replica, beside the
coffin of the elder boy whom she had loved still more, she may
have been unable to suppress her tender feelings for the visitor
who had been absent so long.[1]

A similar dream of another woman patient had a different
explanation. When she was young she had been remarkable
for her ready wit and cheerful disposition; and these characteristics were still to be seen, at all events in the ideas that occurred
to her during the treatment. In the course of a longish dream,
this lady imagined that she saw her only, fifteen-year-old
daughter lying dead 'in a case'. She had half a mind to use the
scene as an objection to the wish-fulfilment theory, though she
herself suspected that the detail of the 'case' must point the way
to another view of the dream.[2] In the course of the analysis she
recalled that at a party the evening before there had been some
talk about the English word 'box' and the various ways in
which it could be translated into German—such as 'Schachtel'
['case'], 'Loge' ['box at the theatre'], 'Kasten' ['chest'], 'Ohrfeige'
['box on the ear'], and so on. Other portions of the same dream
enabled us to discover further that she had guessed that the
English 'box' was related to the German 'Büchse' ['receptacle'],
and that she had then been plagued by a recollection that
'Büchse' is used as a vulgar term for the female genitals. If some
allowance was made for the limits of her knowledge of topo-
graphical anatomy, it might be presumed, therefore, that the
child lying in the case meant an embryo in the womb. After
being enlightened up to this point, she no longer denied that the
dream-picture corresponded to a wish of hers. Like so many
young married women, she had been far from pleased when she
became pregnant; and more than once she had allowed herself
to wish that the child in her womb might die. Indeed, in a fit of
rage after a violent scene with her husband, she had beaten with
her fists on her body so as to hit the child inside it. Thus the dead
child was in fact the fulfilment of a wish, but of a wish that had
been put aside fifteen years earlier. It is scarcely to be wondered

---

[1] [This dream is referred to again on pp. 248 and 463; it is also briefly
recorded in Section IX of Freud, 1901a (*Standard Ed.*, 5, 675).]

[2] Like the smoked salmon in the dream of the abandoned supper-
party. [See above, p. 148.]

at if a wish that was fulfilled after such a long delay was not recognized. Too much had changed in the interval.[1]

I shall have to return to the group of dreams to which the last two examples belong (dreams dealing with the death of relatives of whom the dreamer is fond) when I come to consider 'typical' dreams [p. 248 ff.]. I shall then be able to show from further instances that, in spite of their unwished-for contents, all such dreams must be interpreted as wish-fulfilments.

I owe the following dream, not to a patient, but to an intelligent jurist of my acquaintance. He told it to me, once again, in order to restrain me from rash generalizing on the theory of wishful dreams. 'I dreamt,' said my informant, 'that *I came up to my house with a lady on my arm. A closed carriage was standing in front of it and a man came up to me, showed me his credentials as a police officer and requested me to follow him. I asked him to allow me a little time to put my affairs in order.* Can you suppose that I have a wish to be arrested?'—Of course not, I could only agree. Do you happen to know the charge on which you were arrested? —'Yes, for infanticide, I believe.'—Infanticide? But surely you're aware that that's a crime that can only be committed by a mother on a new-born child?—'Quite true.'[2]—And what were the circumstances in which you had the dream? What happened on the previous evening?—'I would prefer not to tell you. It's a delicate matter.'—Nevertheless I shall have to hear it; otherwise we shall have to give up the idea of interpreting the dream.—'Very well then, listen. I didn't spend last night at home but with a lady who means a great deal to me. When we woke up in the morning there was a further passage between us, after which I went to sleep again and had the dream I described to you.'—Is she a married woman?—'Yes.'—And you don't want to have a child by her?—'Oh, no; that might give us away.'—So you don't practice normal intercourse?—'I take the precaution of withdrawing before ejaculation.'—I think

[1] [This dream is further discussed on p. 249 and is also reported briefly in Lecture XIII of Freud's *Introductory Lectures* (1916–17).]

[2] It often happens that the account first given of a dream is incomplete and that the memory of the omitted portions only emerges in the course of analysis. These subsequently added portions regularly turn out to provide the key to the dream's interpretation. Cf. the discussion below on the forgetting of dreams [p. 518 ff.].

I may assume that you had used this device several times
during the night, and that after repeating it in the morning you
felt a little uncertain whether you had carried it out successfully.—'That's possible, no doubt.'—In that case your dream
was the fulfilment of a wish. It gave you a reassurance that you
had not procreated a child, or, what amounts to the same thing,
that you had killed a child. The intermediate links are easily
indicated. You remember that a few days ago we were talking
about marriage difficulties and how inconsistent it is that there
should be no objection to carrying out intercourse in such a
way that no fertilization takes place, whereas any interference
when once the ovum and semen have come together and a
foetus has been formed is punished as a crime. We went on to
recall the mediaeval controversy over the exact point of time
at which the soul enters the foetus, since it is not until after that
that the concept of murder becomes applicable. No doubt, too,
you know Lenau's gruesome poem ['Das tote Glück'] in which
child murder and child prevention are equated.—'Oddly
enough I happened to think of Lenau this morning, quite by
chance, as it seemed.'—An after-echo of your dream. And now
I can show you another incidental wish-fulfilment contained
in your dream. You came up to your house with the lady on
your arm. Thus you were bringing her home,[1] instead of
spending the night in her house as you did in reality. There may
be more than one reason why the wish-fulfilment which constitutes the core of the dream was disguised in such a disagreeable form. Perhaps you have learned from my paper on the
aetiology of anxiety neurosis [Freud, 1895b] that I regard *coitus
interruptus* as one of the aetiological factors in the development
of neurotic anxiety? It would tally with this if, after carrying
out sexual intercourse in this way several times, you were left
in an uneasy mood which afterwards became an element in the
construction of your dream. Moreover, you made use of this
moodiness to help disguise the wish-fulfilment. [Cf. p. 487.]
Incidentally, your reference to infanticide has not been explained. How did you come to light on this specifically feminine
crime?—'I must admit that some years ago I became involved
in an occurrence of that kind. I was responsible for a girl's
trying to avoid the consequence of a love-affair with me by

[1] [The German '*heimführen*' means both 'to bring home' and 'to
marry'.]

means of an abortion. I had nothing to do with her carrying out her intention, but for a long time I naturally felt very nervous in case the business came out.'—I quite understand that. This recollection provides a second reason why you must have been worried by your suspicion that your device might have gone wrong.[1]

A young physician who heard me describe this dream during a course of lectures must have been greatly struck by it, for he promptly re-dreamt it, applying the same pattern of thought to another theme. The day before, he had sent in his income-tax return, which he had filled in perfectly honestly, since he had very little to declare. He then had a dream that *an acquaintance of his came to him from a meeting of the tax commissioners and informed him that, while no objection had been raised to any of the other tax returns, general suspicion had been aroused by his and a heavy fine had been imposed on him.* The dream was a poorly disguised fulfilment of his wish to be known as a doctor with a large income. It recalls the well-known story of the girl who was advised not to accept a suitor because he had a violent temper and would be sure to beat her if they were married. 'If only he'd begun beating me already!' the girl replied. Her wish to be married was so intense that she was ready to take the threatened unpleasantness into the bargain, and even went so far as to turn it into a wish.

The very frequent dreams,[2] which appear to stand in contradiction to my theory because their subject-matter is the frustration of a wish or the occurrence of something clearly unwished-for, may be brought together under the heading of 'counter-wish dreams'. If these dreams are considered as a whole, it seems to me possible to trace them back to two principles; I have not yet mentioned one of these, although it plays a large part not only in people's dreams but in their lives as well. One of the two motive forces leading to such dreams is the wish that I may be wrong. These dreams appear regularly in the course of my treatments when a patient is in a state of resistance to me; and I can count almost certainly on provoking one of them after I have explained to a patient for the first time

[1] [This dream was recorded in Draft I, attached to Freud's letter to Fliess of May 2, 1897 (Freud, 1950a, Letter 61).]

[2] [This paragraph and the next were added in 1909.]

my theory that dreams are fulfilments of wishes.[1] Indeed, it is
to be expected that the same thing will happen to some of the
readers of the present book: they will be quite ready to have one
of their wishes frustrated in a dream if only their wish that I may
be wrong can be fulfilled.

The same point is illustrated by one last dream of the kind
which I will quote from a patient under treatment. This was
the dream of a girl who had succeeded in her struggle to continue her treatment with me against the will of her relatives
and of the authorities whose opinions had been consulted. *She
dreamt that her people forbade her to go on coming to me. She then
reminded me of a promise I had given her that if necessary I would
continue the treatment without a fee. To this I replied: 'I cannot make
any allowances in money matters.'* It must be admitted that it was
not easy to point to the wish-fulfilment in this instance. But in
all such cases one discovers a second riddle, the solution of
which helps one to solve the original one. What was the origin
of the words she put into my mouth? Of course I had said
nothing of the kind to her; but one of her brothers, and the one
by whom she was most influenced, had been good enough to
attribute this sentiment to me. The dream was thus intended
to prove her brother right. And it was not only in her dreams
that she insisted on his being right; the same idea dominated
her whole life and it was the motive of her illness.

A dream[2] which seems at first sight to put special difficulties
in the way of the wish-fulfilment theory was dreamt and interpreted by a physician, and reported by August Stärcke (1911):
'*I saw upon my left index-finger the first indication [Primäraffekt] of
syphilis on the terminal phalange.*' The reflection that, apart from
the dream's unwished-for content, it appears to be clear and
coherent, might dissuade us from analysing it. If, however, we
are prepared to face the trouble involved, we shall find that
'*Primäraffekt*' was equivalent to a '*prima affectio*' (a first love), and
that the repellent ulcer turned out, to quote Stärcke's words, to
'stand for wish-fulfilments that were highly charged with
emotion'.

---

[1] [*Footnote added* 1911:] During the last few years similar 'counter-
wish dreams' have repeatedly been reported to me by people who have
heard me lecturing, as a reaction to first making the acquaintance of my
'wishful' theory of dreams.
[2] [This paragraph was added in 1914.]

The second motive for counter-wish dreams[1] is so obvious that it is easy to overlook it, as I did myself for some considerable time. There is a masochistic component in the sexual constitution of many people, which arises from the reversal of an aggressive, sadistic component into its opposite.[2] Those who find their pleasure, not in having *physical* pain inflicted on them, but in humiliation and mental torture, may be described as 'mental masochists'. It will at once be seen that people of this kind can have counter-wish dreams and unpleasurable dreams, which are none the less wish-fulfilments since they satisfy their masochistic inclinations. I will quote one such dream, produced by a young man who in his earlier years had greatly tormented his elder brother, to whom he had a homosexual attachment. His character having undergone a fundamental change, he had the following dream, which was in three pieces: *I. His elder brother was chaffing him. II. Two grown men were caressing each other with a homosexual purpose. III. His brother had sold the business of which he himself had looked forward to becoming the director.* He awoke from the last dream with the most distressing feelings. Nevertheless it was a masochistic wishful dream, and might be translated thus: 'It would serve me right if my brother were to confront me with this sale as a punishment for all the torments he had to put up with from me.'

I hope that the foregoing examples will be enough (till the next objection is raised) to make it seem plausible that even dreams with a distressing content are to be construed as wish-fulfilments.[3] Nor will anyone regard it as a chance coincidence that the interpretation of these dreams has brought us up each time against topics about which people are loth to speak or to think. The distressing feeling aroused by these dreams is no doubt identical with the repugnance which tends (usually with success) to restrain us from discussing or mentioning such topics, and which each of us has to overcome if we nevertheless

[1] [This paragraph was added in 1909.]

[2] [The author's amended views on this subject will be found in Freud, 1924c.]

[3] [The following sentence was included in the text, in a slightly different form, in 1919 and printed as a footnote in 1925:] I must point out that the subject is not yet finally disposed of; I shall return to it later on. [See p. 556 ff.]

find ourselves compelled to embark on them. But the unpleasurable feeling which thus recurs in dreams does not disprove the existence of a wish. Everyone has wishes that he would prefer not to disclose to other people, and wishes that he will not admit even to himself. On the other hand, we are justified in linking the unpleasurable character of all these dreams with the fact of dream-distortion. And we are justified in concluding that these dreams are distorted and the wish-fulfilment contained in them disguised to the point of being unrecognizable precisely owing to the repugnance felt for the topic of the dream or for the wish derived from it and to an intention to repress them. The distortion in the dream is thus shown in fact to be an act of the censorship. We shall be taking into account everything that has been brought to light by our analysis of unpleasurable dreams if we make the following modification in the formula in which we have sought to express the nature of dreams: *a dream is a (disguised) fulfilment of a (suppressed or repressed) wish.*[1]

There remain to be discussed anxiety-dreams as a special sub-species of dreams with a distressing content. The notion of

---

[1] [*Footnote added* 1914:] A great living writer, who, as I have been told, refuses to hear anything of psycho-analysis or the interpretation of dreams, has independently arrived at an almost identical formula for the nature of dreams. He speaks of a dream as 'the unauthorized emergence of suppressed desires and wishes, under false features and name'. (Spitteler, 1914, 1.)

[*Added* 1911:] I shall anticipate questions which will be discussed later by quoting at this point Otto Rank's enlargement and modification of the above basic formula: 'On the basis and with the help of repressed, infantile sexual material, dreams regularly represent present-day, and also as a rule erotic, wishes as fulfilled, in a veiled and symbolically disguised shape.' (Rank, 1910, [519].)

[*Added* 1925:] I have nowhere stated that I adopted Rank's formula as my own. The shorter version, as stated in the text above, seems to me adequate. But the mere fact of my having mentioned Rank's modification has been enough to unleash countless accusations against psychoanalysis of having asserted that 'all dreams have a sexual content'.

If this sentence is taken in the sense in which it was intended, it merely shows the unconscientious manner in which critics are accustomed to perform their functions, and the readiness with which opponents overlook the clearest statements if they do not give scope to their aggressive inclinations. For only a few pages earlier [p. 127 ff.] I had mentioned the variety of the wishes whose fulfilments are to be found in children's regarding these as wishful dreams will meet with very little sympathy from the unenlightened. Nevertheless I can deal with anxiety-dreams very briefly at this point. They do not present us with a new aspect of the dream-problem; what they face us with is the whole question of neurotic anxiety. The anxiety that we feel in a dream is only *apparently* explained by the dream's content. If we submit the content of the dream to analysis, we find that the anxiety in the dream is no better justified by the dream's content than, let us say, the anxiety in a phobia is justified by the idea to which the phobia relates. No doubt it is true, for instance, that it is possible to fall out of a window and that there is therefore reason for exercising a certain degree of caution in the neighbourhood of a window; but we cannot see why the anxiety felt in a phobia on this subject is so great and pursues the patient far beyond its occasion.[1] We find then that the same thing may be validly asserted both of phobias and of anxiety-dreams: in both cases the anxiety is only superficially attached to the idea that accompanies it; it originates from another source.

Since this intimate connection exists between anxiety in dreams and in neuroses, in discussing the former I must refer to the latter. In a short paper on anxiety-neurosis (Freud, 1895*b*), I argued some time ago that neurotic anxiety is derived from sexual life and corresponds to libido which has been diverted from its purpose and has found no employment.[2] Since dreams (wishes to take part in an excursion or a sail on a lake, or to make up for a missed meal, and so on); and in other passages I had discussed dreams of hunger [p. 131 *n.*], dreams stimulated by thirst [p. 123 f.] or by excretory needs, and dreams of mere convenience [p. 125]. Even Rank himself made no absolute assertion. The words he used were 'also *as a rule* erotic wishes', and what he said can be amply confirmed in the dreams of most adults.

The situation would be different if 'sexual' was being used by my critics in the sense in which it is now commonly employed in psycho-analysis—in the sense of 'Eros'. But my opponents are scarcely likely to have had in mind the interesting problem of whether all dreams are created by 'libidinal' instinctual forces as contrasted with 'destructive' ones. [Cf. Freud, *The Ego and the Id*, Chapter IV (Freud, 1923*b*).]

[1] [This particular form of phobia, the fear of falling out of windows, was referred to by Freud in a letter to Fliess of December 12, 1896 (Freud, 1950*a*, Letter 53), and again much later in his paper on 'Dreams and Telepathy' (Freud, 1922*a*).]

[2] [The author's later views on the relation between libido and anxiety will be found in his *Inhibitions, Symptoms and Anxiety* (1926*d*).]

then this formula has met the test of time; and it enables us now to infer from it that anxiety-dreams are dreams with a sexual content, the libido belonging to which has been transformed into anxiety. There will be an opportunity later to support this assertion by the analysis of some neurotic patients' dreams.[1] In the course, too, of a further attempt to arrive at a theory of dreams, I shall have occasion to discuss once more the determinants of anxiety-dreams and their compatibility with the theory of wish-fulfilment.

[1] [Freud evidently changed his mind on this point: see p. 579 ff., where, however, two anxiety-dreams are analysed and the whole subject of anxiety-dreams is again discussed.]

CHAPTER V

THE MATERIAL AND SOURCES OF DREAMS

WHEN the analysis of the dream of Irma's injection showed us that a dream could be the fulfilment of a wish, our interest was at first wholly absorbed by the question of whether we had come upon a universal characteristic of dreams, and for the time being we stifled our curiosity about any other scientific problems that may have arisen during the work of the interpretation. Having followed one path to its end, we may now retrace our steps and choose another starting-point for our rambles through the problems of dream-life: for the time being, we may leave the topic of wish-fulfilment on one side, though we are still far from having exhausted it.

Now that the application of our procedure for interpreting dreams enables us to disclose a *latent* content in them which is of far greater significance than their *manifest* one, the pressing task at once arises of re-examining one by one the various problems raised by dreams, to see whether we may not now be in a position to find satisfactory solutions for the conundrums and contradictions which seemed intractable so long as we were only acquainted with the manifest content.

In the first chapter I have given a detailed account of the views of the authorities on the relation of dreams with waking life [Section A] and on the origin of the material of dreams [Section C]. No doubt, too, my readers will recall the three characteristics of memory in dreams [Section B], which have been so often remarked on but which have never been explained:

(1) Dreams show a clear preference for the impressions of the immediately preceding days [p. 17 f.]. Cf. Robert [1886, 46], Strümpell [1877, 39], Hildebrandt [1875, 11] and Hallam and Weed [1896, 410 f.].

(2) They make their selection upon different principles from our waking memory, since they do not recall what is essential and important but what is subsidiary and unnoticed. [P. 18 ff.]

(3) They have at their disposal the earliest impressions of our

childhood and even bring up details from that period of our life which, once again, strike us as trivial and which in our waking state we believe to have been long since forgotten. [P. 15 ff.][1]

All these peculiarities shown by dreams in their choice of material have, of course, only been studied by earlier writers in connection with their *manifest* content.

[1] The view adopted by Robert [1886, 9 f.] that the purpose of dreams is to unburden our memory of the useless impressions of daytime [cf. p. 79 ff.] is plainly no longer tenable if indifferent memory images from our childhood appear at all frequently in dreams. Otherwise we could only conclude that dreams perform their function most inadequately.

(A)

RECENT AND INDIFFERENT MATERIAL IN DREAMS

If I examine my own experience on the subject of the origin of the elements included in the content of dreams, I must begin with an assertion that in every dream it is possible to find a point of contact with the experiences of the previous day. This view is confirmed by every dream that I look into, whether my own or anyone else's. Bearing this fact in mind, I am able, on occasion, to begin a dream's interpretation by looking for the event of the previous day which set it in motion; in many instances, indeed, this is the easiest method.[1] In the two dreams which I have analysed in detail in my last chapters (the dream of Irma's injection and the dream of my uncle with a yellow beard) the connection with the previous day is so obvious as to require no further comment. But in order to show the regularity with which such a connection can be traced, I will go through the records of my own dreams and give some instances. I shall only quote enough of the dream to indicate the source we are looking for:

(1) *I was visiting a house into which I had difficulty in gaining admittance . . .; in the meantime I kept a lady* WAITING.
Source: I had had a conversation `᭜ ᭜ ᭜` a female relative the evening before in which I had told `᭜ ᭜ ᭜` that she would have to *wait* for a purchase she wanted to `᭜ ᭜ ᭜` till . . . etc.

(2) *I had written a* MONOGRAPH *on a certain* (indistinct) *species of plant.*
Source: That morning I had seen a *monograph* on the genus Cyclamen in the window of a book-shop. [See below, p. 169 ff.]

(3) *I saw two women in the street,* A MOTHER AND DAUGHTER, *the latter of whom was a patient of mine.*
Source: One of my patients had explained to me the previous evening the difficulties her *mother* was putting in the way of her continuing her treatment.

[1] [The different ways of beginning the interpretation of a dream are discussed in Section I of Freud, 1923c.]

165

(4) *I took out a subscription in S. and R.'s bookshop for a periodical costing* TWENTY FLORINS *a year*.

Source: My wife had reminded me the day before that I still owed her *twenty florins* for the weekly household expenses.

(5) *I received* A COMMUNICATION *from the Social Democratic* COMMITTEE, *treating me as though I were a* MEMBER.

Source: I had received *communications* simultaneously from the Liberal Election *Committee* and from the Council of the Humanitarian League, of which latter body I was in fact *a member*.

(6) *A man standing on* A CLIFF IN THE MIDDLE OF THE SEA, IN THE STYLE OF BÖCKLIN.

Source: Dreyfus on the *Île du Diable;* I had had news at the same time from my relatives in *England*, etc.

The question may be raised whether the point of contact with the dream is invariably the events of the *immediately* preceding day or whether it may go back to impressions derived from a rather more extensive period of the most recent past. It is unlikely that this question involves any matter of theoretical importance; nevertheless I am inclined to decide in favour of the exclusiveness of the claims of the day immediately preceding the dream—which I shall speak of as the 'dream-day'. Whenever it has seemed at first that the source of a dream was an impression two or three days earlier, closer enquiry has convinced me that the impression had been recalled on the previous day and thus that it was possible to show that a reproduction of the impression, occurring on the previous day, could be inserted between the day of the original event and the time of the dream; moreover it has been possible to indicate the contingency on the previous day which may have led to the recalling of the older impression.

On the other hand[1] I do not feel convinced that there is any regular interval of biological significance between the instigating daytime impression and its recurrence in the dream. (Swoboda, 1904, has mentioned an initial period of eighteen hours in this connection.)[2]

---

[1] [This paragraph was added in 1909.]

[2] [*Footnote added* 1911:] As I have mentioned in a postscript to my first chapter (p. 94 f.), Hermann Swoboda [1904] has made a far-reaching application to the mental field of the biological periodic intervals of 23

and 28 days discovered by Wilhelm Fliess [1906]. He has asserted in
particular that these periods determine the emergence of the elements
which appear in dreams. No essential modification in dream-interpretation would be involved if this fact were to be established; it would merely
provide a fresh source of origin of dream-material. I have, however,
recently made some investigations upon my own dreams, to test how far
the 'theory of periodicity' is applicable to them. For this purpose I chose
some specially outstanding dream-elements the time of whose appearance in real life could be determined with certainty.

I. DREAM OF OCTOBER 1ST–2ND, 1910

(Fragment) . . . *Somewhere in Italy. Three daughters were showing me some
small curios, as though we were in an antique shop, and were sitting on my lap. I
commented on one of the objects: 'Why, you got that from me', and saw plainly
before me a small profile relief with the clear-cut features of Savonarola.*

When had I last seen a portrait of Savonarola? My travel-diary
proved that I had been in Florence on September 4th and 5th. While I
was there I thought I would show my travelling companion the medallion bearing the fanatical monk's features, let into the pavement of the
Piazza della Signoria, which marks the place where he was burned. I
pointed it out to him, I believe, on the morning of the 3rd. [Misprinted
'5th' in recent editions.] Between this impression and its reappearance
in the dream 27 + 1 days elapsed—Fliess's 'female period'. Unluckily
for the conclusiveness of this example, however, I must add that on the
actual 'dream-day' I had a visit (for the first time since my return) from
a capable but gloomy-looking medical colleague of mine whom I had
many years before nick-named 'Rabbi Savonarola'. He introduced a
patient to me who was suffering from the effects of an accident to the
Pontebba express, in which I myself had travelled a week earlier, and
my thoughts were thus led back to my recent visit to Italy. The appearance in the content of the dream of the outstanding element 'Savonarola' is thus accounted for by my colleague's visit on the dream-day;
and the interval of 28 days is deprived of its significance.

II. DREAM OF OCTOBER 10TH–11TH, 1910

*I was once more working at chemistry in the University laboratory. Hofrat L.
invited me to come somewhere and walked in front of me along the corridor, holding
a lamp or some other instrument before him in his uplifted hand and with his head
stretched forward in a peculiar attitude, with a clear-sighted (? far-sighted) look
about him. Then we crossed an open space. . .* (The remainder was forgotten.)

The most outstanding point in the content of this dream was the way
in which Hofrat L. held the lamp (or magnifying glass) before him, with
his eyes peering into the distance. It was many years since I had last
seen him; but I knew at once that he was only a substitute figure in the
place of someone else, someone greater than he—Archimedes, whose
statue stands near the Fountain of Arethusa at Syracuse in that very
attitude, holding up his burning-glass and peering out towards the besieging army of the Romans. When did I see that statue for the first (and
last) time? According to my diary it was on the evening of September

17th; and between then and the time of the dream $13 + 10 = 23$ days had elapsed—Fliess's 'male period'.

Unfortunately, when we go into the interpretation of this dream in greater detail, we once again find that the coincidence loses some of its conclusiveness. The exciting cause of the dream was the news I received on the dream-day that the clinic, in whose lecture room I was able by courtesy to deliver my lectures, was shortly to be removed to another locality. I took it for granted that its new situation would be very out of the way and told myself that in that case I might just as well not have a lecture room at my disposal at all. From that point my thoughts must have gone back to the beginning of my career as University Lecturer when I in fact had no lecture room and when my efforts to get hold of one met with little response from the powerfully placed Hofrats and Professors. In those circumstances I had gone to L., who at that time held the office of Dean of the Faculty and who I believed was friendlily disposed to me, to complain of my troubles. He promised to help me, but I heard nothing more from him. In the dream he was Archimedes, giving me a ποῦ στῶ [footing] and himself leading me to the new locality. Anyone who is an adept at interpretation will guess that the dream-thoughts were not exactly free from ideas of vengeance and self-importance. It seems clear, in any case, that without this exciting cause Archimedes would scarcely have found his way into my dream that night; nor am I convinced that the powerful and still recent impression made on me by the statue in Syracuse might not have produced its effect after some different interval of time.

III. Dream of October 2nd–3rd, 1910

(Fragment) . . . *Something about Professor Oser, who had drawn up the menu for me himself, which had a very soothing effect.* . . . (Some more that was forgotten.)

This dream was a reaction to a digestive disturbance that day, which made me consider whether I should go to one of my colleagues to have a dietary prescribed for me. My reason for choosing Oser for that purpose, who had died in the course of the summer, went back to the death of another University teacher whom I greatly admired, which had occurred shortly before (on October 1st). When had Oser died? and when had I heard of his death? According to a paragraph in the papers he had died on August 22nd. I had been in Holland at that time and had my Vienna newspaper sent on to me regularly; so that I must have read of his death August 24th or 25th. But here the interval no longer corresponds to either period. It amounts to $7 + 30 + 2 = 39$ days or possibly 40 days. I could not recall having spoken or thought of Oser in the meantime.

Intervals such as this one, which cannot be fitted into the theory of periodicity without further manipulation, occur far more frequently in my dreams than intervals which *can* be so fitted. The only relation which I find occurs with regularity is the relation which I have insisted upon in the text and which connects the dream with some impression of the dream-day.

Havelock Ellis [1911, 224],[1] who has also given some attention to this point, declares that he was unable to find any such
periodicity in his dreams in spite of looking for it. He records
a dream of being in Spain and of wanting to go to a place called
Daraus, Varaus or Zaraus. On waking he could not recall any
such place-name, and put the dream on one side. A few months
later he discovered that Zaraus was in fact the name of a station
on the line between San Sebastian and Bilbao, through which
his train had passed 250 days before he had the dream.

I believe, then, that the instigating agent of every dream is
to be found among the experiences which one has not yet 'slept
on'. Thus the relations of a dream's content to impressions of
the most recent past (with the single exception of the day immediately preceding the night of the dream) differ in no respect
from its relations to impressions dating from any remoter period.
Dreams can select their material from any part of the dreamer's
life, provided only that there is a train of thought linking the
experience of the dream-day (the 'recent' impressions) with the
earlier ones.

But why this preference for recent impressions? We shall form
some notion on this point, if we submit one of the dreams in the
series I have just quoted [p. 165] to a fuller analysis. For this
purpose I shall choose the

DREAM OF THE BOTANICAL MONOGRAPH

*I had written a monograph on a certain plant. The book lay before me
and I was at the moment turning over a folded coloured plate. Bound up
in each copy there was a dried specimen of the plant, as though it had
been taken from a herbarium.*

ANALYSIS

That morning I had seen a new book in the window of a
book-shop, bearing the title *The Genus Cyclamen*—evidently a
monograph on that plant.

Cyclamens, I reflected, were my wife's *favourite flowers* and I
reproached myself for so rarely remembering to *bring* her *flowers*,
which was what she liked.—The subject of '*bringing flowers*'
recalled an anecdote which I had recently repeated to a circle
of friends and which I had used as evidence in favour of my

[1] [This paragraph was added in 1914.]

theory that forgetting is very often determined by an unconscious purpose and that it always enables one to deduce the
secret intentions of the person who forgets.[1] A young woman
was accustomed to receiving a bouquet of flowers from her
husband on her birthday. One year this token of his affection
failed to appear, and she burst into tears. Her husband came
in and had no idea why she was crying till she told him that
to-day was her birthday. He clasped his hand to his head and
exclaimed: 'I'm so sorry, but I'd quite forgotten. I'll go out at
once and fetch your *flowers*.' But she was not to be consoled; for
she recognized that her husband's forgetfulness was a proof that
she no longer had the same place in his thoughts as she had
formerly.—This lady, Frau L., had met my wife two days before
I had the dream, had told her that she was feeling quite well
and enquired after me. Some years ago she had come to me for
treatment.

I now made a fresh start. Once, I recalled, I really *had* written
something in the nature of a *monograph on a plant*, namely a dis-
sertation on the *coca-plant* [Freud, 1884*e*], which had drawn
Karl Koller's attention to the anaesthetic properties of cocaine.
I had myself indicated this application of the alkaloid in my
published paper, but I had not been thorough enough to pursue
the matter further.[2] This reminded me that on the morning of
the day after the dream—I had not found time to interpret it
till the evening—I had thought about cocaine in a kind of day-
dream. If ever I got glaucoma, I had thought, I should travel
to Berlin and get myself operated on, incognito, in my friend's
[Fliess's] house, by a surgeon recommended by him. The operating surgeon, who would have no idea of my identity, would
boast once again of how easily such operations could be performed since the introduction of cocaine; and I should not give
the slightest hint that I myself had had a share in the discovery.
This phantasy had led on to reflections of how awkward it is,
when all is said and done, for a physician to ask for medical
treatment for himself from his professional colleagues. The
Berlin eye-surgeon would not know me, and I should be able
to pay his fees like anyone else. It was not until I had recalled

---

[1] [The theory was published a few months after the date of the dream,
in Freud (1898*b*), and then incorporated in *The Psychopathology of
Everyday Life* (Freud, 1901*b*).]

[2] [See footnote 2, p. 111.]

this day-dream that I realized that the recollection of a specific event lay behind it. Shortly after Koller's discovery, my father had in fact been attacked by glaucoma; my friend Dr. König-stein, the ophthalmic surgeon, had operated on him; while Dr. Koller had been in charge of the cocaine anaesthesia and had commented on the fact that this case had brought together all of the three men who had had a share in the introduction of cocaine.

My thoughts then went on to the occasion when I had last been reminded of this business of the cocaine. It had been a few days earlier, when I had been looking at a copy of a *Festschrift* in which grateful pupils had celebrated the jubilee of their teacher and laboratory director. Among the laboratory's claims to distinction which were enumerated in this book I had seen a mention of the fact that Koller had made his discovery there of the anaesthetic properties of cocaine. I then suddenly per-ceived that my dream was connected with an event of the previous evening. I had walked home precisely with Dr. König-stein and had got into conversation with him about a matter which never fails to excite my feelings whenever it is raised. While I was talking to him in the entrance-hall, Professor *Gärtner* [Gardener] and his wife had joined us; and I could not help congratulating them both on their *blooming* looks. But Professor Gärtner was one of the authors of the *Festschrift* I have just mentioned, and may well have reminded me of it. More-over, the Frau L., whose disappointment on her birthday I described earlier, was mentioned—though only, it is true, in another connection—in my conversation with Dr. Königstein.

I will make an attempt at interpreting the other determin-ants of the content of the dream as well. There was *a dried specimen of the plant* included in the monograph, as though it had been a *herbarium*. This led me to a memory from my secondary school. Our headmaster once called together the boys from the higher forms and handed over the school's herbarium to them to be looked through and cleaned. Some small *worms*—book-worms—had found their way into it. He does not seem to have had much confidence in my helpfulness, for he handed me only a few sheets. These, as I could still recall, included some Cruci-fers. I never had a specially intimate contact with botany. In my preliminary examination in botany I was also given a Crucifer to identify—and failed to do so. My prospects would not have been too bright, if I had not been helped out by my theoretical knowledge. I went on from the Cruciferae to the Compositae. It occurred to me that artichokes were Compositae, and indeed I might fairly have called them my *favourite flowers*. Being more generous than I am, my wife often brought me back these favourite flowers of mine from the market.

I saw the monograph which I had written *lying before me*. This again led me back to something. I had had a letter from my friend [Fliess] in Berlin the day before in which he had shown his power of visualization: 'I am very much occupied with your dream-book. *I see it lying finished before me and I see myself turning over its pages.*'[1] How much I envied him his gift as a seer! If only *I* could have seen it lying finished before me!

The folded coloured plate. While I was a medical student I was the constant victim of an impulse only to learn things out of *monographs*. In spite of my limited means, I succeeded in getting hold of a number of volumes of the proceedings of medical societies and was enthralled by their *coloured plates*. I was proud of my hankering for thoroughness. When I myself had begun to publish papers, I had been obliged to make my own drawings to illustrate them and I remembered that one of them had been so wretched that a friendly colleague had jeered at me over it. There followed, I could not quite make out how, a recollection from very early youth. It had once amused my father to hand over a book with *coloured plates* (an account of a journey through Persia) for me and my eldest sister to destroy. Not easy to justify from the educational point of view! I had been five years old at the time and my sister not yet three; and the picture of the two of us blissfully pulling the book to pieces (leaf by leaf, like an *artichoke*, I found myself saying) was almost the only plastic memory that I retained from that period of my life. Then, when I became a student, I had developed a passion for collecting and owning books, which was analogous to my liking for learning out of monographs: a *favourite hobby*. (The idea of '*favourite*' had already appeared in connection with cyclamens and artichokes.) I had become a *book-worm*. I had always, from the time I first began to think about myself, referred this first passion of mine back to the childhood memory I have men-

---

[1] [Freud's reply to this letter from Fliess is dated March 10, 1898 (Freud, 1950a, Letter 84); so that the dream must have occurred not more than a day or two earlier.]

tioned. Or rather, I had recognized that the childhood scene was a 'screen memory' for my later bibliophile propensities.[1] And I had early discovered, of course, that passions often lead to sorrow. When I was seventeen I had run up a largish account at the bookseller's and had nothing to meet it with; and my father had scarcely taken it as an excuse that my inclinations might have chosen a worse outlet. The recollection of this experience from the later years of my youth at once brought back to my mind the conversation with my friend Dr. Königstein. For in the course of it we had discussed the same question of my being blamed for being too much absorbed in my *favourite hobbies*.

For reasons with which we are not concerned, I shall not pursue the interpretation of this dream any further, but will merely indicate the direction in which it lay. In the course of the work of analysis I was reminded of my conversation with Dr. Königstein, and I was brought to it from more than one direction. When I take into account the topics touched upon in that conversation, the meaning of the dream becomes intelligible to me. All the trains of thought starting from the dream—the thoughts about my wife's and my own favourite flowers, about cocaine, about the awkwardness of medical treatment among colleagues, about my preference for studying monographs and about my neglect of certain branches of science such as botany —all of these trains of thought, when they were further pursued, led ultimately to one or other of the many ramifications of my conversation with Dr. Königstein. Once again the dream, like the one we first analysed—the dream of Irma's injection— turns out to have been in the nature of a self-justification, a plea on behalf of my own rights. Indeed, it carried the subject that was raised in the earlier dream a stage further and discussed it with reference to fresh material that had arisen in the interval between the two dreams. Even the apparently indifferent form in which the dream was couched turns out to have had significance. What it meant was: 'After all, I'm the man who wrote the valuable and memorable paper (on cocaine)', just as in the earlier dream I had said on my behalf: 'I'm a conscientious and hard-working student.' In both cases what I was insisting was: 'I may allow myself to do this.' There is, however, no need for me to carry the interpretation of the dream any further, since

[1] Cf. my paper on screen memories [Freud, 1899*a*].

my only purpose in reporting it was to illustrate by an example the relation between the content of a dream and the experience of the previous day which provoked it. So long as I was aware only of the dream's *manifest* content, it appeared to be related only to a *single* event of the dream-day. But when the analysis was carried out, a *second* source of the dream emerged in another experience of the same day. The first of these two impressions with which the dream was connected was an indifferent one, a subsidiary circumstance: I had seen a book in a shop-window whose title attracted my attention for a moment but whose subject-matter could scarcely be of interest to me. The second experience had a high degree of psychical importance: I had had a good hour's lively conversation with my friend the eye-surgeon; in the course of it I had given him some information which was bound to affect both of us closely, and I had had memories stirred up in me which had drawn my attention to a great variety of internal stresses in my own mind. Moreover, the conversation had been interrupted before its conclusion because we had been joined by acquaintances.

We must now ask what was the relation of the two impressions of the dream-day to each other and to the dream of the subsequent night. In the manifest content of the dream only the *indifferent* impression was alluded to, which seems to confirm the notion that dreams have a preference for taking up unimportant details of waking life. All the strands of the interpretation, on the other hand, led to the *important* impression, to the one which had justifiably stirred my feelings. If the sense of the dream is judged, as it can only rightly be, by its latent content as revealed by the analysis, a new and significant fact is unexpectedly brought to light. The conundrum of why dreams are concerned only with worthless fragments of waking life seems to have lost all its meaning; nor can it any longer be maintained that waking life is not pursued further in dreams and that dreams are thus psychical activity wasted upon foolish material. The contrary is true: our dream-thoughts are dominated by the same material that has occupied us during the day and we only bother to dream of things which have given us cause for reflection in the daytime.

Why is it, then, that, though the occasion of my dreaming was a daytime impression by which I had been justifiably stirred, I nevertheless actually dreamt of something indifferent?

The most obvious explanation, no doubt, is that we are once more faced by one of the phenomena of dream-distortion, which in my last chapter I traced to a psychical force acting as a censorship. My recollection of the monograph on the genus Cyclamen would thus serve the purpose of being an *allusion* to the conversation with my friend, just as the 'smoked salmon' in the dream of the abandoned supper-party [p. 148 f.] served as an *allusion* to the dreamer's thought of her woman friend. The only question is as to the intermediate links which enabled the impression of the monograph to serve as an allusion to the conversation with the eye-surgeon, since at first sight there is no obvious connection between them. In the example of the abandoned supper-party the connection was given at once: 'smoked salmon', being the friend's favourite dish, was an immediate constituent of the group of ideas which were likely to be aroused in the dreamer's mind by the personality of her friend. In this later example there were two detached impressions which at a first glance only had in common the fact of their having occurred on the same day: I had caught sight of the monograph in the morning and had had the conversation the same evening. The analysis enabled us to solve the problem as follows: connections of this kind, when they are not present in the first instance, are woven retrospectively between the ideational content of one impression and that of the other. I have already drawn attention to the intermediate links in the present case by the words I have italicized in my record of the analysis. If there had been no influences from another quarter, the idea of the monograph on the Cyclamen would only, I imagine, have led to the idea of its being my wife's favourite flower, and possibly also to Frau L.'s absent bouquet. I scarcely think that these background thoughts would have sufficed to evoke a dream. As we are told in *Hamlet*:

> There needs no ghost, my lord, come from the grave
> To tell us this.

But, lo and behold, I was reminded in the analysis that the man who interrupted our conversation was called *Gärtner* [Gardener] and that I had thought his wife looked *blooming*. And even as I write these words I recall that one of my patients, who bore the charming name of *Flora*, was for a time the pivot of our discussion. These must have been the intermediate links, arising from the botanical group of ideas, which formed the bridge between the two experiences of that day, the indifferent and the stirring one. A further set of connections was then established —those surrounding the idea of cocaine, which had every right to serve as a link between the figure of Dr. Königstein and a botanical monograph which I had written; and these connections strengthened the fusion between the two groups of ideas so that it became possible for a portion of the one experience to serve as an allusion to the other one.

I am prepared to find this explanation attacked on the ground of its being arbitrary or artificial. What, it may be asked, would have happened if Professor Gärtner and his wife with her blooming looks had not come up to us or if the patient we were talking about had been called Anna instead of Flora? The answer is simple. If these chains of thought had been absent others would no doubt have been selected. It is easy enough to construct such chains, as is shown by the puns and riddles that people make every day for their entertainment. The realm of jokes knows no boundaries. Or, to go a stage further, if there had been no possibility of forging enough intermediate links between the two impressions, the dream would simply have been different. Another indifferent impression of the same day—for crowds of such impressions enter our minds and are then forgotten— would have taken the place of the 'monograph' in the dream, would have linked up with the subject of the conversation and would have represented it in the content of the dream. Since it was in fact the monograph and not any other idea that was chosen to serve this function, we must suppose that it was the best adapted for the connection. There is no need for us to emulate Lessing's Hänschen Schlau and feel astonished that 'only the rich people own the most money'.[1]

A psychological process by which, according to our account, indifferent experiences take the place of psychically significant ones, cannot fail to arouse suspicion and bewilderment. It will be our task in a later chapter [Chapter VI, Section B (p. 305 ff.)] to make the peculiarities of this apparently irrational operation more intelligible. At this point we are only concerned with the *effects* of a process whose reality I have been driven to assume

[1] [From one of Lessing's *Sinngedichte* (epigrams in verse). A further lengthy discussion of this dream will be found below (p. 282 ff.).]

by innumerable and regularly recurrent observations made in analysing dreams. What takes place would seem to be something in the nature of a 'displacement'—of psychical emphasis, shall we say?—by means of intermediate links; in this way, ideas which originally had only a *weak* charge of intensity take over the charge from ideas which were originally *intensely* cathected [1] and at last attain enough strength to enable them to force an entry into consciousness. Displacements of this kind are no surprise to us where it is a question of dealing with quantities of *affect* or with motor activities in general. When a lonely old maid transfers her affection to animals, or a bachelor becomes an enthusiastic collector, when a soldier defends a scrap of coloured cloth—a flag—with his life's blood, when a few seconds' extra pressure in a hand-shake means bliss to a lover, or when, in *Othello*, a lost handkerchief precipitates an outburst of rage—all of these are instances of psychical displacements to which we raise no objection. But when we hear that a decision as to what shall reach our consciousness and what shall be kept out of it—what we shall *think*, in short—has been arrived at in the same manner and on the same principles, we have an impression of a pathological event and, if such things happen in waking life, we describe them as errors in thought. I will anticipate the conclusions to which we shall later be led, and suggest that the psychical process which we have found at work in dream-displacement, though it cannot be described as a pathological disturbance, nevertheless differs from the normal and is to be regarded as a process of a more *primary* nature. [See below, Chapter VII, Section E, p. 595 ff.]

Thus the fact that the content of dreams includes remnants of trivial experiences is to be explained as a manifestation of dream-distortion (by displacement); and it will be recalled that we came to the conclusion that dream-distortion was the product of a censorship operating in the passage-way between two psychical agencies. It is to be expected that the analysis of a dream will regularly reveal its true, psychically significant source in waking life, though the emphasis has been displaced from the recollection of that source on to that of an indifferent one. This explanation brings us into complete conflict with Robert's theory [p. 78 ff.], which ceases to be of any service to us. For the fact which Robert sets out to explain is a non-

[1] [Charged with psychical energy. See Editor's Introduction, p. xvii f.]

existent one. His acceptance of it rests on a misunderstanding, on his failure to replace the *apparent* content of dreams by their *real* meaning. And there is another objection that can be raised to Robert's theory. If it were really the business of dreams to relieve our memory of the 'dregs' of daytime recollections by a special psychical activity, our sleep would be more tormented and harder worked than our mental life while we are awake. For the number of indifferent impressions from which our memory would need to be protected is clearly immensely large: the night would not be long enough to cope with such a mass. It is far more likely that the process of forgetting indifferent impressions goes forward without the active intervention of our psychical forces.

Nevertheless we must not be in a hurry to take leave of Robert's ideas without further consideration. [See p. 579 f.] We have still not explained the fact that one of the indifferent impressions of waking life, one, moreover, dating from the day preceding the dream, invariably contributes towards the dream's content. The connections between this impression and the true source of the dream in the unconscious are not always there ready-made; as we have seen, they may only be established retrospectively, in the course of the dream-work,[1] with a view, as it were, to making the intended displacement feasible. There must therefore be some compelling force in the direction of establishing connections precisely with a recent, though indifferent, impression; and the latter must possess some attribute which makes it especially suitable for this purpose. For if that were not so, it would be just as easy for the dream-thoughts to displace their emphasis on to an unimportant component in their *own* circle of ideas.

The following observations may help us towards clearing up this point. If in the course of a single day we have two or more experiences suitable for provoking a dream, the dream will make a combined reference to them as a single whole; *it is under a necessity to combine them into a unity*. Here is an instance. One afternoon during the summer I entered a railway compartment in which I found two acquaintances who were strangers to each other. One of them was an eminent medical colleague and the other was a member of a distinguished family with which I had

[1] [This is the first mention of the fundamentally important concept to which the whole of the sixth and longest chapter of the book is devoted.]

professional relations. I introduced the two gentlemen to each other, but all through the long journey they conducted their conversation with me as a go-between, so that I presently found myself discussing various topics alternately, first with the one and then with the other. I asked my doctor friend to use his influence on behalf of a common acquaintance of ours who was just starting a medical practice. The doctor replied that he was convinced of the young man's capacity, but that his homely appearance would make it hard for him to make his way in families of the better class; to which I replied that that was the very reason why he needed influential assistance. Turning to my other fellow-traveller, I enquired after the health of his aunt —the mother of one of my patients—who was lying seriously ill at the time. During the night following the journey I had a dream that the young friend on whose behalf I had pleaded was sitting in a fashionable drawing-room in a select company composed of all the distinguished and wealthy people of my acquaintance and, with the easy bearing of a man of the world, was delivering a funeral oration on the old lady (who was already dead so far as my dream was concerned), the aunt of my second fellow-traveller. (I must confess that I had not been on good terms with that lady.) Thus my dream had, once again, worked out connections between the two sets of impressions of the previous day and had combined them into a single situation.

Many experiences such as this lead me to assert that the dream-work is under some kind of necessity to combine all the sources which have acted as stimuli for the dream into a single unity in the dream itself.[1]

I will now proceed to the question of whether the instigating source of a dream, revealed by analysis, must invariably be a recent (and significant) event or whether an internal experi-

---

[1] The tendency of the dream-work to fuse into a single action all events of interest which occur simultaneously has already been remarked on by several writers; e.g. Delage (1891, 41) and Delbœuf (1885, 237), who speaks of 'rapprochement forcé' ['enforced convergence']. [Freud himself had stated this principle in the passage in Studies on Hysteria (Breuer and Freud, 1895) quoted in the Editor's Introduction (p. xv).—At this point the following sentence was added in 1909 and included in every edition up to that of 1922, after which it was omitted: 'In a later chapter (on the dream-work) we shall come across this compelling impulse towards combining as an instance of "condensation"—another kind of primary psychical process.' (Cf. pp. 228 and 279 ff.)]

ence, that is, the *recollection* of a psychically important event—a train of thought—, can assume the rôle of a dream-instigator. The answer, based upon a large number of analyses, is most definitely in favour of the latter alternative. A dream can be instigated by an internal process which has, as it were, become a recent event, owing to thought-activity during the previous day.

This seems to be the appropriate moment for tabulating the different conditions to which we find that the sources of dreams are subject. The source of a dream may be either—

(*a*) a recent and psychically significant experience which is represented in the dream directly,[1] or

(*b*) several recent and significant experiences which are combined into a single unity by the dream,[2] or

(*c*) one or more recent and significant experiences which are represented in the content of the dream by a mention of a contemporary but indifferent experience,[3] or

(*d*) an internal significant experience (e.g. a memory or a train of thought), which is in that case *invariably* represented in the dream by a mention of a recent but indifferent impression.[4]

It will be seen that in interpreting dreams we find one condition always fulfilled: one component of the content of the dream is a repetition of a recent impression of the previous day. This impression that is to be represented in the dream may either itself belong to the circle of ideas surrounding the actual instigator of the dream—whether as an essential or as a trivial portion of it—or it may be derived from the field of an indifferent impression which has been brought into connection with the ideas surrounding the dream-instigator by more or less numerous links. The apparent multiplicity of governing conditions is in fact merely dependent upon the two alternatives of whether a displacement has or has not taken place; and it is worth pointing out that we are enabled by these alternatives to explain the range of contrast between different dreams just as easily as the medical theory is enabled to do by its hypothesis of brain-cells ranging from partial to total wakefulness. (See above, p. 76 ff.)

It will further be observed, if we consider these four possible

---

[1] As in the dream of Irma's injection [p. 106 ff.] and in the dream of my uncle with the yellow beard [p. 136 ff.].

[2] As in the young doctor's funeral oration [p. 178 f.].

[3] As in the dream of the botanical monograph [p. 169 ff.].

[4] Most of my patients' dreams during analysis are of this kind.

cases, that a psychical element which is significant but not recent (e.g. a train of thought or a memory) can be replaced, for the purpose of forming a dream, by an element which is recent but indifferent, provided only that two conditions are fulfilled: (1) the content of the dream must be connected with a recent experience, and (2) the instigator of the dream must remain a psychically significant process. Only in one case—case (a)—are both of these conditions fulfilled by one and the same impression. It is to be noticed, moreover, that indifferent impressions which are capable of being used for constructing a dream so long as they are recent lose that capacity as soon as they are a day (or at the most a few days) older. From this we must conclude that the freshness of an impression gives it some kind of psychical value for purposes of dream-construction equivalent in some way to the value of emotionally coloured memories or trains of thought. The basis of the value which thus attaches to recent impressions in connection with the construction of dreams will only become evident in the course of our subsequent psychological discussions.[1]

In this connection it will be noticed, incidentally, that modifications in our mnemic and ideational material may take place during the night unobserved by our consciousness. We are often advised that before coming to a final decision on some subject we should 'sleep on it', and this advice is evidently justified. But here we have passed from the psychology of dreams to that of sleep, and this is not the last occasion on which we shall be tempted to do so.[2]

An objection, however, may be raised which threatens to upset these last conclusions. If indifferent impressions can only

[1] See the passage on 'transference' in Chapter VII [p. 562 ff.].

[2] [*Footnote added* 1919:] An important contribution to the part played by recent material in the construction of dreams has been made by Pötzl (1917) in a paper which carries a wealth of implications. In a series of experiments Pötzl required the subjects to make a drawing of what they had consciously noted of a picture exposed to their view in a tachistoscope [an instrument for exposing an object to view for an extremely short time]. He then turned his attention to the dreams dreamt by the subjects during the following night and required them once more to make drawings of appropriate portions of these dreams. It was shown unmistakably that those details of the exposed picture which had not been noted by the subject provided material for the construction of the dream, whereas those details which had been consciously perceived and recorded in the drawing made after the exposure did not recur in the

find their way into a dream provided they are recent, how does it happen that the content of dreams also includes elements from an earlier period of life which at the time when they were recent possessed, to use Strümpell's words [1877, 40 f.], no psychical value, and should therefore have been long since forgotten—elements, that is to say, which are neither fresh nor psychically significant?

This objection can be completely dealt with by a reference to the findings of the psycho-analysis of neurotics. The explanation is that the displacement which replaces psychically important by indifferent material (alike in dreaming and in thinking) has in these cases already taken place at the early period of life in question and since then become fixed in the memory. These particular elements which were originally indifferent are indifferent no longer, since taking over (by means of displacement) the value of psychically significant material. Nothing that has *really* remained indifferent can be reproduced in a dream.

The reader will rightly conclude from the foregoing arguments that I am asserting that there are no indifferent dream-instigators—and consequently no 'innocent' dreams. Those are, in the strictest and most absolute sense, my opinions—if I leave on one side the dreams of children and perhaps brief reactions in dreams to sensations felt during the night. Apart from this, what we dream is either manifestly recognizable as psychically significant, or it is distorted and cannot be judged till the dream has been interpreted, after which it will once more be found to be significant. Dreams are never concerned with trivialities; we do not allow our sleep to be disturbed by trifles.[1] The appar-

manifest content of the dream. The material that was taken over by the dream-work was modified by it for the purposes of dream-construction in its familiar 'arbitrary' (or, more properly, 'autocratic') manner. The questions raised by Pötzl's experiment go far beyond the sphere of dream-interpretation as dealt with in the present volume. In passing, it is worth remarking on the contrast between this new method of studying the formation of dreams experimentally and the earlier, crude technique for introducing into the dream stimuli which interrupted the subject's sleep. [Cf. p. 223 n.]

[1] [*Footnote added* 1914:] Havelock Ellis, a friendly critic of this book, writes (1911, 166): 'This is the point at which many of us are no longer able to follow Freud.' Havelock Ellis has not, however, carried out any analyses of dreams and refuses to believe how impossible it is to base one's judgement on their manifest content.

ently innocent dreams turn out to be quite the reverse when we take the trouble to analyse them. They are, if I may say so, wolves in sheep's clothing. Since this is another point upon which I may expect to be contradicted, and since I am glad of an opportunity of showing dream-distortion at work, I will select a number of 'innocent' dreams from my records and submit them to analysis.

I

An intelligent and cultivated young woman, reserved and undemonstrative in her behaviour, reported as follows: *I dreamt that I arrived too late at the market and could get nothing either from the butcher or from the woman who sells vegetables.* An innocent dream, no doubt; but dreams are not as simple as that, so I asked to be told it in greater detail. She thereupon gave me the following account. *She dreamt she was going to the market with her cook, who was carrying the basket. After she had asked for something, the butcher said to her: 'That's not obtainable any longer', and offered her something else, adding 'This is good too'. She rejected it and went on to the woman who sells vegetables, who tried to get her to buy a peculiar vegetable that was tied up in bundles but was of a black colour. She said: 'I don't recognize that; I won't take it.'*

The dream's connection with the previous day was quite straightforward. She had actually gone to the market too late and had got nothing. The situation seemed to shape itself into the phrase '*Die Fleischbank war schon geschlossen*' ['the meat-shop was closed']. I pulled myself up: was not that, or rather its opposite, a vulgar description of a certain sort of slovenliness in a man's dress?[1] However, the dreamer herself did not use the phrase; she may perhaps have avoided using it. Let us endeavour, then, to arrive at an interpretation of the details of the dream.

When anything in a dream has the character of direct speech, that is to say, when it is said or heard and not merely thought (and it is easy as a rule to make the distinction with certainty), then it is derived from something actually spoken in waking life—though, to be sure, this something is merely treated as raw material and may be cut up and slightly altered and, more

[1] ['*Du hast deine Fleischbank offen*' ('your meat-shop's open'): Viennese slang for 'your flies are undone'.]

especially, divorced from its context.[1] In carrying out an interpretation, one method is to start from spoken phrases of this kind. What, then, was the origin of the butcher's remark '*That's not obtainable any longer*'? The answer was that it came from me myself. A few days earlier I had explained to the patient that the earliest experiences of childhood were '*not obtainable any longer as such*', but were replaced in analysis by 'transferences' and dreams.[2] So *I* was the butcher and she was rejecting these transferences into the present of old habits of thinking and feeling.— What, again, was the origin of her own remark in the dream '*I don't recognize that; I won't take it*'? For the purposes of the analysis this had to be divided up. '*I don't recognize that*' was something she had said the day before to her cook, with whom she had had a dispute; but at the time she had gone on: '*Behave yourself properly!*' At this point there had clearly been a displacement. Of the two phrases that she had used in the dispute with her cook, she had chosen the insignificant one for inclusion in the dream. But it was only the suppressed one, '*Behave yourself properly!*' that fitted in with the rest of the content of the dream: those would have been the appropriate words to use if someone had ventured to make improper suggestions and had forgotten 'to close his meat-shop'. The allusions underlying the incident with the vegetable-seller were a further confirmation that our interpretation was on the right track. A vegetable that is sold tied up in bundles (lengthways, as the patient added afterwards) and is also black, could only be a dream-combination of asparagus and black (Spanish) radishes. No knowledgeable person of either sex will ask for an interpretation of asparagus. But the other vegetable—'*Schwarzer Rettig*' ['black radish']—can be taken as an exclamation—'*Schwarzer, rett' dich!*' ['Blacky! Be off!']—[3];

---

[1] See my discussion of speeches in dreams in my chapter on the dream-work [p. 418 ff.]. Only one writer on the subject seems to have recognized the source of spoken phrases occurring in dreams, namely Delbœuf (1885, 226), who compares them to *clichés*. [This dream is briefly recorded in Section VII of Freud's short essay *On Dreams* (1901*a*); *Standard Ed.*, 5, 668.]

[2] [This passage is referred to in a footnote to a discussion of childhood memories in Section V of Freud's case history of the 'Wolf Man' (1918*b*).]

[3] [It seems probable that this is a reminiscence of a picture puzzle or rebus of the kind so common in the pages of *Fliegende Blätter* and similar comic papers.]

and accordingly it too seems to hint at the same sexual topic which we suspected at the very beginning, when we felt inclined to introduce the phrase about the meat-shop being closed into the original account of the dream. We need not enquire now into the full meaning of the dream. So much is quite clear: it *had* a meaning and that meaning was far from innocent.[1]

II

Here is another innocent dream, dreamt by the same patient, and in a sense a counterpart to the last one. *Her husband asked her: 'Don't you think we ought to have the piano tuned?' And she replied: 'It's not worth while; the hammers need reconditioning in any case.'*

Once again this was a repetition of a real event of the previous day. Her husband had asked this question and she had made some such reply. But what was the explanation of her dreaming it? She told me that the piano was a *disgusting* old *box*, that it made an *ugly noise*, that it had been in her husband's possession before their marriage,[2] and so on. But the key to the solution was only given by her words: '*It's not worth while.*' These were derived from a visit she had paid the day before to a woman friend. She had been invited to take off her jacket, but had refused with the words: 'Thank you, but *it's not worth while*; I can only stop a minute.' As she was telling me this, I recollected that during the previous day's analysis she had suddenly caught hold of her jacket, one of the buttons having come undone. Thus it was as though she were saying: 'Please don't look; *it's not worth while.*' In the same way the 'box' ['*Kasten*'] was a

---

[1] If anyone is curious to know, I may add that the dream concealed a phantasy of my behaving in an improper and sexually provocative manner, and of the patient putting up a defence against my conduct. If this interpretation seems incredible, I need only point to the numerous instances in which doctors have charges of the same kind brought against them by hysterical women. But in such cases the phantasy emerges into consciousness undisguised and in the form of a delusion, instead of being distorted and appearing only as a dream.—[*Added* 1909:] This dream occurred at the beginning of the patient's psycho-analytic treatment. It was not until later that I learnt that she had been repeating in it the initial trauma from which her neurosis had arisen. I have since then come across the same behaviour in other patients; having been exposed to a sexual assault in their childhood, they seek, as it were, to bring about a repetition of it in their dreams.

[2] This last was a substitute for the opposite idea, as the course of the analysis will make clear.

substitute for a 'chest' ['*Brustkasten*']; and the interpretation of the dream led us back at once to the time of her physical development at puberty, when she had begun to be dissatisfied by her figure. We can hardly doubt that it led back to still earlier times, if we take the word '*disgusting*' into account and the '*ugly noise*', and if we remember how often—both in *doubles entendres* and in dreams—the lesser hemispheres of a woman's body are used, whether as contrasts or as substitutes, for the larger ones.

III

I will interrupt this series for a moment and insert a short innocent dream produced by a young man. He dreamt that *he was putting on his winter overcoat once more, which was a dreadful thing.* The ostensible reason for this dream was a sudden return of cold weather. If we look more closely, however, we shall notice that the two short pieces that make up the dream are not in complete harmony. For what could there be 'dreadful' about putting on a heavy or thick overcoat in cold weather? Moreover, the innocence of the dream was decidedly upset by the first association that occurred to the dreamer in the analysis. He recalled that a lady confided to him the day before that her youngest child owed its existence to a torn condom. On that basis he was able to reconstruct his thoughts. A thin condom was dangerous, but a thick one was bad. The condom was suitably represented as an overcoat, since one slips into both of them. But an occurrence such as the lady described to him would certainly be 'dreadful' for an unmarried man.

And now let us return to our innocent lady dreamer.

IV

She was putting a candle into a candlestick; but the candle broke so that it wouldn't stand up properly. The girls at her school said she was clumsy; but the mistress said it was not her fault.

Yet again the occasion for the dream was a real event. The day before she had actually put a candle into a candlestick, though it did not break. Some transparent symbolism was being used in this dream. A candle is an object which can excite the female genitals; and, if it is broken, so that it cannot stand up properly, it means that the man is impotent. ('*It was not her fault.*') But could a carefully brought-up young woman, who had been screened from the impact of anything ugly, have known that a candle might be put to such a use? As it happened, she was able to indicate how it was that she obtained this piece of knowledge. Once when they were in a rowing boat on the Rhine, another boat had passed them with some students in it. They were in high spirits and were singing, or rather shouting, a song:

> Wenn die Königin von Schweden,
> Bei geschlossenen Fensterläden
> Mit Apollokerzen . . .[1]

She either failed to hear or did not understand the last word and had to get her husband to give her the necessary explanation. The verse was replaced in the content of the dream by an innocent recollection of some job she had done clumsily when she was at school, and the replacement was made possible owing to the common element of *closed shutters*. The connection between the topics of masturbation and impotence is obvious enough. The 'Apollo' in the latent content of this dream linked it with an earlier one in which the virgin Pallas figured. Altogether far from innocent.

V

In order that we may not be tempted to draw conclusions too easily from dreams as to the dreamer's actual life, I will add one more dream of the same patient's, which once more has an innocent appearance. '*I dreamt*,' she said, '*of what I really did yesterday: I filled a small trunk so full of books that I had difficulty in shutting it and I dreamt just what really happened.*' In this instance the narrator herself laid the chief emphasis on the agreement between the dream and reality. [Cf. pp. 21 *n.* and 372.] All such judgements on a dream and comments upon it, though they have made themselves a place in waking thought, invariably form in fact part of the latent content of the dream, as we shall find confirmed by other examples later on [p. 445 ff.]. What we were being told, then, was that what the dream described had really happened the day before. It would take up too much

---

[1] ['When the Queen of Sweden, behind closed shutters, . . . with Apollo candles.' 'Apollo candles' was the trade name of a familiar brand of candles. This is an extract from a well-known students' song, which has innumerable similar stanzas. The missing word is '*onaniert*' ('masturbates').]

space to explain how it was that the idea occurred to me of making use of the English language in the interpretation. It is enough to say that once again what was in question was a little 'box' (cf. the dream of the dead child in the 'case', p. 154 f.) which was so full that nothing more could get into it. Anyhow, nothing bad this time.

In all of these 'innocent' dreams the motive for the censorship is obviously the sexual factor. This, however, is a subject of prime importance which I must leave on one side.

INFANTILE MATERIAL AS A SOURCE OF DREAMS

Like every other writer on the subject, with the exception of Robert, I have pointed out as a third peculiarity of the content of dreams that it may include impressions which date back to earliest childhood, and which seem not to be accessible to waking memory. It is naturally hard to determine how rarely or how frequently this occurs, since the origin of the dream-elements in question is not recognized after waking. Proof that what we are dealing with are impressions from childhood must therefore be established by external evidence and there is seldom an opportunity for doing this. A particularly convincing example is that given by Maury [1878, 143 f., quoted on p. 16 f. above] of the man who determined one day to revisit his old home after an absence of more than twenty years. During the night before his departure he dreamt that he was in a totally unknown place and there met an unknown man in the street and had a conversation with him. When he reached his home, he found that the unknown place was a real one in the immediate neighbourhood of his native town, and the unknown man in the dream turned out to be a friend of his dead father's who was still living there. This was conclusive evidence that he had seen both the man and the place in his childhood. This dream is also to be interpreted as a dream of impatience like that of the girl with the concert-ticket in her pocket (p. 152 f.), that of the child whose father had promised to take her on an excursion to the Hameau (cf. p. 129 f.), and similar ones. The motives which led the dreamers to reproduce one particular impression from their childhood rather than any other cannot, of course, be discovered without an analysis.

Someone who attended a course of lectures of mine and boasted that his dreams very seldom underwent distortion reported to me that not long before he had dreamt of seeing *his former tutor in bed with the nurse* who had been with his family till his eleventh year. In the dream he had identified the locality where the scene occurred. His interest had been aroused and he had reported the dream to his elder brother, who had laughingly confirmed the truth of what he had dreamt. His brother remembered it very well, as he had been six years old at the time. The lovers had been in the habit of making the elder boy drunk with beer, whenever circumstances were favourable for intercourse during the night. The younger boy—the dreamer—, who was then three years old and slept in the room with the nurse, was not regarded as an impediment. [See also p. 198.]

There is another way in which it can be established with certainty without the assistance of interpretation that a dream contains elements from childhood. This is where the dream is of what has been called the 'recurrent' type: that is to say, where a dream was first dreamt in childhood and then constantly reappears from time to time during adult sleep.[1] I am able to add to the familiar examples of such dreams a few from my own records, though I have never myself experienced one. A physician in his thirties told me that from the earliest days of his childhood to the present time a yellow lion frequently appeared in his dreams; he was able to give a minute description of it. This lion out of his dreams made its appearance one day in bodily form, as a china ornament that had long disappeared. The young man then learnt from his mother that this object had been his favourite toy during his early childhood, though he himself had forgotten the fact.[2]

If we turn now from the manifest content of dreams to the dream-thoughts which only analysis uncovers, we find to our

[1] [See above, p. 44 n. Some remarks on 'recurrent' dreams will be found in Freud's 'Fragment of an Analysis of a Case of Hysteria' (1905e), at the end of the synthesis of Dora's first dream (Section II). Cf. below, p. 579 n.]

[2] [The following further dream appeared at this point in the first edition (1900) only. A note in *Ges. Schriften*, 3 (1925), 38, remarks that it was rightly omitted in all subsequent editions: 'Dreams of this sort are of a *typical* character and correspond not to memories but to phantasies, whose meaning it is not hard to guess.' Here are the cancelled sentences: 'One of my women patients dreamt the same dream—a scene filled with anxiety—four or five times during her thirty-eighth year. She was being pursued, fled into a room, shut the door, and then opened it again to take out the key, which was on the outside of the door. She had a feeling that if she failed something frightful would happen. She got hold of the key, locked the door from the inside and gave a sigh of relief. I cannot say to what age we should assign this little scene, in which, of course, she had only played the part of an audience.']

astonishment that experiences from childhood also play a part in dreams whose content would never have led one to suppose it. I owe a particularly agreeable and instructive example of a dream of this kind to my respected colleague of the yellow lion. After reading Nansen's narrative of his polar expedition, he had a dream of being in a field of ice and of giving the gallant explorer galvanic treatment for an attack of sciatica from which he was suffering. In the course of analysing the dream, he thought of a story dating from his childhood, which alone, incidentally, made the dream intelligible. One day, when he was a child of three or four, he had heard the grown-ups talking of voyages of discovery and had asked his father whether that was a serious illness. He had evidently confused '*Reisen*' ['voyages'] with '*Reissen*' ['gripes'], and his brothers and sisters saw to it that he never forgot this embarrassing mistake.

There was a similar instance of this when, in the course of my analysis of the dream of the monograph on the genus Cyclamen [see above, p. 172], I stumbled upon the childhood memory of my father, when I was a boy of five, giving me a book illustrated with coloured plates to destroy. It may perhaps be doubted whether this memory really had any share in determining the form taken by the content of the dream or whether it was not rather that the process of analysis built up the connection subsequently. But the copious and intertwined associative links warrant our accepting the former alternative: cyclamen—favourite flower—favourite food—artichokes; pulling to pieces like an artichoke, leaf by leaf (a phrase constantly ringing in our ears in relation to the piecemeal dismemberment of the Chinese Empire)—herbarium—book-worms, whose favourite food is books. Moreover I can assure my readers that the ultimate meaning of the dream, which I have not disclosed, is intimately related to the subject of the childhood scene.

In the case of another group of dreams, analysis shows us that the actual wish which instigated the dream, and the fulfilment of which is represented by the dream, is derived from childhood; so that, to our surprise, *we find the child and the child's impulses still living on in the dream.*

At this point I shall once more take up the interpretation of a dream which we have already found instructive—the dream of my friend R. being my uncle. [See p. 137 ff.] We have followed its interpretation to the point of recognizing clearly as one of its motives my wish to be appointed to a professorship; and we explained the affection I felt in the dream for my friend R. as a product of opposition and revolt against the slanders upon my two colleagues which were contained in the dream-thoughts. The dream was one of my own; I may therefore continue its analysis by saying that my feelings were not yet satisfied by the solution that had so far been reached. I knew that my waking judgement upon the colleagues who were so ill-used in the dream-thoughts would have been a very different one; and the force of my wish not to share their fate in the matter of the appointment struck me as insufficient to explain the contradiction between my waking and dreaming estimates of them. If it was indeed true that my craving to be addressed with a different title was as strong as all that, it showed a pathological ambition which I did not recognize in myself and which I believed was alien to me. I could not tell how other people who believed they knew me would judge me in this respect. It might be that I was really ambitious; but, if so, my ambition had long ago been transferred to objects quite other than the title and rank of *professor extraordinarius*.

What, then, could have been the origin of the ambitiousness which produced the dream in me? At that point I recalled an anecdote I had often heard repeated in my childhood. At the time of my birth an old peasant-woman had prophesied to my proud mother that with her first-born child she had brought a great man into the world. Prophecies of this kind must be very common: there are so many mothers filled with happy expectations and so many old peasant-women and others of the kind who make up for the loss of their power to control things in the present world by concentrating it on the future. Nor can the prophetess have lost anything by her words. Could this have been the source of my thirst for grandeur? But that reminded me of another experience, dating from my later childhood, which provided a still better explanation. My parents had been in the habit, when I was a boy of eleven or twelve, of taking me with them to the Prater.[1] One evening, while we were sitting in a restaurant there, our attention had been attracted by a man who was moving from one table to another and, for a small

[1] [The famous park on the outskirts of Vienna.]

consideration, improvising a verse upon any topic presented to him. I was despatched to bring the poet to our table and he showed his gratitude to the messenger. Before enquiring what the chosen topic was to be, he had dedicated a few lines to myself; and he had been inspired to declare that I should probably grow up to be a Cabinet Minister. I still remembered quite well what an impression this second prophecy had made on me. Those were the days of the '*Bürger*' Ministry.[1] Shortly before, my father had brought home portraits of these middle-class professional men—Herbst, Giskra, Unger, Berger and the rest—and we had illuminated the house in their honour. There had even been some Jews among them. So henceforth every industrious Jewish schoolboy carried a Cabinet Minister's portfolio in his satchel. The events of that period no doubt had some bearing on the fact that up to a time shortly before I entered the University it had been my intention to study Law; it was only at the last moment that I changed my mind. A ministerial career is definitely barred to a medical man. But now to return to my dream. It began to dawn on me that my dream had carried me back from the dreary present to the cheerful hopes of the days of the '*Bürger*' Ministry, and that the wish that it had done its best to fulfil was one dating back to those times. In mishandling my two learned and eminent colleagues because they were Jews, and in treating the one as a simpleton and the other as a criminal, I was behaving as though I were the Minister, I had put myself in the Minister's place. Turning the tables on His Excellency with a vengeance! He had refused to appoint me *professor extraordinarius* and I had retaliated in the dream by stepping into his shoes.[2]

In another instance it became apparent that, though the wish which instigated the dream was a present-day one, it had received a powerful reinforcement from memories that stretched far back into childhood. What I have in mind is a series of dreams which are based upon a longing to visit Rome. For a long time to come, no doubt, I shall have to continue to satisfy that

[1] [The 'Middle-class Ministry'—a government of liberal complexion, elected after the new Austrian constitution was established in 1867.]

[2] [In an amusing letter to Fliess of March 11, 1902 (Freud, 1950*a*, Letter 152), Freud tells the story of how he came actually to be appointed to a professorship, two years after the publication of this book.]

longing in my dreams: for at the season of the year when it is possible for me to travel, residence in Rome must be avoided for reasons of health.[1] For instance, I dreamt once that I was looking out of a railway-carriage window at the Tiber and the Ponte Sant' Angelo. The train began to move off, and it occurred to me that I had not so much as set foot in the city. The view that I had seen in my dream was taken from a well-known engraving which I had caught sight of for a moment the day before in the sitting-room of one of my patients. Another time someone led me to the top of a hill and showed me Rome half-shrouded in mist; it was so far away that I was surprised at my view of it being so clear. There was more in the content of this dream than I feel prepared to detail; but the theme of 'the promised land seen from afar' was obvious in it. The town which I saw in this way for the first time, shrouded in mist, was —Lübeck, and the prototype of the hill was—at Gleichenberg.[2] In a third dream I had at last got to Rome, as the dream itself informed me; but I was disappointed to find that the scenery was far from being of an urban character. *There was a narrow stream of dark water; on one side of it were black cliffs and on the other meadows with big white flowers. I noticed a Herr Zucker* (whom I knew slightly) *and determined to ask him the way to the city.* I was clearly making a vain attempt to see in my dream a city which I had never seen in my waking life. Breaking up the landscape in the dream into its elements, I found that the white flowers took me to Ravenna, which I have visited and which, for a time at least, superseded Rome as capital of Italy. In the marshes round Ravenna we found the loveliest water-lilies growing in black water. Because we had had such difficulty in picking them out of the water, the dream made them grow in meadows like the narcissi at our own Aussee. The dark cliff, so close to the water, reminded me vividly of the valley of the Tepl near Karlsbad. '*Karlsbad*' enabled me to explain the curious detail of my having asked Herr Zucker the way. The material out of which the dream was woven included at this point two of those

---

[1] [*Footnote added* 1909:] I discovered long since that it only needs a little courage to fulfil wishes which till then have been regarded as unattainable; [*added* 1925:] and thereafter became a constant pilgrim to Rome. [The correspondence with Fliess (Freud, 1950a) gives repeated evidence of the emotional importance to Freud of the idea of visiting Rome. He first fulfilled this wish in the summer of 1901 (Letter 146).]

[2] [An Austrian spa in Styria, not far from Graz.]

facetious Jewish anecdotes which contain so much profound and
often bitter worldly wisdom and which we so greatly enjoy quoting in our talk and letters.[1] Here is the first one: the *'constitution'*
story. An impecunious Jew had stowed himself away without a
ticket in the fast train to *Karlsbad*. He was caught, and each time
tickets were inspected he was taken out of the train and treated
more and more severely. At one of the stations on his *via
dolorosa* he met an acquaintance, who asked him where he was
travelling to. 'To Karlsbad,' was his reply, 'if my constitution
can stand it.' My memory then passed on to another story: of
a Jew who could not speak French and had been recommended
when he was in Paris to ask the way to the rue Richelieu. Paris
itself had for many long years been another goal of my longings;
and the blissful feelings with which I first set foot on its pavement seemed to me a guarantee that others of my wishes would
be fulfilled as well. 'Asking the way', moreover, was a direct
allusion to *Rome*, since it is well known that all roads lead there.
Again, the name *Zucker* [sugar] was once more an allusion to
Karlsbad; for we are in the habit of prescribing treatment there
for anyone suffering from the *constitutional* complaint of diabetes.[2]
The instigation to this dream had been a proposal made by my
friend in Berlin that we should meet in Prague at Easter. What
we were going to discuss there would have included something
with a further connection with 'sugar' and 'diabetes'.

A fourth dream, which occurred soon after the last one, took
me to Rome once more. I saw a street-corner before me and was
surprised to find so many posters in German stuck up there.[3] I
had written to my friend with prophetic foresight the day before
to say that I thought Prague might not be an agreeable place
for a German to walk about in. Thus the dream expressed at the
same time a wish to meet him in Rome instead of in a Bohemian

---

[1] [In a letter to Fliess of June 12, 1897 (Freud, 1950*a*, Letter 65),
Freud mentions that he is making a collection of these anecdotes, of
which he was to make great use in his book on jokes (Freud, 1905*c*).
The first of the present anecdotes is alluded to more than once in his
letters, and Rome and Karlsbad come to be identified as symbols of
unattainable aims (e.g. in Letters 112 and 130).]

[2] [The German word for 'diabetes' is *'Zuckerkrankheit'* ('sugar-
disease').]

[3] [This dream is discussed in a letter to Fliess of December 3, 1897
(Freud, 1950*a*, Letter 77). The meeting in Prague was probably in the
early part of the same year (see Letter 58, of February 8, 1897).]

town, and a desire, probably dating back to my student days, that the German language might be better tolerated in Prague. Incidentally, I must have understood Czech in my earliest childhood, for I was born in a small town in Moravia which has a Slav population. A Czech nursery rhyme, which I heard in my seventeenth year, printed itself on my memory so easily that I can repeat it to this day, though I have no notion what it means. Thus there was no lack of connections with my early childhood in these dreams either.

It was on my last journey to Italy, which, among other places, took me past Lake Trasimene, that finally—after having seen the Tiber and sadly turned back when I was only fifty miles from Rome—I discovered the way in which my longing for the eternal city had been reinforced by impressions from my youth. I was in the act of making a plan to by-pass Rome next year and travel to Naples, when a sentence occurred to me which I must have read in one of our classical authors:[1] 'Which of the two, it may be debated, walked up and down his study with the greater impatience after he had formed his plan of going to Rome—Winckelmann, the Vice-Principal, or Hannibal, the Commander-in-Chief?' I had actually been following in Hannibal's footsteps. Like him, I had been fated not to see Rome; and he too had moved into the Campagna when everyone had expected him in Rome. But Hannibal, whom I had come to resemble in these respects, had been the favourite hero of my later school days. Like so many boys of that age, I had sympathized in the Punic Wars not with the Romans but with the Carthaginians. And when in the higher classes I began to understand for the first time what it meant to belong to an alien race, and anti-semitic feelings among the other boys warned me that I must take up a definite position, the figure of the semitic general rose still higher in my esteem. To my youthful mind Hannibal and Rome symbolized the conflict between the tenacity of Jewry and the organization of the Catholic church. And the increasing importance of the effects of the anti-semitic movement upon our emotional life helped to fix the thoughts and feelings of those early days. Thus the wish to go to Rome

[1] [Footnote added 1925:] The author in question must no doubt have been Jean Paul.—[His decision to visit Rome was the turning-point in the career of Winckelmann, the eighteenth-century founder of classical archaeology.]

had become in my dream-life a cloak and symbol for a number of other passionate wishes. Their realization was to be pursued with all the perseverance and single-mindedness of the Carthaginian, though their fulfilment seemed at the moment just as little favoured by destiny as was Hannibal's lifelong wish to enter Rome.

At that point I was brought up against the event in my youth whose power was still being shown in all these emotions and dreams. I may have been ten or twelve years old, when my father began to take me with him on his walks and reveal to me in his talk his views upon things in the world we live in. Thus it was, on one such occasion, that he told me a story to show me how much better things were now than they had been in his days. 'When I was a young man', he said, 'I went for a walk one Saturday in the streets of your birthplace; I was well dressed, and had a new fur cap on my head. A Christian came up to me and with a single blow knocked off my cap into the mud and shouted: "Jew! get off the pavement!" ' 'And what did you do?' I asked. 'I went into the roadway and picked up my cap,' was his quiet reply. This struck me as unheroic conduct on the part of the big, strong man who was holding the little boy by the hand. I contrasted this situation with another which fitted my feelings better: the scene in which Hannibal's father, Hamilcar Barca,[1] made his boy swear before the household altar to take vengeance on the Romans. Ever since that time Hannibal had had a place in my phantasies.

I believe I can trace my enthusiasm for the Carthaginian general a step further back into my childhood; so that once more it would only have been a question of a transference of an already formed emotional relation on to a new object. One of the first books that I got hold of when I had learnt to read was Thiers' history of the Consulate and Empire. I can still remember sticking labels on the flat backs of my wooden soldiers with the names of Napoleon's marshals written on them. And at that time my declared favourite was already Masséna (or to give the name its Jewish form, Manasseh).[2] (No

---

[1] [*Footnote added* 1909:] In the first edition the name of Hasdrubal appeared instead: a puzzling mistake, which I have explained in my *Psychopathology of Everyday Life* (1901b), Chapter X (2).

[2] [*Footnote added* 1930:] Incidentally, doubts have been thrown on the Marshal's Jewish origin.

doubt this preference was also partly to be explained by the fact that my birthday fell on the same day as his, exactly a hundred years later.)[1] Napoleon himself lines up with Hannibal owing to their both having crossed the Alps. It may even be that the development of this martial ideal is traceable still further back into my childhood: to the times when, at the age of three, I was in a close relation, sometimes friendly but sometimes warlike, with a boy a year older than myself, and to the wishes which that relation must have stirred up in the weaker of us.[2]

The deeper one carries the analysis of a dream, the more often one comes upon the track of experiences in childhood which have played a part among the sources of that dream's latent content.

We have already seen (on p. 21) that a dream very seldom reproduces recollections in such a way that they constitute, without abbreviation or modification, the *whole* of its manifest content. Nevertheless there are some undoubted instances of this happening: and I can add a few more, relating, once more, to childhood scenes. One of my patients was presented in a dream with an almost undistorted reproduction of a sexual episode, which was at once recognizable as a true recollection. His memory of the event had, in fact, never been completely lost in waking life, though it had become greatly obscured, and its revival was a consequence of work previously done in analysis. At the age of twelve, the dreamer had gone to visit a school friend who was laid up in bed, when the latter, by what was probably an accidental movement, uncovered his body. At the sight of his friend's genitals, my patient had been overcome by some sort of compulsion and had uncovered himself too and caught hold of the other's penis. His friend looked at him with indignation and astonishment; whereupon, overcome by embarrassment, he let go. This scene was repeated in a dream twenty-three years later, including all the details of his feelings at the time. It was modified, however, to this extent, that the dreamer assumed the passive instead of the active role, while the figure of his school-friend was replaced by someone belonging to his contemporary life. [See also p. 189.]

---

[1] [This sentence was added in 1914.]

[2] [A fuller account of this will be found on pp. 424 f. and 483 f.]

It is true that as a rule the childhood scene is only represented in the dream's manifest content by an allusion, and has to be arrived at by an interpretation of the dream. Such instances when they are recorded, cannot carry much conviction, since as a rule there is no other evidence of these childhood experiences having occurred: if they date back to a very early age they are no longer recognized as memories. The general justification for inferring the occurrence of these childhood experiences from dreams is provided by a whole number of factors in psychoanalytic work, which are mutually consistent and thus seem sufficiently trustworthy. If I record some of these inferred childhood experiences torn from their context for the purposes of dream-interpretation, they may perhaps create little impression, especially as I shall not even be able to quote all the material on which the interpretations were based. Nevertheless I shall not allow this to deter me from relating them.

I

All the dreams of one of my women patients were characterized by her being 'rushed': she would be in a violent rush to get somewhere in time not to miss a train, and so on. In one dream *she was going to call on a woman friend; her mother told her to take a cab and not to walk; but she ran instead and kept on falling down.*—The material which came up in analysis led to memories of *rushing* about and romping as a child. One particular dream recalled the favourite children's game of saying a sentence '*Die Kuh rannte, bis sie fiel*' ['The cow ran till it fell'] so quickly that it sounds as though it were a single [nonsensical] word—another *rush* in fact. All these innocent rushings-about with little girl friends were remembered because they took the place of other, less innocent ones.

II

Here is another woman patient's dream: *She was in a big room in which all sorts of machines were standing, like what she imagined an orthopaedic institute to be. She was told I had no time and that she must have her treatment at the same time as five others. She refused, however, and would not lie down in the bed—or whatever it was—that was meant for her. She stood in the corner and waited for me to say it wasn't true. Meanwhile the others were laughing at her and saying it was just her way of 'carrying on'.*—Simultaneously, it was as though she was making a lot of small squares.

The first part of the content of this dream related to the treatment and was a transference on to me. The second part contained an allusion to a scene in childhood. The two parts were linked together by the mention of the bed.

The *orthopaedic institute* referred back to a remark I had made in which I had compared the treatment, alike in its length and in its nature, to an *orthopaedic* one. When I started her treatment I had been obliged to tell her that for the time being *I had not much time for her*, though later I should be able to give her a whole hour daily. This had stirred up her old sensitiveness, which is a principal trait in the character of children inclined to hysteria: they are insatiable for love. My patient had been the youngest of a family of six children (hence: *at the same time as five others*) and had therefore been her father's favourite; but even so she seems to have felt that her adored father devoted too little of his time and attention to her.—Her *waiting for me to say it wasn't true* had the following origin. A young tailor's apprentice had brought her a dress and she had given him the money for it. Afterwards she had asked her husband whether if the boy lost the money she would have to pay it over again. Her husband, to *tease* her, had said that was so. (The *teasing* in the dream.) She kept on asking over and over again and *waited for him to say after all it wasn't true*. It was then possible to infer that in the latent content of the dream she had had a thought of whether she would have to pay me twice as much if I gave her twice as much time—a thought which she felt was avaricious or *filthy*. (Uncleanliness in childhood is often replaced in dreams by avariciousness for money; the link between the two is the word 'filthy'.[1]) If the whole passage about *waiting for me to say*, etc., was intended in the dream as a circumlocution for the word 'filthy', then her '*standing in the corner*' and '*not lying down in the bed*' would fit in with it as constituents of a scene from her childhood: a scene in which she had dirtied her bed and been punished by being made to stand in the corner, with a threat that her father would not love her any more and her brothers and sisters would laugh at her, and so on.—The *small squares* related to her little niece, who had shown her the arithmetical trick of arranging the digits in nine squares (I believe this is correct) so that they add up in all directions to fifteen.

[1] [This point was later enlarged upon by Freud (1908*b*). But it already occurs in a letter to Fliess of December 22, 1897 (Freud, 1950*a*, Letter 79).]

III

A man dreamt as follows: *He saw two boys struggling—barrel-maker's boys, to judge by the implements lying around. One of the boys threw the other down; the boy on the ground had ear-rings with blue stones. He hurried towards the offender with his stick raised, to chastise him. The latter fled for protection to a woman, who was standing by a wooden fence, as though she was his mother. She was a woman of the working classes and her back was turned to the dreamer. At last she turned round and gave him a terrible look so that he ran off in terror. The red flesh of the lower lids of her eyes could be seen standing out.*

The dream had made copious use of trivial events of the previous day. He had in fact seen two boys in the street, one of whom threw the other down. When he hurried up to stop the fight they had both taken to their heels.—*Barrel-maker's boys.* This was only explained by a subsequent dream in which he used the phrase '*knocking the bottom out of a barrel*'.—From his experience he believed that *ear-rings with blue stones* were mostly worn by prostitutes. A line from a well-known piece of doggerel about *two boys* then occurred to him: 'The other boy was called Marie' (i.e. was a girl).—*The woman standing.* After the scene with the two boys he had gone for a walk along the bank of the Danube and had profited by the loneliness of the spot to micturate against *a wooden fence.* Further on, a respectably dressed elderly lady had smiled at him in a very friendly manner and had wanted to give him her visiting-card. Since the woman in the dream was standing in the same position as he had been in when he was micturating, it must have been a question of a micturating woman. This tallies with her terrible *look* and the *red flesh standing out*, which could only relate to the gaping of the genitals caused by stooping. This, seen in his childhood, re-appeared in later memory as '*proud flesh*'—as a wound.

The dream combined two opportunities he had had as a little boy of seeing little girls' genitals: when they were *thrown down* and when they were *micturating.* And from the other part of the context it emerged that he had a recollection of being *chastised* or threatened by his father for the sexual curiosity he had evinced on these occasions.

IV

Behind the following dream (dreamt by an elderly lady)

there lay a whole quantity of childhood memories, combined, as best they might be, into a single phantasy.

She went out in a violent rush to do some commissions. In the Graben[1] *she sank down on her knees, as though she was quite broken-down. A large number of people collected round her, especially cab-drivers; but no one helped her up. She made several vain attempts, and she must at last have succeeded, for she was put into a cab which was to take her home. Someone threw a big, heavily-laden basket (like a shopping-basket) in through the window after her.*

This was the same lady who always felt 'rushed' in her dreams, just as she had rushed and romped about when she was a child. [See above, p. 199.] The first scene in the dream was evidently derived from the sight of a horse fallen down; in the same way the word '*broken-down*' referred to horse-racing. In her youth she had ridden horses, and no doubt when she was still younger she had actually *been* a horse. The *falling down* was related to a memory from very early childhood of the seventeen-year-old son of the house-porter who had fallen down in the street in an epileptic fit and been brought home in a carriage. She had of course only *heard* about this, but the idea of epileptic fits (of the '*falling* sickness') had obtained a hold on her imagination and had later influenced the form taken by her own hysterical attacks.—If a woman dreams of falling, it almost invariably has a sexual sense: she is imagining herself as a '*fallen woman*'. The present dream in particular scarcely left any room for doubt, since the place where my patient fell was the Graben, a part of Vienna notorious as a promenade for prostitutes. The *shopping-basket* [*Korb*] led to more than one interpretation. It reminded her of the numerous *rebuffs* [*Körbe*][2] which she had dealt out to her suitors, as well as of those which she complained of having later received herself. This also connected with the fact that *no one helped her up*, which she herself explained as a rebuff. The *shopping-basket* further reminded her of phantasies which had already come up in her analysis, in which she was married far beneath her and had to go marketing herself. And lastly it might serve as the mark of a servant. At this point further childhood recollections emerged. First, of a cook who had been dismissed for stealing, and who

---

[1] [One of the principal shopping centres in Vienna.]

[2] [The word '*Korb*' ('basket') is commonly used for the rejection of an offer of marriage.]

had *fallen on her knees* and begged to be forgiven. She herself had been twelve at the time. Then, of a housemaid who had been dismissed on account of a love-affair with the family *coachman* (who incidentally married her subsequently). Thus this memory was also one of the sources of the coachmen (*drivers*)[1] in the dream (who, in contradistinction to the actual coachman, failed to raise the fallen woman). There remained to be explained the fact of the basket being *thrown in after her* and *through the window*. This reminded her of *handing in* luggage to be *sent off* by rail, of the country custom of lovers climbing in through their sweethearts' *window*, and of other little episodes from her life in the country: how a gentleman had thrown some *blue plums* to a lady *through the window* of her room, and how her own younger sister had been scared by the village idiot looking in *through her window*. An obscure memory from her tenth year then began to emerge, of a nurse in the country who had had love-scenes (which the girl might have seen something of) with one of the servants in the house and who, along with her lover, had been *sent off*, *thrown out* (the opposite of the dream-image '*thrown in*')—a story that we had already approached from several other directions. A servant's luggage or trunk is referred to contemptuously in Vienna as 'seven *plums*': 'pack up your seven plums and out you go!'

My records naturally include a large collection of patients' dreams the analysis of which led to obscure or entirely forgotten impressions of childhood, often going back to the first three years of life. But it would be unsafe to apply any conclusions drawn from them to dreams in general. The persons concerned were in every instance neurotics and in particular hysterics; and it is possible that the part played by childhood scenes in their dreams might be determined by the nature of their neurosis and not by the nature of dreams. Nevertheless, in analysing my own dreams—and, after all, I am not doing so on account of any gross pathological symptoms—it happens no less frequently that in the latent content of a dream I come unexpectedly upon a scene from childhood, and that all at once a whole series of my dreams link up with the associations branching out from some experience of my childhood. I have already given some instances of this [pp. 193–8], and I shall

[1] [The German word is the same (*Kutscher*) in both cases.]

have others to give in a variety of connections. I cannot, perhaps, bring this section to a better close than by reporting one or two dreams of mine in which recent occasions and long-forgotten experiences of childhood came together as sources of the dream.

I

Tired and hungry after a journey, I went to bed, and the major vital needs began to announce their presence in my sleep; I dreamt as follows:

I went into a kitchen in search of some pudding. Three women were standing in it; one of them was the hostess of the inn and was twisting something about in her hand, as though she was making Knödel [dumplings]. She answered that I must wait till she was ready. (These were not definite spoken words.) I felt impatient and went off with a sense of injury. I put on an overcoat. But the first I tried on was too long for me. I took it off, rather surprised to find it was trimmed with fur. A second one that I put on had a long strip with a Turkish design let into it. A stranger with a long face and a short pointed beard came up and tried to prevent my putting it on, saying it was his. I showed him then that it was embroidered all over with a Turkish pattern. He asked: 'What have the Turkish (designs, stripes . . .) to do with you?' But we then became quite friendly with each other.

When I began analysing this dream, I thought quite unexpectedly of the first novel I ever read (when I was thirteen, perhaps); as a matter of fact I began at the end of the first volume. I have never known the name of the novel or of its author; but I have a vivid memory of its ending. The hero went mad and kept calling out the names of the three women who had brought the greatest happiness and sorrow into his life. One of these names was *Pélagie*. I still had no notion what this recollection was going to lead to in the analysis. In connection with the three women I thought of the three Fates who spin the destiny of man, and I knew that one of the three women—the inn-hostess in the dream—was the mother who gives life, and furthermore (as in my own case) gives the living creature its first nourishment. Love and hunger, I reflected, meet at a woman's breast. A young man who was a great admirer of feminine beauty was talking once—so the story went—of the good-looking wet-nurse who had suckled him when he was a baby: 'I'm sorry,' he remarked, 'that I didn't make a better use of my opportunity.' I was in the habit of quoting this anecdote to explain the factor of 'deferred action' in the mechanism of the psychoneuroses.[1]—One of the Fates, then, was rubbing the palms of her hands together as though she was making dumplings: a queer occupation for a Fate, and one that cried out for an explanation. This was provided by another and earlier memory of my childhood. When I was six years old and was given my first lessons by my mother, I was expected to believe that we were all made of earth and must therefore return to earth. This did not suit me and I expressed doubts of the doctrine. My mother thereupon rubbed the palms of her hands together—just as she did in making dumplings, except that there was no dough between them—and showed me the blackish scales of *epidermis* produced by the friction as a proof that we were made of earth. My astonishment at this ocular demonstration knew no bounds and I acquiesced in the belief which I was later to hear expressed in the words: '*Du bist der Natur einen Tod schuldig.*'[2] So they really were Fates that I found in the kitchen when I went into it—as I had so often done in my childhood when I was hungry, while my mother, standing by the fire, had admonished me that I must wait till dinner was ready.—And now for the dumplings—the *Knödel*! One at least of my teachers at the University—and precisely the one to whom I owe my histological knowledge (for instance of the *epidermis*)—would infallibly be reminded by the name *Knödl* of a person against whom he had been obliged to take legal action for *plagiarizing* his writings. The idea of plagiarizing—of appropriating whatever one can, even though it belongs to someone else—clearly led on to the second part of the dream, in which I was treated as though I were the thief who had for some time carried on his business of stealing overcoats in the lecture-rooms. I had written down the word 'plagiarizing', without thinking about it, because it

[1] [A reference to a superseded theory of the mechanism of hysteria, described in the later sections of Part II of Freud's early 'Project for a Scientific Psychology' (Freud, 1950a).]

[2] ['Thou owest Nature a death.' Evidently a reminiscence of Prince Hal's remark to Falstaff in *1 Henry IV*, v. 1: 'Thou owest God a death.' Freud uses the same words and ascribes them to Shakespeare in a letter to Fliess of February 6, 1899 (Freud, 1950a, Letter 104).]—Both of the emotions that were attached to these childhood scenes—astonishment and submission to the inevitable—had occurred in a dream which I had had shortly before this one and which had first reminded me of this event in my childhood.

occurred to me; but now I noticed that it could form a bridge [*Brücke*] between different pieces of the dream's manifest content. A chain of associations (*Pélagie—plagiarizing—plagiostomes*[1] or sharks [*Haifische*]—*a fish's swimming-bladder* [*Fischblase*]) connected the old novel with the case of Knödl and with the overcoats, which clearly referred to implements used in sexual technique [see p. 186]. (Cf. Maury's alliterative dreams [on p. 59].) No doubt it was a very far-fetched and senseless chain of thought; but I could never have constructed it in waking life unless it had already been constructed by the dream-work. And, as though the need to set up forced connections regarded *nothing* as sacred, the honoured name of Brücke[2] (cf. the verbal *bridge* above) reminded me of the Institute in which I spent the happiest hours of my student life, free from all other desires—

> So wird's Euch an der Weisheit *Brüsten*
> Mit jedem Tage mehr gelüsten [3]

—in complete contrast to the desires which were now *plaguing* me in my dreams. Finally there came to mind another much respected teacher—his name, Fleischl ['*Fleisch*' = 'meat'], like Knödl, sounded like something to eat—and a distressing scene in which *scales of epidermis* played a part (my mother and the inn-hostess) as well as *madness* (the novel) and a drug from the dispensary[4] which removes *hunger*: cocaine.

I might pursue the intricate trains of thought further along these lines and explain fully the part of the dream which I have not analysed; but I must desist at this point because the personal sacrifice demanded would be too great. I will only pick out one thread, which is qualified to lead us straight to one of the dream-thoughts underlying the confusion. The stranger with the long face and pointed beard who tried to prevent my putting on the overcoat bore the features of a shop-keeper at

---

[1] I have deliberately avoided enlarging upon the plagiostomes; they reminded me of an unpleasant occasion on which I had disgraced myself in connection with this same University teacher.

[2] [For Brücke and Fleischl (below) see footnote, p. 482.]

[3] ['Thus, at the *breasts* of Wisdom clinging,
Thou'lt find each day a greater rapture bringing.'
Goethe, *Faust*, Part I, [Scene 4]
(Bayard Taylor's translation).]

[4] [In German '*lateinische Küche*' (literally, 'Latin kitchen').—Cf. footnote 2, p. 111.]

Spalato from whom my wife had bought a quantity of *Turkish* stuffs. He was called Popović, an equivocal name,[1] on which a humorous writer, Stettenheim, has already made a suggestive comment: 'He told me his name and blushingly pressed my hand.' Once again I found myself misusing a name, as I already had done with Pélagie, Knödl, Brücke and Fleischl. It could scarcely be denied that playing about with names like this was a kind of childish naughtiness. But if I indulged in it, it was as an act of retribution; for my own name had been the victim of feeble witticisms like these on countless occasions.[2] Goethe, I recalled, had remarked somewhere upon people's sensitiveness about their names: how we seem to have grown into them like our *skin*. He had said this *à propos* of a line written on his name by Herder:

'Der du von Göttern abstammst, von Gothen oder vom Kote.'—
'So seid ihr Götterbilder auch zu Staub.'[3]

I noticed that my digression on the subject of the misuse of names was only leading up to this complaint. But I must break off here.—My wife's purchase made at Spalato reminded me of another purchase, made at Cattaro,[4] which I had been too cautious over, so that I had lost an opportunity of making some nice acquisitions. (Cf. the neglected opportunity with the wet-nurse.) For one of the thoughts which my hunger introduced into the dream was this: 'One should never neglect an opportunity, but always take what one can even when it involves doing a small wrong. One should never neglect an opportunity, since life is short and death inevitable.' Because this lesson of 'carpe diem' had among other meanings a sexual one, and because the desire it expressed did not stop short of doing wrong, it had reason to dread the censorship and was obliged to conceal

---

[1] ['*Popo*' is a childish word for 'bottom'.]

[2] ['*Freud*' is the German word for 'joy'.]

[3] [The first of these lines comes from a facetious note written by Herder to Goethe with a request for the loan of some books: 'Thou who art the offspring of gods or of Goths or of dung—(Goethe, send them to me!)' The second line, a further free association of Freud's, is taken from the well-known recognition scene in Goethe's *Iphigenie auf Tauris*. Iphigenia, hearing from Pylades of the death of so many heroes during the siege of Troy, exclaims: 'So you too, divine figures, have turned to dust!']

[4] [Spalato and Cattaro: both towns on the Dalmatian coast.]

itself behind a dream. All kinds of thoughts having a *contrary* sense then found voice: memories of a time when the dreamer was content with *spiritual* food, restraining thoughts of every kind and even threats of the most revolting sexual punishments.

II

The next dream calls for a rather long preamble:

I had driven to the Western Station [in Vienna] to take the train for my summer holiday at Aussee, but had arrived on the platform while an earlier train, going to Ischl, was still standing in the station. There I had seen Count Thun[1] who was once again travelling to Ischl for an audience with the Emperor. Though it was raining, he had arrived in an open carriage. He had walked straight in through the entrance for the Local Trains. The ticket inspector at the gate had not recognized him and had tried to take his ticket, but he had waved the man aside with a curt motion of his hand and without giving any explanation. After the train for Ischl had gone out, I ought by rights to have left the platform again and returned to the waiting room; and it had cost me some trouble to arrange matters so that I was allowed to stop on the platform. I had passed the time in keeping a look-out to see if anyone came along and tried to get a reserved compartment by exercising some sort of 'pull'. I had intended in that case to make a loud protest: that is to say to claim equal rights. Meantime I had been humming a tune to myself which I recognized as Figaro's aria from *Le Nozze di Figaro*:

> Se vuol ballare, signor contino,
> Se vuol ballare, signor contino,
> Il chitarino le suonerò[2]

(It is a little doubtful whether anyone else would have recognized the tune.)

The whole evening I had been in high spirits and in a combative mood. I had chaffed my waiter and my cab-driver

---

[1] [Austrian politician (1847–1916) of reactionary views; an upholder of Bohemian self-government as against the German nationalists; Austrian premier 1898–9.—Ischl, in Upper Austria, where the Court regularly spent the summer months.]

[2] ['If my Lord Count is inclined to go dancing,
If my Lord Count is inclined to go dancing,
I'll be quite ready to play him a tune . . .']

—without, I hope, hurting their feelings. And now all kinds of insolent and revolutionary ideas were going through my head, in keeping with Figaro's words and with my recollections of Beaumarchais' comedy which I had seen acted by the *Comédie française*. I thought of the phrase about the great gentlemen who had taken the trouble to be born, and of the *droit du Seigneur* which Count Almaviva tried to exercise over Susanna. I thought, too, of how our malicious opposition journalists made jokes over Count Thun's name, calling him instead 'Count Nichtsthun'.[1] Not that I envied him. He was on his way to a difficult audience with the Emperor, while *I* was the real Count Do-nothing—just off on my holidays. There followed all sorts of enjoyable plans for the holidays. At this point a gentleman came on to the platform whom I recognized as a Government invigilator at medical examinations, and who by his activities in that capacity had won the flattering nickname of 'Government bedfellow'.[2] He asked to be given a first-class half-compartment to himself in virtue of his official position, and I heard one railwayman saying to another: 'Where are we to put the gentleman with the half first-class ticket?'[3] This, I thought to myself, was a fine example of privilege; after all *I* had paid the full first-class fare. And I did in fact get a compartment to myself, but not in a corridor coach, so that there would be no lavatory available during the night. I complained to an official without any success; but I got my own back on him by suggesting that he should at all events have a hole made in the floor of the compartment to meet the possible needs of passengers. And in fact I did wake up at a quarter to three in the morning with a pressing need to micturate, having had the following dream:

A crowd of people, a meeting of students.—A count (Thun or Taaffe[4]) was speaking. He was challenged to say something about the Germans, and declared with a contemptuous gesture that their favourite flower was colt's foot, and put some sort of dilapidated leaf—or rather

[1] ['Count Do-nothing.' '*Thun*' is the German word for 'to do'.]

[2] ['*Beischläfer*', literally 'one who sleeps with someone' because he used to go to sleep instead of invigilating.]

[3] [Being a government official, he had been able to buy his ticket at half-rates.]

[4] [Austrian politician (1833–95); premier 1870–1 and 1879–93. Like Count Thun, he favoured some degree of independence for the non-German parts of the Empire.]

the crumpled skeleton of a leaf—into his buttonhole. I fired up—so I fired up,[1] though I was surprised at my taking such an attitude.

(Then, less distinctly:) *It was as though I was in the Aula;[2] the entrances were cordoned off and we had to escape. I made my way through a series of beautifully furnished rooms, evidently ministerial or public apartments, with furniture upholstered in a colour between brown and violet; at last I came to a corridor, in which a housekeeper was sitting, an elderly stout woman. I avoided speaking to her, but she evidently thought I had a right to pass, for she asked whether she should accompany me with the lamp. I indicated to her, by word or gesture, that she was to stop on the staircase; and I felt I was being very cunning in thus avoiding inspection at the exit. I got downstairs and found a narrow and steep ascending path, along which I went.*

(Becoming indistinct again) . . . *It was as though the second problem was to get out of the town, just as the first one had been to get out of the house. I was driving in a cab and ordered the driver to drive me to a station. 'I can't drive with you along the railway-line itself', I said, after he had raised some objection, as though I had overtired him. It was as if I had already driven with him for some of the distance one normally travels by train. The stations were cordoned off. I wondered whether to go to Krems or Znaim,[3] but reflected that the Court would be in residence there, so I decided in favour of Graz, or some such place. I was now sitting in the compartment, which was like a carriage on the Stadtbahn* [the suburban railway]; *and in my buttonhole I had a peculiar plaited, long-shaped object, and beside it some violet-brown violets made of a stiff material. This greatly struck people.* (At this point the scene broke off.)

Once more I was in front of the station, but this time in the company of an elderly gentleman. I thought of a plan for remaining unrecognized; and then saw that this plan had already been put into effect. It was as though thinking and experiencing were one and the same thing. He appeared to be blind, at all events with one eye, and I handed him a male glass urinal (which we had to buy or had bought in town). So I was a sick-nurse and had to give him the urinal because he was blind.

[1] This repetition crept into my record of the dream, apparently through inadvertence. I have let it stand, since the analysis showed that it was significant. [The German is '*ich fahre auf*'; '*fahren*' also means 'to drive' or 'to travel' and is used repeatedly in these senses later in the dream. See on this point p. 433 *n.*]

[2] [The great ceremonial hall of the University.]

[3] [Krems in Lower Austria and Znaim in Moravia were neither of them Imperial residences.—Graz is the capital of the province of Styria.]

If the ticket-collector were to see us like that, he would be certain to let us get away without noticing us. Here the man's attitude and his micturating penis appeared in plastic form. (This was the point at which I awoke, feeling a need to micturate.)

The dream as a whole gives one the impression of being in the nature of a phantasy in which the dreamer was carried back to the Revolutionary year 1848. Memories of that year had been recalled to me by the [Emperor Francis Joseph's] Jubilee in 1898, as well as by a short trip which I had made to *the Wachau*, in the course of which I had visited Emmersdorf,[1] the place of retirement of the student-leader Fischhof, to whom certain elements in the manifest content of the dream may allude. My associations then led me to England and to my brother's house there. He used often to tease his wife with the words 'Fifty Years Ago' (from the title of one of Lord Tennyson's poems),[2] which his children used then to correct to *'fifteen years ago'*. This revolutionary phantasy, however, which was derived from ideas aroused in me by seeing Count Thun, was like the façade of an Italian church in having no organic relation with the structure lying behind it. But it differed from those façades in being disordered and full of gaps, and in the fact that portions of the interior construction had forced their way through into it at many points.

The first situation in the dream was an amalgam of several scenes, which I can separate out. The insolent attitude adopted by the Count in the dream was copied from a scene at my secondary school when I was *fifteen years* old. We had hatched a conspiracy against an unpopular and ignorant master, the moving spirit of which had been one of my school-fellows who

---

[1] [The Wachau is a stretch of the Danube valley some fifty miles above Vienna.—*Footnote added* 1925:] This is a mistake, but not a slip this time. I only learnt later that the Emmersdorf in the Wachau is not to be identified with the place of the same name which was the refuge of the revolutionary leader Fischhof. [A reference to this mistake will be found in *The Psychopathology of Everyday Life* (Freud, 1901*b*), Chapter X (3).]

[2] [No poem by Tennyson seems to bear this title. The reference is perhaps to his ode 'On the Jubilee of Queen Victoria', in which the words 'fifty years' (though not 'fifty years ago') occur repeatedly. Or, alternatively, the allusion may be to the second 'Locksley Hall': 'Sixty Years After'.]

since those days seemed to have taken *Henry VIII* of *England* as his model. The leadership in the chief assault was allotted to me, and the signal for open revolt was a discussion on the significance of the Danube to Austria (cf. *the Wachau*). One of our fellow-conspirators had been the only aristocratic boy in the class, who, on account of his remarkable length of limb, was called 'the Giraffe'. He was standing up, like the Count in my dream, having been taken to task by the school tyrant, the *German language* master. The *favourite flower* and the *putting into his buttonhole* of something in the nature of a flower (which last made me think of some orchids which I had brought the same day for a woman friend and also of a rose of Jericho[1]) were a striking reminder of the scene in one of Shakespeare's historical plays [*3 Henry VI*, I, 1] which represented the beginning of the Wars of the *Red* and *White* Roses. (The mention of *Henry VIII* opened the way to this recollection.)—From there it was only a short step to red and white carnations. (Two little couplets, one in *German* and the other in *Spanish*, slipped into the analysis at this point:

> Rosen, Tulpen, Nelken,
> alle Blumen welken.

> *Isabelita*, no llores,
> que se marchitan las flores.[2]

The appearance of a *Spanish* couplet led back to *Figaro*.) Here in Vienna white carnations had become an emblem of antisemitism, and red ones of the Social Democrats. Behind this lay a recollection of a piece of anti-semitic provocation during a railway journey in the lovely Saxon countryside (cf. *Anglo-Saxon*).—The third scene which contributed to the formation of the first situation in the dream dated from my early student days. There was a discussion in a *German* students' club on the relation of philosophy to the natural sciences. I was a green youngster, full of materialistic theories, and thrust myself forward to give expression to an extremely one-sided point of view. Thereupon someone who was my senior and my superior, someone who has since then shown his ability as a leader of men and an organizer of large groups (and who also, incident-

---

[1] [The 'Resurrection plant', whose dried fronds unfold under moisture.]

[2] ['Roses, tulips, carnations: every flower fades.' (Lines often found in nineteenth century 'common-place books'.)—'*Isabelita*, do not weep because the flowers fade.']

ally, bears a name derived from the Animal Kingdom[1]), stood up and gave us a good talking-to: he too, he told us, had fed swine in his youth and returned repentant to his father's house. *I fired up* (as I did in the dream) and replied boorishly ['*saugrob*', literally 'swinishly gross'] that since I now knew that he had fed *swine* in his youth I was no longer *surprised* at the tone of his speeches. (In the dream I was *surprised* at my German-nationalist attitude. [Cf. p. 323.]) There was a general uproar and I was called upon from many sides to withdraw my remarks, but I refused to do so. The man I had insulted was too sensible to look upon the incident as a *challenge*, and let the affair drop.

The remaining elements of this first situation in the dream were derived from deeper layers. What was the meaning of the Count's pronouncement about colt's foot? To find the answer, I followed a train of associations: colt's foot ['*Huflattich*', literally 'hoof lettuce']—lettuce—salad—dog-in-the-manger ['*Salathund*', literally 'salad dog']. Here was a whole collection of terms of abuse: 'Gir-affe' ['*Affe*' is the German for 'ape'], 'swine', 'dog'—and I could have arrived at 'donkey' if I had made a détour through another name and insulted yet another academic teacher. Moreover, I translated 'colt's foot'—whether rightly or wrongly I could not tell—by the French '*pisse-en-lit*'.[2] This information was derived from Zola's *Germinal*, in which a child was told to pick some of that plant for salad. The French word for 'dog'—'*chien*'—reminded me of the major function ('*chier*' in French, compared with '*pisser*' for the minor one). Soon, I thought, I should have collected examples of impropriety in all three states of matter—solid, liquid and gaseous; —for this same book, *Germinal*, which had plenty to do with the approaching revolution, contained an account of a very peculiar sort of competition—for the production of a gaseous excretion known by the name of '*flatus*'.[3] I now saw that the path leading to *flatus* had been prepared far ahead: from *flowers*, through the *Spanish* couplet, *Isabelita*, *Isabella* and Ferdinand, *Henry VIII*, *English* history, and the Armada which sailed against *England*,

---

[1] [Presumably Viktor Adler ('eagle'), the Austrian social democrat leader (1852–1918). Cf. '*Adler*' on p. 214 below.]

[2] ['*Pissenlit*' actually means 'dandelion'.]

[3] Not in fact in *Germinal* but in *La terre*: a mistake which I only observed after I had completed the analysis.—Notice the occurrence of the same letters in '*Huflattich*' ['colt's foot'] and '*flatus*'.

after whose defeat a medal was struck, bearing the inscription 'Flavit et dissipati sunt'[1], since the storm-blast had scattered the Spanish fleet. I had thought, half seriously, of using those words as the heading to the chapter on 'Therapy', if ever I got so far as producing a detailed account of my theory and treatment of hysteria.

Turning now to the second episode of the dream, I am unable to deal with it in such detail—out of consideration for the censorship. For I was putting myself in the place of an exalted personage of those revolutionary times, who also had an adventure with an eagle [*Adler*] and is said to have suffered from incontinence of the bowels, and so on. I thought to myself that *I should not be justified in passing* the censorship at this point, even though the greater part of the story was told me by a Hofrat (a *consiliarius aulicus* [court councillor]—cf. *Aula*). The series of public rooms in the dream were derived from His Excellency's saloon carriage, of which I had succeeded in getting a glimpse. But the 'rooms' [*Zimmer*] also meant 'women' [*Frauenzimmer*], as is often the case in dreams[2]—in this instance 'public women'. In the figure of the housekeeper I was showing my lack of gratitude towards a witty elderly lady and ill repaying her hospitality and the many good stories that I heard while I was stopping in her house.—The allusion to the lamp went back to Grillparzer,[3] who introduced a charming episode of a similar kind, which he had actually experienced, into his tragedy about Hero and Leander, *Des Meeres und der Liebe Wellen* ['*The Waves of the Sea and of Love*']—the Armada and the *storm*.[4]

I must also refrain from any detailed analysis of the two

[1] ['He blew and they were scattered.'—*Footnote added* 1925:] An unsolicited biographer, Dr. Fritz Wittels [1924, 21; Engl. trans. (1924), 28] has charged me with having omitted the name of Jehovah from the above motto. [*Added* 1930:] The English medallion bears the deity's name in Hebrew lettering on a cloud in the background. It is so placed that it can be taken as being part either of the design or of the inscription.—[The idea of using the words as a motto at the head of a chapter on therapy is mentioned in a letter to Fliess of January 3, 1897 (Freud, 1950a, Letter 54).]

[2] ['*Frauenzimmer*', literally 'women's apartment', is commonly used in German as a slightly derogatory word for 'woman'. Cf. p. 354.]

[3] [The well-known Austrian dramatist (1791–1872).]

[4] [*Footnote added* 1911:] In an interesting paper, Silberer (1910) has tried to show from this part of my dream that the dream-work can succeed in reproducing not only the latent dream-thoughts but also the

remaining episodes of the dream.[1] I will merely pick out the elements leading to the two childhood scenes on whose account alone I embarked upon a discussion of this dream. It will rightly be suspected that what compels me to make this suppression is sexual material; but there is no need to rest content with this explanation. After all, there are many things which one has to keep secret from other people but of which one makes no secret to oneself; and the question here is not as to why I am obliged to conceal the solution but as to the motives for the *internal* censorship which hid the true content of the dream from myself. I must therefore explain that the analysis of these three [last] episodes of the dream showed that they were impertinent boastings, the issue of an absurd megalomania which had long been suppressed in my waking life and a few of whose ramifications had even made their way into the dream's manifest content (e.g. '*I felt I was being very cunning*'), and which incidentally accounted for my exuberant spirits during the evening before I had the dream. The boasting extended to all spheres; for instance, the mention of *Graz* went back to the slang phrase 'What's the price of Graz?', which expresses the self-satisfaction of a person who feels extremely well-off. The first episode of the dream may also be included among the boastings by anyone who will bear in mind the great Rabelais' incomparable account of the life and deeds of Gargantua and his son Pantagruel.

Here is the material relating to the two childhood scenes which I have promised my readers. I had bought a *new* trunk for the journey, of a *brownish violet* colour. This colour appears more than once in the dream: the *violet-brown violets made of a stiff material* and beside them a thing known as a '*Mädchenfänger*' ['girl-catcher'][2]—and the furniture in the ministerial apart-

psychical processes that take place during the formation of dreams. (This is what he terms 'the functional phenomenon'.) [See below, p. 503 ff.—*Added* 1914:] But he is, I think, overlooking the fact that 'the psychical processes that take place during the formation of dreams' were, like the rest, part of the *material* of my thoughts. In this boastful dream I was evidently proud of having discovered those processes.

[1] [The first of these is in fact further analysed on p. 431 ff.]

[2] [This word, ordinarily used in the sense of 'rake' (see footnote on p. 217), seems here to be the slang name of some sort of buttonhole. Cf. corresponding terms such as 'fascinator' and 'beau-catcher' used in America for women's head-dresses.]

ments. It is commonly believed by children that *people are struck by anything new*. The following scene from my childhood has been described to me, and my memory of the description has taken the place of my memory of the scene itself. It appears that when I was two years old I still occasionally *wetted the bed*, and when I was reproached for this I *consoled* my father by promising to buy him a nice *new red* bed in N., the nearest town of any size. This was the origin of the parenthetical phrase in the dream to the effect that *we had bought or had to buy the* urinal in town: one must keep one's promises. (Notice, too, the juxtaposition in symbolism of the male urinal and the female trunk or box. [Cf. p. 154.]) This promise of mine exhibited all the megalomania of childhood. We have already come across the significant part played in dreams by children's difficulties in connection with micturition (cf. the dream reported on p. 201). We have also learned from the psycho-analysis of neurotic subjects the intimate connection between bed-wetting and the character trait of ambition.[1]

When I was seven or eight years old there was another domestic scene, which I can remember very clearly. One evening before going to sleep I disregarded the rules which modesty lays down and obeyed the calls of nature in my parents' bedroom while they were present. In the course of his reprimand, my father let fall the words: 'The boy will come to nothing.' This must have been a frightful blow to my ambition, for references to this scene are still constantly recurring in my dreams and are always linked with an enumeration of my achievements and successes, as though I wanted to say: 'You see, I *have* come to something.' This scene, then, provided the material for the final episode of the dream, in which—in revenge, of course—the roles were interchanged. The older man (clearly my father, since his blindness in one eye referred to his unilateral glaucoma[2]) was now micturating in front of me, just as I had in front of him in my childhood. In the reference to his glaucoma I was reminding him of the cocaine,

---

[1] [This sentence was added in 1914. The first mention of the connection seems to have been made in the last paragraph of Freud's paper on 'Character and Anal Erotism' (1908b).]

[2] There is another interpretation. He was one-eyed like Odin, the father-god.—*Odhins Trost* [*Odin's Consolation*, a mythological novel by Felix Dahn (1880)].—The *consolation* I offered him in the first childhood scene of buying him a new bed.

which had helped him in the operation [cf. p. 170 f.], as though I had in that way kept my promise. Moreover, I was making fun of him; I had to hand him the urinal because he was blind, and I revelled in allusions to my discoveries in connection with the theory of hysteria, of which I felt so proud.[1]

---

[1] Here is some further interpretative material. Handing him the glass [urinal] reminded me of the story of the peasant at the optician's, trying glass after glass and still not being able to read.—(Peasant-*catcher* [*Bauernfänger*, 'sharper']: girl-*catcher* [*Mädchenfänger*] in the preceding episode of the dream.)—The way in which the father in Zola's *La terre* was treated among the peasants after he had grown feeble-minded.— The tragic requital that lay in my father's soiling his bed like a child during the last days of his life [cf. p. 429]; hence my appearance in the dream as a *sick-nurse*.—'*Here it was as though thinking and experiencing were one and the same thing.*' This recalled a strongly revolutionary literary play by Oskar Panizza ['*Das Liebeskonzil*' (1895)], in which God the Father is ignominiously treated as a paralytic old man. In his case will and deed were represented as one and the same thing, and he had to be restrained from cursing and swearing by one of his archangels, a kind of Ganymede, because his imprecations would be promptly fulfilled.— My making *plans* was a reproach against my father dating from a later period. And indeed the whole rebellious content of the dream, with its *lèse majesté* and its derision of the higher authorities, went back to rebellion against my father. A Prince is known as the father of his country; the father is the oldest, first, and for children the only authority, and from his autocratic power the other social authorities have developed in the course of the history of human civilization—except in so far as the 'matriarchy' calls for a qualification of this assertion.—The phrase '*thinking and experiencing were one and the same thing*' had a reference to the explanation of hysterical symptoms, and the '*male urinal*' belonged in the same connection. I need not explain to a Viennese the principle of the '*Gschnas*'. It consists in constructing what appear to be rare and precious objects out of trivial and preferably comic and worthless materials (for instance, in making armour out of saucepans, wisps of straw and dinner rolls)—a favourite pastime at bohemian parties here in Vienna. I had observed that this is precisely what hysterical subjects do: alongside what has really happened to them, they unconsciously build up frightful or perverse imaginary events which they construct out of the most innocent and everyday material of their experience. It is to these phantasies that their symptoms are in the first instance attached and not to their recollections of real events, whether serious or equally innocent. This revelation had helped me over a number of difficulties and had given me particular pleasure. What made it possible for me to refer to this by means of the dream-element of the 'male urinal' was as follows. I had been told that at the latest '*Gschnas*'-night a poisoned chalice belonging to Lucrezia Borgia had been exhibited; its central and principal constituent had been a *male urinal* of the type used in hospitals.

The two scenes of micturition from my childhood were in any case closely linked to the topic of megalomania; but their emergence while I was travelling to Aussee was further assisted by the chance circumstance that there was no lavatory attached to my compartment and that I had reason to anticipate the predicament which in fact arose in the morning. I awoke with the sensations of a physical need. One might, I think, be inclined to suppose that these sensations were the actual provoking agent of the dream; but I would prefer to take another view, namely that the desire to micturate was only called up by the dream-thoughts. It is quite unusual for me to be disturbed in my sleep by physical needs of any kind, especially at the hour at which I awoke on this occasion—a quarter to three in the morning. And I may meet a further objection by remarking that upon other journeys under more comfortable conditions I have scarcely ever felt a need to micturate when I have woken up early. But in any case it will do no harm to leave the point unresolved.[1]

My experiences in analysing dreams have drawn my attention to the fact that trains of thought reaching back to earliest childhood lead off even from dreams which seem at first sight to have been completely interpreted, since their sources and instigating wish have been discovered without difficulty. I have therefore been compelled to ask myself whether this characteristic may not be a further essential precondition of dreaming. Stated in general terms, this would imply that every dream was linked in its manifest content with recent experiences and in its latent content with the most ancient experiences. And I have in fact been able to show in my analysis of hysteria that these ancient experiences have remained recent in the proper sense of the word up to the immediate present. It is still extremely hard to demonstrate the truth of this suspicion; and I shall have to return in another connection (Chapter VII, [p. 553 ff.]) to a consideration of the probable part played by the earliest experiences of childhood in the formation of dreams.

Of the three characteristics of memory in dreams enumerated at the beginning of this chapter, one—the preference for non-essential material in the content of dreams—has been satisfactorily cleared up by being traced back to dream-distortion.

[1] [This dream is further discussed on p. 432 ff.]

We have been able to confirm the existence of the other two—
the emphasis upon recent and upon infantile material—but we
have not been able to account for them on the basis of the
motives that lead to dreaming. These two characteristics, whose
explanation and appreciation remain to be discovered, must
be kept in mind. Their proper place must be looked for elsewhere—either in the psychology of the state of sleep or in the
discussion of the structure of the mental apparatus upon which
we shall later embark, after we have learnt that the interpretation of dreams is like a window through which we can get a
glimpse of the interior of that apparatus. [See Chapter VII.]

There is, however, another inference following from these
last dream-analyses to which I will draw attention at once.
Dreams frequently seem to have more than one meaning. Not
only, as our examples have shown, may they include several
wish-fulfilments one alongside the other; but a succession of
meanings or wish-fulfilments may be superimposed on one another, the bottom one being the fulfilment of a wish dating
from earliest childhood. And here again the question arises
whether it might not be more correct to assert that this occurs
'invariably' rather than 'frequently'.[1]

---

[1] [*Footnote added* 1914:] The fact that the meanings of dreams are
arranged in superimposed layers is one of the most delicate, though also
one of the most interesting, problems of dream-interpretation. Anyone
who forgets this possibility will easily go astray and be led into making
untenable assertions upon the nature of dreams. Yet it is still a fact that
far too few investigations have been made into this matter. Hitherto the
only thorough piece of research has been Otto Rank's [1912a] into the
fairly regular stratification of symbols in dreams provoked by pressure
of the bladder. [See below, p. 402 f.]

THE SOMATIC SOURCES OF DREAMS

If one tries to interest an educated layman in the problem of dreams and, with that end in view, asks him what in his opinion are the sources from which they arise, one finds as a rule that he feels confident of possessing the answer to this part of the question. He thinks at once of the effects produced on the construction of dreams by digestive disturbances or difficulties—'dreams come from indigestion' [cf. p. 22]—, by postures accidentally assumed by the body and by other small incidents during sleep. It never seems to occur to him that when all these factors have been taken into account anything is left over that needs explaining.

I have already discussed at length in the opening chapter (Section C) the part assigned by scientific writers to somatic sources of stimulation in the formation of dreams; so that here I need only recall the results of that enquiry. We found that three different kinds of somatic sources of stimulation were distinguished: objective sensory stimuli arising from external objects, internal states of excitation of the sense organs having only a subjective basis, and somatic stimuli derived from the interior of the body. We noticed moreover that the authorities were inclined to push into the background, or to exclude entirely, any possible *psychical* sources of dreams, as compared with these somatic stimuli (cf. p. 41). In our examination of the claims made on behalf of somatic sources of stimulation we arrived at the following conclusions. The significance of *objective* excitations of the sense organs (consisting partly of chance stimuli during sleep and partly of excitations such as cannot fail to impinge even upon a sleeping mind) is established from numerous observations and has been experimentally confirmed (cf. p. 24 f.). The part played by *subjective* sensory excitations seems to be demonstrated by the recurrence in dreams of hypnagogic sensory images (cf. p. 31 f.). And lastly it appears that, though it is impossible to prove that the images and ideas occurring in our dreams can be traced back to *internal* somatic stimuli to the extent to which this has been asserted to be the case, nevertheless this origin finds support in the universally recognized influence exercised upon our dreams by states of excitation in our digestive, urinary and sexual organs [cf. p. 37].

It would appear, then, that 'nervous stimulation' and 'somatic stimulation' are the somatic sources of dreams—that is to say, according to many writers, their sole source.

On the other hand, we have already found a number of doubts expressed, which seemed to imply a criticism, not indeed of the *correctness*, but of the *adequacy* of the theory of somatic stimulation.

However secure the supporters of this theory might feel in its factual basis—especially as far as accidental and external nervous stimuli are concerned, since these can be traced in the content of dreams without any trouble at all—not one of them could fail to perceive that it is impossible to attribute the wealth of ideational material in dreams to external nervous stimuli alone. Miss Mary Whiton Calkins (1893, 312) examined her own and another person's dreams for six weeks with this question in mind. She found that in only 13·2 per cent and 6·7 per cent of them respectively was it possible to trace the element of external sense-perception; while only two cases in the collection were derivable from organic sensations. Here we have statistical confirmation of what I had been led to suspect from a hasty survey of my own experiences.

It has often been proposed to separate off 'dreams due to nervous stimulation' from other forms of dreams as a sub-species that has been thoroughly investigated. Thus Spitta [1882, 233] divides dreams into 'dreams due to nervous stimulation' and 'dreams due to association'. This solution was, however, bound to remain unsatisfactory so long as it was impossible to demonstrate the link between the somatic sources of a dream and its ideational content. Thus, in addition to the first objection—the insufficient frequency of external sources of stimulation—there was a second one—the insufficient explanation of dreams afforded by such sources. We have a right to expect the supporters of this theory to give us explanations of two points: first, why it is that the external stimulus of a dream is not perceived in its true character but is invariably misunderstood (cf. the alarm-clock dreams on p. 27 f.); and secondly, why it is that the reaction of the perceiving mind to these misunderstood stimuli should lead to results of such unpredictable variety.

By way of answer to these questions, Strümpell (1877, 108 f.) tells us that, because the mind is withdrawn from the external world during sleep, it is unable to give a correct interpretation of objective sensory stimuli and is obliged to construct illusions on the basis of what is in many respects an indeterminate impression. To quote his own words: 'As soon as a sensation or complex of sensations or a feeling or a psychical process of any kind arises in the mind during sleep as a result of an external or internal nervous stimulus and is perceived by the mind, that process calls up sensory images from the circle of experiences left over in the mind from the waking state—that is to say, earlier perceptions—which are either bare or accompanied by their appropriate psychical values. The process surrounds itself, as it were, with a larger or smaller number of images of this kind and through them the impression derived from the nervous stimulus acquires its psychical value. We speak here (just as we usually do in the case of waking behaviour) of the sleeping mind "interpreting" the impressions made by the nervous stimulus. The outcome of this interpretation is what we describe as a "dream due to nervous stimulation", that is, a dream whose components are determined by a nervous stimulus producing its psychical effects in the mind according to the laws of reproduction.' [Cf. pp. 29 f., 54 and 58.]

Wundt [1874, 656 f.] is saying something essentially identical with this theory when he asserts that the ideas occurring in dreams are derived, for the most part at least, from sensory stimuli, including especially coenaesthetic sensations, and are for that reason mainly imaginative illusions and probably only to a small extent pure mnemic ideas intensified into hallucinations. [Cf. p. 40 f.] Strümpell (1877, 84) has hit upon an apt simile for the relation which subsists on this theory between the contents of a dream and its stimuli, when he writes that 'it is as though the ten fingers of a man who knows nothing of music were wandering over the keys of a piano'. [Cf. pp. 78 and 122.] Thus a dream is not, on this view, a mental phenomenon based on psychical motives, but the outcome of a physiological stimulus which is expressed in psychical symptoms because the apparatus upon which the stimulus impinges is capable of no

other form of expression. A similar presupposition also underlies, for instance, the famous analogy by means of which
Meynert attempted to explain obsessive ideas: the analogy of a
clock-face on which certain figures stand out by being more
prominently embossed than the rest.[1]

However popular the theory of the somatic stimulation of
dreams may have become and however attractive it may seem,
its weak point is easily displayed. Every somatic dream-
stimulus which requires the sleeping mental apparatus to interpret it by the construction of an illusion may give rise to an
unlimited number of such attempts at interpretation—that is to
say, it may be represented in the content of the dream by an
immense variety of ideas.[2] But the theory put forward by
Strümpell and Wundt is incapable of producing any motive
governing the relation between an external stimulus and the
dream-idea chosen for its interpretation—is incapable, that is,
of explaining what Lipps (1883, 170) describes as the 'remarkable choice often made' by these stimuli 'in the course of their
productive activity'. Objections have further been raised
against the presupposition upon which the whole theory of
illusion is based—the presupposition that the sleeping mind is
incapable of recognizing the true nature of objective sensory
stimuli. Burdach, the physiologist, showed us long ago that even
in sleep the mind is very well able to interpret correctly the
sense impressions that reach it and to react in accordance with
that correct interpretation; for he recalled the fact that particular sense impressions which seem important to the sleeper
can be excepted from the general neglect to which such impressions are subjected during sleep (as in the case of a nursing
mother or wet-nurse and her charge), and that a sleeper is
much more certain to be woken by the sound of his own name
than by any indifferent auditory impression—all of which
implies that the mind distinguishes between sensations during

---

[1] [This has not been traced in Meynert's published writings.]

[2] [Footnote added 1914]: Mourly Vold [1910–12] has produced a
two-volume work containing detailed and precise reports of a series
of experimentally produced dreams. [Cf. p. 38 f.] I should recommend a study of this work to anyone who wishes to convince himself
of how little light is thrown on the content of individual dreams by
the conditions of the experiments described in it and of how little help
in general is afforded by such experiments towards an understanding
of the problems of dreams. [See, however, p. 181 f. n.]

sleep (cf. p. 53). Burdach went on to infer from these observations that what we must presume during the state of sleep is not an *incapacity to interpret* sensory stimuli but a *lack of interest* in them. The same arguments which were used by Burdach in 1830 were brought forward once more without any modifications by Lipps in 1883 in his criticism of the theory of somatic stimulation. Thus the mind seems to behave like the sleeper in the anecdote. When someone asked him if he was asleep, he replied 'No'. But when his questioner went on to say: 'Then lend me ten florins', he took refuge in a subterfuge and replied: 'I'm asleep.'

The inadequacy of the theory of the somatic stimulation of dreams can be demonstrated in other ways. Observation shows that external stimuli do not necessarily compel me to dream, even though such stimuli appear in the content of my dream when and if I do dream. Supposing, let us say, that I am subjected to a tactile stimulus while I am asleep. A variety of different reactions are then open to me. I may disregard it, and when I wake up I may find, for instance, that my leg is uncovered or that there is some pressure on my arm; pathology provides very numerous instances in which various powerfully exciting sensory and motor stimuli can remain without effect during sleep. Or again, I may be aware of the sensation in my sleep—I may be aware of it, as one might say, 'through' my sleep—(which is what happens as a rule in the case of painful stimuli) but without my weaving the pain into a dream. And thirdly, I may react to the stimulus by waking up so as to get rid of it.[1] It is only as a fourth possibility that the nervous stimulus may cause me to dream. Yet the other possibilities are realized at least as frequently as this last one of constructing a dream. And this could not happen unless the motive for dreaming lay *elsewhere than in somatic sources of stimulation.*

Certain other writers—Scherner [1861] and Volkelt [1875], the philosopher, who adopted Scherner's views—formed a just estimate of the gaps which I have here indicated in the explanation of dreams as being due to somatic stimulation. These writers attempted to define more precisely the mental activities

---

[1] [*Footnote added* 1919:] Cf. Landauer (1918) on behaviour during sleep. Anyone can observe persons asleep carrying out actions which obviously have a meaning. A man asleep is not reduced to complete idiocy; on the contrary, he is capable of logical and deliberate acts.

which lead to the production of such variegated dream-images from the somatic stimuli; in other words, they sought to regard dreaming once again as something essentially *mental*—as a psychical activity. [Cf. p. 83 ff.] Scherner did not merely depict the psychical characteristics unfolded in the production of dreams in terms charged with poetic feeling and glowing with life; he believed, too, that he had discovered the principle according to which the mind deals with the stimuli presented to it. On his view, the dream-work, when the imagination is set free from the shackles of daytime, seeks to give a *symbolic* representation of the nature of the organ from which the stimulus arises and of the nature of the stimulus itself. Thus he provides a kind of 'dream-book' to serve as a guide to the interpretation of dreams, which makes it possible to deduce from the dream-images inferences as to the somatic feelings, the state of the organs and the character of the stimuli concerned. 'Thus the image of a cat expresses a state of angry ill-temper, and the image of a smooth and lightly-coloured loaf of bread stands for physical nudity.' [Volkelt, 1875, 32.] The human body as a whole is pictured by the dream-imagination as a house and the separate organs of the body by portions of a house. In 'dreams with a dental stimulus', an entrance-hall with a high, vaulted roof corresponds to the oral cavity and a stair-case to the descent from the throat to the oesophagus. 'In dreams due to headaches, the top of the head is represented by the ceiling of a room covered with disgusting, toad-like spiders.' [Ibid., 33 f.] A variety of such symbols are employed by dreams to represent the same organ. 'Thus the breathing lung will be symbolically represented by a blazing furnace, with flames roaring with a sound like the passage of air; the heart will be represented by hollow boxes or baskets, the bladder by round, bag-shaped objects or, more generally, by hollow ones.' [Ibid., 34.] 'It is of special importance that at the end of a dream the organ concerned or its function is often openly re-vealed, and as a rule in relation to the dreamer's own body. Thus a dream with a dental stimulus usually ends by the dreamer picturing himself pulling a tooth out of his mouth.' [Ibid., 35.]

This theory of dream-interpretation cannot be said to have been very favourably received by other writers on the subject. Its main feature seems to be its extravagance; and there has even been hesitation in recognizing such justification as, in my opinion, it can lay claim to. As will have been seen, it involves a revival of dream-interpretation by means of *symbolism*—the same method that was employed in antiquity, except that the field from which interpretations are collected is restricted within the limits of the human body. Its lack of any technique of interpreting that can be grasped scientifically must greatly narrow the application of Scherner's theory. It seems to leave the door open to arbitrary interpretations, especially as in its case, too, the same stimulus can be represented in the dream-content in a variety of different ways. Thus even Scherner's disciple, Volkelt, found himself unable to confirm the view that the body was represented by a house. Objections are also bound to arise from the fact that once again the mind is saddled with the dream-work as a useless and aimless function; for, according to the theory we are discussing, the mind is content with making phantasies about the stimulus with which it is occupied, without the remotest hint at anything in the nature of *disposing* of the stimulus.

There is one particular criticism, however, which is gravely damaging to Scherner's theory of the symbolization of somatic stimuli. These stimuli are present at all times and it is generally held that the mind is more accessible to them during sleep than when it is awake. It is difficult to understand, then, why the mind does not dream continuously all through the night, and, indeed, dream every night of all the organs. An attempt may be made to avoid this criticism by adding the further condition that in order to arouse dream-activity it is necessary for *special* excitations to proceed from the eyes, ears, teeth, intestines, etc. But the difficulty then arises of proving the objective nature of such increases of stimulus—which is only possible in a small number of cases. If dreams of flying are a symbolization of the rising and sinking of the lobes of the lungs [cf. p. 37 f.], then, as Strümpell [1877, 119] has already pointed out, either such dreams would have to be much more frequent than they are or it would be necessary to prove an increase in the activity of breathing in the course of them. There is a third possibility, which is the most probable of all, namely that special motives may be temporarily operative which direct the attention to visceral sensations that are uniformly present at all times. This possibility, however, carries us beyond the scope of Scherner's theory.

The value of the views put forward by Scherner and Volkelt lies in the fact that they draw attention to a number of characteristics of the content of dreams which call for explanation and seem to promise fresh discoveries. It is perfectly true that dreams contain symbolizations of bodily organs and functions, that water in a dream often points to a urinary stimulus, and that the male genitals can be represented by an upright stick or a pillar, and so on. In the case of dreams in which the field of vision is full of movement and bright colours, in contrast to the drabness of other dreams, it is scarcely possible not to interpret them as 'dreams with a visual stimulus'; nor can one dispute the part played by illusions in the case of dreams characterized by noise and a confusion of voices. Scherner [1861, 167] reports a dream of two rows of pretty, fair-haired boys standing opposite each other on a bridge, and of their attacking each other and then going back to their original position, till at last the dreamer saw himself sitting down on a bridge and pulling a long tooth out of his jaw. Similarly Volkelt [1875, 52] reports a dream in which two rows of drawers in a cupboard played a part and which once more ended with the dreamer pulling out a tooth. Dream-formations such as these, which are recorded in great numbers by the two authors, forbid our dismissing Scherner's theory as an idle invention without looking for its kernel of truth. [See p. 346.] The task, then, that faces us is to find an explanation of another kind for the supposed symbolization of what is alleged to be a dental stimulus.[1]

Throughout the whole of this discussion of the theory of the somatic sources of dreams I have refrained from making use of the argument based upon my dream-analyses. If it can be proved, by a procedure which other writers have not employed upon their dream-material, that dreams possess a value of their own as psychical acts, that wishes are the motive for their construction and that experiences of the preceding day provide the immediate material for their content, then any other theory of dreams, which neglects so important a procedure of research and accordingly represents dreams as a useless and puzzling psychical reaction to somatic stimuli, stands condemned without there being any necessity for specific criticisms. Otherwise— and this seems highly improbable—there would have to be two

[1] [These dreams are further considered on p. 385 ff.]

quite different kinds of dreaming, one of which has come only under *my* observation and the other only under that of the earlier authorities. All that remains, therefore, is to find a place in my theory of dreams for the facts upon which the current theory of the somatic stimulation of dreams is based.

We have already taken the first step in this direction by advancing the thesis (see p. 178 f.) that the dream-work is under the necessity of combining into a unity all instigations to dreaming which are active simultaneously. We found that, when two or more experiences capable of creating an impression are left over from the previous day, the wishes derived from them are combined in a single dream, and similarly that the psychically significant impression and the indifferent experiences from the previous day are brought together in the dream-material, provided always that it is possible to set up communicating ideas between them. Thus a dream appears to be a reaction to everything that is simultaneously present in the sleeping mind as currently active material. So far as we have hitherto analysed the material of dreams, we have seen it as a collection of psychical residues and memory-traces, to which (on account of the preference shown for recent and infantile material) we have been led to attribute a hitherto indefinable quality of being 'currently active'. We can foresee, then, without any great difficulty, what will happen if fresh material in the form of sensations is added during sleep to these currently active memories. It is once again owing to the fact of their being currently active that these sensory excitations are of importance for the dream; they are united with the other currently active psychical material to furnish what is used for the construction of the dream. To put it another way, stimuli arising during sleep are worked up into a wish-fulfilment the other constituents of which are the familiar psychical 'day's residues'. This combination *need* not occur; as I have already pointed out, there is more than one way of reacting to a somatic stimulus during sleep. When it *does* occur, it means that it has been possible to find ideational material to serve as the content of the dream of such a sort as to be able to represent both kinds of source of the dream—the somatic and the psychical.

The essential nature of the dream is not altered by the fact of somatic material being added to its psychical sources: a dream remains the fulfilment of a wish, no matter in what way the expression of that wish-fulfilment is determined by the currently active material.

I am prepared to leave room at this point for the operation of a number of special factors which can lend a varying importance to external stimuli in relation to dreams. As I picture it, a combination of individual factors, physiological and accidental, produced by the circumstances of the moment, is what determines how a person shall behave in particular cases of comparatively intense objective stimulation during sleep. The habitual or accidental depth of his sleep, taken in conjunction with the intensity of the stimulus, will make it possible in one case for him to suppress the stimulus so that his sleep is not interrupted and in another case will compel him to wake up or will encourage an attempt to overcome the stimulus by weaving it into a dream. In accordance with these various possible combinations, external objective stimuli will find expression in dreams with greater or less frequency in one person than in another. In my own case, since I am an excellent sleeper and obstinately refuse to allow anything to disturb my sleep, it very rarely happens that external causes of excitation find their way into my dreams; whereas psychical motives obviously cause me to dream very easily. In fact I have only noted a single dream in which an objective and painful source of stimulus is recognizable; and it will be most instructive to examine the effect which the external stimulus produced in this particular dream.

I was riding on a grey horse, timidly and awkwardly to begin with, as though I were only reclining upon it. I met one of my colleagues, P., who was sitting high on a horse, dressed in a tweed suit, and who drew my attention to something (probably to my bad seat). I now began to find myself sitting more and more firmly and comfortably on my highly intelligent horse, and noticed that I was feeling quite at home up there. My saddle was a kind of bolster, which completely filled the space between its neck and crupper. In this way I rode straight in between two vans. After riding some distance up the street, I turned round and tried to dismount, first in front of a small open chapel that stood in the street frontage. Then I actually did dismount in front of another chapel that stood near it. My hotel was in the same street; I might have let the horse go to it on its own, but I preferred to lead it there. It was as though I should have felt ashamed to arrive at it on horseback. A hotel 'boots' was standing in front of the hotel; he showed me a note of mine that had been found, and laughed at me over it. In the note was written, doubly under-lined: 'No food', and then another remark (indistinct) such as 'No work', together with a vague idea that I was in a strange town in which I was doing no work.

It would not be supposed at first sight that this dream originated under the influence, or rather under the compulsion, of a painful stimulus. But for some days before I had been suffering from boils which made every movement a torture; and finally a boil the size of an apple had risen at the base of my scrotum, which caused me the most unbearable pain with every step I took. Feverish lassitude, loss of appetite and the hard work with which I nevertheless carried on—all these had combined with the pain to depress me. I was not properly capable of discharging my medical duties. There was, however, one activity for which, in view of the nature and situation of my complaint, I should certainly have been less fitted than for any other, and that was—riding. And this was precisely the activity in which the dream landed me: it was the most energetic denial of my illness that could possibly be imagined. I cannot in fact ride, nor have I, apart from this, had dreams of riding. I have only sat on a horse once in my life and that was without a saddle, and I did not enjoy it. But in this dream I was riding as though I had no boil on my perineum—or rather *because I wanted not to have one.* My saddle, to judge from its description, was the poultice which had made it possible for me to fall asleep. Under its assuaging influence I had probably been unaware of my pain during the first hours of sleep. The painful feelings had then announced themselves and sought to wake me; whereupon the dream came and said soothingly: 'No! Go on sleeping! There's no need to wake up. You haven't got a boil; for you're riding on a horse, and it's quite certain that you couldn't ride if you had a boil in that particular place.' And the dream was successful. The pain was silenced, and I went on sleeping.

But the dream was not content with 'suggesting away' my boil by obstinately insisting upon an idea that was inconsistent with it and so behaving like the hallucinatory delusion of the mother who had lost her child or the merchant whose losses had robbed him of his fortune.[1] The details of the sensation which

[1] Cf. the passage in Griesinger [1861, 106, referred to on p. 91 f.] and my remarks in my second paper on the neuro-psychoses of defence (Freud, 1896b). [Actually the reference seems to be to a paragraph near the end of Freud's *first* paper on that subject (Freud, 1894a).]

was being repudiated and of the picture which was employed
in order to repress that sensation also served the dream as a
means of connecting *other* material that was currently active
in my mind with the situation in the dream and of giving that
material representation. I was riding on a *grey* horse, whose
colour corresponded precisely to the *pepper-and-salt* colour of
the suit my colleague P. was wearing when I had last met him
in the country. The cause of my boils had been ascribed to my
eating *highly-spiced* food—an aetiology that was at least pre-
ferable to the *sugar* [diabetes] which might also occur to one in
connection with boils. My friend P. liked to ride *the high horse*
over me ever since he had taken over one of my women patients
on whom I had pulled off some remarkable *feats*. (In the
dream I began by riding tangentially—like the *feat* of a trick-
rider.) But in fact, like the horse in the anecdote of the Sunday
horseman,[1] this patient had taken me wherever she felt inclined.
Thus the horse acquired the symbolic meaning of a woman
patient. (It was *highly intelligent* in the dream.) '*I felt quite at
home up there*' referred to the position I had occupied in this
patient's house before I was replaced by P. Not long before, one
of my few patrons among the leading physicians in this city had
remarked to me in connection with this same house: 'You struck
me as being firmly in the saddle there.' It was a remarkable
feat, too, to be able to carry on my psychotherapeutic work for
eight or ten hours a day while I was having so much pain.
But I knew that I could not go on long with my peculiarly
difficult work unless I was in completely sound physical health;
and my dream was full of gloomy allusions to the situation in
which I should then find myself. (The *note* which neurasthenics
bring with them to show the doctor; *no work, no food*.) In the
course of further interpretation I saw that the dream-work had
succeeded in finding a path from the wishful situation of riding
to some scenes of quarrelling from my very early childhood which
must have occurred between me and a nephew of mine, a year
my senior, who was at present living in England. [Cf. p. 424 f.]
Furthermore, the dream had derived some of its elements from
my travels in Italy: the street in the dream was composed of
impressions of Verona and Siena. A still deeper interpretation

---

[1] [In a letter to Fliess of July 7, 1898 (Freud, 1950a, Letter 92), Freud
describes 'the famous principle of Itzig, the Sunday horseman: "Itzig,
where are you riding to?"—"Don't ask *me*! Ask the horse!"']

led to sexual dream-thoughts, and I recalled the meaning which references to Italy seem to have had in the dreams of a woman patient who had never visited that lovely country: '*gen Italien* [to Italy]'—'*Genitalien* [genitals]'; and this was connected, too, with the house in which I had preceded my friend P. as physician, as well as with the situation of my boil.

In another dream[1] I similarly succeeded in warding off a threatened interruption of my sleep which came this time from a sensory stimulus. In this case it was only by chance, however, that I was able to discover the link between the dream and its accidental stimulus and thus to understand the dream. One morning at the height of summer, while I was staying at a mountain resort in the Tyrol, I woke up knowing I had had a dream that *the Pope was dead*. I failed to interpret this dream— a non-visual one—and only remembered as part of its basis that I had read in a newspaper a short time before that his Holiness was suffering from a slight indisposition. In the course of the morning, however, my wife asked me if I had heard the frightful noise made by the pealing of bells that morning. I had been quite unaware of them, but I now understood my dream. It had been a reaction on the part of my need for sleep to the noise with which the pious Tyrolese had been trying to wake me. I had taken my revenge on them by drawing the inference which formed the content of the dream, and I had then continued my sleep without paying any more attention to the noise.

The dreams quoted in earlier chapters included several which might serve as instances of the working-over of such so-called nervous stimuli. My dream of drinking water in great gulps [p. 123] is an example. The somatic stimulus was apparently its only source, and the wish derived from the sensation (the thirst, that is) was apparently its only motive. The case is similar with other simple dreams in which a somatic stimulus seems able by itself to construct a wish. The dream of the woman patient who threw off the cooling apparatus from her cheek during the night [p. 125] presents an unusual method of re-

---

[1] [This paragraph was added in 1914. The dream had already been very briefly recorded in Freud, 1913*h* (No. 1); it will also be found in Lecture V of Freud, 1916–17.]

acting to a painful stimulus with a wish-fulfilment: it appears as though the patient succeeded temporarily in making herself analgesic, while ascribing her pains to someone else.

My dream of the three Fates [p. 204 ff.] was clearly a hunger dream. But it succeeded in shifting the craving for nourishment back to a child's longing for his mother's breast, and it made use of an innocent desire as a screen for a more serious one which could not be so openly displayed. My dream about Count Thun [p. 208 ff.] showed how an accidental physical need can be linked up with the most intense (but at the same time the most intensely suppressed) mental impulses. And a case such as that related by Garnier (1872, 1, 476) of how the First Consul wove the noise of an exploding bomb into a battle dream before he woke up from it [p. 26] reveals with quite special clarity the nature of the sole motive that leads mental activity to concern itself with sensations during sleep. A young barrister,[1] fresh from his first important bankruptcy proceedings, who dropped asleep one afternoon, behaved in just the same way as the great Napoleon. He had a dream of a certain G. Reich of *Husyatin* [a town in Galicia] whom he had come across during a bankruptcy case; the name 'Husyatin' kept on forcing itself on his notice, till he woke up and found that his wife (who was suffering from a bronchial catarrh) was having a violent fit of coughing [in German '*husten*'].

Let us compare this dream of the first Napoleon (who, incidentally, was an extremely sound sleeper) with that of the sleepy student who was roused by his landlady and told that it was time to go to the hospital, and who proceeded to dream that he was in bed at the hospital and then slept on, under the pretext that as he was already in the hospital there was no need for him to get up and go there [p. 125]. This latter dream was clearly a dream of convenience. The dreamer admitted his motive for dreaming without any disguise; but at the same time he gave away one of the secrets of dreaming in general. All dreams are in a sense dreams of convenience: they serve the purpose of prolonging sleep instead of waking up. *Dreams are the* GUARDIANS *of sleep and not its disturbers.* We shall have occasion elsewhere to justify this view of them in relation to awakening factors of a *psychical* kind [see below, p. 578 f.]; but we are already in a position to show that it is applicable to the part played by

[1] [This sentence and the next were added in 1909.]

objective external stimuli. Either the mind pays no attention at all to occasions for sensation during sleep—if it is able to do this despite the intensity of the stimuli and the significance which it knows attaches to them; or it makes use of a dream in order to deny the stimuli; or, thirdly, if it is obliged to recognize them, it seeks for an interpretation of them which will make the currently active sensation into a component part of a situation which is wished for and which is consistent with sleeping. The currently active sensation is woven into a dream *in order to rob it of reality*. Napoleon could sleep on—with a conviction that what was trying to disturb him was only a dream-memory of the thunder of the guns at Arcole.[1]

Thus the wish to sleep (which the conscious ego is concentrated upon, and which, together with the dream-censorship and the 'secondary revision' which I shall mention later [p. 488 ff.], *constitute the conscious ego's share in dreaming) must in every case be reckoned as one of the motives for the formation of dreams, and every successful dream is a fulfilment of that wish.*[2] We shall discuss elsewhere [p. 570 ff.] the relations subsisting between this universal, invariably present and unchanging wish to sleep and the other wishes, of which now one and now another is fulfilled by the content of the dream. But we have found in the wish to sleep the factor that is able to fill the gap in the theory of Strümpell and Wundt [p. 223 f.] and to explain the perverse and capricious manner in which external stimuli are interpreted. The correct interpretation, which the sleeping mind is perfectly capable of making, would involve an active interest and would require that sleep should be brought to an end; for that reason, of all the possible interpretations, only those are admitted which are consistent with the absolute censorship exercised by the wish to sleep. 'It is the nightingale and not the lark.' For if it were the lark it would mean the end of the lovers' night. Among the interpretations of the stimulus which are accordingly

[1] The two sources from which I know this dream do not agree in their account of it.

[2] [The portion of this sentence in brackets was not included in the first or second edition (1900 and 1909). The phrase 'which the conscious ego is concentrated upon, and which, together with the dream-censorship, constitute the conscious ego's contribution to dreaming' was added in 1911. The phrase 'and the "secondary revision" which I shall mention later' was added as a footnote in 1914 and incorporated in the text in 1930.]

admissible, that one is then selected which can provide the best link with the wishful impulses lurking in the mind. Thus everything is unambiguously determined and nothing is left to arbitrary decision. The misinterpretation is not an illusion but, as one might say, an evasion. Here once again, however, just as when, in obedience to the dream-censorship, a substitution is effected by displacement, we have to admit that we are faced by an act which deviates from normal psychical processes.

When external nervous stimuli and internal somatic stimuli are intense enough to force psychical attention to themselves, then—provided that their outcome *is* dreaming and not waking up—they serve as a fixed point for the formation of a dream, a nucleus in its material; a wish-fulfilment is then looked for that shall correspond to this nucleus, just as (see above [p. 228]) intermediate ideas are looked for between two psychical dream-stimuli. To that extent it is true that in a number of dreams the content of the dream is dictated by the somatic element. In this extreme instance it may even happen that a wish which is not actually a currently active one is called up for the sake of constructing a dream. A dream, however, has no alternative but to represent a wish in the situation of having been fulfilled; it is, as it were, faced with the problem of looking for a wish which can be represented as fulfilled by the currently active sensation. If this immediate material is of a painful or distressing kind, that does not necessarily mean that it cannot be used for the construction of a dream. The mind has wishes at its disposal whose fulfilment produces unpleasure. This seems self-contradictory; but it becomes intelligible when we take into account the presence of two psychical agencies and a censorship between them.

As we have seen, there are 'repressed' wishes in the mind, which belong to the first system and whose fulfilment is opposed by the second system. In saying that there are such wishes I am not making a historical statement to the effect that they once existed and were later abolished. The theory of repression, which is essential to the study of the psychoneuroses, asserts that these repressed wishes *still* exist—though there is a simultaneous inhibition which holds them down. Linguistic usage hits the mark in speaking of the 'suppression' [i.e. the 'pressing down'] of these impulses. The psychical arrangements that make it possible for such impulses to force their way to realization remain in being and in working order. Should it happen, however, that a suppressed wish of this kind is carried into effect, and that its inhibition by the second system (the system that is admissible to consciousness) is defeated, this defeat finds expression as unpleasure. In conclusion: if sensations of an unpleasurable nature arising from somatic sources occur during sleep, the dream-work makes use of that event in order to represent—subject to the continuance of the censorship to a greater or less degree—the fulfilment of some wish which is normally suppressed.[1]

This state of affairs is what makes possible one group of anxiety-dreams,—dream-structures unpropitious from the point of view of the wish-theory. A second group of them reveal a different mechanism; for anxiety in dreams may be psycho-neurotic anxiety: it may originate from psychosexual excitations—in which case the anxiety corresponds to repressed libido. Where this is so, the anxiety, like the whole anxiety-dream, has the significance of a neurotic symptom, and we come near the limit at which the wish-fulfilling purpose of dreams breaks down. [See pp. 160 ff. and 579 ff.] But there are some anxiety-dreams[—those of the first group—]in which the feeling of anxiety is determined somatically—where, for instance, there happens to be difficulty in breathing owing to disease of the lungs or heart;—and in such cases the anxiety is exploited in order to assist the fulfilment in the form of dreams of energetically suppressed wishes which, if they had been dreamt about for *psychical* reasons, would have led to a similar release of anxiety. But there is no difficulty in reconciling these two apparently different groups. In both groups of dreams two psychical factors are involved: an inclination towards an affect and an ideational content; and these are intimately related to each other. If one of them is currently active, it calls up the other even in a dream; in the one case the somatically determined anxiety calls up the suppressed ideational content, and in the other the ideational content with its accompanying sexual excitation, having been set free from repression, calls up a release of anxiety. We can put it that in the first case a somatically determined affect is given a psychical interpreta-

[1] [This whole subject is further discussed in Section C of Chapter VII; see especially p. 557 ff. Cf. also pp. 267 and 487.]

tion; while in the other case, though the whole is psychically determined, the content which had been suppressed is easily replaced by a somatic interpretation appropriate to anxiety. The difficulties which all this offers to our understanding have little to do with dreams: they arise from the fact that we are here touching on the problem of the generation of anxiety and on the problem of repression.

There can be no doubt that physical coenaesthesia [or diffuse general sensibility, see p. 35] is among the internal somatic stimuli which can dictate the content of dreams. It can do so, not in the sense that it can provide the dream's content, but in the sense that it can force upon the dream-thoughts a choice of the material to be represented in the content by putting forward one part of the material as being appropriate to its own character and by holding back another part. Apart from this, the coenaesthetic feelings left over from the preceding day link themselves up, no doubt, with the psychical residues which have such an important influence on dreams. This general mood may persist unchanged in the dream or it may be mastered, and thus, if it is unpleasurable, may be changed into its opposite.[1]

Thus, in my opinion, somatic sources of stimulation during sleep (that is to say, sensations during sleep), unless they are of unusual intensity, play a similar part in the formation of dreams to that played by recent but indifferent impressions left over from the previous day. I believe, that is, that they are brought in to help in the formation of a dream if they fit in appropriately with the ideational content derived from the dream's psychical sources, but otherwise not. They are treated like some cheap material always ready to hand, which is employed whenever it is needed, in contrast to a precious material which itself prescribes the way in which it shall be employed. If, to take a simile, a patron of the arts brings an artist some rare stone, such as a piece of onyx, and asks him to create a work of art from it, then the size of the stone, its colour and markings, help to decide what head or what scene shall be represented in it. Whereas in the case of a uniform and plentiful material such as marble or sandstone, the artist merely follows some idea that is present in his own mind. It is only in this way, so it seems to

[1] [Cf. p. 487 ff.—This last sentence was added in 1914.]

me, that we can explain the fact that dream-content provided by somatic stimuli of no unusual intensity fails to appear in every dream or every night. [Cf. p. 226.][1]

I can perhaps best illustrate my meaning by an example, which, moreover, will bring us back to dream-interpretation.

One day I had been trying to discover what might be the meaning of the feelings of being inhibited, of being glued to the spot, of not being able to get something done, and so on, which occur so often in dreams and are so closely akin to feelings of anxiety. That night I had the following dream:

I was very incompletely dressed and was going upstairs from a flat on the ground floor to a higher storey. I was going up three steps at a time and was delighted at my agility. Suddenly I saw a maid-servant coming down the stairs—coming towards me, that is. I felt ashamed and tried to hurry, and at this point the feeling of being inhibited set in: I was glued to the steps and unable to budge from the spot.

ANALYSIS.—The situation in the dream is taken from everyday reality. I occupy two flats in a house in Vienna, which are connected only by the public staircase. My consulting-room and study are on the upper ground floor and my living rooms are one storey higher. When, late in the evening, I have finished my work down below, I go up the stairs to my bedroom. On the evening before I had the dream, I had in fact made this short journey in rather disordered dress—that is to say, I had taken off my collar and tie and cuffs. In the dream this had been turned into a higher degree of undress, but, as usual, an indeterminate one. [Cf. p. 245.] I usually go upstairs two or three steps at a time; and this was recognized in the dream itself as a wish-fulfilment: the ease with which I achieved it reassured me as to the functioning of my heart. Further, this method of going upstairs was an effective contrast to the inhibition in the second half of the dream. It showed me—what needed no proving—that dreams find no difficulty in representing motor acts carried out to perfection. (One need only recall dreams of flying.)

---

[1] [*Footnote added* 1914:] Rank has shown in a number of papers [1910, 1912a and 1912b] that certain arousal dreams produced by organic stimuli (dreams with a urinary stimulus and dreams of emission or orgasm) are especially suited to demonstrate the struggle between the need to sleep and the claims of organic needs, as well as the influence of the latter upon the content of dreams. [See p. 402 f.]

The staircase up which I was going, however, was not the one in my house. At first I failed to recognize it and it was only the identity of the person who met me that made it clear to me what locality was intended. This person was the maid-servant of the old lady whom I was visiting twice a day in order to give her injections [cf. p. 118]; and the staircase, too, was just like the one in her house which I had to go up twice a day.

Now how did this staircase and this female figure come to be in my dream? The feeling of shame at not being completely dressed is no doubt of a sexual nature; but the maid-servant whom I dreamt about was older than I am, surly and far from attractive. The only answer to the problem that occurred to me was this. When I paid my morning visits to this house I used as a rule to be seized with a desire to clear my throat as I went up the stairs and the product of my expectoration would fall on the staircase. For on neither of these floors was there a spittoon; and the view I took was that the cleanliness of the stairs should not be maintained at my expense but should be made possible by the provision of a spittoon. The concierge, an equally elderly and surly woman (but of cleanly instincts, as I was prepared to admit), looked at the matter in a different light. She would lie in wait for me to see whether I should again make free of the stairs, and, if she found that I did, I used to hear her grumbling audibly; and for several days afterwards she would omit the usual greeting when we met. The day before I had the dream the concierge's party had received a reinforcement in the shape of the maid-servant. I had, as usual, concluded my hurried visit to the patient, when the servant stopped me in the hall and remarked: 'You might have wiped your boots, doctor, before you came into the room to-day. You've made the red carpet all dirty again with your feet.' This was the only claim the staircase and the maid-servant had to appearing in my dream.

There was an internal connection between my running up the stairs and my spitting on the stairs. Pharyngitis as well as heart trouble are both regarded as punishments for the vice of smoking. And on account of that habit my reputation for tidiness was not of the highest with the authorities in my own house any more than in the other; so that the two were fused into one in the dream.

I must postpone my further interpretation of this dream till

I can explain the origin of the typical dream of being incompletely dressed. I will only point out as a provisional conclusion to be drawn from the present dream that a sensation of inhibited movement in dreams is produced whenever the particular context requires it. The cause of this part of the dream's content cannot have been that some special modification in my powers of movement had occurred during my sleep, since only a moment earlier I had seen myself (almost as though to confirm this fact) running nimbly up the stairs.[1]

[1] [The feeling of inhibition in dreams is discussed at length on p. 335 ff. The present dream is further analysed on p. 247 f. It was reported in a letter to Fliess of May 31, 1897. (Freud, 1950a, Letter 64.)]

(D)

TYPICAL DREAMS

We are not in general in a position to interpret another person's dream unless he is prepared to communicate to us the unconscious thoughts that lie behind its content. The practical applicability of our method of interpreting dreams is in consequence severely restricted.[1] We have seen that, as a general rule, each person is at liberty to construct his dream-world according to his individual peculiarities and so to make it unintelligible to other people. It now appears, however, that, in complete contrast to this, there are a certain number of dreams which almost everyone has dreamt alike and which we are accustomed to assume must have the same meaning for everyone. A special interest attaches, moreover, to these typical dreams because they presumably arise from the same sources in every case and thus seem particularly well qualified to throw light on the sources of dreams.

It is therefore with quite particular anticipations that we shall attempt to apply our technique of dream-interpretation to these typical dreams; and it is with great reluctance that we shall have to confess that our art disappoints our expectations precisely in relation to this material. If we attempt to interpret a typical dream, the dreamer fails as a rule to produce the associations which would in other cases have led us to understand it, or else his associations become obscure and insufficient so that we cannot solve our problem with their help. We shall learn in a later portion of this work [Section E of Chapter VI,

---

[1] [*Footnote added* 1925:] This assertion that our method of interpreting dreams cannot be applied unless we have access to the dreamer's associative material requires supplementing: our interpretative activity is in one instance independent of these associations—if, namely, the dreamer has employed *symbolic* elements in the content of the dream. In such cases we make use of what is, strictly speaking, a second and auxiliary method of dream-interpretation. (See below [p. 359 f.].) [In the edition of 1911 only, the following footnote appeared at this point: 'Apart from cases in which the dreamer makes use of symbols which are familiar to us for the purpose of representing his latent dream-thoughts (see below).']

p. 351 ff.] why this is so and how we can make up for this defect in our technique. My readers will also discover why it is that at the present point I am able to deal only with a few members of the group of typical dreams and must postpone my consideration of the rest until this later point in my discussion. [See p. 384 ff.][1]

(a) EMBARRASSING DREAMS OF BEING NAKED

Dreams of being naked or insufficiently dressed in the presence of strangers sometimes occur with the additional feature of there being a complete absence of any such feeling as shame on the dreamer's part. We are only concerned here, however, with those dreams of being naked in which one *does* feel shame and embarrassment and tries to escape or hide, and is then overcome by a strange inhibition which prevents one from moving and makes one feel incapable of altering one's distressing situation. It is only with this accompaniment that the dream is typical; without it, the gist of its subject-matter may be included in every variety of context or may be ornamented with individual trimmings. Its essence [in its typical form] lies in a distressing feeling in the nature of shame and in the fact that one wishes to hide one's nakedness, as a rule by locomotion, but finds one is unable to do so. I believe the great majority of my readers will have found themselves in this situation in dreams.

The nature of the undress involved is customarily far from clear. The dreamer may say 'I was in my chemise', but this is rarely a distinct picture. The kind of undress is usually so vague that the description is expressed as an alternative: 'I was in my chemise or petticoat.' As a rule the defect in the dreamer's toilet is not so grave as to appear to justify the shame to which it gives rise. In the case of a man who has worn the Emperor's uniform, nakedness is often replaced by some breach of the dress regulations: 'I was walking in the street without my sabre and saw some officers coming up', or 'I was without my necktie', or 'I was wearing civilian check trousers', and so on.

The people in whose presence one feels ashamed are almost

---

[1] [This paragraph in its present form dates from 1914. It was in the edition of that year (the fourth) that the section on symbolism was added to Chapter VI. This led to considerable alterations in the present section, much of the material in which was transferred to the new section. (See Editor's Introduction, p. xiii.)]

always strangers, with their features left indeterminate. In the typical dream it never happens that the clothing which causes one so much embarrassment is objected to or so much as noticed by the onlookers. On the contrary, they adopt indifferent or (as I observed in one particularly clear dream) solemn and stiff expressions of face. This is a suggestive point.

The embarrassment of the dreamer and the indifference of the onlookers offer us, when taken together, a contradiction of the kind that is so common in dreams. It would after all be more in keeping with the dreamer's feelings if strangers looked at him in astonishment and derision or with indignation. But this objectionable feature of the situation has, I believe, been got rid of by wish-fulfilment, whereas some force has led to the retention of the other features; and the two portions of the dream are consequently out of harmony with each other. We possess an interesting piece of evidence that the dream in the form in which it appears—partly distorted by wish-fulfilment—has not been rightly understood. For it has become the basis of a fairy tale which is familiar to us all in Hans Andersen's version, *The Emperor's New Clothes*, and which has quite recently been put into verse by Ludwig Fulda[1] in his ['dramatic fairy tale'] *Der Talisman*. Hans Andersen's fairy tale tells us how two impostors weave the Emperor a costly garment which, they say, will be visible only to persons of virtue and loyalty. The Emperor walks out in this invisible garment, and all the spectators, intimidated by the fabric's power to act as a touchstone, pretend not to notice the Emperor's nakedness.

This is just the situation in our dream. It is hardly rash to assume that the unintelligibility of the dream's content as it exists in the memory has led to its being recast in a form designed to make sense of the situation. That situation, however, is in the process deprived of its original meaning and put to extraneous uses. But, as we shall see later, it is a common thing for the conscious thought-activity of a second psychical system to misunderstand the content of a dream in this way, and this misunderstanding must be regarded as one of the factors in determining the final form assumed by dreams.[2]

---

[1] [German playwright, 1862–1939.]

[2] [This process of 'secondary revision' forms the subject of Section I of Chapter VI (p. 488 ff.). Its application to this same fairy tale is discussed in a letter to Fliess of July 7, 1897 (Freud, 1950*a*, Letter 66).]

Moreover we shall learn that similar misunderstandings (taking place, once again, within one and the same psychical personality) play a major part in the construction of obsessions and phobias.

In the case of our dream we are in a position to indicate the material upon which the misinterpretation is based. The impostor is the dream and the Emperor is the dreamer himself; the moralizing purpose of the dream reveals an obscure knowledge of the fact that the latent dream-content is concerned with forbidden wishes that have fallen victim to repression. For the context in which dreams of this sort appear during my analyses of neurotics leaves no doubt that they are based upon memories from earliest childhood. It is only in our childhood that we are seen in inadequate clothing both by members of our family and by strangers—nurses, maid-servants, and visitors; and it is only then that we feel no shame at our nakedness.[1] We can observe how undressing has an almost intoxicating effect on many children even in their later years, instead of making them feel ashamed. They laugh and jump about and slap themselves, while their mother, or whoever else may be there, reproves them and says: 'Ugh! Shocking! You mustn't ever do that!' Children frequently manifest a desire to exhibit. One can scarcely pass through a country village in our part of the world without meeting some child of two or three who lifts up his little shirt in front of one—in one's honour, perhaps. One of my patients has a conscious memory of a scene in his eighth year, when at bed-time he wanted to dance into the next room where his little sister slept, dressed in his night-shirt, but was prevented by his nurse. In the early history of neurotics an important part is played by exposure to children of the opposite sex; in paranoia delusions of being observed while dressing and undressing are to be traced back to experiences of this kind; while among persons who have remained at the stage of perversion there is one class in which this infantile impulse has reached the pitch of a symptom—the class of 'exhibitionists'.[2]

---

[1] A child plays a part in the fairy tale as well; for it was a small child who suddenly exclaimed: 'But he has nothing on!'

[2] [This allusion to the perversions as remnants of infantile sexual activity foreshadows Freud's analysis of the sexual instinct in his *Three Essays* (1905d).]

When we look back at this unashamed period of childhood it seems to us a Paradise; and Paradise itself is no more than a group phantasy of the childhood of the individual. That is why mankind were naked in Paradise and were without shame in one another's presence; till a moment arrived when shame and anxiety awoke, expulsion followed, and sexual life and the tasks of cultural activity began. But we can regain this Paradise every night in our dreams. I have already [p. 218] expressed a suspicion that impressions of earliest childhood (that is, from the prehistoric epoch until about the end of the third year of life) strive to achieve reproduction, from their very nature and irrespectively perhaps of their actual content, and that their repetition constitutes the fulfilment of a wish. Thus dreams of being naked are dreams of exhibiting.[1]

The core of a dream of exhibiting lies in the figure of the dreamer himself (not as he was as a child but as he appears at the present time) and his inadequate clothing (which emerges indistinctly, whether owing to superimposed layers of innumerable later memories of being in undress or as a result of the censorship). Added to these are the figures of the people in whose presence the dreamer feels ashamed. I know of no instance in which the actual spectators of the infantile scene of exhibiting have appeared in the dream; a dream is scarcely ever a simple memory. Curiously enough, the people upon whom our sexual interest was directed in childhood are omitted in all the reproductions which occur in dreams, in hysteria and in obsessional neurosis. It is only in paranoia that these spectators reappear and, though they remain invisible, their presence is inferred with fanatical conviction. What takes their place in dreams—'a lot of strangers' who take no notice of the spectacle that is offered—is nothing more nor less than the wishful contrary of the single familiar individual before whom the dreamer exposed himself. Incidentally, 'a lot of strangers' frequently appear in dreams in many other connections, and they always stand as the

---

[1] [*Footnote added* 1911:] Ferenczi [1910] has recorded a number of interesting dreams of being naked dreamt by *women*. There was no difficulty in tracing these back to the infantile desire to exhibit; but they differed in some respects from the 'typical' dreams of being naked which I have discussed in the text.—[The penultimate sentence in the paragraph above seems to adumbrate some of the ideas put forward twenty years later in *Beyond the Pleasure Principle* (Freud, 1920g).]

wishful contrary of 'secrecy'.[1] It is to be noticed that even in paranoia, where the original state of things is restored, this reversal into a contrary is observed. The subject feels that he is no longer alone, he has no doubt that he is being observed, but the observers are 'a lot of strangers' whose identity is left curiously vague.

In addition to this, repression plays a part in dreams of exhibiting; for the distress felt in such dreams is a reaction on the part of the second system against the content of the scene of exhibiting having found expression in spite of the ban upon it. If the distress was to be avoided, the scene should never have been revived.

We shall return later [p. 335 ff.] to the feeling of being inhibited. It serves admirably in dreams to represent a conflict in the will or a negative. The unconscious purpose requires the exhibiting to proceed; the censorship demands that it shall be stopped.

There can be no doubt that the connections between our typical dreams and fairy tales and the material of other kinds of creative writing are neither few nor accidental. It sometimes happens that the sharp eye of a creative writer has an analytic realization of the process of transformation of which he is habitually no more than the tool. If so, he may follow the process in a reverse direction and so trace back the imaginative writing to a dream. One of my friends has drawn my attention to the following passage in Gottfried Keller's *Der grüne Heinrich* [Part III, Chapter 2]: 'I hope, my dear Lee, that you may never learn from your own personal experience the peculiar and *piquant* truth of the plight of Odysseus when he appeared, naked and covered with mud, before the eyes of Nausicaä and her maidens! Shall I tell you how that can happen? Let us look into our example. If you are wandering about in a foreign land, far from your home and from all that you hold dear, if you have seen and heard many things, have known sorrow and care, and are wretched and forlorn, then without fail you will dream one night that you are coming near to your home; you will see it gleaming and shining in the fairest colours, and the sweetest, dearest and most beloved forms will move towards you. Then

---

[1] [This point is also mentioned towards the end of Freud's paper on 'Screen Memories' (1899a).—*Footnote added* 1909:] For obvious reasons the presence of 'the whole family' in a dream has the same significance.

suddenly you will become aware that you are in rags, naked and dusty. You will be seized with a nameless shame and dread, you will seek to find covering and to hide yourself,.and you will awake bathed in sweat. This, so long as men breathe, is the dream of the unhappy wanderer; and Homer has evoked the picture of his plight from the deepest and eternal nature of man.'

The deepest and eternal nature of man, upon whose evocation in his hearers the poet is accustomed to rely, lies in those impulses of the mind which have their roots in a childhood that has since become prehistoric. Suppressed and forbidden wishes from childhood break through in the dream behind the exile's unobjectionable wishes which are capable of entering consciousness; and that is why the dream which finds concrete expression in the legend of Nausicaä ends as a rule as an anxiety-dream.

My own dream (recorded on p. 238) of running upstairs and of soon afterwards finding myself glued to the steps was equally a dream of exhibiting, since it bears the essential marks of being one. It should be possible, therefore, to trace it back to experiences during my childhood, and if these could be discovered they should enable us to judge how far the maid-servant's behaviour to me—her accusing me of dirtying the carpet— helped to give her her place in my dream. I can, as it happens, provide the necessary particulars. In a psycho-analysis one learns to interpret propinquity in time as representing connection in subject-matter. [See below, p. 314.] Two thoughts which occur in immediate sequence without any apparent connection are in fact part of a single unity which has to be discovered; in just the same way, if I write an '*a*' and a '*b*' in succession, they have to be pronounced as a single syllable '*ab*'. The same is true of dreams. The staircase dream to which I have referred was one of a series of dreams; and I understood the interpretation of the other members of the series. Since this particular dream was surrounded by the others it must have dealt with the same subject. Now these other dreams were based on a recollection of a nurse in whose charge I had been from some date during my earliest infancy till I was two and a half. I even retain an obscure conscious memory of her. According to what I was told not long ago by my mother, she was old and ugly, but very sharp and efficient. From what I can infer from my own dreams her treatment of me was not always excessive in its amiability and her words could be harsh if I failed to reach the required standard of cleanliness. And thus the maid-servant, since she had undertaken the job of carrying on this educational work, acquired the right to be treated in my dream as a reincarnation of the prehistoric old nurse. It is reasonable to suppose that the child loved the old woman who taught him these lessons, in spite of her rough treatment of him.[1]

(β) DREAMS OF THE DEATH OF PERSONS OF WHOM THE DREAMER IS FOND

Another group of dreams which may be described as typical are those containing the death of some loved relative—for instance, of a parent, of a brother or sister, or of a child. Two classes of such dreams must at once be distinguished: those in which the dreamer is unaffected by grief, so that on awakening he is astonished at his lack of feeling, and those in which the dreamer feels deeply pained by the death and may even weep bitterly in his sleep.

We need not consider the dreams of the first of these classes, for they have no claim to be regarded as 'typical'. If we analyse them, we find that they have some meaning other than their apparent one, and that they are intended to conceal some other wish. Such was the dream of the aunt who saw her sister's only son lying in his coffin. (See p. 152.) It did not mean that she wished her little nephew dead; as we have seen, it merely con-cealed a wish to see a particular person of whom she was fond and whom she had not met for a long time—a person whom she had once before met after a similarly long interval beside the coffin of another nephew. This wish, which was the true content of the dream, gave no occasion for grief, and no grief, therefore, was felt in the dream. It will be noticed that the affect felt in the dream belongs to its latent and not to its

---

[1] Here is an 'over-interpretation' of the same dream. Since '*spuken* [haunting]' is an activity of *spirits*, '*spucken* [spitting] on the stairs' might be loosely rendered as '*esprit d'escalier*'. This last phrase is equivalent to lack of ready repartee ['*Schlagfertigkeit*', literally 'readiness to strike']—a failing to which I must in fact plead guilty. Was my nurse, I wonder, equally wanting in that quality? [This nurse is referred to at the end of Chapter IV of *The Psychopathology of Everyday Life* (Freud, 1901*b*) and in greater detail in his letters to Fliess of October 3 and 4 and October 15, 1897 (Freud, 1950*a*, Letters 70 and 71).]

manifest content, and that the dream's *affective* content has remained untouched by the distortion which has overtaken its *ideational* content.[1]

Very different are the dreams of the other class—those in which the dreamer imagines the death of a loved relative and is at the same time painfully affected. The meaning of such dreams, as their content indicates, is a wish that the person in question may die. And since I must expect that the feelings of all of my readers and any others who have experienced similar dreams will rebel against my assertion, I must try to base my evidence for it on the broadest possible foundation.

I have already discussed a dream which taught us that the wishes which are represented in dreams as fulfilled are not always present-day wishes. They may also be wishes of the past which have been abandoned, overlaid and repressed, and to which we have to attribute some sort of continued existence only because of their re-emergence in a dream. They are not dead in our sense of the word but only like the shades in the Odyssey, which awoke to some sort of life as soon as they had tasted blood. In the dream of the dead child in the 'case' (p. 154) what was involved was a wish which had been an immediate one fifteen years earlier and was frankly admitted as having existed at that time. I may add—and this may not be without its bearing upon the theory of dreams—that even behind this wish there lay a memory from the dreamer's earliest childhood. When she was a small child—the exact date could not be fixed with certainty—she had heard that her mother had fallen into a deep depression during the pregnancy of which she had been the fruit and had passionately wished that the child she was bearing might die. When the dreamer herself was grown-up and pregnant, she merely followed her mother's example.

If anyone dreams, with every sign of pain, that his father or mother or brother or sister has died, I should never use the dream as evidence that he wishes for that person's death *at the present time*. The theory of dreams does not require as much as that; it is satisfied with the inference that this death has been wished for at some time or other during the dreamer's childhood. I fear, however, that this reservation will not appease the

[1] [See the discussion on affects in dreams in Chapter VII, Section H (especially p. 463).]

objectors; they will deny the possibility of their *ever* having had such a thought with just as much energy as they insist that they harbour no such wishes now. I must therefore reconstruct a portion of the vanished mental life of children on the basis of the evidence of the present.[1]

Let us first consider the relation of children to their brothers and sisters. I do not know why we presuppose that that relation must be a loving one; for instances of hostility between adult brothers and sisters force themselves upon everyone's experience and we can often establish the fact that the disunity originated in childhood or has always existed. But it is further true that a great many adults, who are on affectionate terms with their brothers and sisters and are ready to stand by them to-day, passed their childhood on almost unbroken terms of enmity with them. The elder child ill-treats the younger, maligns him and robs him of his toys; while the younger is consumed with impotent rage against the elder, envies and fears him, or meets his oppressor with the first stirrings of a love of liberty and a sense of justice. Their parents complain that the children do not get on with one another, but cannot discover why. It is easy to see that the character of even a good child is not what we should wish to find it in an adult. Children are completely egoistic; they feel their needs intensely and strive ruthlessly to satisfy them—especially as against the rivals, other children, and first and foremost as against their brothers and sisters. But we do not on that account call a child 'bad', we call him 'naughty'; he is no more answerable for his evil deeds in our judgement than in the eyes of the law. And it is right that this should be so; for we may expect that, before the end of the period which we count as childhood, altruistic impulses and morality will awaken in the little egoist and (to use Meynert's terms [e.g. 1892, 169 ff.]) a secondary ego will overlay and inhibit the primary one. It is true, no doubt, that morality does not set in simultaneously all along the line and that the length of non-moral childhood varies in different individuals. If this morality fails to develop, we like to talk of 'degeneracy', though what in fact faces us is an inhibition in development. After the

[1] [*Footnote added* 1909:] Cf. my 'Analysis of a Phobia in a Five-Year-Old Boy' (1909*b*) and my paper 'On the Sexual Theories of Children' (1908*c*).

primary character has already been overlaid by later development, it can still be laid bare again, at all events in part, in cases of hysterical illness. There is a really striking resemblance between what is known as the hysterical character and that of a naughty child. Obsessional neurosis, on the contrary, corresponds to a super-morality imposed as a reinforcing weight upon fresh stirrings of the primary character.

Many people, therefore, who love their brothers and sisters and would feel bereaved if they were to die, harbour evil wishes against them in their unconscious, dating from earlier times; and these are capable of being realized in dreams.

It is of quite particular interest, however, to observe the behaviour of small children up to the age of two or three or a little older towards their younger brothers and sisters. Here, for instance, was a child who had so far been the only one; and now he was told that the stork had brought a new baby. He looked the new arrival up and down and then declared decisively: 'The stork can take him away again!'[1] I am quite seriously of the opinion that a child can form a just estimate of the set-back he has to expect at the hands of the little stranger. A lady of my acquaintance, who is on very good terms to-day with a sister four years her junior, tells me that she greeted the news of her first arrival with this qualification: 'But all the same I shan't give her my red cap.' Even if a child only comes to realize the situation later on, his hostility will date from that moment. I know of a case in which a little girl of less than three tried to strangle an infant in its cradle because she felt that its continued presence boded her no good. Children at that time of life are capable of jealousy of any degree of intensity and obviousness. Again, if it should happen that the baby sister does in fact disappear after a short while, the elder child will find the whole affection of the household once more concentrated upon himself. If after that the stork should bring yet another baby, it

[1] [Footnote added 1909:] The three-and-a-half-year-old Hans (whose phobia was the subject of the analysis mentioned in the preceding footnote) exclaimed shortly after the birth of a sister, while he was suffering from a feverish sore throat: 'I don't want a baby sister!' [Freud, 1909b, Section I.] During his neurosis eighteen months later he frankly confessed to a wish that his mother might drop the baby into the bath so that she would die. [Ibid., Section II (April 11).] At the same time, Hans was a good-natured and affectionate child, who soon grew fond of this same sister and particularly enjoyed taking her under his wing.

seems only logical that the little favourite should nourish a wish that his new competitor may meet with the same fate as the earlier one, so that he himself may be as happy as he was originally and during the interval.[1] Normally, of course, this attitude of a child towards a younger brother or sister is a simple function of the difference between their ages. Where the gap in time is sufficiently long, an elder girl will already begin to feel the stirring of her maternal instincts towards the helpless new-born baby.

Hostile feelings towards brothers and sisters must be far more frequent in childhood than the unseeing eye of the adult observer can perceive.[2]

In the case of my own children, who followed each other in rapid succession, I neglected the opportunity of carrying out observations of this kind; but I am now making up for this neglect by observing a small nephew, whose autocratic rule was upset, after lasting for fifteen months, by the appearance of a female rival. I am told, it is true, that the young man behaves in the most chivalrous manner to his little sister, that he kisses her hand and strokes her; but I have been able to convince myself that even before the end of his second year he made use of his powers of speech for the purpose of criticizing someone whom he could not fail to regard as superfluous. Whenever the conversation touched upon her he used to intervene in it and exclaim petulantly: 'Too 'ickle! too 'ickle!' During the last few

---

[1] [*Footnote added* 1914:] Deaths that are experienced in this way in childhood may quickly be forgotten in the family; but psycho-analytic research shows that they have a very important influence on subsequent neuroses.

[2] [*Footnote added* 1914:] Since this was written, a large number of observations have been made and recorded in the literature of psycho-analysis upon the originally hostile attitude of children towards their brothers and sisters and one of their parents. The [Swiss] author and poet Spitteler has given us a particularly genuine and naïve account of this childish attitude, derived from his own childhood [1914, 40]: 'Moreover there was a second Adolf there: a little creature who they alleged was my brother, though I could not see what use he was and still less why they made as much fuss of him as of me myself. I was sufficient so far as I was concerned; why should I want a brother? And he was not merely useless, he was positively in the way. When I pestered my grandmother, he wanted to pester her too. When I was taken out in the perambulator, he sat opposite to me and took up half the space, so that we were bound to kick each other with our feet.'

months the baby's growth has made enough progress to place
her beyond this particular ground for contempt, and the little
boy has found a different basis for his assertion that she does not
deserve so much attention: at every suitable opportunity he
draws attention to the fact that she has no teeth.[1] We all of us
recollect how the eldest girl of another of my sisters, who was
then a child of six, spent half an hour in insisting upon each of
her aunts in succession agreeing with her: 'Lucie can't understand that yet, can she?' she kept asking. Lucie was her rival
—two and a half years her junior.

In none of my women patients, to take an example, have I
failed to come upon this dream of the death of a brother or
sister, which tallies with an increase in hostility. I have only
found a single exception; and it was easy to interpret this as a
confirmation of the rule. On one occasion during an analytic
session I was explaining this subject to a lady, since in view of
her symptom its discussion seemed to me relevant. To my
astonishment she replied that she had never had such a dream.
Another dream, however, occurred to her, which ostensibly had
no connection with the topic—a dream which she had first
dreamt when she was four years old and at that time the
youngest of the family, and which she had dreamt repeatedly
since: *A whole crowd of children—all her brothers, sisters and cousins
of both sexes—were romping in a field. Suddenly they all grew wings,
flew away and disappeared.* She had no idea what this dream meant;
but it is not hard to recognize that in its original form it had
been a dream of the death of all her brothers and sisters, and
had been only slightly influenced by the censorship. I may
venture to suggest the following analysis. On the occasion of the
death of one of this crowd of children (in this instance the
children of two brothers had been brought up together as a
single family) the dreamer, not yet four years old at the time,
must have asked some wise grown-up person what became of
children when they were dead. The reply must have been:
'They grow wings and turn into little angels.' In the dream
which followed upon this piece of information all the dreamer's
brothers and sisters had wings like angels and—which is the

---

[1] [*Footnote added* 1909:] Little Hans, when he was three and a half,
gave vent to a crushing criticism of his sister in the same words. It was
because of her lack of teeth, he supposed, that she was unable to talk.
[Freud, 1909*b*, Section I.]

main point—flew away. Our little baby-killer was left alone, strange to say: the only survivor of the whole crowd! We can hardly be wrong in supposing that the fact of the children romping in a *field* before flying away points to butterflies. It is as though the child was led by the same chain of thought as the peoples of antiquity to picture the soul as having a butterfly's wings.

At this point someone will perhaps interrupt: 'Granted that children have hostile impulses towards their brothers and sisters, how can a child's mind reach such a pitch of depravity as to wish for the *death* of his rivals or of playmates stronger than himself, as though the death penalty were the only punishment for every crime?' Anyone who talks like this has failed to bear in mind that a child's idea of being 'dead' has nothing much in common with ours apart from the word. Children know nothing of the horrors of corruption, of freezing in the ice-cold grave, of the terrors of eternal nothingness—ideas which grown-up people find it so hard to tolerate, as is proved by all the myths of a future life. The fear of death has no meaning to a child; hence it is that he will play with the dreadful word and use it as a threat against a playmate: 'If you do that again, you'll die, like Franz!' Meanwhile the poor mother gives a shudder and re-members, perhaps, that the greater half of the human race fail to survive their childhood years. It was actually possible for a child, who was over eight years old at the time, coming home from a visit to the Natural History Museum, to say to his mother: 'I'm so fond of you, Mummy: when you die I'll have you stuffed and I'll keep you in this room, so that I can see you *all* the time.' So little resemblance is there between a child's idea of being dead and our own![1]

To children, who, moreover, are spared the sight of the scenes of suffering which precede death, being 'dead' means approximately the same as being 'gone'—not troubling the sur-vivors any longer. A child makes no distinction as to how this absence is brought about: whether it is due to a journey, to a

---

[1] [*Footnote added* 1909:] I was astonished to hear a highly intelligent boy of ten remark after the sudden death of his father: 'I know father's dead, but what I can't understand is why he doesn't come home to supper.'—[*Added* 1919:] Further material on this subject will be found in the first [seven] volumes of the periodical *Imago* [1912–21], under the standing rubric of '*Vom wahren Wesen der Kinderseele*' ['The True Nature of the Child Mind'], edited by Frau Dr. H. von Hug-Hellmuth.

D. TYPICAL DREAMS   255

dismissal, to an estrangement, or to death.[1] If, during a child's
prehistoric epoch, his nurse has been dismissed, and if soon
afterwards his mother has died, the two events are superimposed
on each other in a single series in his memory as revealed in
analysis. When people are absent, children do not miss them
with any great intensity; many mothers have learnt this to their
sorrow when, after being away from home for some weeks on a
summer holiday, they are met on their return by the news that
the children have not once asked after their mummy. If their
mother does actually make the journey to that 'undiscover'd
country, from whose bourn no traveller returns', children seem
at first to have forgotten her, and it is only later on that they
begin to call their dead mother to mind.

Thus if a child has reasons for wishing the absence of another,
there is nothing to restrain him from giving his wish the form
of the other child being dead. And the psychical reaction to
dreams containing death-wishes proves that, in spite of the
different content of these wishes in the case of children, they are
nevertheless in some way or other the same as wishes expressed
in the same terms by adults.[2]

If, then, a child's death-wishes against his brothers and sisters
are explained by the childish egoism which makes him regard
them as his rivals, how are we to explain his death-wishes
against his parents, who surround him with love and fulfil his
needs and whose preservation that same egoism should lead him
to desire?

[1] [*Footnote added* 1919:] An observation made by a parent who had a
knowledge of psycho-analysis caught the actual moment at which his
highly intelligent four-year-old daughter perceived the distinction
between being 'gone' and being 'dead'. The little girl had been troublesome at meal-time and noticed that one of the maids at the pension
where they were staying was looking at her askance. 'I wish Josefine was
dead,' was the child's comment to her father. 'Why dead?' enquired her
father soothingly; 'wouldn't it do if she went away?' 'No,' replied the
child; 'then she'd come back again.' The unbounded self-love (the nar-
cissism) of children regards any interference as an act of *lèse majesté*; and
their feelings demand (like the Draconian code) that any such crime shall
receive the one form of punishment which admits of no degrees.

[2] [The adult attitude to death is discussed by Freud more particularly in the second essay of his *Totem and Taboo* (1912–13), Section 3(*c*),
in his paper on 'The Three Caskets' (1913*f*) and in the second part of
his 'Thoughts on War and Death' (1915*b*).]

A solution of this difficulty is afforded by the observation that dreams of the death of parents apply with preponderant frequency to the parent who is of the same sex as the dreamer: that men, that is, dream mostly of their father's death and women of their mother's. I cannot pretend that this is universally so, but the preponderance in the direction I have indicated is so evident that it requires to be explained by a factor of general importance.[1] It is as though—to put it bluntly—a sexual preference were making itself felt at an early age: as though boys regarded their fathers and girls their mothers as their rivals in love, whose elimination could not fail to be to their advantage.

Before this idea is rejected as a monstrous one, it is as well in this case, too, to consider the real relations obtaining—this time between parents and children. We must distinguish between what the cultural standards of filial piety demand of this relation and what everyday observation shows it in fact to be. More than one occasion for hostility lies concealed in the relation between parents and children—a relation which affords the most ample opportunities for wishes to arise which cannot pass the censorship.

Let us consider first the relation between father and son. The sanctity which we attribute to the rules laid down in the Decalogue has, I think, blunted our powers of perceiving the real facts. We seem scarcely to venture to observe that the majority of mankind disobey the Fifth Commandment. Alike in the lowest and in the highest strata of human society filial piety is wont to give way to other interests. The obscure information which is brought to us by mythology and legend from the primaeval ages of human society gives an unpleasing picture of the father's despotic power and of the ruthlessness with which he made use of it. Kronos devoured his children, just as the wild boar devours the sow's litter; while Zeus emasculated his father[2] and made himself ruler in his place. The more un-

[1] [*Footnote added* 1925:] The situation is often obscured by the emergence of a self-punitive impulse, which threatens the dreamer, by way of a moral reaction, with the loss of the parent whom he loves.

[2] [*Footnote added* 1909:] Or so he is reported to have done according to some myths. According to others, emasculation was only carried out by Kronos on his father Uranus. [This passage is discussed in Chapter X (3) of *The Psychopathology of Everyday Life* (Freud, 1901*b*).] For the mythological significance of this theme, cf. Rank, 1909, [*added* 1914:] and Rank, 1912*c*, Chapter IX, Section 2.—[These sentences in the text are, of course,

restricted was the rule of the father in the ancient family, the more must the son, as his destined successor, have found himself in the position of an enemy, and the more impatient must he have been to become ruler himself through his father's death. Even in our middle-class families fathers are as a rule inclined to refuse their sons independence and the means necessary to secure it and thus to foster the growth of the germ of hostility which is inherent in their relation. A physician will often be in a position to notice how a son's grief at the loss of his father cannot suppress his satisfaction at having at length won his freedom. In our society to-day fathers are apt to cling desperately to what is left of a now sadly antiquated *potestas patris familias*; and an author who, like Ibsen, brings the immemorial struggle between fathers and sons into prominence in his writings may be certain of producing his effect.

Occasions for conflict between a daughter and her mother arise when the daughter begins to grow up and long for sexual liberty, but finds herself under her mother's tutelage; while the mother, on the other hand, is warned by her daughter's growth that the time has come when she herself must abandon her claims to sexual satisfaction.

All of this is patent to the eyes of everyone. But it does not help us in our endeavour to explain dreams of a parent's death in people whose piety towards their parents has long been unimpeachably established. Previous discussions, moreover, will have prepared us to learn that the death-wish against parents dates back to earliest childhood.

This supposition is confirmed with a certainty beyond all doubt in the case of psychoneurotics when they are subjected to analysis. We learn from them that a child's sexual wishes —if in their embryonic stage they deserve to be so described— awaken very early, and that a girl's first affection is for her father[1] and a boy's first childish desires are for his mother. Accordingly, the father becomes a disturbing rival to the boy and the mother to the girl; and I have already shown in the case of brothers and sisters how easily such feelings can lead to a death-wish. The parents too give evidence as a rule of

an early hint at the line of thought developed later by Freud in his *Totem and Taboo* (1912–13).]

[1] [Freud's views on this point were later modified, Cf. Freud, 1925*j* and 1931*b*.]

sexual partiality: a natural predilection usually sees to it that a man tends to spoil his little daughters, while his wife takes her sons' part; though both of them, where their judgement is not disturbed by the magic of sex, keep a strict eye upon their children's education. The child is very well aware of this partiality and turns against that one of his parents who is opposed to showing it. Being loved by an adult does not merely bring a child the satisfaction of a special need; it also means that he will get what he wants in every other respect as well. Thus he will be following his own sexual instinct and at the same time giving fresh strength to the inclination shown by his parents if his choice between them falls in with theirs.

The signs of these infantile preferences are for the most part overlooked; yet some of them are to be observed even after the first years of childhood. An eight-year-old girl of my acquaintance, if her mother is called away from the table, makes use of the occasion to proclaim herself her successor: '*I*'m going to be Mummy now. Do you want some more greens, Karl? Well, help yourself, then!' and so on. A particularly gifted and lively girl of four, in whom this piece of child psychology is especially transparent, declared quite openly: 'Mummy can go away now. Then Daddy must marry me and I'll be his wife.' Such a wish occurring in a child is not in the least inconsistent with her being tenderly attached to her mother. If a little boy is allowed to sleep beside his mother when his father is away from home, but has to go back to the nursery and to someone of whom he is far less fond as soon as his father returns, he may easily begin to form a wish that his father should *always* be away, so that he himself could keep his place beside his dear, lovely Mummy. One obvious way of attaining this wish would be if his father were dead; for the child has learnt one thing by experience— namely that 'dead' people, such as Grandaddy, are always away and never come back.

Though observations of this kind on small children fit in perfectly with the interpretation I have proposed, they do not carry such complete conviction as is forced upon the physician by psycho-analyses of adult neurotics. In the latter case dreams of the sort we are considering are introduced into the analysis in such a context that it is impossible to avoid interpreting them as *wishful* dreams.

One day one of my women patients was in a distressed and tearful mood. 'I don't want ever to see my relations again,' she said, 'they must think me horrible.' She then went on, with almost no transition, to say that she remembered a dream, though of course she had no idea what it meant. When she was four years old she had a dream that *a lynx or fox*[1] *was walking on the roof; then something had fallen down or she had fallen down; and then her mother was carried out of the house dead*—and she wept bitterly. I told her that this dream must mean that when she was a child she had wished she could see her mother dead, and that it must be on account of the dream that she felt her relations must think her horrible. I had scarcely said this when she produced some material which threw light on the dream. 'Lynx-eye' was a term of abuse that had been thrown at her by a street-urchin when she was a very small child. When she was three years old, a tile off the roof had fallen on her mother's head and made it bleed violently.

I once had an opportunity of making a detailed study of a young woman who passed through a variety of psychical conditions. Her illness began with a state of confusional excitement during which she displayed a quite special aversion to her mother, hitting and abusing her whenever she came near her bed, while at the same period she was docile and affectionate towards a sister who was many years her senior. This was followed by a state in which she was lucid but somewhat apathetic and suffered from badly disturbed sleep. It was during this phase that I began treating her and analysing her dreams. An immense number of these dreams were concerned, with a greater or less degree of disguise, with the death of her mother: at one time she would be attending an old woman's funeral, at another she and her sister would be sitting at table dressed in mourning. There could be no question as to the meaning of these dreams. As her condition improved still further, hysterical phobias developed. The most tormenting of these was a fear that something might have happened to her mother. She was obliged to hurry home, wherever she might be, to convince herself that her mother was still alive. This case, taken in conjunction with what I had learnt from other sources, was highly instructive: it exhibited, translated as it were into different

[1] [The German names for these animals are very much alike: '*Luchs*' and '*Fuchs*'.]

languages, the various ways in which the psychical apparatus reacted to one and the same exciting idea. In the confusional state, in which, as I believe, the second psychical agency was overwhelmed by the normally suppressed first one, her unconscious hostility to her mother found a powerful *motor* expression. When the calmer condition set in, when the rebellion was suppressed and the domination of the censorship re-established, the only region left open in which her hostility could realize the wish for her mother's death was that of dreaming. When a normal state was still more firmly established, it led to the production of her exaggerated worry about her mother as a hysterical counter-reaction and defensive phenomenon. In view of this it is no longer hard to understand why hysterical girls are so often attached to their mothers with such exaggerated affection.

On another occasion I had an opportunity of obtaining a deep insight into the unconscious mind of a young man whose life was made almost impossible by an obsessional neurosis. He was unable to go out into the street because he was tortured by the fear that he would kill everyone he met. He spent his days in preparing his alibi in case he might be charged with one of the murders committed in the town. It is unnecessary to add that he was a man of equally high morals and education. The analysis (which, incidentally, led to his recovery) showed that the basis of this distressing obsession was an impulse to murder his somewhat over-severe father. This impulse, to his astonishment, had been consciously expressed when he was seven years old, but it had, of course, originated much earlier in his childhood. After his father's painful illness and death, the patient's obsessional self-reproaches appeared—he was in his thirty-first year at the time—taking the shape of a phobia transferred on to strangers. A person, he felt, who was capable of wanting to push his own father over *a* precipice from the top of a mountain was not to be trusted to respect the lives of those less closely related to him; he was quite right to shut himself up in his room.[1]

In my experience, which is already extensive, the chief part in the mental lives of all children who later become psychoneurotics is played by their parents. Being in love with the one parent and hating the other are among the essential constituents

[1] [This patient is referred to again on p. 457.]

of the stock of psychical impulses which is formed at that time and which is of such importance in determining the symptoms of the later neurosis. It is not my belief, however, that psychoneurotics differ sharply in this respect from other human beings who remain normal—that they are able, that is, to create something absolutely new and peculiar to themselves. It is far more probable—and this is confirmed by occasional observations on normal children—that they are only distinguished by exhibiting on a magnified scale feelings of love and hatred to their parents which occur less obviously and less intensely in the minds of most children.

This discovery is confirmed by a legend that has come down to us from classical antiquity: a legend whose profound and universal power to move can only be understood if the hypothesis I have put forward in regard to the psychology of children has an equally universal validity. What I have in mind is the legend of King Oedipus and Sophocles' drama which bears his name.

Oedipus, son of Laïus, King of Thebes, and of Jocasta, was exposed as an infant because an oracle had warned Laïus that the still unborn child would be his father's murderer. The child was rescued, and grew up as a prince in an alien court, until, in doubts as to his origin, he too questioned the oracle and was warned to avoid his home since he was destined to murder his father and take his mother in marriage. On the road leading away from what he believed was his home, he met King Laïus and slew him in a sudden quarrel. He came next to Thebes and solved the riddle set him by the Sphinx who barred his way. Out of gratitude the Thebans made him their king and gave him Jocasta's hand in marriage. He reigned long in peace and honour, and she who, unknown to him, was his mother bore him two sons and two daughters. Then at last a plague broke out and the Thebans made enquiry once more of the oracle. It is at this point that Sophocles' tragedy opens. The messengers bring back the reply that the plague will cease when the murderer of Laïus has been driven from the land.

> But he, where is he? Where shall now be read ·
> The fading record of this ancient guilt?[1]

The action of the play consists in nothing other than the process

[1] [Lewis Campbell's translation (1883), line 108 f.]

of revealing, with cunning delays and ever-mounting excitement—a process that can be likened to the work of a psycho-analysis—that Oedipus himself is the murderer of Laïus, but further that he is the son of the murdered man and of Jocasta. Appalled at the abomination which he has unwittingly perpetrated, Oedipus blinds himself and forsakes his home. The oracle has been fulfilled.

Oedipus Rex is what is known as a tragedy of destiny. Its tragic effect is said to lie in the contrast between the supreme will of the gods and the vain attempts of mankind to escape the evil that threatens them. The lesson which, it is said, the deeply moved spectator should learn from the tragedy is submission to the divine will and realization of his own impotence. Modern dramatists have accordingly tried to achieve a similar tragic effect by weaving the same contrast into a plot invented by themselves. But the spectators have looked on unmoved while a curse or an oracle was fulfilled in spite of all the efforts of some innocent man: later tragedies of destiny have failed in their effect.

If *Oedipus Rex* moves a modern audience no less than it did the contemporary Greek one, the explanation can only be that its effect does not lie in the contrast between destiny and human will, but is to be looked for in the particular nature of the material on which that contrast is exemplified. There must be something which makes a voice within us ready to recognize the compelling force of destiny in the *Oedipus*, while we can dismiss as merely arbitrary such dispositions as are laid down in [Grillparzer's] *Die Ahnfrau* or other modern tragedies of destiny. And a factor of this kind is in fact involved in the story of King Oedipus. His destiny moves us only because it might have been ours—because the oracle laid the same curse upon us before our birth as upon him. It is the fate of all of us, perhaps, to direct our first sexual impulse towards our mother and our first hatred and our first murderous wish against our father. Our dreams convince us that that is so. King Oedipus, who slew his father Laïus and married his mother Jocasta, merely shows us the fulfilment of our own childhood wishes. But, more fortunate than he, we have meanwhile succeeded, in so far as we have not become psychoneurotics, in detaching our sexual impulses from our mothers and in forgetting our jealousy of our fathers. Here is one in whom these primaeval wishes of our childhood

have been fulfilled, and we shrink back from him with the whole
force of the repression by which those wishes have since that
time been held down within us. While the poet, as he unravels
the past, brings to light the guilt of Oedipus, he is at the same
time compelling us to recognize our own inner minds, in which
those same impulses, though suppressed, are still to be found.
The contrast with which the closing Chorus leaves us confronted—

> . . . Fix on Oedipus your eyes,
> Who resolved the dark enigma, noblest champion and most wise.
> Like a star his envied fortune mounted beaming far and wide:
> Now he sinks in seas of anguish, whelmed beneath a raging tide . . .[1]

—strikes as a warning at ourselves and our pride, at us who
since our childhood have grown so wise and so mighty in our
own eyes. Like Oedipus, we live in ignorance of these wishes,
repugnant to morality, which have been forced upon us by
Nature, and after their revelation we may all of us well seek to
close our eyes to the scenes of our childhood.[2]

There is an unmistakable indication in the text of Sophocles'
tragedy itself that the legend of Oedipus sprang from some
primaeval dream-material which had as its content the distressing disturbance of a child's relation to his parents owing to

---

[1] [Lewis Campbell's translation, line 1524 ff.]

[2] [*Footnote added* 1914:] None of the findings of psycho-analytic
research has provoked such embittered denials, such fierce opposition—
or such amusing contortions—on the part of critics as this indication of
the childhood impulses towards incest which persist in the unconscious.
An attempt has even been made recently to make out, in the face of all
experience, that the incest should only be taken as 'symbolic'.—Ferenczi (1912) has proposed an ingenious 'over-interpretation' of the
Oedipus myth, based on a passage in one of Schopenhauer's letters.—
[*Added* 1919:] Later studies have shown that the 'Oedipus complex',
which was touched upon for the first time in the above paragraphs in
the *Interpretation of Dreams*, throws a light of undreamt-of importance on
the history of the human race and the evolution of religion and morality. (See my *Totem and Taboo*, 1912–13 [Essay IV].)—[Actually the
gist of this discussion of the Oedipus complex and of the *Oedipus Rex*, as
well as of what follows on the subject of *Hamlet*, had already been put
forward by Freud in a letter to Fliess as early as October 15th, 1897.
(See Freud, 1950a, Letter 71.) A still earlier hint at the discovery of the
Oedipus complex was included in a letter of May 31st, 1897. (Ibid.,
Draft N.)—The actual term 'Oedipus complex' seems to have been first
used by Freud in his published writings in the first of his 'Contributions
to the Psychology of Love' (1910h).]

the first stirrings of sexuality. At a point when Oedipus, though he is not yet enlightened, has begun to feel troubled by his recollection of the oracle, Jocasta consoles him by referring to a dream which many people dream, though, as she thinks, it has no meaning:

> Many a man ere now in dreams hath lain
> With her who bare him. He hath least annoy
> Who with such omens troubleth not his mind.[1]

To-day, just as then, many men dream of having sexual relations with their mothers, and speak of the fact with indignation and astonishment. It is clearly the key to the tragedy and the complement to the dream of the dreamer's father being dead. The story of Oedipus is the reaction of the imagination to these two typical dreams. And just as these dreams, when dreamt by adults, are accompanied by feelings of repulsion, so too the legend must include horror and self-punishment. Its further modification originates once again in a misconceived secondary revision of the material, which has sought to exploit it for theological purposes. (Cf. the dream-material in dreams of exhibiting, p. 243 f.) The attempt to harmonize divine omnipotence with human responsibility must naturally fail in connection with this subject-matter just as with any other.

Another of the great creations of tragic poetry, Shakespeare's *Hamlet*, has its roots in the same soil as *Oedipus Rex*.[2] But the changed treatment of the same material reveals the whole difference in the mental life of these two widely separated epochs of civilization: the secular advance of repression in the emotional life of mankind. In the *Oedipus* the child's wishful phantasy that underlies it is brought into the open and realized as it would be in a dream. In *Hamlet* it remains repressed; and —just as in the case of a neurosis—we only learn of its existence from its inhibiting consequences. Strangely enough, the overwhelming effect produced by the more modern tragedy has turned out to be compatible with the fact that people have remained completely in the dark as to the hero's character. The play is built up on Hamlet's hesitations over fulfilling the task of revenge that is assigned to him; but its text offers no

---

[1] [Lewis Campbell's translation, line 982 ff.]

[2] [This paragraph was printed as a footnote in the first edition (1900) and included in the text from 1914 onward.]

reasons or motives for these hesitations and an immense variety of attempts at interpreting them have failed to produce a result. According to the view which was originated by Goethe and is still the prevailing one to-day, Hamlet represents the type of man whose power of direct action is paralysed by an excessive development of his intellect. (He is 'sicklied o'er with the pale cast of thought'.) According to another view, the dramatist has tried to portray a pathologically irresolute character which might be classed as neurasthenic. The plot of the drama shows us, however, that Hamlet is far from being represented as a person incapable of taking any action. We see him doing so on two occasions: first in a sudden outburst of temper, when he runs his sword through the eavesdropper behind the arras, and secondly in a premeditated and even crafty fashion, when, with all the callousness of a Renaissance prince, he sends the two courtiers to the death that had been planned for himself. What is it, then, that inhibits him in fulfilling the task set him by his father's ghost? The answer, once again, is that it is the peculiar nature of the task. Hamlet is able to do anything—except take vengeance on the man who did away with his father and took that father's place with his mother, the man who shows him the repressed wishes of his own childhood realized. Thus the loathing which should drive him on to revenge is replaced in him by self-reproaches, by scruples of conscience, which remind him that he himself is literally no better than the sinner whom he is to punish. Here I have translated into conscious terms what was bound to remain unconscious in Hamlet's mind; and if anyone is inclined to call him a hysteric, I can only accept the fact as one that is implied by my interpretation. The distaste for sexuality expressed by Hamlet in his conversation with Ophelia fits in very well with this: the same distaste which was destined to take possession of the poet's mind more and more during the years that followed, and which reached its extreme expression in *Timon of Athens*. For it can of course only be the poet's own mind which confronts us in Hamlet. I observe in a book on Shakespeare by Georg Brandes (1896) a statement that *Hamlet* was written immediately after the death of Shakespeare's father (in 1601), that is, under the immediate impact of his bereavement and, as we may well assume, while his childhood feelings about his father had been freshly revived. It is known, too, that Shakespeare's own son who died at an early age bore the name of 'Hamnet', which is identical with 'Hamlet'. Just as *Hamlet* deals with the relation of a son to his parents, so *Macbeth* (written at approximately the same period) is concerned with the subject of childlessness. But just as all neurotic symptoms, and, for that matter, dreams, are capable of being 'over-interpreted' and indeed need to be, if they are to be fully understood, so all genuinely creative writings are the product of more than a single motive and more than a single impulse in the poet's mind, and are open to more than a single interpretation. In what I have written I have only attempted to interpret the deepest layer of impulses in the mind of the creative writer.[1]

I cannot leave the subject of typical dreams of the death of loved relatives, without adding a few more words to throw light on their significance for the theory of dreams in general. In these dreams we find the highly unusual condition realized of a dream-thought formed by a repressed wish entirely eluding censorship and passing into the dream without modification. There must be special factors at work to make this event possible, and I believe that the occurrence of these dreams is facilitated by two such factors. Firstly, there is no wish that seems more remote from us than this one: 'we couldn't even *dream*'—so we believe—of wishing such a thing. For this reason the dream-censorship is not armed to meet such a monstrosity, just as Solon's penal code contained no punishment for parricide. Secondly, in this case the repressed and unsuspected wish

---

[1] [*Footnote added* 1919:] The above indications of a psycho-analytic explanation of *Hamlet* have since been amplified by Ernest Jones and defended against the alternative views put forward in the literature of the subject. (See Jones, 1910*a* [and, in a completer form, 1949].)— [*Added* 1930:] Incidentally, I have in the meantime ceased to believe that the author of Shakespeare's works was the man from Stratford. [See Freud, 1930*e*.]—[*Added* 1919:] Further attempts at an analysis of *Macbeth* will be found in a paper of mine [Freud, 1916*d*] and in one by Jekels (1917).—[The first part of this footnote was included in a different form in the edition of 1911 but omitted from 1914 onwards: 'The views on the problem of *Hamlet* contained in the above passage have since been confirmed and supported with fresh arguments in an extensive study by Dr. Ernest Jones of Toronto (1910*a*). He has also pointed out the relation between the material in *Hamlet* and the myths of the birth of heroes discussed by Rank (1909).'—Freud further discussed *Hamlet* in a posthumously published sketch dealing with 'Psychopathic Characters on the Stage' (1942*b*), probably written in 1905 or 1906.]

is particularly often met half-way by a residue from the previous day in the form of a *worry* about the safety of the person concerned. This worry can only make its way into the dream by availing itself of the corresponding wish; while the wish can disguise itself behind the worry that has become active during the day. [Cf. p. 555 f.] We may feel inclined to think that things are simpler than this and that one merely carries on during the night and in dreams with what one has been turning over in one's mind during the day; but if so we shall be leaving dreams of the death of people of whom the dreamer is fond completely in the air and without any connection with our explanation of dreams in general, and we shall thus be clinging quite unnecessarily to a riddle which is perfectly capable of solution.

It is also instructive to consider the relation of these dreams to anxiety-dreams. In the dreams we have been discussing, a repressed wish has found a means of evading censorship—and the distortion which censorship involves. The invariable concomitant is that painful feelings are experienced in the dream. In just the same way anxiety-dreams only occur if the censorship has been wholly or partly overpowered; and, on the other hand, the overpowering of the censorship is facilitated if anxiety has already been produced as an immediate sensation arising from somatic sources. [Cf. above, p. 235 ff.] We can thus plainly see the purpose for which the censorship exercises its office and brings about the distortion of dreams: it does so *in order to prevent the generation of anxiety or other forms of distressing affect.*

I have spoken above [p. 250] of the egoism of children's minds, and I may now add, with a hint at a possible connection between the two facts, that dreams have the same characteristic. All of them are completely egoistic:[1] the beloved ego appears in all of them, even though it may be disguised. The wishes that are fulfilled in them are invariably the ego's wishes, and if a dream seems to have been provoked by an altruistic interest, we are only being deceived by appearances. Here are a few analyses of instances which seem to contradict this assertion.

I

A child of under four years old reported having dreamt that *he had seen a big dish with a big joint of roast meat and vegetables on*

[1] [Cf. end of footnote below, pp. 270-1. See also p. 322 ff.]

it. All at once the joint had been eaten up—whole and without being cut up. He had not seen the person who ate it.[1]

Who can the unknown person have been whose sumptuous banquet of meat was the subject of the little boy's dream? His experiences during the dream-day must enlighten us on the subject. By doctor's orders he had been put on a milk diet for the past few days. On the evening of the dream-day he had been naughty, and as a punishment he had been sent to bed without his supper. He had been through this hunger-cure once before and had been very brave about it. He knew he would get nothing, but would not allow himself to show by so much as a single word that he was hungry. Education had already begun to have an effect on him: it found expression in this dream, which exhibits the beginning of dream-distortion. There can be no doubt that the person whose wishes were aimed at this lavish meal—a meat meal, too—was himself. But since he knew he was not allowed it, he did not venture to sit down to the meal himself, as hungry children do in dreams. (Cf. my little daughter Anna's dream of strawberries on p. 130.) The person who ate the meal remained anonymous.

II

I dreamt one night that I saw in the window of a book-shop a new volume in one of the series of monographs for connoisseurs which I am in the habit of buying—monographs on great artists, on world history, on famous cities, etc. *The new series was called 'Famous Speakers' or 'Speeches' and its first volume bore the name of Dr. Lecher.*

[1] [This dream, which was dreamt by Fliess's son Robert, is mentioned in Freud's letters to Fliess of August 8 and 20, 1899. (Freud, 1950a, Letters 114 and 116.)]—The appearance in dreams of things of great size and in great quantities and amounts, and of exaggeration generally, may be another childish characteristic. Children have no more ardent wish than to be big and grown-up and to get as much of things as grown-up people do. They are hard to satisfy, know no such word as 'enough' and insist insatiably on a repetition of things which they have enjoyed or whose taste they liked. It is only the civilizing influence of education that teaches them moderation and how to be content or resigned. Everyone knows that neurotics are equally inclined to be extravagant and immoderate. [Children's love of repetition was alluded to by Freud towards the end of the sixth section of Chapter VII of his book on jokes (Freud, 1905c) and again discussed near the beginning of Chapter V of *Beyond the Pleasure Principle* (1920g).]

When I came to analyse this, it seemed to me improbable that I should be concerned in my dreams with the fame of Dr. Lecher, the non-stop speaker of the German Nationalist obstructionists in Parliament. The position was that a few days earlier I had taken on some new patients for psychological treatment, and was now obliged to talk for ten or eleven hours every day. So it was I myself who was a non-stop speaker.

III

Another time I had a dream that a man I knew on the staff of the University said to me: '*My son, the Myops.*' Then followed a dialogue made up of short remarks and rejoinders. After this, however, there was yet a third piece of dream in which I myself and my sons figured. So far as the dream's latent content was concerned, Professor M. and his son were men of straw—a mere screen for me and my eldest son. I shall have to return to this dream later, on account of another of its features. [See p. 441 ff.]

IV

The dream which follows is an instance of really low egoistic feelings concealed behind affectionate worry.

My friend Otto was looking ill. His face was brown and he had protruding eyes.

Otto is my family doctor, and I owe him more than I can ever hope to repay: he has watched over my children's health for many years, he has treated them successfully when they have been ill, and, in addition, whenever circumstances have given him an excuse, he has given them presents. [See p. 116.] He had visited us on the dream-day, and my wife had remarked that he looked tired and strained. That night I had my dream, which showed him with some of the signs of Basedow's [Graves'] disease. Anyone who interprets this dream without regard for my rules will conclude that I was worried about my friend's health and that this worry was realized in the dream. This would not only contradict my assertion that dreams are wishfulfilments, but my other assertion, too, that they are accessible only to egoistic impulses. But I should be glad if anyone interpreting the dream in this way would be good enough to explain to me why my fears on Otto's behalf should have lighted on *Basedow's* disease—a diagnosis for which his actual appearance gives not the slightest ground. My analysis, on the other hand, brought up the following material from an occurrence six years earlier. A small group of us, which included Professor R., were driving in pitch darkness through the forest of N., which lay some hours' drive from the place at which we were spending our summer holidays. The coachman, who was not perfectly sober, spilt us, carriage and all, over an embankment, and it was only by a piece of luck that we all escaped injury. We were obliged, however, to spend the night in a neighbouring inn, at which the news of our accident brought us a lot of sympathy. A gentleman, with unmistakable signs of Basedow's disease—incidentally, just as in the dream, only the brown discoloration of the skin of the face and the protruding eyes, but no goitre—placed himself entirely at our disposal and asked what he could do for us. Professor R. replied in his decisive manner: 'Nothing except to lend me a night-shirt.' To which the fine gentleman rejoined: 'I'm sorry, but I can't do that', and left the room.

As I continued my analysis, it occurred to me that Basedow was the name not only of a physician but also of a famous educationalist. (In my waking state I no longer felt quite so certain about this.[1]) But my friend Otto was the person whom I had asked to watch over my children's physical education, especially at the age of puberty (hence the night-shirt), in case anything happened to me. By giving my friend Otto in the dream the symptoms of our noble helper, I was evidently saying that if anything happened to me he would do just as little for the children as Baron L. had done on that occasion in spite of his kind offers of assistance. This seems to be sufficient evidence of the egoistic lining of the dream.[2]

---

[1] [Though in fact it was correct. He was an eighteenth-century follower of Rousseau.]

[2] [*Footnote added* 1911:] When Ernest Jones was giving a scientific lecture on the egoism of dreams before an American audience, a learned lady objected to this unscientific generalization, saying that the author of the present work could only judge of the dreams of Austrians and had no business to speak of the dreams of Americans. So far as she was concerned, she was certain that all her dreams were strictly altruistic.— [*Added* 1925:] By way of excuse for this patriotic lady, I may remark that the statement that dreams are entirely egoistic [p. 267] must not be misunderstood. Since anything whatever that occurs in preconscious thought can pass into a dream (whether into its actual content or into the latent dream-thoughts) that possibility is equally open to altruistic impulses. In the same way, an affectionate or erotic impulse towards someone else, if it is present in the unconscious, can appear in a dream.

But where was its wish-fulfilment to be found? Not in my avenging myself on my friend Otto, whose fate it seems to be to be ill-treated in my dreams[1]; but in the following consideration. At the same time as I represented Otto in the dream as Baron L., I had identified myself with someone else, namely Professor R.; for just as in the anecdote R. had made a request to Baron L., so I had made a request to Otto. And that is the point. Professor R., with whom I should really not venture to compare myself in the ordinary way, resembled me in having followed an independent path outside the academic world and had only achieved his well-merited title late in life. So once again I was wanting to be a Professor! Indeed the words 'late in life' were themselves a wish-fulfilment; for they implied that I should live long enough to see my boys through the age of puberty myself.[2]

[(γ) OTHER TYPICAL DREAMS]

I have no experience of my own of other kinds of typical dreams, in which the dreamer finds himself flying through the air to the accompaniment of agreeable feelings or falling with feelings of anxiety; and whatever I have to say on the subject is derived from psycho-analyses.[3] The information provided by the latter forces me to conclude that these dreams, too, reproduce impressions of childhood; they relate, that is, to games involving movement, which are extraordinarily attractive to children. There cannot be a single uncle who has not shown a child how to fly by rushing across the room with him in his outstretched arms, or who has not played at letting him fall by riding him on his knee and then suddenly stretching out his leg, or by holding him up high and then suddenly pretending to drop him. Children are delighted by such experiences and never tire of asking to have them repeated, especially if there is some-

---

The truth in the assertion made in the text above is thus restricted to the fact that among the unconscious instigators of a dream we very frequently find egoistic impulses which seem to have been overcome in waking life.

[1] [Cf. the dream of Irma's injection in Chapter II (p. 118 ff.).]

[2] [This dream is further discussed on pp. 555 and 560.]

[3] [The first sentence of this paragraph appeared in the original edition (1900) but was thereafter dropped until 1925. The remainder of the paragraph, together with the next one, were added in 1909, and in 1914 transferred to Chapter VI, Section E (where they will also be found, on p. 393 below). In the 1930 edition they were included in *both* places.]

thing about them that causes a little fright or giddiness. In after years they repeat these experiences in dreams; but in the dreams they leave out the hands which held them up, so that they float or fall unsupported. The delight taken by young children in games of this kind (as well as in swings and see-saws) is well known; and when they come to see acrobatic feats in a circus their memory of such games is revived.[1] Hysterical attacks in boys sometimes consist merely in reproductions of feats of this kind, carried out with great skill. It not uncommonly happens that these games of movement, though innocent in themselves, give rise to sexual feelings.[2] Childish 'romping' ['*Hetzen*'], if I may use a word which commonly describes all such activities, is what is being repeated in dreams of flying, falling, giddiness and so on; while the pleasurable feelings attached to these experiences are transformed into anxiety. But often enough, as every mother knows, romping among children actually ends in squabbling and tears.

Thus I have good grounds for rejecting the theory that what provokes dreams of flying and falling is the state of our tactile feelings during sleep or sensations of the movement of our lungs, and so on. [Cf. p. 37 f.] In my view these sensations are themselves reproduced as part of the memory to which the dream goes back: that is to say, they are part of the *content* of the dream and not its source.

I cannot, however, disguise from myself that I am unable

[1] [*Footnote added* 1925:] Analytic research has shown us that in addition to pleasure derived from the organs concerned, there is another factor which contributes to the delight taken by children in acrobatic performances and to their repetition in hysterical attacks. This other factor is a memory-image, often unconscious, of an observation of sexual intercourse, whether between human beings or animals.

[2] A young medical colleague, who is quite free from any kind of nervous trouble, has given me the following information on this point: 'I know from my own experience that in my childhood I had a peculiar sensation in my genitals when I was on a swing and especially when the downward motion reached its greatest momentum. And though I cannot say I really enjoyed this sensation I must describe it as a pleasurable one.'—Patients have often told me that the first pleasurable erections that they can remember occurred in their boyhood while they were climbing about.—Psycho-analysis makes it perfectly certain that the first sexual impulses frequently have their roots in games involving romping and wrestling played during childhood. [This topic was elaborated by Freud in the last section of the second of his *Three Essays on the Theory of Sexuality* (1905*d*).]

to produce any complete explanation of this class of typical dreams.[1] My material has left me in the lurch precisely at this point. I must, however, insist upon the general assertion that all the tactile and motor sensations which occur in these typical dreams are called up immediately there is any psychical reason for making use of them and that they can be disregarded when no such need for them arises. [Cf. pp. 237–8.] I am also of the opinion that the relation of these dreams to infantile experiences has been established with certainty from the indications I have found in the analyses of psychoneurotics. I am not able to say, however, what other meanings may become attached to the recollection of such sensations in the course of later life—different meanings, perhaps, in every individual case, in spite of the typical appearance of the dreams; and I should be glad to be able to fill up the gap by a careful analysis of clear instances. If anyone feels surprised that, in spite of the frequency precisely of dreams of flying, falling and pulling out teeth, etc., I should be complaining of lack of material on this particular topic, I must explain that I myself have not experienced any dreams of the kind since I turned my attention to the subject of dream-interpretation. The dreams of neurotics, moreover, of which I might otherwise avail myself, cannot always be interpreted—not, at least, in many cases, so as to reveal the whole of their concealed meaning; a particular psychical force, which was concerned with the original constructing of the neurosis and is brought into operation once again when attempts are made at resolving it, prevents us from interpreting such dreams down to their last secret.

[δ] EXAMINATION DREAMS

Everyone who has passed the matriculation examination at the end of his school studies complains of the obstinacy with which he is pursued by anxiety-dreams of having failed, or of being obliged to take the examination again, etc. In the case of those who have obtained a University degree this typical dream is replaced by another one which represents them as having failed in their University Finals; and it is in vain that they

[1] [In the original edition (1900) the following paragraph (the first on examination dreams) *preceded* this one, and the present paragraph concluded the chapter. Thereafter this paragraph was altogether omitted until 1925.]

object, even while they are still asleep, that for years they have been practising medicine or working as University lecturers or heads of offices. The ineradicable memories of the punishments that we suffered for our evil deeds in childhood become active within us once more and attach themselves to the two crucial points in our studies—the '*dies irae, dies illa*' of our stiffest examinations. The 'examination anxiety' of neurotics owes its intensification to these same childhood fears. After we have ceased to be school-children, our punishments are no longer inflicted on us by our parents or by those who brought us up or later by our schoolmasters. The relentless causal chains of real life take charge of our further education, and now we dream of Matriculation or Finals (and who has not trembled on those occasions, even if he was well-prepared for the examination?) whenever, having done something wrong or failed to do something properly, we expect to be punished by the event—whenever, in short, we feel the burden of responsibility.

For a further explanation of examination dreams[1] I have to thank an experienced colleague [Stekel], who once declared at a scientific meeting that so far as he knew dreams of Matriculation only occur in people who have successfully passed it and never in people who have failed in it. It would seem, then, that anxious examination dreams (which, as has been confirmed over and over again, appear when the dreamer has some responsible activity ahead of him next day and is afraid there may be a fiasco) search for some occasion in the past in which great anxiety has turned out to be unjustified and has been contradicted by the event. This, then, would be a very striking instance of the content of a dream being misunderstood by the waking agency. [See pp. 243-4.] What is regarded as an indignant protest against the dream: 'But I'm a doctor, etc., already!' would in reality be the consolation put forward by the dream, and would accordingly run: 'Don't be afraid of tomorrow! Just think how anxious you were before your Matriculation, and yet nothing happened to you. You're a doctor, etc., already.' And the anxiety which is attributed to the dream would really have arisen from the day's residues.

Such tests as I have been able to make of this explanation on

---

[1] [This paragraph and the next one were added in 1909. In the editions of 1909 and 1911 only, the words 'the true explanation' took the place of 'a further explanation'.]

myself and on other people, though they have not been sufficiently numerous, have confirmed its validity. For instance, I
myself failed in Forensic Medicine in my Finals; but I have
never had to cope with this subject in dreams, whereas I have
quite often been examined in Botany, Zoology or Chemistry. I
went in for the examination in these subjects with well-founded
anxiety; but, whether by the grace of destiny or of the examiners,
I escaped punishment. In my dreams of school examinations, I
am invariably examined in History, in which I did brilliantly
—though only, it is true, because [in the oral examination] my
kindly master (the one-eyed benefactor of another dream, see
p. 17) did not fail to notice that on the paper of questions
which I handed him back I had run my finger-nail through the
middle one of the three questions included, to warn him not to
insist upon that particular one. One of my patients, who decided
not to sit for his Matriculation the first time but passed it later,
and who subsequently failed in his army examination and never
got a commission, has told me that he often dreams of the
former of these examinations but never of the latter.[1]

The interpretation of examination dreams is faced by the
difficulty which I have already referred to as characteristic of
the majority of typical dreams [p. 241].[2] It is but rarely that the
material with which the dreamer provides us in associations is
sufficient to interpret the dream. It is only by collecting a considerable number of examples of such dreams that we can arrive
at a better understanding of them. Not long ago I came to the
conclusion that the objection, 'You're a doctor, etc., already',
does not merely conceal a consolation but also signifies a
reproach. This would have run: 'You're quite old now, quite far

---

[1] [At this point in the 1909 edition the following paragraph appeared:
'The colleague whom I have mentioned above (Dr. Stekel) has drawn
attention to the fact that the word we use for Matriculation, "*Matura*",
also means "maturity"; he claims to have observed that "*Matura*"
dreams very often appear when a sexual test lies ahead for the next day,
when, that is, the fiasco that is dreaded may lie in an insufficient release
of potency.' In the 1911 edition the following sentence was added: 'A
German colleague has, as I think rightly, objected to this that the name
of this examination in Germany—"*Abiturium*"—does not bear this
double meaning.' This whole paragraph was omitted from 1914 onwards. In 1925 it was replaced by the new final paragraph of the
chapter. The subject was discussed by Stekel himself in 1909, 464 and
471.]

[2] [This paragraph was added in 1914.]

advanced in life, and yet you go on doing these stupid, childish things.' This mixture of self-criticism and consolation would thus correspond to the latent content of examination dreams. If so, it would not be surprising if the self-reproaches for being 'stupid' and 'childish' in these last examples referred to the repetition of reprehensible sexual acts.

Wilhelm Stekel,[1] who put forward the first interpretation of dreams of Matriculation ['*Matura*'], was of the opinion that they regularly related to sexual tests and sexual maturity. My experience has often confirmed his view.[2]

---

[1] [This paragraph was added in 1925.]

[2] [In the 1909 and 1911 editions this chapter was continued with a discussion of other kinds of 'typical' dreams. But from 1914 onwards this further discussion was transferred to Chapter VI, Section E, after the newly introduced material dealing with dream-symbolism. See p. 384 below. (Cf. Editor's Introduction, p. xiii.)]

CHAPTER VI

THE DREAM-WORK [1]

EVERY attempt that has hitherto been made to solve the problem of dreams has dealt directly with their *manifest* content as it is presented in our memory. All such attempts have endeavoured to arrive at an interpretation of dreams from their manifest content or (if no interpretation was attempted) to form a judgement as to their nature on the basis of that same manifest content. We are alone in taking something else into account. We have introduced a new class of psychical material between the manifest content of dreams and the conclusions of our enquiry: namely, their *latent* content, or (as we say) the 'dream-thoughts', arrived at by means of our procedure. It is from these dream-thoughts and not from a dream's manifest content that we disentangle its meaning. We are thus presented with a new task which had no previous existence: the task, that is, of investigating the relations between the manifest content of dreams and the latent dream-thoughts, and of tracing out the processes by which the latter have been changed into the former.

The dream-thoughts and the dream-content are presented to us like two versions of the same subject-matter in two different languages. Or, more properly, the dream-content seems like a transcript of the dream-thoughts into another mode of expression, whose characters and syntactic laws it is our business to discover by comparing the original and the translation. The dream-thoughts are immediately comprehensible, as soon as we have learnt them. The dream-content, on the other hand, is expressed as it were in a pictographic script, the characters of which have to be transposed individually into the language of the dream-thoughts. If we attempted to read these characters according to their pictorial value instead of according to their symbolic relation, we should clearly be led into error. Suppose I have a picture-puzzle, a rebus, in front of me. It depicts a house with a boat on its roof, a single letter of the alphabet, the

[1] [Lecture XI of Freud's *Introductory Lectures* (1916–17) deals with the dream-work on a much less extensive scale.]

figure of a running man whose head has been conjured away, and so on. Now I might be misled into raising objections and declaring that the picture as a whole and its component parts are nonsensical. A boat has no business to be on the roof of a house, and a headless man cannot run. Moreover, the man is bigger than the house; and if the whole picture is intended to represent a landscape, letters of the alphabet are out of place in it since such objects do not occur in nature. But obviously we can only form a proper judgement of the rebus if we put aside criticisms such as these of the whole composition and its parts and if, instead, we try to replace each separate element by a syllable or word that can be represented by that element in some way or other. The words which are put together in this way are no longer nonsensical but may form a poetical phrase of the greatest beauty and significance. A dream is a picture-puzzle of this sort and our predecessors in the field of dream-interpretation have made the mistake of treating the rebus as a pictorial composition: and as such it has seemed to them non-sensical and worthless.

(A)

THE WORK OF CONDENSATION

The first thing that becomes clear to anyone who compares the dream-content with the dream-thoughts is that a work of *condensation* on a large scale has been carried out. Dreams are brief, meagre and laconic in comparison with the range and wealth of the dream-thoughts. If a dream is written out it may perhaps fill half a page. The analysis setting out the dream-thoughts underlying it may occupy six, eight or a dozen times as much space. This relation varies with different dreams; but so far as my experience goes its direction never varies. As a rule one underestimates the amount of compression that has taken place, since one is inclined to regard the dream-thoughts that have been brought to light as the complete material, whereas if the work of interpretation is carried further it may reveal still more thoughts concealed behind the dream. I have already had occasion to point out [cf. p. 218 f.] that it is in fact never possible to be sure that a dream has been completely interpreted.[1] Even if the solution seems satisfactory and without gaps, the possibility always remains that the dream may have yet another meaning. Strictly speaking, then, it is impossible to determine the amount of condensation.

There is an answer, which at first sight seems most plausible, to the argument that the great lack of proportion between the dream-content and the dream-thoughts implies that the psychical material has undergone an extensive process of condensation in the course of the formation of the dream. We very often have an impression that we have dreamt a great deal all through the night and have since forgotten most of what we dreamt. On this view, the dream which we remember when we wake up would only be a fragmentary remnant of the total dream-work; and this, if we could recollect it in its entirety, might well be as extensive as the dream-thoughts. There is undoubtedly some truth in this: there can be no question that dreams can be reproduced most accurately if we try to recall them as soon as we wake up and that our memory of them becomes more and

[1] [This subject is discussed at length in Freud, 1925*i*, Section A.]

more incomplete towards evening. But on the other hand it can be shown that the impression that we have dreamt a great deal more than we can reproduce is very often based on an illusion, the origin of which I shall discuss later. [Cf. pp. 489 and 517.] Moreover the hypothesis that condensation occurs during the dream-work is not affected by the possibility of dreams being forgotten, since this hypothesis is proved to be correct by the quantities of ideas which are related to each individual piece of the dream which has been retained. Even supposing that a large piece of the dream has escaped recollection, this may merely have prevented our having access to another group of dream-thoughts. There is no justification for supposing that the lost pieces of the dream would have related to the same thoughts which we have already reached from the pieces of the dream that have survived.[1]

In view of the very great number of associations produced in analysis to each individual element of the content of a dream, some readers may be led to doubt whether, as a matter of principle, we are justified in regarding as part of the dream-thoughts all the associations that occur to us during the subsequent analysis—whether we are justified, that is, in supposing that all these thoughts were already active during the state of sleep and played a part in the formation of the dream. Is it not more probable that new trains of thought have arisen in the course of the analysis which had no share in forming the dream? I can only give limited assent to this argument. It is no doubt true that some trains of thought arise for the first time during the analysis. But one can convince oneself in all such cases that these new connections are only set up between thoughts which were already linked in some other way in the dream-thoughts.[2] The new connections are, as it were, loop-lines or short-circuits, made possible by the existence of other and deeper-lying connecting paths. It must be allowed that the great bulk of the thoughts which are revealed in analysis were already active during the process of forming the dream; for, after working

[1] [Footnote added 1914:] The occurrence of condensation in dreams has been hinted at by many writers. Du Prel (1885, 85) has a passage in which he says it is absolutely certain that there has been a process of condensation of the groups of ideas in dreams.

[2] [This question is mentioned again on p. 311 and discussed at very much greater length in the last part of Section A of Chapter VII (p. 526 f.). See especially p. 532.]

through a string of thoughts which seem to have no connection with the formation of a dream, one suddenly comes upon one which is represented in its content and is indispensable for its interpretation, but which could not have been reached except by this particular line of approach. I may here recall the dream of the botanical monograph [p. 169 ff.], which strikes one as the product of an astonishing amount of condensation, even though I have not reported its analysis in full.

How, then, are we to picture psychical conditions during the period of sleep which precedes dreams? Are all the dream-thoughts present alongside one another? or do they occur in sequence? or do a number of trains of thought start out simultaneously from different centres and afterwards unite? There is no need for the present, in my opinion, to form any plastic idea of psychical conditions during the formation of dreams. It must not be forgotten, however, that we are dealing with an *unconscious* process of thought, which may easily be different from what we perceive during purposive reflection accompanied by consciousness.

The unquestionable fact remains, however, that the formation of dreams is based on a process of condensation. How is that condensation brought about?

When we reflect that only a small minority of all the dream-thoughts revealed are represented in the dream by one of their ideational elements, we might conclude that condensation is brought about by *omission*: that is, that the dream is not a faithful translation or a point-for-point projection of the dream-thoughts, but a highly incomplete and fragmentary version of them. This view, as we shall soon discover, is a most inadequate one. But we may take it as a provisional starting-point and go on to a further question. If only a few elements from the dream-thoughts find their way into the dream-content, what are the conditions which determine their selection?

In order to get some light on this question we must turn our attention to those elements of the dream-content which must have fulfilled these conditions. And the most favourable material for such an investigation will be a dream to the construction of which a particularly intense process of condensation has contributed. I shall accordingly begin by choosing for the purpose the dream which I have already recorded on p. 169 ff.

THE DREAM OF THE BOTANICAL MONOGRAPH

CONTENT OF THE DREAM.—*I had written a monograph on an (unspecified) genus of plants. The book lay before me and I was at the moment turning over a folded coloured plate. Bound up in the copy there was a dried specimen of the plant.*

The element in this dream which stood out most was the *botanical monograph*. This arose from the impressions of the dream-day: I had in fact seen a monograph on the genus Cyclamen in the window of a book-shop. There was no mention of this genus in the content of the dream; all that was left in it was the monograph and its relation to botany. The 'botanical monograph' immediately revealed its connection with the *work upon cocaine* which I had once written. From 'cocaine' the chains of thought led on the one hand to the *Festschrift* and to certain events in a University laboratory, and on the other hand to my friend Dr. Königstein, the eye surgeon, who had had a share in the introduction of cocaine. The figure of Dr. Königstein further reminded me of the interrupted conversation which I had had with him the evening before and of my various reflections upon the payment for medical services among colleagues. This conversation was the actual currently active instigator of the dream; the monograph on the cyclamen was also a currently active impression, but one of an indifferent nature. As I perceived, the 'botanical monograph' in the dream turned out to be an 'intermediate common entity' between the two experiences of the previous day: it was taken over unaltered from the indifferent impression and was linked with the psychically significant event by copious associative connections.

Not only the compound idea, 'botanical monograph', however, but each of its components, 'botanical' and 'monograph' separately, led by numerous connecting paths deeper and deeper into the tangle of dream-thoughts. 'Botanical' was related to the figure of Professor *Gärtner* [Gardener], the *blooming* looks of his wife, to my patient *Flora* and to the lady [Frau L.] of whom I had told the story of the forgotten *flowers*. Gärtner led in turn to the laboratory and to my conversation with Königstein. My two patients [Flora and Frau L.] had been mentioned in the course of this conversation. A train of thought joined the lady with the flowers to my wife's *favourite flowers* and thence to the title of the monograph which I had seen for a moment during the day. In addition to these, 'botanical' recalled an episode at my secondary school and an examination while I was at the University. A fresh topic touched upon in my conversation with Dr. Königstein—my *favourite* hobbies—was joined, through the intermediate link of what I jokingly called my *favourite flower*, the artichoke, with the train of thought proceeding from the forgotten flowers. Behind 'artichokes' lay, on the one hand, my thoughts about Italy[1] and, on the other hand, a scene from my childhood which was the opening of what have since become my intimate relations with books. Thus 'botanical' was a regular nodal point in the dream. Numerous trains of thought converged upon it, which, as I can guarantee, had appropriately entered into the context of the conversation with Dr. Königstein. Here we find ourselves in a factory of thoughts where, as in the 'weaver's masterpiece',—

> Ein Tritt tausend Fäden regt,
> Die Schifflein herüber hinüber schiessen,
> Die Fäden ungesehen fliessen,
> Ein Schlag tausend Verbindungen schlägt.[2]

So, too, 'monograph' in the dream touches upon two subjects: the one-sidedness of my studies and the costliness of my favourite hobbies.

This first investigation leads us to conclude that the elements 'botanical' and 'monograph' found their way into the content of the dream because they possessed copious contacts with the majority of the dream-thoughts, because, that is to say, they constituted 'nodal points' upon which a great number of the dream-thoughts converged, and because they had several meanings in connection with the interpretation of the dream. The explanation of this fundamental fact can also be put in another way: each of the elements of the dream's content turns out to have been 'overdetermined'—to have been represented in the dream-thoughts many times over.

[1] [This seems to be a reference to an element in the dream-thoughts not previously mentioned.]

[2] [. . . a thousand threads one treadle throws,
Where fly the shuttles hither and thither,
Unseen the threads are knit together,
And an infinite combination grows.
                    Goethe, *Faust*, Part I [Scene 4]
                    (Bayard Taylor's translation).

We discover still more when we come to examine the remaining constituents of the dream in relation to their appearance in the dream-thoughts. The *coloured plate* which I was unfolding led (see the analysis, p. 172 f.) to a new topic, my colleagues' criticisms of my activities, and to one which was already represented in the dream, my favourite hobbies; and it led, in addition, to the childhood memory in which I was pulling to pieces a book with coloured plates. The *dried specimen of the plant* touched upon the episode of the herbarium at my secondary school and specially stressed that memory.

The nature of the relation between dream-content and dream-thoughts thus becomes visible. Not only are the elements of a dream determined by the dream-thoughts many times over, but the individual dream-thoughts are represented in the dream by several elements. Associative paths lead from one element of the dream to several dream-thoughts, and from one dream-thought to several elements of the dream. Thus a dream is not constructed by each individual dream-thought, or group of dream-thoughts, finding (in abbreviated form) separate representation in the content of the dream—in the kind of way in which an electorate chooses parliamentary representatives; a dream is constructed, rather, by the whole mass of dream-thoughts being submitted to a sort of manipulative process in which those elements which have the most numerous and strongest supports acquire the right of entry into the dream-content—in a manner analogous to election by *scrutin de liste*. In the case of every dream which I have submitted to an analysis of this kind I have invariably found these same fundamental principles confirmed: the elements of the dream are constructed out of the whole mass of dream-thoughts and each one of those elements is shown to have been determined many times over in relation to the dream-thoughts.

It will certainly not be out of place to illustrate the connection between dream-content and dream-thoughts by a further example, which is distinguished by the specially ingenious interweaving of their reciprocal relations. It is a dream produced by one of my patients—a man whom I was treating for claustrophobia. It will soon become clear why I have chosen to give this exceptionally clever dream-production the title of

II

'A LOVELY DREAM'

He was driving with a large party to X Street, in which there was an unpretentious inn. (This is not the case.) *There was a play being acted inside it. At one moment he was audience, at another actor. When it was over, they had to change their clothes so as to get back to town. Some of the company were shown into rooms on the ground floor and others into rooms on the first floor. Then a dispute broke out. The ones up above were angry because the ones down below were not ready, and they could not come downstairs. His brother was up above and he was down below and he was angry with his brother because they were so much pressed.* (This part was obscure.) *Moreover, it had been decided and arranged even when they first arrived who was to be up above and who was to be down below. Then he was walking by himself up the rise made by X Street in the direction of town. He walked with such difficulty and so laboriously that he seemed glued to the spot. An elderly gentleman came up to him and began abusing the King of Italy. At the top of the rise he was able to walk much more easily.*

His difficulty in walking up the rise was so distinct that after waking up he was for some time in doubt whether it was a dream or reality.

We should not think very highly of this dream, judging by its manifest content. In defiance of the rules, I shall begin its interpretation with the portion which the dreamer described as being the most distinct.

The difficulty which he dreamt of and probably actually experienced during the dream—the laborious climbing up the rise accompanied by dyspnoea—was one of the symptoms which the patient had in fact exhibited years before and which had at that time been attributed, along with certain other symptoms, to tuberculosis. (The probability is that this was hysterically simulated.) The peculiar sensation of inhibited movement that occurs in this dream is already familiar to us from dreams of exhibiting [see p. 242 ff.] and we see once more that it is material available at any time for any other representational purpose. [Cf. p. 335 ff.] The piece of the dream-content which described how the climb began by being difficult and became easy at the end of the rise reminded me, when I heard it, of the masterly introduction to Alphonse Daudet's *Sappho*. That well-known passage describes how a young man carries his mistress upstairs in his arms; at first she is as light as a feather, but the higher he climbs the heavier grows her weight. The whole scene foreshadows the course of their love-affair, which was intended by Daudet as a warning to young men not to allow their affections to be seriously engaged by girls of humble origin and a dubious past.[1] Though I knew that my patient had been involved in a love-affair which he had recently broken off with a lady on the stage, I did not expect to find my guess at an interpretation justified. Moreover the situation in *Sappho* was the *reverse* of what it had been in the dream. In the dream the climbing had been difficult to begin with and had afterwards become easy; whereas the symbolism in the novel only made sense if something that had been begun lightly ended by becoming a heavy burden. But to my astonishment my patient replied that my interpretation fitted in very well with a piece he had seen at the theatre the evening before. It was called *Rund um Wien* [*Round Vienna*] and gave a picture of the career of a girl who began by being respectable, who then became a *demi-mondaine* and had *liaisons* with men in high positions and so '*went up in the world*', but who ended by '*coming down in the world*'. The piece had moreover reminded him of another, which he had seen some years earlier, called *Von Stufe zu Stufe* [*Step by Step*], and which had been advertised by a poster showing a staircase with a flight of *steps*.

To continue with the interpretation. The actress with whom he had had this latest, eventful *liaison* had lived in X Street. There is nothing in the nature of an inn in that street. But when he was spending part of the summer in Vienna on the lady's account he had put up [German '*abgestiegen*', literally '*stepped down*'] at a small hotel in the neighbourhood. When he left the hotel he had said to his cab-driver: 'Anyhow I'm lucky not to have picked up any vermin.' (This, incidentally, was another of his phobias.) To this the driver had replied: 'How could anyone put up at such a place! It's not a hotel, it's only an *inn*.'

The idea of an inn at once recalled a quotation to his mind:

> Bei einem *Wirte* wundermild,
> Da war ich jüngst zu Gaste.[2]

---

[1] [*Footnote added* 1911:] What I have written below in the section on symbolism about the significance of dreams of climbing [p. 355 *n*.] throws light upon the imagery chosen by the novelist.

[2] [Literally: 'I was lately a guest at an *inn* with a most gentle host.' (Uhland, *Wanderlieder*, 8, 'Einkehr'.)]

The host in Uhland's poem was an *apple-tree*; and a second quotation now carried on his train of thought:

FAUST (*mit der Jungen tanzend*):

> Einst hatt' ich *einen schönen Traum*;
> Da sah ich einen *Apfelbaum*,
> Zwei schöne Äpfel glänzten dran,
> Sie reizten mich, *ich stieg hinan*.

DIE SCHÖNE:

> Der Äpfelchen begehrt ihr sehr,
> Und schon vom Paradiese her.
> Von Freuden fühl' ich mich bewegt,
> Dass auch mein Garten solche trägt.[1]

There cannot be the faintest doubt what the apple-tree and the apples stood for. Moreover, lovely breasts had been among the charms which had attracted the dreamer to his actress.

The context of the analysis gave us every ground for supposing that the dream went back to an impression in childhood. If so, it must have referred to the wet-nurse of the dreamer, who was by now a man almost thirty years old. For an infant the breasts of his wet-nurse are nothing more nor less than an inn. The wet-nurse, as well as Daudet's Sappho, seem to have been allusions to the mistress whom the patient had recently dropped.

The patient's (elder) brother also appeared in the content of the dream, the brother being *up above* and the patient himself *down below*. This was once again the *reverse* of the actual situation; for, as I knew, the brother had lost his social position while the patient had maintained his. In repeating the content of the dream to me, the dreamer had avoided saying that his brother was up above and he himself 'on the ground floor'. That would have put the position too clearly, since here in

---

[1] [FAUST (*dancing with the Young Witch*):

> A lovely dream once came to me,
> And I beheld an *apple-tree*,
> On which two lovely apples shone;
> They charmed me so, *I climbed thereon*.

THE LOVELY WITCH:

> Apples have been desired by you,
> Since first in Paradise they grew;
> And I am moved with joy to know
> That such within my garden grow.

> > Goethe, *Faust*, Part I [Scene 21, Walpurgisnacht]
> > (Bayard Taylor's translation, slightly modified).]

Vienna if we say someone is '*on the ground floor*' we mean that he has lost his money and his position—in other words, that he has '*come down in the world*'. Now there must have been a reason for some of this part of the dream being represented by its *reverse*. Further, the reversal must hold good of some other relation between dream-thoughts and dream-content as well [cf. below, p. 326 f.]; and we have a hint of where to look for this reversal. It must evidently be at the end of the dream, where once again there was a *reversal* of the difficulty in going upstairs as described in *Sappho*. We can then easily see what reversal is intended. In *Sappho* the man carried a woman who was in a sexual relation to him; in the dream-thoughts the position was *reversed*, and a woman was carrying a man. And since this can only happen in childhood, the reference was once more to the wet-nurse bearing the weight of the infant in her arms. Thus the end of the dream made a simultaneous reference to Sappho and to the wet-nurse.

Just as the author of the novel, in choosing the name 'Sappho', had in mind an allusion to Lesbian practices, so too the pieces of the dream that spoke of people '*up above*' and '*down below*' alluded to phantasies of a sexual nature which occupied the patient's mind and, as suppressed desires, were not without a bearing on his neurosis. (The interpretation of the dream did not itself show us that what were thus represented in the dream were phantasies and not recollections of real events; an analysis only gives us the *content* of a thought and leaves it to us to determine its reality. Real and imaginary events appear in dreams at first sight as of equal validity; and that is so not only in dreams but in the production of more important psychical structures.)[1]

A 'large party' meant, as we already know [see p. 245 f.], a secret. His brother was simply the representative (introduced into the childhood scene by a 'retrospective phantasy')[2] of all his later rivals for a woman's affection. The episode of the gentleman who abused the King of Italy related once again, *via* the medium of a recent and in itself indifferent experience, to

---

[1] [Freud is probably referring here to the discovery which he had recently made that the infantile sexual traumas apparently revealed in his analyses of neurotic patients were in fact very often phantasies. See Freud, 1906*a*.]

[2] [Phantasies of this kind had been discussed by Freud previously, in the latter part of his paper on 'Screen Memories' (1899*a*).]

people of lower rank pushing their way into higher society. It was just as though the child at the breast was being given a warning parallel to the one which Daudet had given to young men.[1]

To provide a third opportunity for studying condensation in the formation of dreams, I will give part of the analysis of another dream, which I owe to an elderly lady undergoing psycho-analytic treatment. As was to be expected from the severe anxiety-states from which the patient suffered, her dreams contained a very large number of sexual thoughts, the first realization of which both surprised and alarmed her. Since I shall not be able to pursue the interpretation of the dream to the end, its material will appear to fall into several groups without any visible connection.

III

'THE MAY-BEETLE[2] DREAM'

CONTENT OF THE DREAM.—*She called to mind that she had two may-beetles in a box and that she must set them free or they would suffocate. She opened the box and the may-beetles were in an exhausted state. One of them flew out of the open window; but the other was crushed by the casement while she was shutting it at someone's request. (Signs of disgust.)*

ANALYSIS.—Her husband was temporarily away from home, and her fourteen-year-old daughter was sleeping in the bed beside her. The evening before, the girl had drawn her attention to a moth which had fallen into her tumbler of water; but she had not taken it out and felt sorry for the poor creature next morning. The book she had been reading during the evening had told how some boys had thrown a cat into boiling water, and had described the animal's convulsions. These were the two precipitating causes of the dream—in themselves indifferent.

[1] The imaginary nature of the situation relating to the dreamer's wet-nurse was proved by the objectively established fact that in his case the wet-nurse had been his mother. I may recall in this connection the anecdote, which I repeated on p. 204, of the young man who regretted that he had not made better use of his opportunities with his wet-nurse. A regret of the same kind was no doubt the source of the present dream.

[2] [The commoner English equivalent for the German '*Maikäfer*' is 'cockchafer'. For the purposes of this dream, however, a literal translation is to be preferred.]

She then pursued the subject of *cruelty to animals* further. Some years before, while they were spending the summer at a particular place, her daughter had been very cruel to animals. She was collecting butterflies and asked the patient for some *arsenic* to kill them with. On one occasion a moth with a pin through its body had gone on flying about the room for a long time; another time some caterpillars which the child was keeping to turn into chrysalises starved to death. At a still more tender age the same child used to tear the wings off *beetles* and butterflies. But to-day she would be horrified at all these cruel actions—she had grown so kind-hearted.

The patient reflected over this contradiction. It reminded her of another contradiction, between appearance and character, as George Eliot displays it in *Adam Bede*: one girl who was pretty, but vain and stupid, and another who was ugly, but of high character; a nobleman who seduced the silly girl, and a working man who felt and acted with true nobility. How impossible it was, she remarked, to recognize that sort of thing in people! Who would have guessed, to look at *her*, that she was tormented by sensual desires?

In the same year in which the little girl had begun collecting butterflies, the district they were in had suffered from a serious plague of *may-beetles*. The children were furious with the beetles and *crushed* them unmercifully. At that time my patient had seen a man who tore the wings off may-beetles and then ate their bodies. She herself had been born in *May* and had been married in *May*. Three days after her marriage she had written to her parents at home saying how happy she was. But it had been far from true.

The evening before the dream she had been rummaging among some old letters and had read some of them—some serious and some comic—aloud to her children. There had been a most amusing letter from a piano-teacher who had courted her when she was a girl, and another from an admirer *of noble birth*.[1]

She blamed herself because one of her daughters had got hold of a 'bad' book by Maupassant.[2] The *arsenic* that the girl had

---

[1] This had been the true instigator of the dream.

[2] An interpolation is required at this point: 'books of that kind are *poison* to a girl'. The patient herself had dipped into forbidden books a great deal when she was young.

asked for reminded her of the *arsenic pills* which restored the Duc de Mora's youthful strength in [Daudet's] *Le Nabab*.

'Set them free' made her think of a passage in the *Magic Flute*:

> Zur Liebe kann ich dich nicht zwingen,
> Doch geb ich dir *die Freiheit* nicht.[1]

'May-beetles' also made her think of Kätchen's words:

> Verliebt ja wie ein *Käfer* bist du mir.[2]

And in the middle of all this came a quotation from *Tannhäuser*:

> Weil du von *böser Lust* beseelt . . .[3]

She was living in a perpetual worry about her absent husband. Her fear that something might happen to him on his journey was expressed in numerous waking phantasies. A short time before, in the course of her analysis, she had lighted among her unconscious thoughts upon a complaint about her husband 'growing senile'. The wishful thought concealed by her present dream will perhaps best be conjectured if I mention that, some days before she dreamt it, she was horrified, in the middle of her daily affairs, by a phrase in the imperative mood which came into her head and was aimed at her husband: 'Go and hang yourself!' It turned out that a few hours earlier she had read somewhere or other that when a man is hanged he gets a powerful erection. The wish for an erection was what had emerged from repression in this horrifying disguise. 'Go and hang yourself!' was equivalent to: 'Get yourself an erection at any price!' Dr. Jenkins's arsenic pills in *Le Nabab* fitted in here. But my patient was also aware that the most powerful aphrodisiac, cantharides (commonly known as 'Spanish flies'), was prepared

---

[1] [Fear not, to love I'll ne'er compel thee;
  Yet 'tis too soon to *set thee free*.
         (Sarastro to Pamina in the *Finale* to Act I.—
                     E. J. Dent's translation.)]

[2] ['You are madly in love with me.' Literally: 'You are in love with me like a *beetle*.' From Kleist's *Kätchen von Heilbronn*, IV, 2.]—A further train of thought led to the same poet's *Penthesilea*, and to the idea of *cruelty* to a lover.

[3] [Literally: 'Because thou wast inspired by such *evil pleasure*.' This is presumably a recollection of the opening phrase of the Pope's condemnation reported by Tannhäuser in the last scene of the opera. The actual words are: 'Hast du so böse Lust getheilt'—'Since thou hast shared such evil pleasure'.]

from *crushed beetles*. This was the drift of the principal part of
the dream's content.

The opening and shutting of *windows* was one of the main
subjects of dispute between her and her husband. She herself
was aerophilic in her sleeping habits; her husband was aero-
phobic. *Exhaustion* was the chief symptom which she complained
of at the time of the dream.

In all three of the dreams which I have just recorded, I have
indicated by italics the points at which one of the elements of
the dream-content reappears in the dream-thoughts, so as to
show clearly the multiplicity of connections arising from the
former. Since, however, the analysis of none of these dreams has
been traced to its end, it will perhaps be worth while to consider
a dream whose analysis has been recorded exhaustively, so as
to show how its content is over-determined. For this purpose I
will take the dream of Irma's injection [p. 106 ff.]. It will be easy
to see from that example that the work of condensation makes
use of more than one method in the construction of dreams.

The principal figure in the dream-content was my patient
Irma. She appeared with the features which were hers in real
life, and thus, in the first instance, represented herself. But the
position in which I examined her by the window was derived
from someone else, the lady for whom, as the dream-thoughts
showed, I wanted to exchange my patient. In so far as Irma
appeared to have a diphtheritic membrane, which recalled my
anxiety about my eldest daughter, she stood for that child and,
behind her, through her possession of the same name as my
daughter, was hidden the figure of my patient who succumbed
to poisoning. In the further course of the dream the figure of
Irma acquired still other meanings, without any alteration
occurring in the visual picture of her in the dream. She turned
into one of the children whom we had examined in the neurological department of the children's hospital, where my two
friends revealed their contrasting characters. The figure of my
own child was evidently the stepping-stone towards this transition. The same 'Irma's' recalcitrance over opening her mouth
brought an allusion to another lady whom I had once examined,
and, through the same connection, to my wife. Moreover, the
pathological changes which I discovered in her throat involved
allusions to a whole series of other figures.

None of these figures whom I lighted upon by following up 'Irma' appeared in the dream in bodily shape. They were concealed behind the dream figure of 'Irma', which was thus turned into a collective image with, it must be admitted, a number of contradictory characteristics. Irma became the representative of all these other figures which had been sacrificed to the work of condensation, since I passed over to *her*, point by point, everything that reminded me of *them*.

There is another way in which a 'collective figure' can be produced for purposes of dream-condensation, namely by uniting the actual features of two or more people into a single dream-image. It was in this way that the Dr. M. of my dream was constructed. He bore the name of Dr. M., he spoke and acted like him; but his physical characteristics and his malady belonged to someone else, namely to my eldest brother. One single feature, his pale appearance, was doubly determined, since it was common to both of them in real life.

Dr. R. in my dream about my uncle with the yellow beard [p. 136 ff.] was a similar composite figure. But in his case the dream-image was constructed in yet another way. I did not combine the features of one person with those of another and in the process omit from the memory-picture certain features of each of them. What I did was to adopt the procedure by means of which Galton produced family portraits: namely by projecting two images on to a single plate, so that certain features common to both are emphasized, while those which fail to fit in with one another cancel one another out and are indistinct in the picture. In my dream about my uncle the fair beard emerged prominently from a face which belonged to two people and which was consequently blurred; incidentally, the beard further involved an allusion to my father and myself through the intermediate idea of growing grey.

The construction of collective and composite figures is one of the chief methods by which condensation operates in dreams. I shall presently have occasion to deal with them in another context. [See p. 320 f.]

The occurrence of the idea of 'dysentery' in the dream of Irma's injection also had a multiple determination: first owing to its phonetic similarity to 'diphtheria' [see p. 114], and secondly owing to its connection with the patient whom I had sent to the East and whose hysteria was not recognized.

Another interesting example of condensation in this dream
was the mention in it of 'propyls' [p. 115 ff.]. What was contained in the dream-thoughts was not 'propyls' but 'amyls'. It
might be supposed that a single displacement had taken place at
this point in the construction of the dream. This was indeed the
case. But the displacement served the purposes of condensation,
as is proved by the following addition to the analysis of the dream.
When I allowed my attention to dwell for a moment longer on
the word 'propyls', it occurred to me that it sounded like
'Propylaea'. But there are Propylaea not only in Athens but in
Munich.[1] A year before the dream I had gone to Munich to visit
a friend who was seriously ill at the time—the same friend who
was unmistakably alluded to in the dream by the word 'trimethylamin' which occurred immediately after 'propyls'.

I shall pass over the striking way in which here, as elsewhere
in dream-analyses, associations of the most various inherent
importance are used for laying down thought-connections as
though they were of equal weight, and shall yield to the temptation to give, as it were, a plastic picture of the process by which
the amyls in the dream-thoughts were replaced by propyls in
the dream-content.

On the one hand we see the group of ideas attached to my
friend Otto, who did not understand me, who sided against me,
and who made me a present of liqueur with an aroma of amyl.
On the other hand we see—linked to the former group by its
very contrast—the group of ideas attached to my friend in
Berlin [Wilhelm Fliess], who *did* understand me, who would
take my side, and to whom I owed so much valuable information, dealing, amongst other things, with the chemistry of the
sexual processes.

The recent exciting causes—the actual instigators of the
dream—determined what was to attract my attention in the
'Otto' group; the amyl was among these selected elements,
which were predestined to form part of the dream-content. The
copious 'Wilhelm' group was stirred up precisely through being
in contrast to 'Otto', and those elements in it were emphasized
which echoed those which were already stirred up in 'Otto'.
All through the dream, indeed, I kept on turning from someone
who annoyed me to someone else who could be agreeably contrasted with him; point by point, I called up a friend against an

    [1] [A ceremonial portico on the model of the Athenian one.]

opponent. Thus the amyl in the 'Otto' group produced memories from the field of chemistry in the other group; in this manner the trimethylamin, which was supported from several directions, found its way into the dream-content. 'Amyls' itself might have entered the dream-content unmodified; but it came under the influence of the 'Wilhelm' group. For the whole range of memories covered by that name was searched through in order to find some element which could provide a two-sided determination for 'amyls'. 'Propyls' was closely associated with 'amyls', and Munich from the 'Wilhelm' group with its 'propylaea' came half-way to meet it. The two groups of ideas converged in 'propyls-propylaea'; and, as though by an act of compromise, this intermediate element was what found its way into the dream-content. Here an intermediate common entity had been constructed which admitted of multiple determination. It is obvious, therefore, that multiple determination must make it easier for an element to force its way into the dream-content. In order to construct an intermediate link of this kind, attention is without hesitation displaced from what is actually intended on to some neighbouring association.

Our study of the dream of Irma's injection has already enabled us to gain some insight into the processes of condensation during the formation of dreams. We have been able to observe certain of their details, such as how preference is given to elements that occur several times over in the dream-thoughts, how new unities are formed (in the shape of collective figures and composite structures), and how intermediate common entities are constructed. The further questions of the *purpose* of condensation and of the factors which tend to produce it will not be raised till we come to consider the whole question of the psychical processes at work in the formation of dreams. [See p. 330 and Chapter VII, Section E, especially p. 595 ff.] We will be content for the present with recognizing the fact that dream-condensation is a notable characteristic of the relation between dream-thoughts and dream-content.

The work of condensation in dreams is seen at its clearest when it handles words and names. It is true in general that words are frequently treated in dreams as though they were things, and for that reason they are apt to be combined in just

the same way as are presentations of things.[1] Dreams of this
sort offer the most amusing and curious neologisms.[2]

I

On one occasion a medical colleague had sent me a paper he
had written, in which the importance of a recent physiological
discovery was, in my opinion, overestimated, and in which,
above all, the subject was treated in too emotional a manner.
The next night I dreamt a sentence which clearly referred to
this paper: '*It's written in a positively norekdal style.*' The analysis
of the word caused me some difficulty at first. There could be
no doubt that it was a parody of the [German] superlatives
'*kolossal*' and '*pyramidal*'; but its origin was not so easy to guess.
At last I saw that the monstrosity was composed of the two
names 'Nora' and 'Ekdal'—characters in two well-known plays
of Ibsen's. [*A Doll's House* and *The Wild Duck*.] Some time
before, I had read a newspaper article on Ibsen by the same
author whose latest work I was criticizing in the dream.

II

One of my women patients told me a short dream which
ended in a meaningless verbal compound. She dreamt she was
with her husband at a peasant festivity and said: '*This will end
in a general "Maistollmütz"*.' In the dream she had a vague feeling that it was some kind of pudding made with maize—a sort
of polenta. Analysis divided the word into '*Mais*' ['maize'],
'*toll*' ['mad'], '*mannstoll*' ['nymphomaniac'—literally 'mad for
men'] and *Olmütz* [a town in Moravia]. All these fragments
were found to be remnants of a conversation she had had at
table with her relatives. The following words lay behind '*Mais*'
(in addition to a reference to the recently opened Jubilee Exhi-
bition[3]): '*Meissen*' (a Meissen [Dresden] porcelain figure representing a bird); '*Miss*' (her relatives' English governess had

[1] [The relation between presentations of words and of things was
discussed by Freud very much later, in the last pages of his paper on the
Unconscious (1915*e*).]

[2] [A dream involving a number of verbal conceits is reported by
Freud in Chapter V (10) of his *Psychopathology of Everyday Life* (1901*b*).
—The examples which follow are, as will be seen, for the most part
untranslatable. See Editor's Introduction (p. xxii).]

[3] [To commemorate the jubilee of the Emperor Francis Joseph,
which was celebrated in 1898.]

just gone to *Olmütz*); and '*mies*' (a Jewish slang term, used jokingly to mean 'disgusting'). A long chain of thoughts and associations led off from each syllable of this verbal hotch-potch.

III

A young man, whose door-bell had been rung late one night by an acquaintance who wanted to leave a visiting-card on him, had a dream that night: *A man had been working till late in the evening to put his house-telephone in order. After he had gone, it kept on ringing—not continuously, but with detached rings. His servant fetched the man back, and the latter remarked: 'It's a funny thing that even people who are "tutelrein" as a rule are quite unable to deal with a thing like this.'*

It will be seen that the indifferent exciting cause of the dream only covers one element of it. That episode only obtained any importance from the fact that the dreamer put it in the same series as an earlier experience which, though equally indifferent in itself, was given a substitutive meaning by his imagination. When he was a boy, living with his father, he had upset a glass of water over the floor while he was half-asleep. The flex of the house-telephone had been soaked through and its *continuous ringing* had disturbed his father's sleep. Since the continuous ringing corresponded to getting wet, the '*detached rings*' were used to represent drops falling. The word '*tutelrein*' could be analysed in three directions, and led in that way to three of the subjects represented in the dream-thoughts. '*Tutel*' is a legal term for 'guardianship' ['tutelage']. '*Tutel*' (or possibly '*Tuttel*') is also a vulgar term for a woman's breast. The remaining portion of the word, '*rein*' ['clean'], combined with the first part of '*Zimmertelegraph*' ['house-telephone'], forms '*zimmerrein*' ['house-trained']—which is closely connected with making the floor wet, and, in addition, sounded very much like the name of a member of the dreamer's family.[1]

[1] In waking life this same kind of analysis and synthesis of syllables—a syllabic chemistry, in fact—plays a part in a great number of jokes: 'What is the cheapest way of obtaining silver? You go down an avenue of silver poplars [*Pappeln*, which means both "poplars" and "babbling"] and call for silence. The babbling then ceases and the silver is released.' The first reader and critic of this book—and his successors are likely to follow his example—protested that 'the dreamer seems to be too ingenious and amusing'. This is quite true so long as it refers only to the

IV

In a confused dream of my own of some length, whose central point seemed to be a sea voyage, it appeared that the next stopping place was called '*Hearsing*' and the next after that '*Fliess*'. This last word was the name of my friend in B[erlin], who has often been the goal of my travels. 'Hearsing' was a compound. One part of it was derived from the names of places on the suburban railway near Vienna, which so often end in 'ing': Hietzing, Liesing, Mödling (Medelitz, '*meae deliciae*', was its old name—that is '*meine Freud*' ['my delight']). The other part was derived from the English word 'hearsay'. This suggested slander and established the dream's connection with its indifferent instigator of the previous day: a poem in the periodical *Fliegende Blätter* about a slanderous dwarf called 'Sagter Hatergesagt' ['He-says Says-he']. If the syllable 'ing' were to be added to the name 'Fliess' we should get 'Vlissingen', which was in fact the stopping-place on the sea voyage made by my brother whenever he visited us from England. But the English name for Vlissingen is 'Flushing', which in English means 'blushing' and reminded me of the patients I have treated for ereutophobia, and also of a recent paper on that neurosis by Bechterew which had caused me some annoyance.

V

On another occasion I had a dream which consisted of two separate pieces. The first piece was the word '*Autodidasker*',

dreamer; it would only be an objection if it were to be extended to the dream-interpreter. In waking reality I have little claim to be regarded as a wit. If my dreams seem amusing, that is not on my account, but on account of the peculiar psychological conditions under which dreams are constructed; and the fact is intimately connected with the theory of jokes and the comic. Dreams become ingenious and amusing because the direct and easiest pathway to the expression of their thoughts is barred: they are forced into being so. The reader can convince himself that my patients' dreams seem at least as full of jokes and puns as my own, or even fuller.—[*Added* 1909:] Nevertheless this objection led me to compare the technique of jokes with the dream-work; and the results are to be found in the book which I published on *Jokes and their Relation to the Unconscious* (1905c) [in particular in Chapter VI.—Towards the end of this chapter Freud remarks that dream-jokes are bad jokes, and explains why this should be so. The same point is made in Lecture XV of the *Introductory Lectures* (1916–17.)—The 'first reader' referred to above was Fliess, and the question is dealt with in a letter to him of September 11, 1899 (Freud, 1950a. Letter 118).]

which I recalled vividly. The second piece was an exact reproduction of a short and harmless phantasy which I had produced
some days before. This phantasy was to the effect that when I
next saw Professor N. I must say to him: 'The patient about
whose condition I consulted you recently is in fact only suffering
from a neurosis, just as you suspected.' Thus the neologism
'Autodidasker' must satisfy two conditions: firstly, it must bear
or represent a composite meaning; and secondly, that meaning
must be solidly related to the intention I had reproduced from
waking life of making amends to Professor N.

The word 'Autodidasker' could easily be analysed into 'Autor'
[author], 'Autodidakt' [self-taught] and 'Lasker', with which I
also associated the name of Lassalle.[1] The first of these words
led to the precipitating cause of the dream—this time a significant one. I had given my wife several volumes by a well-
known [Austrian] writer who was a friend of my brother's, and
who, as I have learnt, was a native of my own birthplace:
J. J. David. One evening she had told me of the deep impression that had been made on her by the tragic story in one of
David's books of how a man of talent went to the bad; and our
conversation had turned to a discussion of the gifts of which we
saw signs in our own children. Under the impact of what she
had been reading, my wife expressed concern about the children, and I consoled her with the remark that those were the
very dangers which could be kept at bay by a good upbringing.
My train of thought was carried further during the night; I took
up my wife's concern and wove all kinds of other things into it.
A remark made by the author to my brother on the subject of
marriage showed my thoughts a by-path along which they
might come to be represented in the dream. This path led to
Breslau, where a lady with whom we were very friendly had
gone to be married and settle down. The concern I felt over the
danger of coming to grief over a woman—for that was the kernel
of my dream-thoughts—found an example in Breslau in the
cases of Lasker and Lassalle which made it possible to give a
simultaneous picture of the two ways in which this fatal influ-

---

[1] [Ferdinand Lassalle, founder of the German Social Democratic movement, was born at Breslau in 1825 and died in 1864. Eduard Lasker
(1829-1884), born at Jarotschin, not far from Breslau, was one of the
founders of the National Liberal Party in Germany. Both were of
Jewish origin.]

ence can be exercised.¹ '*Cherchez la femme*', the phrase in which these thoughts could be summarized, led me, taken in another sense, to my still unmarried brother, whose name is Alexander. I now perceived that 'Alex', the shortened form of the name by which we call him, has almost the same sound as an anagram of 'Lasker', and that this factor must have had a share in leading my thoughts along the by-path by way of Breslau.

The play which I was making here upon names and syllables had a still further sense, however. It expressed a wish that my brother might have a happy domestic life, and it did so in this way. In Zola's novel of an artist's life, *L'œuvre*, the subject of which must have been close to my dream-thoughts, its author, as is well known, introduced himself and his own domestic happiness as an episode. He appears under the name of 'Sandoz'. The transformation was probably arrived at as follows. If 'Zola' is written backwards (the sort of thing children are so fond of doing), we arrive at 'Aloz'. No doubt this seemed too undisguised. He therefore replaced 'Al', which is the first syllable of 'Alexander' by 'Sand', which is the third syllable of the same name; and in this way 'Sandoz' came into being. My own 'Autodidasker' arose in much the same fashion.

I must now explain how my phantasy of telling Professor N. that the patient we had both examined was only suffering from a neurosis made its way into the dream. Shortly before the end of my working year, I began the treatment of a new patient who quite baffled my powers of diagnosis. The presence of a grave organic disease—perhaps some degeneration of the spinal cord —strongly suggested itself but could not be established. It would have been tempting to diagnose a neurosis (which would have solved every difficulty), if only the patient had not repudiated with so much energy the sexual history without which I refuse to recognize the presence of a neurosis. In my embarrassment I sought help from the physician whom I, like many other people, respect more than any as a man and before whose authority I am readiest to bow. He listened to my doubts, told me they were justified, and then gave his opinion: 'Keep the man under observation; it must be a neurosis.' Since I knew he

---

¹ Lasker died of tabes, that is, as a result of an infection (syphilis) contracted from a woman; Lassalle, as everyone knows, fell in a duel on account of a woman. [George Meredith's *Tragic Comedians* is based on his story.]

did not share my views on the aetiology of the neuroses, I did not produce my counter-argument, but I made no concealment of my scepticism. A few days later I informed the patient that I could do nothing for him and recommended him to seek other advice. Whereupon, to my intense astonishment, he started apologizing for having lied to me. He had been too much ashamed of himself, he said, and went on to reveal precisely the piece of sexual aetiology which I had been expecting and without which I had been unable to accept his illness as a neurosis. I was relieved but at the same time humiliated. I had to admit that my consultant, not being led astray by considering the anamnesis, had seen more clearly than I had. And I proposed to tell him as much when I next met him—to tell him that *he* had been right and *I* wrong.

This was precisely what I did in the dream. But what sort of a wish-fulfilment can there have been in confessing that I was wrong? To be wrong was, however, just what I *did* wish. I wanted to be wrong in my fears, or, more precisely, I wanted my wife, whose fears I had adopted in the dream-thoughts, to be wrong. The subject round which the question of right or wrong revolved in the dream was not far removed from what the dream-thoughts were really concerned with. There was the same alternative between organic and functional damage caused by a woman, or, more properly, by sexuality: tabetic paralysis or neurosis? (The manner of Lassalle's death could be loosely classed in the latter category.)

In this closely knit and, when it was carefully interpreted, very transparent dream, Professor N. played a part not only on account of this analogy and of my wish to be wrong, and on account of his incidental connections with Breslau and with the family of our friend who had settled there after her marriage— but also on account of the following episode which occurred at the end of our consultation. When he had given his opinion and so concluded our medical discussion, he turned to more personal subjects: 'How many children have you got now?'—'Six.'—He made a gesture of admiration and concern.—'Girls or boys?'— 'Three and three: they are my pride and my treasure.'—'Well, now, be on your guard! Girls are safe enough, but bringing up boys leads to difficulties later on.'—I protested that mine had been very well behaved so far. Evidently this second diagnosis, on the future of my boys, pleased me no more than the earlier

one, according to which my patient was suffering from a neurosis.
Thus these two impressions were bound up together by their
contiguity, by the fact of their having been experienced both at
once; and in taking the story of the neurosis into my dream, I
was substituting it for the conversation about upbringing,
which had more connection with the dream-thoughts, since it
touched so closely upon the worries later expressed by my wife.
So even my fear that N. might be right in what he said about
the difficulty of bringing up boys had found a place in the
dream, for it lay concealed behind the representation of my
wish that I myself might be wrong in harbouring such fears.
The same phantasy served unaltered to represent both of the
opposing alternatives.

VI

'Early this morning,[1] between dreaming and waking, I
experienced a very nice example of verbal condensation. In the
course of a mass of dream-fragments that I could scarcely
remember, I was brought up short, as it were, by a word which
I saw before me as though it were half written and half printed.
The word was *"erzefilisch"*, and it formed part of a sentence
which slipped into my conscious memory apart from any context and in complete isolation: "That has an *erzefilisch* influence
on the sexual emotions." I knew at once that the word ought
really to have been *"erzieherisch"* ["educational"]. And I was in
doubt for some time whether the second *"e"* in *"erzefilisch"*
should not have been an *"i"*.[2] In that connection the word
"syphilis" occurred to me and, starting to analyse the dream
while I was still half asleep, I racked my brains in an effort to
make out how that word could have got into my dream, since
I had nothing to do with the disease either personally or pro-
fessionally. I then thought of *"erzehlerisch"* [another nonsense

---

[1] Quoted from Marcinowski [1911]. [This paragraph was added in
1914.]

[2] [This ingenious example of condensation turns upon the pronun-
ciation of the second syllable—the stressed syllable—of the nonsense
word. If it is *'ze'*, it is pronounced roughly like the English 'tsay', thus
resembling the second syllable of *'erzählen'* and of the invented *'erzehlerisch'*. If it is *'zi'*, it is pronounced roughly like the English 'tsee', thus
resembling the second syllable of *'erzieherisch'*, as well as (less closely) the
first syllable of 'syphilis'.]

word], and this explained the *"e"* of the second syllable of *"erzefilisch"* by reminding me that the evening before I had been asked by our governess [*Erzieherin*] to say something to her on the problem of prostitution, and had given her Hesse's book on prostitution in order to influence her emotional life—for this had not developed quite normally; after which I had talked [*erzählt*] a lot to her on the problem. I then saw all at once that the word "syphilis" was not to be taken literally, but stood for "poison"—of course in relation to sexual life. When translated, therefore, the sentence in the dream ran quite logically: "My talk [*Erzählung*] was intended to have an educational [*erzieherisch*] influence on the emotional life of our governess [*Erzieherin*]; but I fear it may at the same time have had a poisonous effect." *"Erzefilisch"* was compounded from *"erzäh-"* and *"erzieh-"*.'

The verbal malformations in dreams greatly resemble those which are familiar in paranoia but which are also present in hysteria and obsessions. The linguistic tricks performed by children,[1] who sometimes actually treat words as though they were objects and moreover invent new languages and artificial syntactic forms, are the common source of these things in dreams and psychoneuroses alike.

The analysis of the nonsensical verbal forms that occur in dreams [2] is particularly well calculated to exhibit the dream-work's achievements in the way of condensation. The reader should not conclude from the paucity of the instances which I have given that material of this kind is rare or observed at all exceptionally. On the contrary, it is very common. But as a result of the fact that dream-interpretation is dependent upon psycho-analytic treatment, only a very small number of instances are observed and recorded and the analyses of such instances are as a rule only intelligible to experts in the pathology of the neuroses. Thus a dream of this kind was reported by Dr. von Karpinska (1914) containing the nonsensical verbal form: *'Svingnum elvi'*. It is also worth mentioning those cases in which a word appears in a dream which is not in itself meaningless but which has lost its proper meaning and combines a number of other meanings to which it is related in just the same way as a 'meaningless' word would be. This is what occurred, for

[1] [See Chapter IV of Freud's book on jokes (1905c).]
[2] [This paragraph was added in 1916.]

instance, in the ten-year-old boy's dream of a 'category' which was recorded by Tausk (1913). 'Category' in that case meant 'female genitals', and to 'categorate' meant the same as 'to micturate'.

Where spoken sentences occur in dreams and are expressly distinguished as such from thoughts, it is an invariable rule that the words spoken in the dream are derived from spoken words remembered in the dream-material. The text of the speech is either retained unaltered or expressed with some slight displacement. A speech in a dream is often put together from various recollected speeches, the text remaining the same but being given, if possible, several meanings, or one different from the original one. A spoken remark in a dream is not infrequently no more than an allusion to an occasion on which the remark in question was made.[1]

[1] [*Footnote added* 1909:] Not long ago I found a single exception to this rule in the case of a young man who suffered from obsessions while retaining intact his highly developed intellectual powers. The spoken words which occurred in his dreams were not derived from remarks which he had heard or made himself. They contained the undistorted text of his obsessional thoughts, which in his waking life only reached his consciousness in a modified form. [This young man was the subject of Freud's case history of an obsessional neurotic (the 'Rat Man'); a reference to this point will be found there (Freud, 1909d) near the beginning of Section II(A).—The question of spoken words in dreams is dealt with much more fully below on p. 418 ff.]

(B)

THE WORK OF DISPLACEMENT

In making our collection of instances of condensation in dreams, the existence of another relation, probably of no less importance, had already become evident. It could be seen that the elements which stand out as the principal components of the manifest content of the dream are far from playing the same part in the dream-thoughts. And, as a corollary, the converse of this assertion can be affirmed: what is clearly the essence of the dream-thoughts need not be represented in the dream at all. The dream is, as it were, differently centred from the dream-thoughts—its content has different elements as its central point. Thus in the dream of the botanical monograph [p. 169 ff.], for instance, the central point of the dream-content was obviously the element 'botanical'; whereas the dream-thoughts were concerned with the complications and conflicts arising between colleagues from their professional obligations, and further with the charge that I was in the habit of sacrificing too much for the sake of my hobbies. The element 'botanical' had no place whatever in this core of the dream-thoughts, unless it was loosely connected with it by an antithesis—the fact that botany never had a place among my favourite studies. In my patient's *Sappho* dream [p. 285 ff.] the central position was occupied by climbing up and down and being up above and down below; the dream-thoughts, however, dealt with the dangers of sexual relations with people of an inferior social class. So that only a single element of the dream-thoughts seems to have found its way into the dream-content, though that element was expanded to a disproportionate extent. Similarly, in the dream of the may-beetles [p. 289 ff.], the topic of which was the relations of sexuality to cruelty, it is true that the factor of cruelty emerged in the dream-content; but it did so in another connection and without any mention of sexuality, that is to say, divorced from its context and consequently transformed into something extraneous. Once again, in my dream about my uncle [p. 136 ff.], the fair beard which formed its centre-point seems to have had no connection in its meaning with my ambitious wishes which, as we saw, were the core of the dream-thoughts. Dreams such as these give a justifiable impression of 'displacement'. In complete contrast to these examples, we can see that in the dream of Irma's injection [p. 106 ff.] the different elements were able to retain, during the process of constructing the dream, the approximate place which they occupied in the dream-thoughts. This further relation between the dream-thoughts and the dream-content, wholly variable as it is in its sense or direction, is calculated at first to create astonishment. If we are considering a psychical process in normal life and find that one out of its several component ideas has been picked out and has acquired a special degree of vividness in consciousness, we usually regard this effect as evidence that a specially high amount of psychical value—some particular degree of interest —attaches to this predominant idea. But we now discover that, in the case of the different elements of the dream-thoughts, a value of this kind does not persist or is disregarded in the process of dream-formation. There is never any doubt as to which of the elements of the dream-thoughts have the highest psychical value; we learn that by direct judgement. In the course of the formation of a dream these essential elements, charged, as they are, with intense interest, may be treated as though they were of small value, and their place may be taken in the dream by other elements, of whose small value in the dream-thoughts there can be no question. At first sight it looks as though no attention whatever is paid to the psychical intensity[1] of the various ideas in making the choice among them for the dream, and as though the only thing considered is the greater or less degree of multiplicity of their determination. What appears in dreams, we might suppose, is not what is *important* in the dream-thoughts but what occurs in them several times over. But this hypothesis does not greatly assist our understanding of dream-formation, since from the nature of things it seems clear that the two factors of multiple determination and inherent psychical value must necessarily operate in the same sense. The ideas which are most important among the dream-thoughts will almost certainly be those which occur most often in them, since the different dream-thoughts will, as it were, radiate out from

---

[1] *Psychical* intensity or value or the degree of interest of an idea is of course to be distinguished from *sensory* intensity or the intensity of the image presented.

them. Nevertheless a dream can reject elements which are thus both highly stressed in themselves and reinforced from many directions, and can select for its content other elements which possess only the second of these attributes.

In order to solve this difficulty we shall make use of another impression derived from our enquiry [in the previous section] into the overdetermination of the dream-content. Perhaps some of those who have read that enquiry may already have formed an independent conclusion that the overdetermination of the elements of dreams is no very important discovery, since it is a self-evident one. For in analysis we start out from the dream-elements and note down all the associations which lead off from them; so that there is nothing surprising in the fact that in the thought-material arrived at in this way we come across these same elements with peculiar frequency. I cannot accept this objection; but I will myself put into words something that sounds not unlike it. Among the thoughts that analysis brings to light are many which are relatively remote from the kernel of the dream and which look like artificial interpolations made for some particular purpose. That purpose is easy to divine. It is precisely *they* that constitute a connection, often a forced and far-fetched one, between the dream-content and the dream-thoughts; and if these elements were weeded out of the analysis the result would often be that the component parts of the dream-content would be left not only without overdetermination but without any satisfactory determination at all. We shall be led to conclude that the multiple determination which decides what shall be included in a dream is not always a primary factor in dream-construction but is often the secondary product of a psychical force which is still unknown to us. Nevertheless multiple determination must be of importance in choosing what particular elements shall enter a dream, since we can see that a considerable expenditure of effort is used to bring it about in cases where it does not arise from the dream-material unassisted.

It thus seems plausible to suppose that in the dream-work a psychical force is operating which on the one hand strips the elements which have a high psychical value of their intensity, and on the other hand, *by means of overdetermination*, creates from elements of low psychical value new values, which afterwards find their way into the dream-content. If that is so, *a transference and displacement of psychical intensities* occurs in the process of

dream-formation, and it is as a result of these that the difference
between the text of the dream-content and that of the dream-
thoughts comes about. The process which we are here presuming is nothing less than the essential portion of the dream-
work; and it deserves to be described as 'dream-displacement'.
Dream-displacement and dream-condensation are the two
governing factors to whose activity we may in essence ascribe
the form assumed by dreams.

Nor do I think we shall have any difficulty in recognizing the
psychical force which manifests itself in the facts of dream-
displacement. The consequence of the displacement is that the
dream-content no longer resembles the core of the dream-
thoughts and that the dream gives no more than a distortion
of the dream-wish which exists in the unconscious. But we are
already familiar with dream-distortion. We traced it back to
the censorship which is exercised by one psychical agency in the
mind over another. [See p. 141 ff.] Dream-displacement is one
of the chief methods by which that distortion is achieved. *Is
fecit cui profuit.*[1] We may assume, then, that dream-displacement
comes about through the influence of the same censorship—that
is, the censorship of endopsychic defence.[2]

The question of the interplay of these factors—of displacement, condensation and overdetermination—in the construction of dreams, and the question which is a dominant factor
and which a subordinate one—all of this we shall leave aside
for later investigation. [See e.g. p. 405 ff.] But we can state
provisionally a second condition which must be satisfied by
those elements of the dream-thoughts which make their way
into the dream: *they must escape the censorship imposed by resistance.*[3]
And henceforward in interpreting dreams we shall take dream-
displacement into account as an undeniable fact.

[1] [The old legal tag: 'He did the deed who gained by it.']

[2] [*Footnote added* 1909:] Since I may say that the kernel of my theory of
dreams lies in my derivation of dream-distortion from the censorship, I
will here insert the last part of a story from *Phantasien eines Realisten*
[*Phantasies of a Realist*] by 'Lynkeus' (Vienna, 2nd edition, 1900 [1st
edition, 1899]), in which I have found this principal feature of my
theory once more expounded. [See above, Postscript, 1909, to Chapter I,
p. 94 f.; also Freud, 1923*f* and 1932*c*.] The title of the story is 'Träumen
wie Wachen' ['Dreaming like Waking']:

'About a man who has the remarkable attribute of never dreaming
nonsense. . .

' "This splendid gift of yours, for dreaming as though you were waking, is a consequence of your virtues, of your kindness, your sense of justice, and your love of truth; it is the moral serenity of your nature which makes me understand all about you."

' "But when I think the matter over properly", replied the other, "I almost believe that everyone is made like me, and that no one at all ever dreams nonsense. Any dream which one can remember clearly enough to describe it afterwards—any dream, that is to say, which is not a fever-dream—must *always* make sense, and it cannot possibly be otherwise. For things that were mutually contradictory could not group themselves into a single whole. The fact that time and space are often thrown into confusion does not affect the true content of the dream, since no doubt neither of them are of significance for its real essence. We often do the same thing in waking life. Only think of fairy tales and of the many daring products of the imagination, which are full of meaning and of which only a man without intelligence could say: 'This is nonsense, for it's impossible.' "

' "If only one always knew how to interpret dreams in the right way, as you have just done with mine!" said his friend.

' "That is certainly no easy task; but with a little attention on the part of the dreamer himself it should no doubt always succeed.—You ask why it is that for the most part it does *not* succeed? In you other people there seems always to be something that lies concealed in your dreams, something unchaste in a special and higher sense, a certain secret quality in your being which it is hard to follow. And that is why your dreams so often seem to be without meaning or even to be nonsense. But in the deepest sense this is not in the least so; indeed, it cannot be so at all—for it is always the same man, whether he is awake or dreaming." '

³ [The first condition being that they must be overdetermined. (See p. 307.)]

(C)

THE MEANS OF REPRESENTATION IN DREAMS

In the process of transforming the latent thoughts into the manifest content of a dream we have found two factors at work: dream-condensation and dream-displacement. As we continue our investigation we shall, in addition to these, come across two further determinants which exercise an undoubted influence on the choice of the material which is to find access to the dream.

But first, even at the risk of appearing to bring our progress to a halt, I should like to take a preliminary glance at the processes involved in carrying out the interpretation of a dream. I cannot disguise from myself that the easiest way of making those processes clear and of defending their trustworthiness against criticism would be to take some particular dream as a sample, go through its interpretation (just as I have done with the dream of Irma's injection in my second chapter), and then collect the dream-thoughts which I have discovered and go on to reconstruct from them the process by which the dream was formed—in other words, to complete a dream-analysis by a dream-synthesis. I have in fact carried out that task for my own instruction on several specimens; but I cannot reproduce them here, since I am forbidden to do so for reasons connected with the nature of the psychical material involved—reasons which are of many kinds and which will be accepted as valid by any reasonable person. Such considerations interfered less in the *analysis* of dreams, since an analysis could be incomplete and nevertheless retain its value, even though it penetrated only a small way into the texture of the dream. But in the case of the *synthesis* of a dream I do not see how it can be convincing unless it is complete. I could only give a complete synthesis of dreams dreamt by people unknown to the reading public. Since, however, this condition is fulfilled only by my patients, who are neurotics, I must postpone this part of my exposition of the subject till I am able—in another volume—to carry the psychological elucidation of neuroses to a point at which it can make contact with our present topic.[1]

[1] [*Footnote added* 1909:] Since writing the above words, I have published a complete analysis and synthesis of two dreams in my 'Fragment

310

My attempts at building up dreams by synthesis from the dream-thoughts have taught me that the material which emerges in the course of interpretation is not all of the same value. One part of it is made up of the essential dream-thoughts —those, that is, which completely replace the dream, and which, if there were no censorship of dreams, would be sufficient in themselves to replace it. The other part of the material is usually to be regarded as of less importance. Nor is it possible to support the view that all the thoughts of this second kind had a share in the formation of the dream. [See pp. 280 and 532.] On the contrary, there may be associations among them which relate to events that occurred *after* the dream, between the times of dreaming and interpreting. This part of the material includes all the connecting paths that led from the manifest dream-content to the latent dream-thoughts, as well as the intermediate and linking associations by means of which, in the course of the process of interpretation, we came to discover these connecting paths.[1]

We are here interested only in the essential dream-thoughts. These usually emerge as a complex of thoughts and memories

of the Analysis of a Case of Hysteria' [Freud, 1905e (Sections II and III). See also the synthesis of the 'Wolf Man's' dream in Section IV of Freud (1918b).—*Added* 1914:] Otto Rank's analysis, 'Ein Traum, der sich selbst deutet' ['A Dream which Interprets Itself', 1910], deserves mention as the most complete interpretation that has been published of a dream of considerable length.

[1] [The last four sentences (beginning with 'the other part of the material') date in their present form from 1919. In editions earlier than that, this passage ran as follows: 'The other part of the material may be brought together under the term "collaterals". As a whole, they constitute the paths over which the true wish, which arises from the dream-thoughts, passes before becoming the dream-wish. The first set of these "collaterals" consist in derivatives from the dream-thoughts proper; they are, schematically regarded, displacements from what is essential to what is inessential. A second set of them comprise the thoughts that connect these inessential elements (which have become important owing to displacement) with one another, and extend from them to the dream-content. Finally, a third set consist in the associations and trains of thought by means of which the work of interpretation leads us from the dream-content to the second group of collaterals. It need not be supposed that the whole of this third set were necessarily also concerned in the formation of the dream.' With reference to this passage Freud remarks in *Ges. Schr.*, 3 (1925), 55, that he has dropped the term 'collaterals'. In fact, however, the term has survived below on p. 532.]

of the most intricate possible structure, with all the attributes of the trains of thought familiar to us in waking life. They are not infrequently trains of thought starting out from more than one centre, though having points of contact. Each train of thought is almost invariably accompanied by its contradictory counterpart, linked with it by antithetical association.

The different portions of this complicated structure stand, of course, in the most manifold logical relations to one another. They can represent foreground and background, digressions and illustrations, conditions, chains of evidence and counter-arguments. When the whole mass of these dream-thoughts is brought under the pressure of the dream-work, and its elements are turned about, broken into fragments and jammed together —almost like pack-ice—the question arises of what happens to the logical connections which have hitherto formed its framework. What representation do dreams provide for 'if', 'because', 'just as', 'although', 'either—or', and all the other conjunctions without which we cannot understand sentences or speeches?

In the first resort our answer must be that dreams have no means at their disposal for representing these logical relations between the dream-thoughts. For the most part dreams disregard all these conjunctions, and it is only the substantive content of the dream-thoughts that they take over and manipulate.[1] The restoration of the connections which the dream-work has destroyed is a task which has to be performed by the interpretative process.

The incapacity of dreams to express these things must lie in the nature of the psychical material out of which dreams are made. The plastic arts of painting and sculpture labour, indeed, under a similar limitation as compared with poetry, which can make use of speech; and here once again the reason for their incapacity lies in the nature of the material which these two forms of art manipulate in their effort to express something. Before painting became acquainted with the laws of expression by which it is governed, it made attempts to get over this handicap. In ancient paintings small labels were hung from the mouths of the persons represented, containing in written characters the speeches which the artist despaired of representing pictorially.

At this point an objection may perhaps be raised in dispute

[1] [A qualification of this statement will be found below, p. 450 n.]

of the idea that dreams are unable to represent logical relations. For there are dreams in which the most complicated intellectual operations take place, statements are contradicted or confirmed, ridiculed or compared, just as they are in waking thought. But here again appearances are deceitful. If we go into the interpretation of dreams such as these, we find that the whole of this *is part of the material of the dream-thoughts and is not a representation of intellectual work performed during the dream itself.* What is reproduced by the ostensible thinking in the dream is the *subject-matter* of the dream-thoughts and not the *mutual relations between them,* the assertion of which constitutes thinking. I shall bring forward some instances of this. [See p. 441 ff.] But the easiest point to establish in this connection is that all spoken sentences which occur in dreams and are specifically described as such are unmodified or slightly modified reproductions of speeches which are also to be found among the recollections in the material of the dream-thoughts. A speech of this kind is often no more than an allusion to some event included among the dream-thoughts, and the meaning of the dream may be a totally different one. [See p. 418 ff.]

Nevertheless, I will not deny that critical thought-activity which is not a mere repetition of material in the dream-thoughts *does* have a share in the formation of dreams. I shall have to elucidate the part played by this factor at the end of the present discussion. It will then become apparent that this thought-activity is not produced by the dream-thoughts but by the dream itself after it has already, in a certain sense, been completed. [See the last Section of this Chapter (p. 488).]

Provisionally, then, it may be said that the logical relations between the dream-thoughts are not given any separate representation in dreams. For instance, if a contradiction occurs in a dream, it is either a contradiction of the dream itself or a contradiction derived from the subject-matter of one of the dream-thoughts. A contradiction in a dream can only correspond in an exceedingly indirect manner to a contradiction *between* the dream-thoughts. But just as the art of painting eventually found a way of expressing, by means other than the floating labels, at least the *intention* of the words of the personages represented—affection, threats, warnings, and so on— so too there is a possible means by which dreams can take account of some of the logical relations between their dream-

thoughts, by making an appropriate modification in the method
of representation characteristic of dreams. Experience shows
that different dreams vary greatly in this respect. While some
dreams completely disregard the logical sequence of their
material, others attempt to give as full an indication of it as
possible. In doing so dreams depart sometimes more and sometimes less widely from the text that is at their disposal for
manipulation. Incidentally dreams vary similarly in their treatment of the *chronological* sequence of the dream-thoughts, if such
a sequence has been established in the unconscious (as, for
instance, in the dream of Irma's injection. [P. 106 ff.]).

What means does the dream-work possess for indicating these
relations in the dream-thoughts which it is so hard to represent?
I will attempt to enumerate them one by one.

In the first place, dreams take into account in a general way
the connection which undeniably exists between all the portions
of the dream-thoughts by combining the whole material into a
single situation or event. They reproduce *logical connection* by
simultaneity in time. Here they are acting like the painter who, in
a picture of the School of Athens or of Parnassus, represents in
one group all the philosophers or all the poets. It is true that
they were never in fact assembled in a single hall or on a
single mountain-top; but they certainly form a group in the
conceptual sense.

Dreams carry this method of reproduction down to details.
Whenever they show us two elements close together, this
guarantees that there is some specially intimate connection
between what correspond to them among the dream-thoughts.
In the same way, in our system of writing, 'ab' means that the
two letters are to be pronounced in a single syllable. If a gap is
left between the 'a' and the 'b', it means that the 'a' is the last
letter of one word and the 'b' is the first of the next one.[1] So,
too, collocations in dreams do not consist of any chance, disconnected portions of the dream-material, but of portions which
are fairly closely connected in the dream-thoughts as well.

For representing *causal relations* dreams have two procedures

[1] [This simile is a favourite one of Freud's. He uses it above on p. 247
and again in the middle of Section I of the case history of Dora (1905c).
It is possibly derived from a lyric of Goethe's ('Schwer in Waldes
Busch') in which the same image occurs.]

which are in essence the same. Suppose the dream-thoughts run like this: 'Since this was so and so, such and such was bound to happen.' Then the commoner method of representation would be to introduce the dependent clause as an introductory dream and to add the principal clause as the main dream. If I have interpreted aright, the temporal sequence may be reversed. But the more extensive part of the dream always corresponds to the principal clause.

One of my women patients once produced an excellent instance of this way of representing causality in a dream which I shall later record fully. [See p. 347 ff.; also discussed on pp. 319 and 325.] It consisted of a short prelude and a very diffuse piece of dream which was centred to a marked degree on a single theme and might be entitled 'The Language of Flowers'.

The introductory dream was as follows: *She went into the kitchen, where her two maids were, and found fault with them for not having got her 'bite of food' ready. At the same time she saw a very large quantity of common kitchen crockery standing upside down in the kitchen to drain; it was piled up in heaps. The two maids went to fetch some water and had to step into a kind of river which came right up to the house or into the yard.* The main dream then followed, beginning thus: *She was descending from a height over some strangely constructed palisades, and felt glad that her dress was not caught in them* ... etc.

The introductory dream related to the dreamer's parents' home. No doubt she had often heard her mother using the words that occurred in the dream. The heaps of common crockery were derived from a modest hardware shop which was located in the same building. The other part of the dream contained a reference to her father, who used always to run after the maids and who eventually contracted a fatal illness during a flood. (The house stood near a river-bank.) Thus the thought concealed behind the introductory dream ran as follows: 'Because I was born in this house, in such mean and depressing circumstances . . .' The main dream took up the same thought and presented it in a form modified by wish-fulfilment: 'I am of high descent.' Thus the actual underlying thought was: 'Because I am of such low descent, the course of my life has been so and so.'

The division of a dream into two unequal parts does not

invariably, so far as I can see, signify that there is a causal relation between the thoughts behind the two parts. It often seems as though the same material were being represented in the two dreams from different points of view. (This is certainly the case where a series of dreams during one night end in an emission or orgasm—a series in which the somatic need finds its way to progressively clearer expression.)[1] Or the two dreams may have sprung from separate centres in the dream-material, and their content may overlap, so that what is the centre in one dream is present as a mere hint in the other, and *vice versa*. But in a certain number of dreams a division into a shorter preliminary dream and a longer sequel does in fact signify that there is a causal relation between the two pieces.

The other method of representing a causal relation is adapted to less extensive material and consists in one image in the dream, whether of a person or thing, being transformed into another. The existence of a causal relation is only to be taken seriously if the transformation actually occurs before our eyes and not if we merely notice that one thing has appeared in the place of another.

I have said that the two methods of representing a causal relation were in essence the same. In both cases causation is represented by temporal sequence: in one instance by a sequence of dreams and in the other by the direct transformation of one image into another. In the great majority of cases, it must be confessed, the causal relation is not represented at all but is lost in the confusion of elements which inevitably occurs in the process of dreaming.

The alternative 'either—or' cannot be expressed in dreams in any way whatever. Both of the alternatives are usually inserted in the text of the dream as though they were equally valid. The dream of Irma's injection contains a classic instance of this. Its latent thoughts clearly ran [see p. 119]: 'I am not responsible for the persistence of Irma's pains; the responsibility lies *either* in her recalcitrance to accepting my solution, *or* in the unfavourable sexual conditions under which she lives and which I cannot alter, *or* in the fact that her pains are not hysterical at

[1] [This sentence was added in 1914. The point is further mentioned on p. 335 and discussed at greater length on pp. 402–3. The whole subject of dreams occurring on the same night is dealt with on p. 333 ff.]

all but of an organic nature.' The dream, on the other hand, fulfilled *all* of these possibilities (which were almost mutually exclusive), and did not hesitate to add a fourth solution, based on the dream-wish. After interpreting the dream, I proceeded to insert the 'either—or' into the context of the dream-thoughts.

If, however, in reproducing a dream, its narrator feels inclined to make use of an 'either—or'—e.g. 'it was either a garden or a sitting-room'—what was present in the dream-thoughts was not an alternative but an 'and', a simple addition. An 'either—or' is mostly used to describe a dream-element that has a quality of vagueness—which, however, is capable of being resolved. In such cases the rule for interpretation is: treat the two apparent alternatives as of equal validity and link them together with an 'and'.

For instance, on one occasion a friend of mine was stopping in Italy and I had been without his address for a considerable time. I then had a dream of receiving a telegram containing this address. I saw it printed in blue on the telegraph form. The first word was vague:

'*Via*', perhaps ⎫
or '*Villa*' ⎬ ; the second was clear: '*Secerno*'.
or possibly even ('*Casa*') ⎭

The second word sounded like some Italian name and reminded me of discussions I had had with my friend on the subject of etymology. It also expressed my anger with him for having kept his address *secret* from me for so long. On the other hand, each of the three alternatives for the first word turned out on analysis to be an independent and equally valid starting-point for a chain of thoughts.[1]

During the night before my father's funeral I had a dream of a printed notice, placard or poster—rather like the notices forbidding one to smoke in railway waiting-rooms—on which appeared either

'You are requested to close the eyes'
or, 'You are requested to close an eye'.

---

[1] [This dream will be found described in greater detail in Freud's letter to Fliess (the friend in question) of April 28, 1897. See Freud, 1950*a*, Letter 60.]

I usually write this in the form:

the

'You are requested to close   eye(s).'

an

Each of these two versions had a meaning of its own and led in a different direction when the dream was interpreted. I had chosen the simplest possible ritual for the funeral, for I knew my father's own views on such ceremonies. But some other members of the family were not sympathetic to such puritanical simplicity and thought we should be disgraced in the eyes of those who attended the funeral. Hence one of the versions: 'You are requested to close an eye', i.e. to 'wink at' or 'overlook'. Here it is particularly easy to see the meaning of the vagueness expressed by the 'either—or'. The dream-work failed to establish a unified wording for the dream-thoughts which could at the same time be ambiguous, and the two main lines of thought consequently began to diverge even in the manifest content of the dream.[1]

In a few instances the difficulty of representing an alternative is got over by dividing the dream into two pieces of equal length.

The way in which dreams treat the category of contraries and contradictories is highly remarkable. It is simply disregarded. 'No' seems not to exist so far as dreams are concerned.[2] They show a particular preference for combining contraries into a unity or for representing them as one and the same thing. Dreams feel themselves at liberty, moreover, to represent any element by its wishful contrary; so that there is no way of deciding at a first glance whether any element that admits of a contrary is present in the dream-thoughts as a positive or as a negative.[3]

---

[1] [This dream is reported by Freud in a letter to Fliess of November 2, 1896. (See Freud, 1950a, Letter 50.) It is there stated to have occurred during the night *after* the funeral. In its first wording the dream referred to closing the dead man's eyes as a filial duty.]

[2] [Qualifications of this assertion occur on pp. 326, 337 and 434.]

[3] [*Footnote added* 1911:] I was astonished to learn from a pamphlet by K. Abel, *The Antithetical Meaning of Primal Words* (1884) (cf. my review of it, 1910e)—and the fact has been confirmed by other philologists—that the most ancient languages behave exactly like dreams in this respect. In the first instance they have only a single word to describe the two contraries at the extreme ends of a series of qualities or activities (e.g. 'strong-weak', 'old-young', 'far-near', 'bind-sever'); they only form

In one of the dreams recorded just above, the first clause of which has already been interpreted ('because my descent was such and such' [see p. 315]), the dreamer saw herself climbing down over some palisades holding a blossoming branch in her hand. In connection with this image she thought of the angel holding a spray of lilies in pictures of the Annunciation —her own name was Maria—and of girls in white robes walking in Corpus Christi processions, when the streets are decorated with green branches. Thus the blossoming branch in the dream without any doubt alluded to sexual innocence. However, the branch was covered with *red* flowers, each of which was like a camellia. By the end of her walk—so the dream went on—the blossoms were already a good deal faded. There then followed some unmistakable allusions to menstruation. Accordingly, the same branch which was carried like a lily and as though by an innocent girl was at the same time an allusion to the *Dame aux camélias* who, as we know, usually wore a white camellia, except during her periods, when she wore a red one. The same blossoming branch (cf. 'des Mädchens Blüten' ['the maiden's blossoms'] in Goethe's poem 'Der Müllerin Verrat') represented both sexual innocence and its contrary. And the same dream which expressed her joy at having succeeded in passing through life immaculately gave one glimpses at certain points (e.g. in the fading of the blossoms) of the contrary train of ideas—of her having been guilty of various sins against sexual purity (in her childhood, that is). In analysing the dream it was possible clearly to distinguish the two trains of thought, of which the consoling one seemed the more superficial and the self-reproachful one the deeper-lying—trains of thought which were diametrically opposed to each other but whose similar though contrary elements were represented by the same elements in the manifest dream.[1]

One and one only of these logical relations is very highly favoured by the mechanism of dream-formation; namely, the

distinct terms for the two contraries by a secondary process of making small modifications in the common word. Abel demonstrates this particularly from Ancient Egyptian; but he shows that there are distinct traces of the same course of development in the Semitic and Indo-Germanic languages as well. [See also p. 471.]

[1] [The dream is fully reported on p. 347 below.]

relation of similarity, consonance or approximation—the relation of 'just as'. This relation, unlike any other, is capable of
being represented in dreams in a variety of ways.[1] Parallels or
instances of 'just as' inherent in the material of the dream-
thoughts constitute the first foundations for the construction of
a dream; and no inconsiderable part of the dream-work consists in creating fresh parallels where those which are already
present cannot find their way into the dream owing to the
censorship imposed by resistance. The representation of the
relation of similarity is assisted by the tendency of the dream-
work towards condensation.

Similarity, consonance, the possession of common attributes
—all these are represented in dreams by unification, which may
either be present already in the material of the dream-thoughts
or may be freshly constructed. The first of these possibilities may
be described as 'identification' and the second as 'composition'.
Identification is employed where *persons* are concerned; composition where *things* are the material of the unification. Nevertheless composition may also be applied to persons. Localities
are often treated like persons.

In identification, only one of the persons who are linked by a
common element succeeds in being represented in the manifest
content of the dream, while the second or remaining persons
seem to be suppressed in it. But this single covering figure
appears in the dream in all the relations and situations which
apply either to him or to the figures which he covers. In composition, where this is extended to persons, the dream-image
contains features which are peculiar to one or other of the
persons concerned but not common to them; so that the combination of these features leads to the appearance of a new
unity, a composite figure. The actual process of composition can
be carried out in various ways. On the one hand, the dream-
figure may bear the name of one of the persons related to it—
in which case we simply know directly, in a manner analogous
to our waking knowledge, that this or that person is intended
—while its visual features may belong to the other person. Or,
on the other hand, the dream-image itself may be composed of
visual features belonging in reality partly to the one person and
partly to the other. Or again the second person's share in the

---

[1] [*Footnote added* 1914:] Cf. Aristotle's remark on the qualifications of
a dream-interpreter quoted above on p. 97 *n.* 2.

dream-image may lie, not in its visual features, but in the gestures that we attribute to it, the words that we make it speak, or the situation in which we place it. In this last case the distinction between identification and the construction of a composite figure begins to lose its sharpness.[1] But it may also happen that the formation of a composite figure of this kind is unsuccessful. If so, the scene in the dream is attributed to *one* of the persons concerned, while the other (and usually the more important one) appears as an attendant figure without any other function. The dreamer may describe the position in such a phrase as: 'My mother was there as well.' (Stekel.) An element of this kind in the dream-content may be compared to the 'determinatives' used in hieroglyphic script, which are not meant to be pronounced but serve merely to elucidate other signs.

The common element which justifies, or rather causes, the combination of the two persons may be represented in the dream or may be omitted from it. As a rule the identification or construction of a composite person takes place for the very purpose of avoiding the representation of the common element. Instead of saying: '*A* has hostile feelings towards me and so has *B*', I make a composite figure out of *A* and *B* in the dream, or I imagine *A* performing an act of some other kind which is characteristic of *B*. The dream-figure thus constructed appears in the dream in some quite new connection, and the circumstance that it represents both *A* and *B* justifies me in inserting at the appropriate point in the dream the element which is common to both of them, namely a hostile attitude towards me. It is often possible in this way to achieve quite a remarkable amount of condensation in the content of a dream; I can save myself the need for giving a direct representation of very complicated circumstances relating to one person, if I can find another person to whom some of these circumstances apply equally. It is easy to see, too, how well this method of representation by means of identification can serve to evade the censorship due to resistance, which imposes such severe conditions upon the dream-work. What the censorship objects to

---

[1] [On the subject of composite figures cf. also p. 293 ff. The next three sentences were added in 1911. The final sentence of the paragraph was added in 1914.—'Identification' in this passage is evidently being used in a sense different from that discussed on p. 149 ff.]

may lie precisely in certain ideas which, in the material of the dream-thoughts, are attached to a particular person; so I proceed to find a second person, who is also connected with the objectionable material, but only with part of it. The contact between the two persons upon this censorable point now justifies me in constructing a composite figure characterized by indifferent features derived from both. This figure, arrived at by identification or composition, is then admissible to the dream-content without censorship, and thus, by making use of dream-condensation, I have satisfied the claims of the dream-censorship.

When a common element between two persons is represented in a dream, it is usually a hint for us to look for another, concealed common element whose representation has been made impossible by the censorship. A displacement in regard to the common element has been made in order, as it were, to facilitate its representation. The fact that the composite figure appears in the dream with an indifferent common element leads us to conclude that there is another far from indifferent common element present in the dream-thoughts.

Accordingly, identification or the construction of composite figures serves various purposes in dreams: firstly to represent an element common to two persons, secondly to represent a *displaced* common element, and thirdly, too, to express a merely *wishful* common element. Since wishing that two persons had a common element frequently coincides with exchanging one for the other, this latter relation is also expressed in dreams by means of identification. In the dream of Irma's injection, I wished to exchange her for another patient: I wished, that is, that the other woman might be my patient just as Irma was. The dream took this wish into account by showing me a person who was called Irma, but who was examined in a position in which I had only had occasion to see the other woman [p. 109 f.]. In the dream about my uncle an exchange of this kind became the central point of the dream: I identified myself with the Minister by treating and judging my colleagues no better than he did. [P. 193.]

It is my experience, and one to which I have found no exception, that every dream deals with the dreamer himself. Dreams are completely egoistic.[1] Whenever my own ego does

[1] [*Footnote added* 1925:] Cf. the footnote on pp. 270–1.

not appear in the content of the dream, but only some extraneous person, I may safely assume that my own ego lies concealed, by identification, behind this other person; I can insert my ego into the context. On other occasions, when my own ego *does* appear in the dream, the situation in which it occurs may teach me that some other person lies concealed, by identification, behind my ego. In that case the dream should warn me to transfer on to myself, when I am interpreting the dream, the concealed common element attached to this other person. There are also dreams in which my ego appears along with other people who, when the identification is resolved, are revealed once again as my ego. These identifications should then make it possible for me to bring into contact with my ego certain ideas whose acceptance has been forbidden by the censorship. Thus my ego may be represented in a dream several times over, now directly and now through identification with extraneous persons. By means of a number of such identifications it becomes possible to condense an extraordinary amount of thought-material.[1] The fact that the dreamer's own ego appears several times, or in several forms, in a dream is at bottom no more remarkable than that the ego should be contained in a conscious thought several times or in different places or connections—e.g. in the sentence 'when *I* think what a healthy child *I* was'.[2]

Identifications in the case of proper names of *localities* are resolved even more easily than in the case of persons, since here there is no interference by the ego, which occupies such a dominating place in dreams. In one of my dreams about Rome (see p. 195 f.), the place in which I found myself was called Rome, but I was astonished at the quantity of German posters at a street-corner. This latter point was a wish-fulfilment, which at once made me think of Prague; and the wish itself may perhaps have dated from a German-nationalist phase which I passed through during my youth, but have since got over.[3] At the time at which I had the dream there was a prospect of my

[1] When I am in doubt behind which of the figures appearing in the dream my ego is to be looked for, I observe the following rule: the person who in the dream feels an emotion which I myself experience in my sleep is the one who conceals my ego.

[2] [This sentence was added in 1925. The point is dealt with further in Freud, 1923c, Section X.]

[3] [Cf. the 'Revolutionary' dream, pp. 210 and 213.]

meeting my friend [Fliess] in Prague; so that the identification
of Rome and Prague can be explained as a wishful common
element: I would rather have met my friend in Rome than in
Prague and would have liked to exchange Prague for Rome for
the purpose of this meeting.

The possibility of creating composite structures stands foremost among the characteristics which so often lend dreams a
fantastic appearance, for it introduces into the content of
dreams elements which could never have been objects of actual
perception.[1] The psychical process of constructing composite
images in dreams is evidently the same as when we imagine or
portray a centaur or a dragon in waking life. The only difference is that what determines the production of the imaginary
figure in waking life is the impression which the new structure
itself is intended to make; whereas the formation of the composite structure in a dream is determined by a factor extraneous
to its actual shape—namely the common element in the dream-
thoughts. Composite structures in dreams can be formed in a
great variety of ways. The most naïve of these procedures merely
represents the attributes of one thing to the accompaniment of
a knowledge that they also belong to something else. A more
painstaking technique combines the features of both objects into
a new image and in so doing makes clever use of any similarities that the two objects may happen to possess in reality.
The new structure may seem entirely absurd or may strike us
as an imaginative success, according to the material and to
the ingenuity with which it is put together. If the objects which
are to be condensed into a single unity are much too incon-
gruous, the dream-work is often content with creating a composite structure with a comparatively distinct nucleus, accompanied by a number of less distinct features. In that case the
process of unification into a single image may be said to have
failed. The two representations are superimposed and produce
something in the nature of a contest between the two visual
images. One might arrive at similar representations in a
drawing, if one tried to illustrate the way in which a general
concept is formed from a number of individual perceptual
images.

Dreams are, of course, a mass of these composite structures.

[1] [Some amusing instances are given at the end of Section IV of
Freud's short essay on dreams (1901*a*); *Standard Ed.*, 5, 651.]

I have given some examples of them in dreams that I have already analysed; and I will now add a few more. In the dream reported below on p. 347 ff. [also above, p. 319], which describes the course of the patient's life 'in the language of flowers', the dream-ego held a blossoming branch in her hand which, as we have seen, stood both for innocence and for sexual sinfulness. The branch, owing to the way in which the blossoms were placed on it, also reminded the dreamer of *cherry*-blossom; the blossoms themselves, regarded individually, were *camellias*, and moreover the general impression was of an *exotic* growth. The common factor among the elements of this composite structure was shown by the dream-thoughts. The blossoming branch was composed of allusions to gifts made to her in order to win, or attempt to win, her favour. Thus she had been given *cherries* in her childhood and, later in life, a *camellia*-plant; while *'exotic'* was an allusion to a much-travelled naturalist who had tried to win her favour with a flower-drawing.—Another of my women patients produced in one of her dreams a thing that was intermediate between a bathing-hut at the seaside, an outside closet in the country and an attic in a town house. The first two elements have in common a connection with people naked and undressed; and their combination with the third element leads to the conclusion that (in her childhood) an attic had also been a scene of undressing.—Another dreamer,[1] a man, produced a composite locality out of two places where 'treatments' are carried out: one of them being my consulting-room and the other the place of entertainment where he had first made his wife's acquaintance.—A girl dreamt, after her elder brother had promised to give her a feast of caviare, that this same brother's legs were *covered all over with black grains of caviare*. The element of *'contagion'* (in the moral sense) and a recollection of a *rash* in her childhood, which had covered her legs all over with *red* spots, instead of black ones, had been combined with the *grains of caviare* into a new concept—namely the concept of *'what she had got from her brother'*. In this dream, as in others, parts of the human body were treated like objects.—In a dream recorded by Ferenczi [1910],[2] a composite image occurred which was made up from the figure of a *doctor* and of a *horse* and was also dressed in a *night-shirt*. The element common to these

---

[1] [This sentence was added in 1909.]

[2] [The remainder of this paragraph was added in 1911.]

three components was arrived at in the analysis after the woman-patient had recognized that the night-shirt was an allusion to her father in a scene from her childhood. In all three cases it was a question of an object of her sexual curiosity. When she was a child she had often been taken by her nurse to a military stud-farm where she had ample opportunities of gratifying what was at that time her still uninhibited curiosity.

I have asserted above [p. 318] that dreams have no means of expressing the relation of a contradiction, a contrary or a 'no'. I shall now proceed to give a first denial of this assertion.[1] One class of cases which can be comprised under the heading of 'contraries' are, as we have seen [p. 322], simply represented by identification—cases, that is, in which the idea of an exchange or substitution can be brought into connection with the contrast. I have given a number of instances of this. Another class of contraries in the dream-thoughts, falling into a category which may be described as 'contrariwise' or 'just the reverse', find their way into dreams in the following remarkable fashion, which almost deserves to be described as a joke. The 'just the reverse' is not itself represented in the dream-content, but reveals its presence in the material through the fact that some piece of the dream-content, which has already been constructed and happens (for some other reason) to be adjacent to it, is—as it were by an afterthought—turned round the other way. The process is more easily illustrated than described. In the interesting 'Up and Down' dream (p. 285 ff.) the representation of the climbing in the dream was the reverse of what it was in its prototype in the dream-thoughts—that is, in the introductory scene from Daudet's *Sappho*: in the dream the climbing was difficult at first but easier later, while in the Daudet scene it was easy at first but more and more difficult later. Further, the 'up above' and 'down below' in the dreamer's relation to his brother were represented the other way round in the dream. This pointed to the presence of a reversed or contrary relation between two pieces of the material in the dream-thoughts; and we found it in the dreamer's childhood phantasy of being carried by his wet-nurse, which was the reverse of the situation in the novel, where the hero was carrying his mistress. So too in my dream of Goethe's attack on Herr M. (see below, p. 439 ff.)

[1] [Others will be found below on pp. 337 and 434.]

there is a similar 'just the reverse' which has to be put straight
before the dream can be successfully interpreted. In the dream
Goethe made an attack on a young man, Herr M.; in the real
situation contained in the dream-thoughts a man of importance,
my friend [Fliess], had been attacked by an unknown young
writer. In the dream I based a calculation on the date of
Goethe's death; in reality the calculation had been made from
the year of the paralytic patient's birth. The thought which
turned out to be the decisive one in the dream-thoughts was
a contradiction of the idea that Goethe should be treated as
though he were a lunatic. 'Just the reverse', said [the underlying meaning of] the dream, 'if you don't understand the book,
it's *you* [the critic] that are feeble-minded, and not the author.'
I think, moreover, that all these dreams of turning things round
the other way include a reference to the contemptuous implications of the idea of 'turning one's back on something'.[1] (E.g. the
dreamer's turning round in relation to his brother in the *Sappho*
dream [p. 287 f.].) It is remarkable to observe, moreover,[2] how
frequently reversal is employed precisely in dreams arising from
repressed homosexual impulses.

Incidentally,[3] reversal, or turning a thing into its opposite, is
one of the means of representation most favoured by the dream-
work and one which is capable of employment in the most
diverse directions. It serves in the first place to give expression
to the fulfilment of a wish in reference to some particular element of the dream-thoughts. 'If only it had been the other way
round!' This is often the best way of expressing the ego's reaction
to a disagreeable fragment of memory. Again, reversal is of
quite special use as a help to the censorship, for it produces a
mass of distortion in the material which is to be represented,
and this has a positively paralysing effect, to begin with, on any
attempt at understanding the dream. For that reason, if a dream
obstinately declines to reveal its meaning, it is always worth
while to see the effect of reversing some particular elements
in its manifest content, after which the whole situation often
becomes immediately clear.

[1] [The German '*Kehrseite*' can mean both 'reverse' and 'backside'. Cf.
the vulgar English phrase 'arse upwards' for 'upside down', 'the wrong
way round'.]

[2] [This sentence was added in 1911.]

[3] [This and the next paragraph were added in 1909.]

And, apart from the reversal of subject-matter, *chronological* reversal must not be overlooked. Quite a common technique of dream-distortion consists in representing the outcome of an event or the conclusion of a train of thought at the beginning of a dream and of placing at its end the premises on which the conclusion was based or the causes which led to the event. Anyone who fails to bear in mind this technical method adopted by dream-distortion will be quite at a loss when confronted with the task of interpreting a dream.[1]

In some instances, indeed,[2] it is only possible to arrive at the meaning of a dream after one has carried out quite a number of reversals of its content in various respects. For instance, in the case of a young obsessional neurotic, there lay concealed behind one of his dreams the memory of a death-wish dating from his childhood and directed against his father, of whom he had been afraid. Here is the text of the dream: *His father was scolding him for coming home so late.* The context in which the dream occurred in the psycho-analytic treatment and the dreamer's associations showed, however, that the original wording must have been that *he* was angry with his *father*, and that in his view his father always came home too *early* (i.e. too soon). He would have preferred it if his father had not come home *at all*, and this was the same thing as a death-wish against his father. (See p. 254 f.) For as a small boy, during his father's temporary absence, he

---

[1] [*Footnote added* 1909:] Hysterical attacks sometimes make use of the same kind of chronological reversal in order to disguise their meaning from observers. For instance, a hysterical girl needed to represent something in the nature of a brief romance in one of her attacks—a romance of which she had had a phantasy in her unconscious after an encounter with someone on the suburban railway. She imagined how the man had been attracted by the beauty of her foot and had spoken to her while she was reading; whereupon she had gone off with him and had had a passionate love-scene. Her attack *began* with a representation of this love-scene by convulsive twitching of her body, accompanied by movements of her lips to represent kissing and tightening of her arms to represent embracing. She then hurried into the next room, sat down on a chair, raised her skirt so as to show her foot, pretended to be reading a book and spoke to me (that is, answered me).—[*Added* 1914:] Cf. in this connection what Artemidorus says: 'In interpreting the images seen in dreams one must sometimes follow them from the beginning to the end and sometimes from the end to the beginning. . .' [Book I, Chapter XI, Krauss's translation (1881), 20.]

[2] [This paragraph was added in 1911.]

had been guilty of an act of sexual aggression against someone, and as a punishment had been threatened in these words: 'Just you wait till your father comes back!'

If we wish to pursue our study of the relations between dream-content and dream-thoughts further, the best plan will be to take dreams themselves as our point of departure and consider what certain *formal* characteristics of the method of representation in dreams signify in relation to the thoughts underlying them. Most prominent among these formal characteristics, which cannot fail to impress us in dreams, are the differences in sensory intensity between particular dream-images and in the distinctness of particular parts of dreams or of whole dreams as compared with one another.

The differences in intensity between particular dream-images cover the whole range extending between a sharpness of definition which we feel inclined, no doubt unjustifiably, to regard as greater than that of reality and an irritating vagueness which we declare characteristic of dreams because it is not completely comparable to any degree of indistinctness which we ever perceive in real objects. Furthermore we usually describe an impression which we have of an indistinct object in a dream as 'fleeting', while we feel that those dream-images which are more distinct have been perceived for a considerable length of time. The question now arises what it is in the material of the dream-thoughts that determines these differences in the vividness of particular pieces of the content of a dream.

We must begin by countering certain expectations which almost inevitably present themselves. Since the material of a dream may include real sensations experienced during sleep, it will probably be presumed that these, or the elements in the dream derived from them, are given prominence in the dream-content by appearing with special intensity; or, conversely, that whatever is very specially vivid in a dream can be traced back to real sensations during sleep. In my experience, however, this has never been confirmed. It is not the case that the elements of a dream which are derivatives of real impressions during sleep (i.e. of nervous stimuli) are distinguished by their vividness from other elements which arise from memories. The factor of reality counts for nothing in determining the intensity of dream-images.

Again, it might be expected that the *sensory* intensity (that is, the vividness) of particular dream-images would be related to the *psychical* intensity of the elements in the dream-thoughts corresponding to them. In the latter, psychical intensity coincides with psychical *value*: the most intense elements are also the most important ones—those which form the centre-point of the dream-thoughts. We know, it is true, that these are precisely elements which, on account of the censorship, cannot as a rule make their way into the content of the dream; nevertheless, it might well be that their immediate derivatives which represent them in the dream might bear a higher degree of intensity, without necessarily on that account forming the centre of the dream. But this expectation too is disappointed by a comparative study of dreams and the material from which they are derived. The intensity of the elements in the one has no relation to the intensity of the elements in the other: the fact is that a complete 'transvaluation of all psychical values' [in Nietzsche's phrase] takes place between the material of the dream-thoughts and the dream. A direct derivative of what occupies a dominating position in the dream-thoughts can often only be discovered precisely in some transitory element of the dream which is quite overshadowed by more powerful images.

The intensity of the elements of a dream turns out to be determined otherwise—and by two independent factors. In the first place, it is easy to see that the elements by which the wish-fulfilment is expressed are represented with special intensity. [See p. 561 f.] And in the second place, analysis shows that the most vivid elements of a dream are the starting-point of the most numerous trains of thought—that the most vivid elements are also those with the most numerous determinants. We shall not be altering the sense of this empirically based assertion if we put it in these terms: the greatest intensity is shown by those elements of a dream on whose formation the greatest amount of condensation has been expended. [Cf. p. 595 f.] We may expect that it will eventually turn out to be possible to express this determinant and the other (namely relation to the wish-fulfilment) in a single formula.

The problem with which I have just dealt—the causes of the greater or less intensity or clarity of particular elements of a dream—is not to be confounded with another problem, which relates to the varying clarity of whole dreams or sections of dreams. In the former case clarity is contrasted with vagueness, but in the latter case it is contrasted with confusion. Nevertheless it cannot be doubted that the increase and decrease of the qualities in the two scales run parallel. A section of a dream which strikes us as perspicuous usually contains intense elements; a dream which is obscure, on the other hand, is composed of elements of small intensity. Yet the problem presented by the scale which runs from what is apparently clear to what is obscure and confused is far more complicated than that of the varying degrees of vividness of dream-elements. Indeed, for reasons which will appear later, the former problem cannot yet be discussed. [See p. 500 f.]

In a few cases we find to our surprise that the impression of clarity or indistinctness given by a dream has no connection at all with the make-up of the dream itself but arises from the material of the dream-thoughts and is a constituent of it. Thus I remember a dream of mine which struck me when I woke up as being so particularly well-constructed, flawless and clear that, while I was still half-dazed with sleep, I thought of introducing a new category of dreams which were not subject to the mechanisms of condensation and displacement but were to be described as 'phantasies during sleep'. Closer examination proved that this rarity among dreams showed the same gaps and flaws in its structure as any other; and for that reason I dropped the category of 'dream-phantasies'.[1] The content of the dream, when it was arrived at, represented me as laying before my friend [Fliess] a difficult and long-sought theory of bisexuality; and the wish-fulfilling power of the dream was responsible for our regarding this theory (which, incidentally, was not given in the dream) as clear and flawless. Thus what I had taken to be a judgement on the completed dream was actually a part, and indeed the essential part, of the dream-content. The dream-work had in this case encroached, as it were, upon my first waking thoughts and had conveyed to me as a *judgement* upon the dream the part of the material of the dream-thoughts which it had not succeeded in representing accurately

[1] [*Footnote added* 1930:] Whether rightly I am now uncertain. [Freud argues in favour of there being such a category in some remarks at the end of the discussion of his first example in his paper on 'Dreams and Telepathy' (1922a).]

in the dream.[1] I once came across a precise counterpart to this in a woman patient's dream during analysis. To begin with she refused altogether to tell it me, 'because it was so indistinct and muddled'. At length, protesting repeatedly that she felt no certainty that her account was correct, she informed me that several people had come into the dream—she herself, her husband and her father—and that it was as though she had not known whether her husband was her father, or who her father was, or something of that sort. This dream, taken in conjunction with her associations during the analytic session, showed beyond a doubt that it was a question of the somewhat commonplace story of a servant-girl who was obliged to confess that she was expecting a baby but was in doubts as to 'who the (baby's) father really was'.[2] Thus here again the lack of clarity shown by the dream was a part of the material which instigated the dream: part of this material, that is, was represented in the *form* of the dream. *The form of a dream or the form in which it is dreamt is used with quite surprising frequency for representing its concealed subject-matter.*[3]

Glosses on a dream, or apparently innocent comments on it, often serve to disguise a portion of what has been dreamt in the subtlest fashion, though in fact betraying it. For instance, a dreamer remarked that at one point 'the dream had been wiped away'; and the analysis led to an infantile recollection of his listening to someone wiping himself after defaecating. Or here is another example which deserves to be recorded in detail. A young man had a very clear dream which reminded him of some phantasies of his boyhood that had remained conscious. He dreamt that it was evening and that he was in a hotel at a summer resort. He mistook the number of his room and went into one in which an elderly lady and her two daughters were undresssing and going to bed. He proceeded: 'Here there are some gaps in the dream; there's something missing. Finally there was a man in the room who tried to throw me out, and I had to have a struggle with him.' He made vain endeavours to

---

[1] [This subject is discussed much more fully below, on p. 445 ff.]

[2] Her accompanying hysterical symptoms were amenorrhoea and great depression (which was this patient's chief symptom). [This dream is discussed on p. 445 f.]

[3] [The last sentence was added in 1909, and from 1914 onwards was printed in spaced type. The next paragraph was added in 1911.]

recall the gist and drift of the boyish phantasy to which the dream was evidently alluding; until at last the truth emerged that what he was in search of was already in his possession in his remark about the obscure part of the dream. The 'gaps' were the genital apertures of the women who were going to bed; and 'there's something missing' described the principal feature of the female genitalia. When he was young he had had a consuming curiosity to see a woman's genitals and had been inclined to hold to the infantile sexual theory according to which women have male organs.

An analogous recollection of another dreamer assumed a very similar shape.[1] He dreamt as follows: '*I was going into the Volks-garten Restaurant with Fräulein K. . . .*, then came an obscure patch, an interruption . . ., *then I found myself in the salon of a brothel, where I saw two or three women, one of them in her chemise and drawers.*'

ANALYSIS.—Fräulein K. was the daughter of his former chief, and, as he himself admitted, a substitute sister of his own. He had seldom had an opportunity of talking to her, but they once had a conversation in which 'it was just as though we had become aware of our sex, it was as though I were to say: "I'm a man and you're a woman." ' He had only once been inside the restaurant in question, with his brother-in-law's sister, a girl who meant nothing at all to him. Another time he had gone with a group of three ladies as far as the entrance of the same restaurant. These ladies were his sister, his sister-in-law and the brother-in-law's sister who has just been mentioned. All of them were highly indifferent to him, but all three fell into the class of 'sister'. He had only seldom visited a brothel—only two or three times in his life.

The interpretation was based on the 'obscure patch' and the 'interruption' in the dream, and put forward the view that in his boyish curiosity he had occasionally, though only seldom, inspected the genitals of a sister who was a few years his junior. Some days later he had a conscious recollection of the misdeed alluded to by the dream.

The content of all dreams that occur during the same night forms part of the same whole; the fact of their being divided into several sections, as well as the grouping and number of those

[1] [This and the two following paragraphs were added in 1914.]

sections—all of this has a meaning and may be regarded as a piece of information arising from the latent dream-thoughts.[1] In interpreting dreams consisting of several main sections or, in general, dreams occurring during the same night, the possibility should not be overlooked that separate and successive dreams of this kind may have the same meaning, and may be giving expression to the same impulses in different material. If so, the first of these homologous dreams to occur is often the more distorted and timid, while the succeeding one will be more confident and distinct.

Pharaoh's dreams in the Bible of the kine and the ears of corn, which were interpreted by Joseph, were of this kind. They are reported more fully by Josephus (*Ancient History of the Jews*, Book 2, Chapter 5) than in the Bible. After the King had related his first dream, he said: 'After I had seen this vision, I awaked out of my sleep; and, being in disorder, and considering with myself what this appearance should be, I fell asleep again, and saw another dream, more wonderful than the foregoing, which did more affright and disturb me . . .' After hearing the King's account of the dream, Joseph replied: 'This dream, O King, although seen under two forms, signifies one and the same event . . .' [Whiston's translation, 1874, 1, 127–8.]

In his 'Contribution to the Psychology of Rumour', Jung (1910*b*) describes how the disguised erotic dream of a school-girl was understood by her school-friends without any interpreting and how it was further elaborated and modified. He remarks in connection with one of these dream stories: 'The final thought in a long series of dream-images contains precisely what the first image in the series had attempted to portray. The censorship keeps the complex at a distance as long as possible by a succession of fresh symbolic screens, displacements, innocent disguises, etc.' (Ibid., 87.) Scherner (1861, 166) was well acquainted with this peculiarity of the method of representation in dreams and describes it, in connection with his theory of organic stimuli [see p. 85 f.], as a special law: 'Lastly, however, in all symbolic dream-structures which arise from par-

---

[1] [This sentence was added in 1909. The remainder of this paragraph, and the three following ones, were added in 1911. Freud deals with the subject again towards the end of Lecture XXIX of his *New Introductory Lectures* (1933*a*). It has already been touched upon on p. 314 ff., and is mentioned again on p. 403, p. 444 *n*. and p. 525.]

ticular nervous stimuli, the imagination observes a general law: at the beginning of a dream it depicts the object from which the stimulus arises only by the remotest and most inexact allusions, but at the end, when the pictorial effusion has exhausted itself, it nakedly presents the stimulus itself, or, as the case may be, the organ concerned or the function of that organ, and therewith the dream, having designated its actual organic cause, achieves its end. . . .'

Otto Rank (1910) has produced a neat confirmation of this law of Scherner's. A girl's dream reported by him was composed of two separate dreams dreamt, with an interval between them, during the same night, the second of which ended with an orgasm. It was possible to carry out a detailed interpretation of this second dream even without many contributions from the dreamer; and the number of connections between the contents of the two dreams made it possible to see that the first dream represented in a more timid fashion the same thing as the second. So that the second, the dream with the orgasm, helped towards the complete explanation of the first. Rank rightly bases upon this example a discussion of the general significance of dreams of orgasm or emission for the theory of dreaming. [See p. 402 ff.]

Nevertheless in my experience it is only rarely that one is in a position to interpret the clarity or confusion of a dream by the presence of certainty or doubt in its material. Later on I shall have to disclose a factor in dream-formation which I have not yet mentioned and which exercises the determining influence upon the scale of these qualities in any particular dream. [See p. 500 f.]

Sometimes, in a dream in which the same situation and setting have persisted for some time, an interruption will occur which is described in these words: 'But then it was as though at the same time it was another place, and there such and such a thing happened.' After a while the main thread of the dream may be resumed, and what interrupted it turns out to be a subordinate clause in the dream-material—an interpolated thought. A conditional in the dream-thoughts has been represented in the dream by simultaneity: 'if' has become 'when'.

What is the meaning of the sensation of inhibited movement

which appears so commonly in dreams and verges so closely upon anxiety? One tries to move forward but finds oneself glued to the spot, or one tries to reach something but is held up by a series of obstacles. A train is on the point of departure but one is unable to catch it. One raises one's hand to avenge an insult but finds it powerless. And so forth. We have already met with this sensation in dreams of exhibiting [p. 242 ff.; cf. also p. 285], but have not as yet made any serious attempt to interpret it. An easy but insufficient answer would be to say that motor paralysis prevails in sleep and that we become aware of it in the sensation we are discussing. But it may be asked why in that case we are not perpetually dreaming of these inhibited movements; and it is reasonable to suppose that this sensation, though one which can be summoned up at any moment during sleep, serves to facilitate some particular kind of representation, and is only aroused when the material of the dream-thoughts needs to be represented in that way.

This 'not being able to do anything' does not always appear in dreams as a sensation but is sometimes simply a part of the content of the dream. A case of this sort seems to me particularly well qualified to throw light on the meaning of this feature of dreaming. Here is an abridged version of a dream in which I was apparently charged with dishonesty. *The place was a mixture of a private sanatorium and several other institutions. A manservant appeared to summon me to an examination. I knew in the dream that something had been missed and that the examination was due to a suspicion that I had appropriated the missing article.* (The analysis showed that the examination was to be taken in two senses and included a medical examination.) *Conscious of my innocence and of the fact that I held the position of a consultant in the establishment, I accompanied the servant quietly. At the door we were met by another servant, who said, pointing to me: 'Why have you brought him? He's a respectable person.' I then went, unattended, into a large hall, with machines standing in it, which reminded me of an Inferno with its hellish instruments of punishment. Stretched out on one apparatus I saw one of my colleagues, who had every reason to take some notice of me; but he paid no attention. I was then told I could go. But I could not find my hat and could not go after all.*

The wish-fulfilment of the dream evidently lay in my being recognized as an honest man and told I could go. There must therefore have been all kinds of material in the dream-thoughts containing a contradiction of this. That I could go was a sign of my absolution. If therefore something happened at the end of the dream which prevented my going, it seems plausible to suppose that the suppressed material containing the contradiction was making itself felt at that point. My not being able to find my hat meant accordingly: 'After all you're *not* an honest man.' Thus the 'not being able to do something' in this dream was a way of expressing a contradiction—a 'no'—; so that my earlier statement [p. 318] that dreams cannot express a 'no' requires correction.[1]

In other dreams, in which the 'not carrying out' of a movement occurs as a *sensation* and not simply as a *situation*, the sensation of the inhibition of a movement gives a more forcible expression to the same contradiction—it expresses a volition which is opposed by a counter-volition. Thus the sensation of the inhibition of a movement represents a *conflict of will*. [Cf. p. 246.] We shall learn later [p. 567 f.] that the motor paralysis accompanying sleep is precisely one of the fundamental determinants of the psychical process during dreaming. Now an impulse transmitted along the motor paths is nothing other than a volition, and the fact of our being so certain that we shall feel that impulse inhibited during sleep is what makes the whole process so admirably suited for representing an act of volition and a 'no' which opposes it. It is also easy to see, on my explanation of anxiety, why the sensation of an inhibition of will approximates so closely to anxiety and is so often linked with it in dreams. Anxiety is a

---

[1] In the complete analysis there was a reference to an event in my childhood, reached by the following chain of association. 'Der Mohr hat seine Schuldigkeit getan, der Mohr *kann gehen*.' ['The Moor has done his duty, the Moor *can go*.' (Schiller, *Fiesco*, III, 4.) '*Schuldigkeit*' ('duty') is actually a misquotation for '*Arbeit*' ('work').] Then came a facetious conundrum: 'How old was the Moor when he had done his duty?'—'One year old, because then he could go ['*gehen*'—both 'to go' and 'to walk'].' (It appears that I came into the world with such a tangle of black hair that my young mother declared I was a little Moor.)—My not being able to find my hat was an occurrence from waking life which was used in more than one sense. Our housemaid, who was a genius at putting things away, had hidden it.—The end of this dream also concealed a rejection of some melancholy thoughts about death: 'I am far from having done my duty, so I must not go yet.'—Birth and death were dealt with in it, just as they had been in the dream of Goethe and the paralytic patient, which I had dreamt a short time before. (See pp. 327, 439 ff. [and 448 ff.].)

libidinal impulse which has its origin in the unconscious and is
inhibited by the preconscious.[1] When, therefore, the sensation
of inhibition is linked with anxiety in a dream, it must be a
question of an act of volition which was at one time capable of
generating libido—that is, it must be a question of a sexual
impulse.

I shall deal elsewhere (see below [p. 488 f.]) with the meaning and psychical significance of the judgement which often
turns up in dreams expressed in the phrase 'after all this is only
a dream'.[2] Here I will merely say in anticipation that it is
intended to detract from the importance of what is being dreamt.
The interesting and allied problem, as to what is meant when
some of the content of a dream is described in the dream itself
as 'dreamt'—the enigma of the 'dream within a dream'—has
been solved in a similar sense by Stekel [1909, 459 ff.], who has
analysed some convincing examples. The intention is, once
again, to detract from the importance of what is 'dreamt' in the
dream, to rob it of its reality. What is dreamt in a dream after
waking from the 'dream within a dream' is what the dream-
wish seeks to put in the place of an obliterated reality. It is safe
to suppose, therefore, that what has been 'dreamt' in the dream
is a representation of the reality, the true recollection, while the
continuation of the dream, on the contrary, merely represents
what the dreamer wishes. To include something in a 'dream
within a dream' is thus equivalent to wishing that the thing
described as a dream had never happened. In other words,[3] if
a particular event is inserted into a dream as a dream by the
dream-work itself, this implies the most decided confirmation of
the reality of the event—the strongest *affirmation* of it. The
dream-work makes use of dreaming as a form of repudiation,
and so confirms the discovery that dreams are wish-fulfilments.[4]

[1] [*Footnote added* 1930:] In the light of later knowledge this statement
can no longer stand. [Cf. p. 161, *n.* 2. See also p. 499 *n.*]

[2] [This paragraph (except for its penultimate sentence and part of its
last sentence) was added in 1911.]

[3] [This sentence was added in 1919.]

[4] [The last clause was added in 1919.]

www.vintage-books.co.uk